TEN YEARS IN THE TUB

ALSO BY NICK HORNBY

Fever Pitch
High Fidelity
About a Boy
Speaking with the Angel (editor)
How to Be Good
Songbook
The Polysyllabic Spree
A Long Way Down
Housekeeping vs. the Dirt
Slam
An Education
Juliet, Naked
Shakespeare Wrote for Money
More Baths Less Talking

TEN
YEARS
IN THE
TUB

A DECADE SOAKING
IN GREAT BOOKS

BELIEVER BOOKS

a division of
McSWEENEY'S

BELIEVER BOOKS

a division of
MᶜSWEENEY'S

849 Valencia Street
San Francisco, CA 94110

Copyright © 2003–2013 Nick Hornby

Cover illustration by Daniel Fishel

These pieces appeared between September 2003 and
June 2013 in the *Believer* magazine.

www.believermag.com

ISBN: 978-1-938073-73-1

CONTENTS

INTRODUCTION
A NOTE FROM JESS WALTER

The crazy lady in 13B leaned over and asked what I was reading. Hoping to avoid one of those torturous airplane conversations, I simply held up the cover of a newish story collection.

"No. I didn't ask *what* you're reading," the woman said. "Why?"

Why? And in a moment of sheer stupefaction I will regret the rest of my life, I made the tragic mistake of looking up from my book.

Over the next two hours, I found out she didn't read much herself, didn't entirely "get books," and wouldn't believe what she read anyway since so much of it came from "media scumbags" who didn't properly "support the troops" and were tools for "those government scumbags" who kept raising her taxes and trying to take away the assault rifles she and her husband needed to protect themselves from "scumbag criminals like that O. J. Simpson."

Wait. She needed an assault rifle to protect herself from O. J. Simpson?

"That son of a bitch," she informed me, "got away with murder."

I wanted to point out that using a phrase like "got away with murder" to describe someone who actually *got away with murder* is a little bit nuts, like owning a china shop, having a bull run through it, and then describing the experience as like… well, you know.

Instead, I sat there pondering her question.

Why do I read?

Looking back, I wish I'd had this "Stuff I've Been Reading" omnibus with me. It's a very heavy book and I could've hit her with it.

Or I could've turned to just about any page.

In the decade that he's been writing this column for the *Believer* (with the occasional month off to watch *Friday Night Lights* or the World Cup—two of the three acceptable excuses for *not* reading, the other being "captured by pirates") Nick Hornby has created the most intelligent, engaging case for reading you're ever likely to encounter.

Funny without being snarky, generous without sacrificing critical heft, Hornby-on-books is, forgive my English, *bloody brilliant*. "Stuff I've Been Reading" is unfailingly smart but without any of the obnoxious showy bits—lit theory, obscure Russian surnames, untranslated French (agreeably psycho-sur-realist, the book nonetheless reflects Spankmeoff's *fromage de l'extrémité arrière*)—that might serve to remind a poor reader that while he attended Eastern Washington University on a partial welding scholarship, the author happens to be a Cambridge man.

Nick, who actually happens to *be* a Cambridge man, has done much more than display his casual genius for the last ten years, however. He's crafted a wise, thoughtful, and wry narrative out of a reading life—"a paper trail of theme and meaning," just as he promised in that very first column (September 2003).

Over those ten years, children are born and grow into readers; trips to America are endured; friends publish books that have to be considered; a beloved partner is "downgraded" to wife. Another beloved, the Arsenal football club, rises and falls like its own season, and in a quietly gut-wrenching moment, sells off its star Thierry Henry—"the man that both my wife and I wish had fathered our children," yet somehow manages to win the Premier League (before another inevitable fall).

DiMaggio-like streaks of prodigious reading (eleven books in one month!) are followed by whiffs, by admissions of guilt, television, and the too-recogniz-able failure of concentration that afflicts our generation, a plague of distraction.

> I was just itchy and scratchy and probably crusty, too, and I began to wonder whether I had simply lost the habit—the skill, even—of reading.

Amid this ongoing consideration of how and why and what we read are real lessons for writers, vital challenges to old tropes and clichés: "I can officially confirm that readers' writers beat writers' writers every time." Or this about our blind worship of spare prose:

> And there's some stuff about the winnowing process I just don't get. Why does it always stop when the work in question has been reduced to sixty or seventy

thousand words?… I'm sure you could get it down to twenty or thirty, if you tried hard enough. In fact, why stop at twenty or thirty? Why write at all? Why not just jot the plot and a couple of themes down on the back of an envelope and leave it at that?

Reading the whole enterprise again, I found it hilarious, surprising, incisive, and—for a certain kind of book lover like you and me and not the lady in 13B—thrilling.

A few confessions:

I did indeed send Nick one of my books with the suggestion that he start a third column: "Books Foisted Upon Me."

Also, I'm something of a Hornby completist. Novels, essays, criticism—I would read the man on anything. I only thank god his literary north pulls him toward music and books and sport, and that he's not into ceramics or polo or necrophilia (anymore). In fact, now that I have the *Believer*'s ear, may I suggest publishing Nick Hornby's Collected Parentheticals:

> (Twice this week I have been sent manuscripts of books that remind their
> editors, according to their covering letters, of my writing. Like a lot of writers,
> I can't really stand my own writing, in the same way that I don't really like
> my own cooking. And, just as when I go out to eat, I tend not to order my
> signature dish—an overcooked and overspiced meat-stewy thing containing
> something inappropriate, like tinned peaches, and a side order of undercooked
> and flavorless vegetables—I really don't want to read anything that I could have
> come up with at my own computer. What I produce on my computer invariably
> turns out to be an equivalent of the undercooked overcooked stewy thing, no
> matter how hard I try to follow the recipe, and you really don't want to eat too
> much of that. I'd love to be sent a book with an accompanying letter that said,
> "This is nothing like your work. But as a man of taste and discernment, we think
> you'll love it anyway.")

But while I am an unapologetic Hornby fan, what I am *not* is a member of the Polysyllabic Spree (my application was rejected because of a perceived susceptibility to cult deprogramming), that robed band of somewhere between six and sixty lit lovers and ritual spankers who first assigned Nick this project.

That puts me in a good spot to evaluate the success of the most controversial aspect of this experiment, the *Believer*'s insistence on "acid-free" criticism, which, while clearly a challenge for Hornby, contributed to a few small but revolutionary ideas that book reviewers and critics had either forgotten or never knew:

1) That it's OK to give up on a book. So, alongside works that brace and embolden, that thrill and surprise, are books "abandoned" and "unfinished"—unnamed big books of this season, or that classic which might simply not be worth the effort.

> Last month, I may inadvertently have given the impression that *No Name* by Wilkie Collins was a lost Victorian classic (the misunderstanding may have arisen because of my loose use of the phrase "lost Victorian classic")… We fought, Wilkie Collins and I. We fought bitterly and with all our might, to a standstill, over a period of about three weeks, on trains and aeroplanes and by hotel swimming pools.

2) That sometimes the fault for a bad read lies not with the book and its author but with the reader. That we are never the same reader twice—sometimes we want the collected letters of some literary giant, sure, but sometimes we want "thrillers that make us walk into lampposts." This is an especially important idea now, during this tyranny of the customer review, when a book can be dismissed with inanities like "It didn't hold my interest," and "It just wasn't my cup of tea," and "I didn't root for the characters." Well, gentle reader: did you ever think maybe the problem is you?

> We are never allowed to forget some books are badly written; we should remember that sometimes they're badly read, too.

3) That the books we buy are almost as important as those we read. From the beginning there were always two columns, Books Bought and Books Read. By my crude math, Nick spent somewhere around ten or fifteen grand on books he hasn't even read. Besides showing that he did his part to support publishing during a tough economic period, this suggests something important about reading. Looking around my own obsessively crowded shelves, I see there are two categories of books I tend to keep: those I love and those I hope one day to read. If the books we read reflect the person we are, the books we *hope to read* might just be who we aspire to be. There is something profound in that.

> All the books we own, both read and unread, are the fullest expression of self we have at our disposal... With each passing year, and with each whimsical purchase, our libraries become more and more able to articulate who we are, whether we read the books or not.

In the end, that's it, of course, books as "the fullest expression of self." That is what our books say about us, about you and me and Nick Hornby and not the lady in 13B. We *are* our books, the ones we struggle with, the ones we put down and the ones we can't, the ones we still hope to read, and, of course, the ones that we love. That, more than anything: the ones we love.

As that other great British-born writer, Zadie Smith, said of Nick Hornby in *Time* magazine a few years ago: "He believes that beautiful songs, beautiful books and yes, the beautiful game, are the great redemptive forces. He loves good stuff so much that one might call him the European Ambassador of Goodness."

Right. Now go troll this big-ass book for some *goodness*. You might find it exists for you, as it does for Ambassador Hornby, in Charles Dickens, in Marilynne Robinson, in Roddy Doyle, in Anne Tyler, about whom Nick uses words that I would suggest describe the ambassador himself: a writer of "simplicity, intelligence, humor, and heart," whose curse may just be "a gift that seems effortless." ✦

SEPTEMBER 2003

BOOKS BOUGHT:

- *Robert Lowell: A Biography*—Ian Hamilton
- *Collected Poems*—Robert Lowell
- *Against Oblivion: Some of the Lives of the 20th-Century Poets*
  —Ian Hamilton
- *In Search of J. D. Salinger*—Ian Hamilton
- *Nine Stories*—J. D. Salinger
- *Franny and Zooey*—J. D. Salinger
- *Raise High the Roof Beam, Carpenters/Seymour: An Introduction*
  —J. D. Salinger
- *The Ern Malley Affair*—Michael Heyward
- *Something Happened*—Joseph Heller
- *Penguin Modern Poets 5*—Corso/Ferlinghetti/Ginsberg

BOOKS READ:

- All the Salingers
- *In Search of Salinger* and *Lowell*
- Some of *Against Oblivion*
- *Pompeii* by Robert Harris (not bought)

So this is supposed to be about the how, and when, and why, and what of reading—about the way that, when reading is going well, one book leads to another and to another, a paper trail of theme and meaning; and how, when it's going badly, when books don't stick or take, when your mood and the mood of the book are fighting like cats, you'd rather do anything but attempt the next paragraph, or reread the last one for the tenth time. "We talked about books," says a character in Charles Baxter's wonderful *Feast of Love,* "how boring they were to read, but how you loved them anyway." Anyone who hasn't felt like that isn't owning up.

But first, some ground rules:

1) I don't want anyone writing in to point out that I spend too much money on books, many of which I will never read. I know that already. I certainly *intend* to read all of them, more or less. My *intentions* are good. Anyway, it's my money. And I'll bet you do it too.

2) Similarly, I don't want anyone pointing out that certain books I write about in this column are by friends—or, in the case of *Pompeii,* by brothers-in-law. A lot of my friends are writers, and so some of my reading time is, inevitably, spent on their books. I won't attempt to disguise the connections, if that makes anyone feel better. Anyway, it's been five years since my brother-in-law, the author of *Fatherland* and *Enigma,* produced a book, so the chances are that I'll have been fired from this magazine before he comes up with another one. (I may have been fired even before *this* one is published, in September.)

3) And don't waste your breath trying to tell me that I'm showing off. This month, maybe, I'm showing off a little. (Or am I? Shouldn't I have read some of these books decades ago? *Franny and Zooey*? Jesus. Maybe I'm doing the opposite: maybe I'm humiliating myself. And maybe you have read all these *and loads of others*, in the last fortnight. I don't know you. What's—ahem—a normal amount, for someone with a job and kids, who watches TV?) But next month I may spend my allotted space desperately trying to explain how come I've only managed three pages of a graphic novel and the sports section of the *Daily Mirror* in four whole weeks—in which case, please don't bother accusing me of philistinism, laziness, or pig-ignorance. I read a lot this month a) because it's the summer, and it's been hot, and I haven't been working very hard, and there's no football on TV and b) because my eldest son, for reasons we don't need to go into, has spent even more time than usual stuck in the toilet, and I have to sit outside on a chair. Thus do books get read.

This month, it went something like:

Against Oblivion → *Lowell* → *In Search of Salinger* → *Nine Stories* → *Raise High the Roof Beam, Carpenters* → *(Pompeii)* → *Seymour: An Introduction* → *Franny and Zooey*

The Robert Lowell–Ian Hamilton thing began with Anthony Lane's intimidatingly brilliant review of Lowell's collected poems in *The New Yorker*: Lane mentioned in passing that Hamilton's biography was still the best available. Even so, I wouldn't have bothered if it hadn't been for several other factors, the most important of which is that my baby son is called Lowell. We named him thus partly after various musicians—Lowell George and the blues singer Lowell Fulson—and partly because of Robert Lowell, whose work we had never read (in our defense, he is no longer terribly well-known here in England, and he isn't taught in school), but whose existence persuaded us, in our untrustworthy hormonal state, that the name had a generic artistic connotation. Our Lowell will almost certainly turn out to be a sales manager for a sportswear firm, whose only contact with literature is when he listens to Tom Clancy audiobooks once a year on holiday—not that there's anything wrong with that.

On top of that, I had recently watched a BBC documentary about Ian Hamilton himself, who was a good poet and a great critic, and a mentor to Barnes, Amis, McEwan, and that whole generation of English writers. (There is, by the way, an exceptionally good new BBC cable channel here, BBC4, which shows documentaries of similar merit and obscurity every night of the week.) And I'd met him a couple of times, and really liked him, not least because he wrote an enthusiastic review of my first book. (Did I mention that he was a great critic?) He died a couple of years ago, and I wish I'd known him better.

I still wouldn't necessarily have tracked down the Lowell biography, however, if I hadn't spent a weekend near Hay-on-Wye. Hay is a weird town on the border of England and Wales which consists almost entirely of secondhand bookshops—there are forty of 'em, within a few hundred yards of each other—and one of which is an immaculately stocked poetry store. That's where I found Hamilton's book, as well as the Penguin Modern Poets collection, purchased because Corso's lovely "Marriage" was read at a friend's wedding recently. I bought the Ern Malley book (for a pound, pure maybe-one-day whimsy, doomed to top-shelf oblivion), and a first edition of *Something Happened* (because it crops up in Dow Mossman's *The Stone Reader*), elsewhere in the town. Buying books is what you do in Hay, in the absence of any other options.

Despite all these various auguries, I hadn't necessarily expected to read every word of the Lowell biography, but Hamilton is such a good writer, and Lowell's life was so tumultuous, that it was gone in a couple of days, like an Elmore Leonard novel. Sometimes, in the hands of the right person, biographies of relatively minor figures (and Lowell's influence seems to be receding fast) are especially compelling: they seem to have their times and cultural environments written through them like a stick of rock, in a way that sui generis major figures sometimes don't. Lowell, it turns out, is the guy you can see just behind Zelig's shoulder: he corresponded with Eliot, hung out with Jackie and Bobby K., and traveled around with Eugene McCarthy in '68. He also beat up his own father, had endless strange, possibly sexless extramarital affairs with innumerable young women, and endured terrible periods of psychosis, frequently accompanied by alarming rants about Hitler. In other words, it's one of those books you thrust on your partner with an incredulous cry of "This is *me!*"

And as a bonus, I felt I learned more about the act of creating poetry from this one book than I did in my entire educational career. (A line from a letter Lowell wrote to Randall Jarrell that I shall endeavour to remember: "In prose you have to be interested in *what* is being said… it's very exciting for me, like going fishing.") In the end, the psychotic periods make for a wearying rhythm to the book, and perhaps Hamilton's criticism of the poems tends to be a little too astringent—the *Collected Poems* runs to twelve hundred pages, but Hamilton seems to argue that we could live without a good eleven hundred and fifty of them. And this is a poet he clearly loves…

But it's a great biography, and now I was off on this Hamilton kick. I bought *Against Oblivion*, his book of little essays about every major twentieth-century poet bar four—Eliot, Auden, Hardy, and Yeats—absent because their work is, in the critic's view, certain to survive; it's in the bathroom, and I've got through half of it. (Shock news: Grown-up critics think e.e. cummings sucks. I honestly

didn't know. I read him at school, put him in the "good" box, and left him there.)
I vaguely remembered the story of Hamilton's attempt to write a biography
of Salinger: it ended up in court, and Salinger actually broke cover to give a
deposition to Hamilton's lawyer. Hamilton admits that Salinger's victory left
gaping holes in the book he wanted to write. He was denied permission to quote
from letters that are freely available for inspection in various libraries. I'm still
glad I read it, though. I learned things—that you could earn $2,000 for a short
story in the 1930s, for example. The stories about Salinger hustling for work,
and dining gaily with the Oliviers in London, make one feel almost giddy, so
unlikely do they sound now; and when the Hamilton mind goes to work on the
stories, it's something to see.

The realization that you could polish off a major author's entire oeuvre in
less than a week was definitely part of the appeal—you won't catch Dickens
being pushed around like that—but it was still tougher work than I thought
it would be. Just about every one of *Nine Stories* is perfect, and *Raise High the
Roof Beam, Carpenters* is fresh and funny, but *Seymour: An Introduction...* Man,
I really didn't want to know about Seymour's ears. Or his eyes. Or whether
he could play sports. The very first time I met him he blew his brains out (in
"A Perfect Day for Bananafish"), so to be brutal, I never really developed as
much curiosity about him as Salinger seems to want of me. But whereas I was
expecting something light and sweet, I ended up with this queasy sense of the
psychodramatic: I knew that I wouldn't be able to separate the stories from the
Story, but I hadn't expected the author to collude in the confusion. Hamilton is
especially good on how Buddy Glass, apparently Salinger's mouthpiece, creates
and perpetuates myths about his alter ego.

I read *Pompeii* in between *Nine Stories* and *Raise High the Roof Beam...* It has
to be a rule, I think, that when a family member gives you his new book, you
stop what you're doing and read it. Having a writer for a brother-in-law could
have turned out really, really badly. He could have been more or less successful
than me. Or he could have written books that I hated, or found impossible to
get through. (Imagine if your brother-in-law wrote *Finnegans Wake*, and you
were really busy at work. Or you weren't really a big reader.) Luckily, his books
are great, and a pleasure to read, and despite my trepidation—I couldn't see how

he was going to pull off a thriller which ends with the biggest deus ex machina the world has ever known—this is, I reckon, his best one. Oh, and he read just about every book there is on volcanology and Roman water systems, as well as every word Pliny wrote, so my admiration for my sister has increased even further. Has she been sitting there listening to stuff about Roman water systems for the last three years? I now understand why her favorite film of recent years is *Legally Blonde*. How could it not be?

I read 55 percent of the books I bought this month—five and a half out of ten. Two of the unread books, however, are volumes of poetry, and, to my way of thinking, poetry books work more like books of reference: They go up on the shelves straight away (as opposed to onto the bedside table), to be taken down and dipped into every now and again. (And, before any outraged poets explode, I'd like to point out that I'm one of the seventy-three people in the world who buys poetry.) And anyway, anyone who is even contemplating ploughing straight through over a thousand pages of Lowell's poetry clearly needs a cable TV subscription, or maybe even some friends, a relationship, and a job. So if it's OK with you, I'm taking the poetry out, and calling it five and a half out of eight—and the Heller I've read before, years ago, so that's six and a half out of eight. I make that eighty one and a quarter percent! I am both erudite and financially prudent! I admit it: I haven't read a book about an Australian literary hoax (which, I repeat, I bought for a quid), and a handful of essays about people like James Wright, Robinson Jeffers, and Norman Cameron. Maybe there are slumbering pockets of ignorance best left undisturbed; no one likes a know-all. ✷

OCTOBER 2003

BOOKS BOUGHT:

* *A Tragic Honesty: The Life and Work of Richard Yates*—Blake Bailey
* *Notes on a Scandal*—Zoë Heller (released in the U.S. as *What Was She Thinking? Notes on a Scandal*)

BOOKS READ:

* *On Being John McEnroe*—Tim Adams
* *Stop-Time*—Frank Conroy
* *The Fortress of Solitude*—Jonathan Lethem
* *Desperate Characters*—Paula Fox
* *Notes on a Scandal*—Zoë Heller
* *Where You're At*—Patrick Neate
* *Feel Like Going Home*—Peter Guralnick
* *The People's Music*—Ian MacDonald
* *A Tragic Honesty*—Blake Bailey (unfinished)
* *How to Stop Smoking and Stay Stopped for Good*—Gillian Riley
* *Quitting Smoking—The Lazy Person's Guide!*—Gillian Riley

If you write books—or a certain kind of book, anyway—you can't resist a scan round the hotel swimming pool when you go on holiday. You just can't help yourself, despite the odds: you need to know, straight off, whether anyone is reading one of yours. You imagine spending your days under a parasol watching, transfixed and humbled, as a beautiful and intelligent young man or woman, almost certainly a future best friend, maybe even spouse, weeps and guffaws through three hundred pages of your brilliant prose, too absorbed even to go for a swim, or take a sip of Evian. I was cured of this particular fantasy a couple of years ago, when I spent a week watching a woman on the other side of the pool reading my first novel, *High Fidelity*. Unfortunately, however, I was on holiday with my sister and brother-in-law, and my brother-in-law provided a gleeful and frankly unfraternal running commentary. "Look! Her lips are moving." "Ha! She's fallen asleep! Again!" "I talked to her in the bar last night. Not a *bright* woman, I'm afraid." At one point, alarmingly, she dropped the book and ran off. "She's gone to put out her eyes!" my brother-in-law yelled triumphantly. I was glad when she'd finished it and moved on to *Harry Potter* or Dr Seuss or whatever else it was she'd packed.

I like to think that, once he'd recovered from the original aesthetic shock, Jonathan Lethem wouldn't have winced too often if he'd watched me reading *The Fortress of Solitude* by the pool this month. I was pinned to my lounger, and my lips hardly moved at all. In fact, I was so determined to read his novel on holiday that the first half of the reading month started with a mess. It went something like, *On Being* **The** *John McEnroe* Stop-Time **Fortress of Solitude**. I'd just started Tim Adams's short book on McEnroe when an advance copy of *Fortress* came in the post, and I started reading that—but because it seemed so good, so much my kind of book, I wanted to save it, and I went back to the McEnroe. Except then the McEnroe turned out to be *too* short, and I'd finished it before the holiday started, so I needed something to fill in, which is why I reread *Stop-Time*. (And *Stop-Time* turned out to be too long, and I didn't get onto *Fortress* until the third day of the seven-day holiday.)

Last month I read a lot of Salinger, and he pops up in all three of these books. Tim Adams remembers reading *Raise High the Roof Beam, Carpenters* while queuing to watch McEnroe at Wimbledon in 1981; the seventeen-year-old Adams had a theory that McEnroe "was, in fact, a latter-day Holden Caulfield, unable and unwilling to grow up... constantly railing against the phonies—dozing linesmen, tournament organizers with walkie-talkies—in authority." Later, he points out that McEnroe went to Buckley Country Day School—"one model for Holden Caulfield's Pencey Prep." Frank Conroy, meanwhile, attended P.S. 6, "of J. D. Salinger fame." (Adams's book is great, by the way. It's witty and smart, and has ideas about sport that don't strain for significance. It's also oddly English, because it's about the collision of McEnroe and Wimbledon—in other words, McEnroe and one version of England—and about how McEnroe was a weirdly timely illustration of Thatcherism. My favorite McEnroe tirade, one I hadn't heard before: "I'm so disgusting you shouldn't watch. Everybody leave!")

And then, at the beginning of *The Fortress of Solitude,* I came across the following, describing a street ball game: "A shot... which cleared the gates on the opposite side of the street was a home run. Henry seemed to be able to do this at will, and the fact that he didn't each time was mysterious." Compare that to this, from *Seymour: An Introduction:* "A home run was scored only when the ball sailed just high and hard enough to strike the wall of the building on the opposite street... Seymour scored a home run nearly every time he was up. When other boys on the block scored one, it was generally regarded as a fluke... but Seymour's failures to get home runs looked like flukes." Weird, huh? (And that's all it is, by the way—there's nothing sinister going on here. Lethem's book is probably over a hundred thousand words long, and bears no resemblance to anything Salinger wrote, aside from this one tiny echo.) All three books are in part about being young and mixed-up and American, and even though this would appear to be a theme so broad that no one can claim it as their own, somehow Salinger has managed to copyright it (and you wouldn't put it past him); there is clearly some law compelling you to acknowledge somewhere in your book, however obliquely, that he got there first.

A confession, for the record: I know Jonathan Lethem. Or rather, I've met him, and we have exchanged emails on occasions. But I don't know him so well that I had to read his book, if you see what I mean. I could easily have got away with not reading it. I could have left the proof copy his publishers sent me sitting around unopened, and no social embarrassment would have ensued. But I wanted to read it; I loved *Motherless Brooklyn,* and I knew a little bit about this book before I started it—I knew, for example, that a lot of funk records and Marvel comics were mentioned by name. In other words, it wasn't just up my street; it was actually knocking on my front door and peering through the letterbox to see if I was in. I was, however, briefly worried about the title, which sounds portentously and alarmingly Literary, until I was reminded that it refers to Superman.

The Fortress of Solitude is one of those rare novels that felt as though it had to be written; in fact, it's one of those novels that deals with something so crucial—namely, the relationship between a middle-class white boy and black culture—that you can't believe it hasn't been written before. Anyone who has grown up listening to black music, or even white music derived from black music, will have some point of connection to this book; but Dylan Ebdus, Lethem's central character, is a kind of walking, talking embodiment of a cultural obsession. He's the only white kid in his street (in Brooklyn, pre-gentrification), and one of a handful of white kids in his school; Mick Jagger would have killed for his experience, and Mick Jagger would have suffered in exactly the same ways.

This is a painful, beautiful, brave, poetic and definitive book (anyone who attempts to enter this territory again will be found out, not least because Lethem clearly knows whereof he speaks), and though it has its flaws, the right reader will not only forgive them but love them—just as the right listener loves the flaws in, say, *The Wild, the Innocent and the E Street Shuffle*. They are the flaws that come of ambition, not of ineptitude. I think this is a book that people might argue about, but it will also be a book that a sizable number of people cherish and defend and reread, despite its density and length, and as an author you can't really ask for much more than that.

Three of the books on the "read" list—by Patrick Neate, Ian McDonald, and Peter Guralnick—I reviewed for the *Times Literary Supplement*, and I'm not going to write about them again at any length here. But *Where It's At* is in part about a middle-class white boy's obsession with hip-hop, and *Feel Like Going Home* is fuelled by a middle-class white boy's love for R&B and blues; reading them only served to underline why *The Fortress of Solitude* is so necessary.

I do seem, however, to have spent a disproportionate amount of time reading about Stuyvesant High School this month. That's where Dylan Ebdus escapes to, and it's also where Frank Conroy went, when he could be bothered. I'm guessing that Stuyvesant is decent enough, but I'm sure its students would be perplexed to hear that an Englishman spent an entire holiday in France reading about alumni both fictional and real. I even ended up checking out the Stuyvesant website, just to see what the place looked like. (It looked like a high school.)

I reread *Stop-Time* because Frank Conroy is so eloquent and moving about books and their power at the end of *The Stone Reader*. I don't reread books very often; I'm too conscious of both my ignorance and my mortality. (I recently discovered that a friend who was rereading *Bleak House* had done no other Dickens apart from *Barnaby Rudge*. That's just weird. I shamed and nagged him into picking up *Great Expectations* instead.) But when I tried to recall anything about it other than its excellence, I failed. Maybe there was something about a peculiar stepfather? Or was that *This Boy's Life*? And I realized that, as this is true of just about every book I consumed between the ages of, say, fifteen and forty, I haven't even read the books I think I've read. I can't tell you how depressing this is. What's the fucking point?

Apart from Stuyvesant and Salinger, the recurring theme of the month was Paula Fox. Fox has given blurbs for both *The Fortress of Solitude* and Zoë Heller's novel; Lethem has given a blurb to *Desperate Characters*. I know I'm wrong about this book, because everyone else in the world, including writers I love, thinks it's fantastic, but it Wasn't For Me. It's brilliantly written, I can see that much, and it made me think, too. But mostly I thought about why I don't know anyone like the people Fox writes about. Why are all my friends so dim and unreflective? Where did I go wrong?

Towards the end of the book, Otto and Sophie, the central couple, go to stay in their holiday home. Sophie opens the door to the house, and is immediately reminded of a friend, an artist who used to visit them there; she thinks about him for a page or so. The reason she's thinking about him is that she's staring at something he loved, a vinegar bottle shaped like a bunch of grapes. The reason she's staring at the bottle is because it's in pieces. And the reason it's in pieces is because someone has broken in and trashed the place, a fact we only discover when Sophie has snapped out of her reverie. At this point, I realized with some regret that not only could I never write a literary novel, but I couldn't even be a character in a literary novel. I can only imagine myself, or any character I created, saying, "Shit! Some bastard has trashed the house!" No rumination about artist friends—just a lot of cursing, and maybe some empty threats of violence.

Zoë Heller's *Notes from a Scandal,* about a fortysomething pottery teacher who has an affair with a fifteen-year-old pupil, was moving along nicely until a character starts talking about football. He tells a teaching colleague that he's been to see Arsenal, and that "Arsenal won Liverpool 3-0." Readers of this column will have realized by now that I know almost nothing about anything, but if I were forced to declare one area of expertise, it would be what people say to each other after football matches. It's not much, I know, but it's mine. And I am positive that no one has ever said "Arsenal won Liverpool 3-0" in the entire history of either Arsenal Football Club or the English language. "Beat," "thrashed," "did" or "done," "trounced," "thumped," "shat all over," "walloped," etc., yes; "won," emphatically, no. And I think that my dismay and disbelief then led me to question other things, and the fabric of the novel started to unravel a little. Can you really find full-time pottery teachers in modern English state schools? Would a contemporary teenager really complain about being treated as "the Kunta Kinte round here" when asked to do some housework? I like Zoë Heller's writing, and this book has a terrific narrative voice which recalls Alan Bennett's work; I just wish I wasn't so picky. This is how picky I am. You know the Arsenal bit? It wasn't just the unconvincing demotic I objected to; it was the score. Arsenal haven't beaten Liverpool 3-0 at Highbury since 1991. What chance did the poor woman have?

I haven't finished the Richard Yates biography yet. I will, however, say this much: it is 613 pages long. Despite the influence Yates had on a generation of writers, it's hard enough finding people who've read the great *Revolutionary Road*, let alone people who will want to read about its author's grandparents. I propose that those intending to write a biography should first go to the National Biography Office to get a permit which tells you the number of pages you get. (There will be no right of appeal.) It's quite a simple calculation. Nobody wants to read a book longer than—what?—nine hundred pages? OK, a thousand, maybe. And you can't really get the job done in less than 250. So you're given maximum length if you're doing Dickens, say—someone who lived to a ripe old age, wrote enormous books, and had a life outside them. And everyone else is calculated using Dickens as a yardstick. By this reckoning, Yates is a three-hun-dred-page man—maybe 315 tops. I'm on page 194 as we speak, and I'm going to stick with it—the book is compelling and warm and gossipy. But on page 48, I found myself reading a paragraph about the choice of gents' outfitters facing the pupils at Yates's school; I felt, personally speaking, that it could have gone.

I reread two other books this month: *How to Stop Smoking and Stay Stopped for Good,* and *Quitting Smoking—The Lazy Person's Guide!* I reread them for obvious reasons; I'll be rereading them again, too. They're good books, I think, sensible and helpful. But they're clearly not perfect. If I do stop smoking, it may be because I don't want to read Gillian Riley anymore. ✳

NOVEMBER 2003

BOOKS BOUGHT:

* *Bush at War*—Bob Woodward
* *Six Days of War*—Michael B. Oren
* *Genome*—Matt Ridley
* *Isaac Newton*—James Gleick
* *God's Pocket*—Pete Dexter
* *The Poet and the Murderer*—Simon Worrall
* *Sputnik Sweetheart*—Haruki Murakami
* *Lie Down in Darkness*—William Styron
* *Leadville*—Edward Platt
* *Master Georgie*—Beryl Bainbridge
* *How to Breathe Underwater*—Julie Orringer (two copies)

BOOKS READ:

* *A Tragic Honesty: The Life and Work of Richard Yates*—Blake Bailey (completed)
* *Wenger: The Making of a Legend*—Jasper Rees
* *How to Breathe Underwater*—Julie Orringer
* *Bush at War*—Bob Woodward (unfinished)
* Unnamed Literary Novel (abandoned)
* Unnamed Work of Nonfiction (abandoned)
* *No Name*—Wilkie Collins (unfinished)

LITERARY CDS BOUGHT AND LISTENED TO:

* *The Spoken Word—Poets*
* *The Spoken Word—Writers*

Unfinished, abandoned, abandoned, unfinished. Well, you can't say I didn't warn you. In the first of these columns, I voiced the suspicion that my then-current reading jag was unsustainable: I was worried, I seem to recall, about the end of the summer, and the forthcoming football season, and it's true that both of these factors have had an adverse effect on book consumption. (Words added to ongoing novel since autumnal return to work: not many, but more than the month before. Football matches watched in the last month: seven whole ones, four of them live in the stadium, and bits and pieces of probably half a dozen others.) Of the two books I started and finished this month, one I read in a day, mostly on a plane, during a day trip to Amsterdam. And it was a book about football.

It is not only sport and work that have slowed me up, however; I would have to say that the ethos of this magazine has inhibited me a little too. As you are probably aware by now, the *Believer* has taken the honorable and commendable view that, if it is attacks on contemporary writers and writing you wish to read, then you can choose from an endless range of magazines and newspapers elsewhere—just about all of them, in fact—and that therefore the *Believer* will contain only acid-free literary criticism.

This position is, however, likely to cause difficulties if your brief is simply to write honestly about the books you have been reading: boredom and, very occasionally, despair is part of the reading life, after all. Last month, mindful of the *Believer*'s raison d'être, I expressed mild disappointment with a couple of the books I had read. I don't remember the exact words; but I said something to the effect that, if I were physically compelled to express a view as to whether the Disappointing Novel was better or worse than *Crime and Punishment,* then I would keep my opinion to myself, no matter how excruciating the pain, such was my respect for the editorial credo. If, however, the torturers threatened my children, then I would—with the utmost reluctance—voice a very slight preference for *Crime and Punishment.*

Uproar ensued. Voicing a slight preference for *Crime and Punishment* over the Disappointing Novel under threat of torture to my children constituted a Snark, it appeared, and I was summoned to appear before the *Believer* committee—twelve rather eerie young men and women (six of each, naturally), all dressed in white robes and smiling maniacally, like a sort of literary equivalent of the Polyphonic Spree. I was given a severe dressing-down, and only avoided a three-issue suspension by promising never to repeat the offense. Anyway, We (i.e. the Polysyllabic Spree) have decided that if it looks as though I might not enjoy a book, I will abandon it immediately, and not mention it by name. This is what happened with the Literary Novel and the Work of Nonfiction—particularly regrettable in the latter case, as I was supposed to be reviewing it for a London newspaper. The loss of income there, and the expense of flying from London to San Francisco to face the Committee (needless to say, those bastards wouldn't stump up), means that this has been an expensive month.

I did, however, finish Blake Bailey's biography of Yates that I started last month. I haven't changed my view that it could easily have afforded to shed a few of its six-hundred-plus pages—Yates doesn't sell his first story until page 133—but I'm glad I stuck with it. Who'd have thought that the author of *Revolutionary Road* wrote speeches for Robert Kennedy, or provided the model for Alton Benes, the insane writer-father of *Seinfeld's* Elaine? (Yates's daughter Monica, an ex-girlfriend of Larry David, was apparently an inspiration for Elaine herself.) And who'd have thought that the author of an acknowledged American classic, as well as several other respected novels and an outstanding collection of short stories, could have ended up living and then dying in such abject penury? *A Tragic Honesty,* like the Ian Hamilton biography of Lowell that I read recently, is a sad and occasionally terrifying account of how creativity can be simultaneously fragile and self-destructive; it also made me grateful that I am writing now, when the antidepressants are better, and we all drink less. Stories about contemporary writers being taken away in a straitjacket are thin on the ground—or no one tells them to me, anyway—but it seemed to happen to Lowell and Yates all the time; there are ten separate page references under "breakdowns" in the index of *A Tragic Honesty.*

Just as frightening to anyone who writes (or who is connected intimately to a writer) is Yates's willingness to cannibalize his life—friends, lovers, family, work—for his fiction: just about everyone he ever met was able to find a thinly disguised, and frequently horrific, version of themselves in a novel or a story somewhere. Those who have read *The Easter Parade* will recall the savagely-drawn portrait of Pookie, the pathetic, vain, drunken mother of the Grimes sisters; when I tell you that Yates's mother was known to everyone as "Dookie," you will understand just how far Yates was prepared to go.

It was something of a relief to turn to Jasper Rees's biography of Arsene Wenger—not just because it's short, but because Wenger's career as a football manager is currently both highly successful and unfinished. I don't often pick up books about football any more—I wrote one once, and though the experience didn't stop me from wanting to watch the sport, as I feared it might, it did stop me from wanting to read about it—but I love Arsene, who, weirdly and neatly, coaches my team, Arsenal, and who would probably feature at about number eight in a list of People Who Have Changed My Life for the Better. He transformed a mediocre, plodding side into a thing of beauty, and on a good day, Arsenal plays the best football that anyone in England has ever seen. He was the first foreign manager to win an English championship, and his influence is such that everyone now wants to employ cool, cerebral Europeans. (The previous fashion was for ranting, red-faced Scotsmen.) Even the English national team has one now, much to the disgust of tabloid sportswriters and the more rabidly patriotic football fan.

I gave an interview to Rees for his book, but despite my contribution, it's a pretty useful overview of his career to date. I couldn't, hand on heart, argue that it transcends the genre, and you probably only really need to read it if you have an Arsenal season ticket. And if there is one single *Believer* reader who is also an Arsenal season ticket holder, I'll buy you a drink next home game. What the hell—I'll buy you a car.

I received *How to Breathe Underwater* and the Wilkie Collins novel in the same Jiffy envelope, sent to me by a friend at Penguin, who publishes all three of us in the UK; this friend is evangelical about both books, and so I began one, loved it, finished it, and then started the other. Usually, of course, I treat personal book recommendations with the suspicion they deserve. I've got enough to read as it is, so my first reaction when someone tells me to read something is to find a way to doubt their credentials, or to try to dredge up a conflicting view from the memory. (Just as stone always blunts scissors, a lukewarm "Oh, it was OK," always beats a "You have to read this." It's less work that way.) But every now and again, the zealous gleam in someone's eye catches the attention, and anyway Joanna, jaded as she is by her work, doesn't make loose or unnecessary recommendations. She keeps her powder dry.

She was right, luckily for her: *How to Breathe Underwater* is an outstanding collection of stories. Orringer writes about the things that everyone writes about—youth, friendship, death, grief, etc.—but her narrative settings are fresh and wonderfully knotty. So while her themes are as solid and as recognizable as oak trees, the stuff growing on the bark you've never seen before. If you wanted to be reductive, "The Smoothest Way Is Full of Stones" would collapse neatly into a coming-of-age story, with a conventional two-girls-and-a-guy triangle at its core. But one of the girls comes from a ferociously orthodox Jewish family, and the other one has a mother who's in the hospital after the loss of a baby, and the boy has this pornographic book stashed away, and the whole thing is so beautifully and complicatedly imagined that you don't want to boil it down to its essence. "Pilgrims," the first story in the book, makes you feel panicky and breathless, and is destined, I suspect, to be taught in creative writing classes everywhere. The moment I'd finished I bought myself a first edition, and then another, for a friend's birthday. It's that sort of book. I'll tell you how much I liked it: one paragraph in the story "When She Is Old and I Am Famous" contained the words "gowns," "pumps," "diva hairdos," "pink chiffon," "silk roses," "couture," and "*Vogue*," and, after the briefest shudder, I read on anyway.

I'm a couple of hundred pages into *No Name,* and so far it's everything I'd hoped it would be. It was sold to me—or given to me free, anyway—as a lost Victorian classic (and I'd never even heard of it), and it really hits the spot: an engrossing, tortuous plot, quirky characters, pathos, the works. If you pick up the Penguin Classics edition, however, don't read the blurb on the back. It more or less blows the first (fantastic) plot twist, on the grounds that it's "revealed early on"—but "early on" turns out to be page ninety-six, not, say, page eight. Note to publishers: Some people read nineteenth-century novels for fun, and a lot of them were written to be read that way too.

I should, perhaps, attempt to explain away the ludicrous number of books bought this month. Most of them were secondhand paperbacks; I bought the Pete Dexter, the Murakami, and *The Poet and the Murderer* on a Saturday afternoon spent wandering up and down Stoke Newington Church Street with the baby, and I bought *Leadville* and *Master Georgie* from a bookstall at a local community festival. *Leadville* is a biography of the A40, one of London's dreariest arterial roads, and the desperately unpromising nature of the material somehow persuades me that the book has to be great. And I'd like to point out that *The Poet and the Murderer* is the second cheap paperback about a literary hoax that I've bought since I started writing this column. I cannot really explain why I keep buying books about literary hoaxes that I never seriously intend to read. It's a quirk of character that had remained hitherto unrevealed to me.

I picked up the Styron in a remainder shop while I was reading the Yates biography—Yates spent years adapting it for a film that was never made. *Genome* and *Six Days of War* I bought on a visit to the *London Review of Books'* slightly scary new shop near the British Museum. I'm not entirely sure why I chose those two in particular, beyond the usual attempts at reinvention that periodically seize one in a bookstore. (When I'm arguing with St. Peter at the Pearly Gates, I'm going to tell him to ignore the Books Read column, and focus on the Books Bought instead. "This is *really* who I am," I'll tell him. "I'm actually much more of a *Genome* guy than an Arsene Wenger guy. And if you let me in, I'm going to prove it, honest.") I got the CDs at the *LRB* shop, too. They're actually pretty amazing: the recordings are taken from the British Library Sound Archive, and all the writers featured were born in the nineteenth century—Conan Doyle, Virginia Woolf, Joyce, Yeats, Kipling, Wodehouse, Tolkien, and, astonishingly, Browning and Tennyson, although to be honest you can't really hear Browning, who was recorded at a dinner party in 1889, trying and failing to remember the words of "How They Brought the Good News from Ghent to Aix." Weirdly, everyone sounds the same, very posh and slightly mad.

I read about a third of *Bush at War*, and I may well return to it at some stage, but the mood that compelled me to begin it passed quickly, and in any case it wasn't quite what I wanted: Woodward's tone is way too matey and sympathetic for me. I did, however, learn that George W. Bush was woken up by the Secret Service at 11:08 p.m. on 9/11. Woken up! He didn't work late that night? And he wasn't too buzzy to get off to sleep? See, if that had been me, I would have been up until about six, drinking and smoking and watching TV, and I would have been useless the next day. It can't be right, can it, that world leaders emerge not through their ability to solve global problems, but to nod off at the drop of a hat? Most decent people can't sleep easily at night, and that, apparently, is precisely why the world is in such a mess. ✷

NOVEMBER 2003 / JANUARY 2004

BOOKS BOUGHT:

* ✫ *Moneyball*—Michael Lewis
* ✫ *Saul and Patsy*—Charles Baxter
* ✫ *Winner of the National Book Award*—Jincy Willett
* ✫ *Jenny and the Jaws of Life*—Jincy Willett
* ✫ *The Sirens of Titan*—Kurt Vonnegut
* ✫ *True Notebooks*—Mark Salzman

BOOKS READ:

* ✫ *No Name*—Wilkie Collins
* ✫ *Moneyball*—Michael Lewis
* ✫ *George and Sam: Autism in the Family*—Charlotte Moore
* ✫ *The Sirens of Titan*—Kurt Vonnegut

First, an apology. Last month, I may inadvertently have given the impression that *No Name* by Wilkie Collins was a lost Victorian classic (the misunderstanding may have arisen because of my loose use of the phrase "lost Victorian classic"), and that everyone should rush out and buy it. I had read over two hundred pages when I gave you my considered verdict; in fact, the last four hundred and eighteen pages nearly killed me, and I wish I were speaking figuratively. We fought, Wilkie Collins and I. We fought bitterly and with all our might, to a standstill, over a period of about three weeks, on trains and aeroplanes and by hotel swimming pools. Sometimes—usually late at night, in bed—he could put me out cold with a single paragraph; every time I got through twenty or thirty pages, it felt to me as though I'd socked him good, but it took a lot out of me, and I had to retire to my corner to wipe the blood and sweat off my reading glasses. And still he kept coming back for more. Only in the last fifty-odd pages, after I'd landed several of these blows, did old Wilkie show any signs of buckling under the assault. He was pretty tough for a man of nearly one hundred and eighty. Hats off to him. Anyway, I'm sorry for the bum steer, and readers of this column insane enough to have run down to their nearest bookstore as a result of my advice should write to the *Believer*, enclosing a receipt, and we will refund your $14. It has to say *No Name* on the ticket, though, because we weren't born yesterday, and we're not stumping up for your Patricia Cornwell novels. You can pay for them yourselves.

In his introduction to my Penguin edition, Mark Ford points out that Collins wrote the closing sections of the novel "in both great pain and desperate anxiety over publishers' deadlines." (In fact, Dickens, who edited the magazine in which *No Name* was originally published, *All the Year Round,* offered to nip down to London and finish the book off for him: "I could take it up any time and do it… so like you as that no-one should find out the difference." That's literature for you.) It is not fair to wonder why Collins bothered: *No Name* has lots going for it, including a driven, complicated, and morally ambiguous central female character, and a tremendous first two hundred pages. But it's certainly reasonable to wonder why a sick man should have wanted to overextend a relatively slight melodrama to the extent that people want to fight him. *No Name* is the story of a woman's attempt to reclaim her rightful inheritance from cruel and heartless relatives, and one of the reasons the book didn't work for me is that one has to quiver with outrage throughout at the prospect of this poor girl having to work for a living, as a governess or something equally demeaning.

It could be, of course, that the book seems bloated because Collins simply wasn't as good at handling magazine serialization as Dickens, and that huge chunks of the novel, which originally came in forty-four parts, were written only to keep the end well away from the beginning. I'm only guessing, but I'd imagine that many subscribers to *All the Year Round* between May 1862 and early January 1863 felt exactly the same way. I'm guessing, in fact, that there were a few cancelled subscriptions, and that *No Name* is the chief reason you can no longer find *All the Year Round* alongside the *Believer* at your nearest newsstand.

There are two sides to every fight, though, and Wilkie would point out that I unwisely attempted to read the second half of *No Name* during a trip to Los Angeles. Has anyone ever attempted a Victorian novel in Los Angeles, and if so, why? In England, we read Victorian novels precisely because they're long, and we have nothing else to do. L.A. is too warm, too bright, there's too much sport on TV, and the sandwiches are too big (and come with chips/"fries"). English people shouldn't attempt to do anything in L.A.; it's all too much. We should just lie in a darkened room with a cold flannel until it's time to come home again.

With the exception of *The Sirens of Titan*, bought secondhand from a Covent Garden market stall, all this month's books were purchased at Book Soup in L.A. (Book Soup and the Tower Records directly opposite have become, in my head, what Los Angeles *is*.) Going to a good U.S. bookshop is still ludicrously exciting (unless I'm on book tour, when the excitement tends to wear off a little): as I don't see American books-pages, I have no idea whether one of my favorite authors—Charles Baxter, for example, on this trip—has a new book out, and there's every chance that it won't be published in the UK for months, if at all. There is enough money in the music and movie industries to ensure that we get to hear about most things that might interest us; books have to remain a secret, to be discovered only when you spend time browsing. This is bad for authors, but good for the assiduous shopper.

Mark Salzman's book about juvenile offenders I read about in the *Believer*. I met Mark after a reading in L.A. some years ago, and one of the many memorable things he told me was that he'd written a large chunk of his last novel almost naked, covered in aluminum foil, with a towel round his head, sitting in a car. His reasons for doing so, which I won't go into here, were sound, and none of them were connected with mental illness, although perhaps inevitably he had caused his wife some embarrassment—especially when she brought friends back to the house. Jincy Willett, whose work I had never heard of, I bought because of her blurbs, which, I'm afraid to say, only goes to show that blurbs do work.

I was in the U.S. for the two epic playoff series, between the Cubs and the Marlins, and the Red Sox and the Yankees, and I became temporarily fixated with baseball. And I'd read something about *Moneyball* somewhere, and it was a staff pick at Book Soup, and when, finally, *No Name* lay vanquished and lifeless at my feet, it was Lewis's book I turned to: it seemed a better fit. *Moneyball* is a rotten title, I think. You expect a subtitle something along the lines of *How Greed Killed America's National Pastime*, but actually the book isn't like that at all—it's the story of how Billy Beane, the GM of the Oakland A's, worked out how to buck the system and win lots of games despite being hampered by one of the smallest payrolls in baseball. He did this by recognizing (*a*) that the stats traditionally used to judge players are almost entirely worthless, and (*b*) that many good players are being discarded by the major leagues simply because they don't *look* like good players.

The latter discovery in particular struck a chord with me, because my football career has been blighted by exactly this sort of prejudice. English scouts visiting my Friday morning five-a-side game have (presumably) discounted me on peripheral grounds of age, weight, speed, amount of time spent lying on the ground weeping with exhaustion, etc.; what they're not looking at is *performance,* which is of course the only thing that counts. They'd have made a film called *Head It Like Hornby* by now if Billy Beane were working over here. (And if I were any good at heading, another overrated and peripheral skill.) Anyway, I understood about one word in every four of *Moneyball,* and it's still the best and most engrossing sports book I've read for years. If you know anything about baseball, you will enjoy it four times as much as I did, which means that you might explode.

I have an autistic son, but I don't often read any books about autism. Most of the time, publishers seem to want to hear from or about autists with special talents, as in *Rain Man* (my son, like the vast majority of autistic kids, and contrary to public perception, has no special talent, unless you count his remarkable ability to hear the opening of a crisp packet from several streets away), or from parents who believe that they have "rescued" or "cured" their autistic child, and there is no cure for autism, although there are a few weird stories, none of which seem applicable to my son's condition. So most books on the subject tend to make me feel alienated, resentful, cynical, or simply baffled. Granted, pretty much any book on any subject seems to make me feel this way, but I reckon that in this case, my personal experience of the subject means I'm entitled to feel anything I want.

I read Charlotte Moore's book because I agreed to write an introduction for it, and I agreed to write an introduction because, in a series of brilliant columns in the *Guardian,* she has managed not only to tell it like it is, but to do so with enormous good humour and wit—*George and Sam* (Moore has three sons, two of whom are autistic) is, believe it or not, the funniest book I've read this year. I'm not sure I would have found it as funny six or seven years ago, when Danny was first diagnosed, and autism wasn't a topic that made me laugh much; but now that I'm used to glancing out of the window on cold wet November nights and suddenly seeing a ten-year-old boy bouncing naked and gleeful on a trampoline, I have come to relish the stories all parents of autistic kids have.

The old cliché "You couldn't make it up" is always dispiriting to anyone who writes fiction—if you couldn't make it up, then it's probably not worth talking or writing about anyway. But autism is worth writing about—not just because it affects an increasingly large number of people, but because of the light the condition shines down on the rest of us. And though you can predict that autistic kids are likely to behave in peculiar obsessive-compulsive ways, the details of these compulsions and obsessions are always completely unimaginable, and frequently charming in their strangeness. Sam, the younger of Moore's two autistic boys, has an obsession with oasthouses—he once escaped from home in order to explore a particularly fine example a mile and a half away. "Its owner, taking an afternoon nap, was startled to be joined in bed by a small boy still wearing his Wellington boots."

George, meanwhile, is compelled to convince everyone that he doesn't eat, even though he does. After his mum has made his breakfast she has to reassure him that it's for Sam, and then turn her back until he's eaten it. (Food has to be smuggled into school, hidden inside his swimming things.) Sam loves white goods, especially washing machines, so during a two-week stay in London he was taken to a different launderette each day, and nearly combusted with excitement; he also likes to look at bottles of lavatory cleaner through frosted glass. George parrots lines he's learned from videotapes: "The Government has let me down," he told his trampoline teacher recently. (For some reason, trampolines are a big part of our lives.) "This would make Ken Russell spit with envy," he remarked enigmatically on another occasion. Oasthouses, washing machines, pretending not to eat when really you do… see? You really couldn't make it up.

I don't want to give the impression that living with an autistic child is *all* fun. If you have a child of the common or garden-variety, I wouldn't recommend, on balance, that you swap him in (most autistic kids are boys) for a child with a hilarious obsession. Hopefully I need hardly add that there's some stuff that… well, that, to understate the case, isn't quite as hilarious. I am merely pointing out, as Moore is doing, that if you are remotely interested in the strangeness and variety and beauty of humankind, then there is a lot in the condition to marvel at. This is the first book about autism I've read that I'd recommend to people who want to know what it is like; it's sensible about education, diet, possible causes, just about everything that affects the quotidian lives of those dealing with the condition. It also made this parent feel better about the compromises one has to make: "This morning George breakfasted on six After Eights [After Eights are "sophisticated" chocolate mints] and some lemon barley-water. I was pleased—*pleased*—because lately he hasn't been eating at all…" In our house it's salt-and-vinegar crisps.

I can imagine *George and Sam* doing a roaring trade with grandparents, aunts, and uncles tough enough to want to know the truth. I read it while listening to Damien Rice's beautiful *O* for the first time, and I had an unexpectedly transcendent moment: the book coloured the music, and the music coloured the book, and I ended up feeling unambivalently happy that my son is who he is; those moments are precious. I hope *George and Sam* finds a U.S. publisher.

A couple of months ago, I became depressed by the realization that I'd forgotten pretty much everything I've ever read. I have, however, bounced back: I am now cheered by the realization that, if I've forgotten everything I've ever read, then I can read some of my favorite books again *as if for the first time*. I remembered the punch line of *The Sirens of Titan,* but everything else was as fresh as a daisy, and Vonnegut's wise, lovely, world-weary novel was a perfect way to cap Charlotte Moore's book: she'd prepared the way beautifully for a cosmic and absurdly reductive view of our planet. I'm beginning to see that our appetite for books is the same as our appetite for food, that our brain tells us when we need the literary equivalent of salads, or chocolate, or meat and potatoes. When I read *Moneyball,* it was because I wanted something quick and light after the 32-oz steak of *No Name*; *The Sirens of Titan* wasn't a reaction against *George and Sam,* but a way of enhancing it. So what's that? Mustard?

MSG? A brandy? It went down a treat, anyway.

Smoking is rubbish, most of the time. But if I'd never smoked, I'd never have met Kurt Vonnegut. We were both at a huge party in New York, and I sneaked out onto the balcony for a cigarette, and there he was, smoking. So we talked—about C. S. Forester, I seem to remember. (That's just a crappy and phony figure of speech. Of course I remember.) So tell your kids not to smoke, but it's only fair to warn them of the down side, too: that they will therefore never get the chance to offer the greatest living writer in America a light. ✷

FEBRUARY 2004

BOOKS BOUGHT:

* ⋆ *Old School*—Tobias Wolff
* ⋆ *Train*—Pete Dexter
* ⋆ *Backroom Boys*—Francis Spufford
* ⋆ *You Are Not a Stranger Here*—Adam Haslett
* ⋆ *Eats, Shoots and Leaves*—Lynn Truss

BOOKS READ:

* ⋆ *Enemies of Promise*—Cyril Connolly
* ⋆ *What Just Happened?*—Art Linson
* ⋆ *Clockers*—Richard Price
* ⋆ *Eats, Shoots and Leaves*—Lynn Truss
* ⋆ *Meat Is Murder*—Joe Pernice
* ⋆ *Dusty in Memphis*—Warren Zanes
* ⋆ *Old School*—Tobias Wolff
* ⋆ *Introducing Time*—Craig Callender and Ralph Edney
* ⋆ PLUS: a couple of stories in *You Are Not a Stranger Here*; a couple of stories in *Sixty Stories* by Donald Barthelme; a couple of stories in *Here's Your Hat What's Your Hurry?* by Elizabeth McCracken.

My first book was published just over eleven years ago and remains in print, and though I observed the anniversary with only a modest celebration (a black-tie dinner for forty of my closest friends, many of whom were kind enough to read out the speeches I had prepared for them), I can now see that I should have made more of a fuss: in *Enemies of Promise*, which was written in 1938, the critic Cyril Connolly attempts to isolate the qualities that make a book last for ten years.

Over the decades since its publication, *Enemies of Promise* has been reduced pretty much to one line: "There is no more sombre enemy of good art than the pram in the hall," which is possibly why I was never previously very interested in reading it. What are you supposed to do if the pram in the hall is already there? You could move it out into the garden, I suppose, if you have a garden, or get rid of it and carry the little bastards everywhere, but maybe I'm being too literal-minded.

Enemies of Promise is about a lot more than the damaging effects of domesticity, however; it's also about prose style, and the perils of success, and journalism, and politics. Anyone who writes, or wants to write, will find something on just about every single page that either endorses a long-held prejudice or outrages, and that makes it a pretty compelling read. (Ironically, the copy I found on the shelf belongs to one of the mothers of my children. I wonder if she knew, when she bought it twenty years ago, that she would one day partially destroy a literary career? Connolly would probably argue that she did. He generally takes a pretty dim view of women, who "make crippling demands on [a writer's] time and money, especially if they set their hearts on his popular success." Bless 'em, eh? I'm presuming, as Connolly does, that you're a man. What would a woman be doing reading a literary magazine anyway?)

Connolly spends the first part of the book dividing writers into two camps, the Mandarin and the Vernacular. (He is crankily thorough in this division, by the way. He even goes through the big books of the twenties year by year, and marks them with a V or an M: "1929—H. Green, *Living* (V); W. Faulkner, *The Sound and the Fury* (M); Hemingway, *A Farewell to Arms* (V); Lawrence, *Pansies* (V); Joyce, *Fragments of a Work in Progress* (M)," and so on. One hesitates to point it out—it's too late now—but shouldn't Connolly have been getting on with his writing, rather than fiddling around with lists? That's one of your enemies, right there.) And then, having thus divided, he spends a lot of time despairing of both camps. "The Mandarin style… is beloved of literary pundits, by those who would make the written word as unlike as possible to the spoken one. It is the title of those writers whose tendency is to make their language convey more than they mean or more than they feel." (Yay, Cyril! Way to go!) Meanwhile, "According to Gide, a good writer should navigate against the current; the practitioners in the new vernacular are swimming with it; the familiarities of the advertisements in the morning paper, the matey leaders in the *Daily Express,* the blather of the film critics, the wisecracks of the newsreel commentators, the know-all autobiographies of political reporters, the thrillers and 'teccies… are all swimming with it too." (Cyril, you utter *ass*. You think Hemingway wrote like that lot? Have another look, mate.) Incidentally, the "know-all autobiographies of political reporters"—that was a whole *genre* in the nineteen-thirties? Boy.

The invention of paperbacks, around the time Connolly was writing *Enemies of Promise*, changed everything. Connolly's ten-year question could fill a book in 1938 because the answer was genuinely complicated then; books really could sit out the vicissitudes of fashion on library shelves, and then dust themselves off and climb back down into readers' laps. Paperbacks and chain bookstores mean that a contemporary version of *Enemies of Promise* would consist of one simple and uninteresting question: "Well, did it sell in its first year?" My first book did OK; meanwhile, books that I reviewed and loved in 1991 and 1992, books every bit as good or better than mine, are out of print, simply because they never found a readership then. They might have passed all the Connolly tests, but they're dead in the water anyway.

You end up muttering back at just about every ornately constructed *pensée* that Connolly utters, but that's one of the joys of this book. At one point, he strings together a few sentences by Hemingway, Isherwood, and Orwell in an attempt to prove that their prose styles are indistinguishable. But the point, surely, is that though you can make Connolly's sentence-by-sentence case easily enough, you'd never confuse a book by Orwell with a book by Hemingway—and that's what they were doing, writing books. Look, here's a plain, flat, vernacular sentence:

> So I bought a little city (it was Galveston, Texas) and told everybody that nobody had to move, we were going to do it just gradually, very relaxed, no big changes overnight.

This is the tremendous first line of Donald Barthelme's story "I Bought a Little City" (V); one fears that Connolly might have spent a lot of time looking at the finger, and ignored what it was pointing at. ("See, he bought a whole *city*, Cyril! Galveston, Texas! Oh, forget it.") The vernacular turned out to be far more adaptable than Connolly could have predicted.

Reading the book now means that one can, if one wants, play Fantasy Literature—match writers off against each other and see who won over the long haul. (M) or (V)? Faulkner or Henry Green? I reckon the surprise champ was

PG Wodehouse, as elegant and resourceful a prose stylist as anyone held up for our inspection here; Connolly is sniffy about him several times over the course of *Enemies of Promise,* and presumes that his stuff won't last five minutes, but he has turned out to be as enduring as anyone apart from Orwell. Jokes, you see. People do like jokes.

The Polysyllabic Spree, the twelve terrifyingly beatific young men and woman who run this magazine, have been quiet of late—they haven't been giving me much trouble, anyway. A friend who works in the same building has heard the ominous rustle of white robes upstairs, however, and he reckons they're planning something pretty big, maybe something like another Jonestown. (That makes sense, if you think about it. The robes, the eerie smiles, "the *Believer*"… if you find a free sachet of powdered drink, or—more likely—an edible poem in this month's issue, don't touch it.) Anyway, while they're thus distracted, I shall attempt to sneak a snark under the wire: Tobias Wolff's *Old School* is too short. Oh, come on, guys! That's different from saying it's too long! Too long means you didn't like it! Too short means you did!

The truth is, I've been reading more short books recently because I need to bump up the numbers in the Books Read column—six of this month's seven were really pretty scrawny. But *Old School* I would have read this month, the month of its publication, no matter how long it was: Wolff's two volumes of memoir, *This Boy's Life* and *In Pharaoh's Army,* are perennial sources of writerly inspiration, and you presumably know how good his stories are. *Old School* is brilliant—painful, funny, exquisitely written, acute about writers and literary ambition. (*Old School* is set right at the beginning of the sixties, in a boys' private school, and you get to meet Robert Frost and Ayn Rand.) But the problem with short novels is that you can take liberties with them: you know you're going to get through them no matter what, so you never set aside the time or the commitment that a bigger book requires. I fucked *Old School* up; I should have read it in a sitting, but I didn't, and I never gave it a chance to leave its mark. We are never allowed to forget that some books are badly written; we should remember that sometimes they're badly read, too.

Eats, Shoots and Leaves (the title refers to a somewhat labored joke about a misplaced comma and a panda) is Britain's number-one best seller at the moment, and it's about punctuation, and no, I don't get it, either. It's a sweet, good-humored book, and it's grammatically sound and all, but, you know... it really is all about how to use a semicolon and all that. What's going on? One writer I know suspects that the book's enormous success is due to the disturbing rise of the Provincial Pedant, but I have a more benign theory: that when you hear about it (and you hear about it a lot, at the moment), you think of someone immediately, someone you know and love, whose punctuation exasperates you and fills them full of self-loathing. I thought of Len, and my partner thought of Emily, neither of whom could place an apostrophe correctly if their lives depended on it. (Names have been changed, by the way, to protect the semiliterate.) And I'm sure Len and Emily will receive a thousand copies each for Christmas and birthdays, and other people will buy a thousand copies for their Lens and Emilys, and in the end the book will sell a quarter of a million copies, *but only two hundred different people will own them.* I enjoyed the fearful bashing that Lynn Truss gives to the entertainment industry—the Hugh Grant movie *Two Weeks Notice* (sic), *Who Framed Roger Rabbit* (sic), the fabricated English pop band Hear'Say (sic)—and the advice she quotes from a newspaper style manual: "Punctuation is a courtesy designed to help readers understand a story without stumbling," which helps to explain a lot of literary fiction. I had never before heard of the Oxford comma (used before the "and" that brings a list to a close), and I didn't know that Jesus never gets a possessive "s," just because of who He is. I never really saw the possessive "s" as profane, or even very secular, but there you go.

The most irritating book of the month (can't you feel the collective heart of the Spree beating a little faster?) was Joe Pernice's *Meat Is Murder.* One can accept, reluctantly, Pernice's apparently inexhaustible ability to knock out brilliant three-minute pop songs—just about any Pernice Brothers record contains half a dozen tunes comparable to Elvis Costello's best work. But now it turns out that he can write fiction too, and so envy and bitterness become unavoidable. *Meat Is Murder* and Warren Zanes's *Dusty in Memphis* are both part of a new and neat little "33-and-a-third" series published by Continuum; Pernice is the only writer who has chosen to write a novella about a favorite album, rather than an essay; his story is set in 1985, and is about high school and suicide and teen depression and, tangentially, the Smiths. Warren Zanes's effort, almost the polar opposite of

Pernice's, is a long, scholarly and convincing piece of nonfiction analyzing the myth of the American South. Endearingly, neither book mentions the relevant records as much as you'd expect: the music is a ghostly rather than physical presence. I liked Art Linson's *What Just Happened?*, one of those scabrous, isn't-Hollywood-awful? books written by someone—a producer, in this case (and indeed in most other cases, e.g. Julia Phillips, Lynda Obst)—who knows what he's talking about. I can't really explain why I picked it up, however; perhaps I wanted to be made grateful that I work in publishing, rather than film, and that's what happened.

Clockers was my big book of the month, the centerpiece around which I can now arrange the short books so that they look functional—pretty, even, if I position them right. I cheated a little, I know—*Clockers* is essentially a thriller, so it didn't feel as though I'd had to work for my 650 pages—but it was still a major reading job. Why isn't Richard Price incredibly famous, like Tom Wolfe? His work is properly plotted, indisputably authentic and serious-minded, and it has soul and moral authority.

Clockers asks—almost in passing, and there's a lot more to it than this—a pretty interesting question: if you choose to work for the minimum wage when everyone around you is pocketing thousands from drug deals, then what does that do to you, to your head and to your heart? Price's central characters, brothers Strike (complicatedly bad, a crack dealer) and Victor (complicatedly good, the minimum wage guy) act out something that feels as inevitable and as durable as a Bible story, except with a lot more swearing and drugs. *Clockers* is—eek—really about the contradictions of capitalism.

I've been trying to write a short story that entails my knowing something about contemporary theories of time—hence *Introducing Time*—but every time I pick up any kind of book about science I start to cry. This actually inhibits my reading pretty badly, due to not being able to see. I'm OK with time theorists up until, say, St. Augustine, and then I start to panic, and the panic then gives way to actual weeping. By my estimation, I should be able to understand Newton by the time I'm 850 years old—by which time I'll probably discover that some smartass has invented a new theory, and he's out of date anyway. The short story should be done some time shortly after that. Anyway, I hope you enjoy it, because it's killing me. ✭

MARCH 2004

So this last month was, as I believe you people say, a bust. I had high hopes for it, too; it was Christmas-time in England, and I was intending to do a little holiday comfort reading—*David Copperfield* and a couple of John Buchan novels, say, while sipping an eggnog and heroically ploughing my way through some enormous animal carcass or other. I've been a father for ten years now, and not once have I been able to sit down and read several hundred pages of Dickens during the Christmas holidays. Why I thought it might be possible this year, now that I have twice as many children, is probably a question best discussed with an analyst: somewhere along the line, I have failed to take something on board. (Hey, great idea: if you have kids, give your partner reading vouchers next Christmas. Each voucher entitles the bearer to two hours' reading-time *while kids are awake*. It might look like a cheapskate present, but parents will appreciate that it costs more in real terms than a Lamborghini.)

If I'm honest, however, it wasn't just snot-nosed children who crawled between and all over me and Richard Hannay. One of the reasons I wanted to write this column, I think, is because I assumed that the cultural highlight of my month would arrive in book form, and that's true, for probably eleven months of the year. Books are, let's face it, better than everything else. If we played Cultural Fantasy Boxing League, and made books go fifteen rounds in the ring against the best that any other art form had to offer, then books would win pretty much every time. Go on, try it. "The Magic Flute" v. *Middlemarch*? *Middlemarch* in six. "The Last Supper" v. *Crime and Punishment*? Fyodor on points. See? I mean, I don't know how scientific this is, but it feels like the novels are walking it. You might get the occasional exception—*Blonde on Blonde* might mash up *The Old Curiosity Shop*, say, and I wouldn't give much for *Pale Fire*'s chances against *Citizen Kane*. And every now and again you'd get a shock, because that happens in sport, so *Back to the Future III* might land a lucky punch on *Rabbit, Run*; but I'm still backing literature twenty-nine times out of thirty. Even if you love movies and music as much as you do books, it's still, in any given four-week period, way, *way* more likely you'll find a great book you haven't read than a great movie you haven't seen, or a great album you haven't heard: the assiduous consumer will eventually exhaust movies and music. Sure, there will always be gaps and blind spots, but I've been watching and listening for a long time, and I'll never again have the feeling everyone has with literature: that we can't get through the good novels published in the last six months, let alone those published since publishing began. This month, however, the cultural highlight of the month was a rock and roll show—two shows, actually, one of which took place in a pub called the Fiddler's Elbow in Kentish Town, North London. The Fiddler's Elbow is not somewhere you would normally expect to find your most memorable drink of the month, let alone your most memorable spiritual moment, but there you go: God really is everywhere. Anyway, against all the odds, and even though they were fighting above their weight, these shows punched the books to the floor. And they were good books, too.

Five or six years ago, a friend in Philly introduced me to a local band called Marah. Their first album had just come out, on an indie label, and it sounded great to me, like the Pogues reimagined by the E Street Band, full of fire and tunes and soul and banjos. There was a buzz about it, and they got picked up by Steve Earle's label E-Squared; their next album got noticed by Greil Marcus and Stephen King (who proudly wore a Marah T-shirt in a photo-shoot) and Springsteen himself, and it looked like they were off and away. Writing this down, I can suddenly see the reason why it didn't happen for them, or at least, why it hasn't happened yet. Steve Earle, Stephen King, Greil Marcus, Bruce, me... none of us is under a hundred years old. The band is young, but their referents, the music they love, is getting on a bit, and in an attempt to address this problem, they attempted to alienate their ancient fans with a noisy modern rock album. They succeeded in the alienation, but not in finding a new audience, so they have been forced to retreat and retrench and rethink. At the end of the Fiddler's Elbow show they passed a hat around, which gives you some indication of the level of retrenchment going on. They'll be OK. Their next album will be spectacular, and they'll sell out Madison Square Garden, and you'll all be boasting that you read a column by a guy who saw them in the Fiddler's Elbow.

Anyway, the two shows I saw that week were spectacular, as good as anything I've seen with the possible exception of the Clash in '79, Prince in '85, and Springsteen on the *River* tour. Dave and Serge, the two brothers who are to Marah what the Gallaghers are to Oasis, played the Fiddler's Elbow as if it were Giants Stadium, and even though it was acoustic, they just about blew the place up. They were standing on chairs and lying on the floor, they were funny, they charmed everyone in the pub apart from an old drunk sitting next to the drum kit (a drummer turned up halfway through the evening with his own set, having played a gig elsewhere first), who put his fingers firmly in his ears during Serge's extended harmonica solo. (His mate, meanwhile, rose unsteadily to his feet and started clapping along.) It was utterly bizarre and very moving: most musicians wouldn't have bothered turning up, let alone almost killing themselves. And I was reminded—and this happened the last time I saw them play, too—how rarely one feels included in a live show. Usually you watch, and listen, and drift off, and the band plays well or doesn't and it doesn't matter much either way. It can actually be a very lonely experience. But I felt a part of the music, and a part of the people I'd gone with, and, to cut this short before the encores, I didn't want to read for about a fortnight afterwards. I wanted to write, but I couldn't because of the holidays, and I wanted to listen to Marah, but

I didn't want to read no book. I was too itchy, too energized, and if young people feel like that every night of the week, then, yes, literature's dead as a dodo. (In an attempt to get myself back on course, I bought Bill Ehrhardt's book *Vietnam-Perkasie,* because he comes Marah-endorsed, and provided the inspiration for "Round Eye Blues," one of their very best songs. I didn't read the thing, though. And their next album is tentatively entitled *20,000 Streets under the Sky,* after a Patrick Hamilton novel—I'm going to order that and not read it, too.)

It wasn't as if I didn't try; it was just that very little I picked up fit very well with my mood. I bought Flaubert's letters after reading the piece about Donald Barthelme's required reading list in the *Believer* [October, 2003], but they weren't right—or at least, they're not if one chooses to read them in chronological order. The young Flaubert wasn't very rock and roll. He was, on this evidence, kind of a prissy, nerdy kid. "friend, I shall send you some of my political speeches, liberal constitutionalist variety," he wrote to Ernest Chevalier in January 1831; he'd just turned nine years old. Nine! Get a life, kid! (Really? You wrote those? They're pretty good books. Well… Get another one, then.) I am probably taking more pleasure than is seemly in his failure to begin the sentence with a capital letter. You know, as in, Jesus, he didn't know the first thing about basic punctuation! How did this loser ever get to be a writer?

Francis Wheen's *How Mumbo-Jumbo Conquered the World* was a better fit, because, well, it rocks: it's fast and smart and very funny, despite being about how we have betrayed the Enlightenment by retreating back to the Dark Ages. Wheen wrote a warm, witty biography of Marx a few years back, and has a unique, sharp, enviable, and trustworthy mind. Here he dishes it out two-fisted to Tony Blair and George W. Bush, Deepak Chopra and Francis Fukuyama, Princess Diana and Margaret Thatcher, Hillary Clinton and Jacques Derrida, and by the end of the book you do have the rather dizzying sensation that you, the author, and maybe Richard Dawkins are the only remotely sane people in the entire world. It's difficult to endorse this book without committing a few cardinal *Believer* sins: as you may have noticed, some of the people that Wheen accuses of talking bullshit are, regrettably, writers, and in a chapter entitled "The Demolition Merchants of Reality," Wheen lumps deconstructionism in with creationism. In other words, he claims there isn't much to choose from between

Pat Buchanan and Jacques Lacan when it comes to mumbo-jumbo, and I'm sorry to say that I laughed a lot. The next chapter, "The Catastrophists," gives homeopathy, astrology, and UFOlogy a good kicking, and you'll find yourself conveniently forgetting the month you gave up coffee and mint because you were taking arnica three times a day. (Did you know that Jacques Benveniste, one of the world's leading homeopathic "scientists," now claims that you can *email* homeopathic remedies? Yeah, see, what you do is you can take the "memory" of the diluted substance out of the water electromagnetically, put it on your computer, email it, and play it back on a sound card into new water. I mean, that could work, right?)

Richard Dawkins, Wheen recalls, once pointed out that if an alternative remedy proves to be efficacious—that is to say, if it is shown to have curative properties in rigorous medical trials—then "it ceases to be an alternative; it simply becomes medicine." In other words, it's only "alternative" so long as it's been shown not to be any bloody good. I found it impossible not to apply this helpful observation to other areas of life. Maybe a literary novel is just a novel that doesn't really work, and an art film merely a film that people don't want to see... *How Mumbo-Jumbo Conquered the World* is a clever-clogs companion to Michael Moore's *Stupid White Men*; and as it's about people of both sexes and every conceivable hue, it's arguably even more ambitious.

I read *Liar's Poker,* Michael Lewis's book about bond-traders in the eighties, for two reasons, one of which was Wheen-inspired: he made me want to try and be more clever, especially about grown-up things like economics. Plus I'd read Lewis's great *Moneyball* a couple of months previously [see "Stuff I've Been Reading," Dec. 2003/Jan. 2004], so I already knew that he was capable of leading me through the minefields of my own ignorance. It turns out, though, that the international money markets are more complicated than baseball. These guys buy and sell mortgages! They buy and sell risk! But I haven't got a clue what any of that actually means! This isn't Michael Lewis's fault—he really did try his best, and in any case you kind of romp through the book anyway: the people are pretty compelling, if completely unlike anyone you might meet in real life. At one point, Lewis describes an older trader throwing a ten-dollar bill at a young colleague about to take a business flight. "Hey, take out some crash insurance for yourself in my name," the older guy says. "I feel lucky." As a metaphor for what happens on the trading floor, that's pretty hard to beat.

Francis Wheen's book and Paul Collins's *Not Even Wrong* were advance reading copies that arrived through the post. I'm never going to complain about receiving free early copies of books, because quite clearly there's nothing to complain about, but it does introduce a rogue element into one's otherwise carefully plotted reading schedule. I had no idea I wanted to read Wheen's book until it arrived, and it was because of Wheen that I read Lewis, and then *Not Even Wrong* turned up and I wanted to read that too, and Buchan's *Greenmantle* got put to one side, I suspect forever. Being a reader is sort of like being president, except reading involves fewer state dinners, usually. You have this agenda you want to get through, but you get distracted by life events, e.g. books arriving in the mail/ World War III, and you are temporarily deflected from your chosen path.

Having said that I hardly ever read books about autism. I have now read two in the last few weeks. Paul Collins, occasionally of this parish, is another parent of an autistic kid, and *Not Even Wrong,* like Charlotte Moore's *George and Sam,* is a memoir of sorts. The two books are complementary, though; while writing unsentimentally but movingly about his son Morgan's diagnosis and the family's response, Collins trawls around, as is his wont, for historical and contemporary illustration and resonance, and finds plenty. There's Peter the Wild Boy, who became part of the royal household in the early eighteenth century, and who met Pope, Addison, Steele, Swift, and Defoe—he almost certainly played for our team. (Autistic United? Maybe Autistic Wanderers is better.) And Collins finds a lot of familiar traits among railway-timetable collectors, and Microsoft boffins, and outsider artists… I'm happy that we're living through these times of exceptionally written and imaginative memoirs, despite the incessant whine you hear from the books pages; Collins's engaging, discursive book isn't as raw as some, but in place of rawness there is thoughtfulness, and thoughtfulness is never a bad thing. I even learned stuff, and you can't often say that of a memoir.

New Year, New Me, another quick read of Gillian Riley's *How to Give Up Smoking and Stay Stopped for Good.* I have now come to think of Riley as our leading cessation theorist; she's brilliant, but now I need someone who deals with the practicalities. ✱

APRIL 2004

Last month I was banging on about how books were better than anything—how just about any decent book you picked would beat up anything else, any film or painting or piece of music, you cared to match it up with. Anyway, like most theories advanced in this column, it turned out to be utter rubbish. I read four really good books this month, but even so, my cultural highlights of the last four weeks were not literary. I went to a couple of terrific exhibitions at the Royal Academy (and that's a hole in my argument right there—one book might beat up one painting, but what chance has one book, or even four books, got against the collected works of Guston and Vuillard?); I saw Jose Antonio Reyes score his first goal for Arsenal against Chelsea, a thirty-yard screamer, right in the top corner; and someone sent me a superlative Springsteen bootleg, a '75 show at the Main Point in Bryn Mawr with strings, and a cover of "I Want You," and I don't know what else. Like I said, I loved the books that I read this month, but when that Reyes shot hit the back of the net, I was four feet in the air. (The Polysyllabic Spree hates sport, especially soccer, because it requires people to expose their arms and legs, and the Spree believes that all body parts must be covered at all times. So even though I'm not allowed to talk about Reyes at any length, he does look to be some player.) Anyway, Patrick Hamilton didn't even get me to move my feet. I just sat there—lay there, most of the time—throughout the whole thing. So there we are, then. Books: pretty good, but not as good as other stuff, like goals, or bootlegs.

I spent a long time resisting *The Curious Incident of the Dog in the Night-Time* because I got sent about fifteen copies, by publishers and agents and magazines and newspapers, and it made me recalcitrant and reluctant, truculent, maybe even perverse. I got sent fifteen copies because the narrator of *The Curious Incident* has Asperger's syndrome, which places him on the autistic spectrum, although way over the other side from my son. I can see why publishers do this, but the books that arrive in the post tend to be a distorted and somewhat unappetizing version of one's life and work. And what one wants to read, most of the time, is something that bears no reference to one's life and work.

(Twice this week I have been sent manuscripts of books that remind their editors, according to their covering letters, of my writing. Like a lot of writers, I can't really stand my own writing, in the same way that I don't really like my own cooking. And, just as when I go out to eat, I tend not to order my signature dish—an overcooked and overspiced meat-stewy thing containing something inappropriate, like tinned peaches, and a side order of undercooked and flavor-less vegetables—I really don't want to read anything that I could have come up with at my own computer. What I produce on my computer invariably turns out to be an equivalent of the undercooked overcooked stewy thing, no matter how hard I try to follow the recipe, and you really don't want to eat too much of that. I'd love to be sent a book with an accompanying letter that said, "This is nothing like your work. But as a man of taste and discernment, we think you'll love it anyway." That never happens.)

Anyway, I finally succumbed to Mark Haddon's book, simply because it had been recommended to me so many times as a piece of fiction, rather than as a recognizable portrait of my home life. It's the third book about autism I've read in three months, and each book—this one, Charlotte Moore's *George and Sam,* and Paul Collins's *Not Even Wrong*—contains a description of the classic test devised to demonstrate the lack of a theory of mind in autistic children. I'll quote Paul Collins's succinct summary:

> Sally and Anne have a box and a basket in front of them. Sally puts a marble in the basket. Then she leaves the room. While Sally is gone, Anne takes the marble out of the basket and puts it in the box. When Sally comes back in, where will she look for her marble?

If you ask ordinary kids, even ordinary three-year-olds, to observe Sally and Anne and then answer the question, they'll tell you that Sally will look in the basket. An autistic kid, however, will always tell you that Sally should look in the box, because an autistic kid is unable to imagine that someone else knows (or feels, or thinks) anything different from himself. In *The Curious Incident*, Christopher attempts to solve a murder-mystery, and one would imagine that of all the career-paths closed off to autists, the path leading to a desk at the FBI is probably the least accessible. If you are profoundly unable to put yourself in someone else's shoes, then a job involving intuition and empathy, second-guessing and psychology is probably not the job for you. Haddon has Christopher, his narrator, refer to the theory-of-mind experiment, and it's the one moment in the book where the author nearly brings his otherwise smartly imagined world crashing about his and our ears. Christopher talks about his own failure in the test, and then says, "That was because when I was little I didn't understand about other people having minds. And Julie said to Mother and Father that I would always find this very difficult. Because I decided it was a kind of puzzle, and if something is a puzzle there is always a way of solving it."

"I decided it was a kind of puzzle..." Hold on a moment: that means—what?—that every Asperger's kid could do this, if they so chose? That the most debilitating part of the condition—effectively, the condition itself—could be removed by an application of will? This is dangerous territory, and I'm not sure Haddon crosses it with absolute conviction. *The Curious Incident...* is an absorbing, entertaining, moving book, but when truth gets bent out of shape in this way in order to serve the purposes of a narrative, then maybe it's a book that can't properly be described as a work of art? I don't know. I'm just asking the question. Happily, the detective element of the novel has been pretty much forgotten by the second half, and one description—of Christopher trying and failing to get on a crowded tube train, and then another, and then another, until

hours and hours pass—is unforgettable, and very, very real.

In an online interview, Haddon quotes one of his Amazon reviewers, someone who hated his novel, saying "the most worrying thing about the book is that Christopher says he dislikes fiction, and yet the whole book is fiction." And that, says the author, "puts at least part of the problem in a nutshell." It doesn't, I don't think, because the Amazon reviewer is too dim to put anything in a nutshell. I suspect, in fact, that the Amazon reviewer couldn't put anything in the boot of his car, let alone a nutshell. (Presumably you couldn't write a book about someone who couldn't read, either, or someone who didn't like paper, because the whole book is paper. Oh, man, I hate Amazon reviewers. Even the nice ones, who say nice things. They're bastards too.) But Haddon is right if what he's saying is that picking through a book of this kind for inconsistencies is a mug's game, and I'm sorry if that's what I've done. The part that made me wince a little seemed more fundamental than an inconsistency, though.

This comes up again in Patrick Hamilton's brilliant *Hangover Square,* where the central character suffers from some kind of schizophrenia. At periodic intervals he kind of blacks out, even though he remains conscious throughout the attacks. ("It was as though a shutter had fallen"; "as though one had blown one's nose too hard and the outer world had become suddenly dim"; "as though he had been watching a talking film, and all at once the sound-track had failed"—because George Bone cannot properly recall the last attack, he searches for fresh ways to describe each new one.) And of course it doesn't quite make sense, because he doesn't know what he's doing when the attacks occur, except he does, really; and he doesn't know who anyone is anymore, except he manages to retain just enough information to make Hamilton's plot work. And it really doesn't matter, because this book isn't about schizophrenia. It's about an exhausted city on the brink of war—it's set in London at the beginning of 1939—and about shiftless drunken fuckups, and it feels astonishingly contemporary and fresh. You may remember that I wanted to read Hamilton because my current favorite rock-and-roll band is naming an album after one of his books, and if that seems like a piss-poor (and laughably unliterary) reason to dig out a neglected minor classic, well, I'm sorry. But I got there in the end, and I'm glad I did. Thank you, Marah. Oh, and George Bone in schizophrenic mode has a hilarious and unfathomable obsession with a town called Maidenhead, which is where I grew up, and which has been for the most part overlooked, and wisely so, throughout the entire history of the English novel. Bone thinks that when he gets to Maidenhead, everything's going to be all right. Good luck with that, George!

I bought Mark Salzman's *True Notebooks* a couple of months ago, after an interview with the author in this magazine. I am beginning belatedly to realize that discovering books through reading about them in the *Believer,* and then writing about them in the *Believer*—as I have done once or twice before—is a circular process that doesn't do you any favors. You'd probably like to read about a book you didn't read about a while back. Anyway, as the interview implied, this is a pretty great book, but, *boy* is it sad.

True Notebooks is about Mark Salzman's gig teaching writing at Central Juvenile Hall in LA, where just about every kid is awaiting trial on a gang-related murder charge. Salzman's just the right person to attempt a book of this kind. He's empathetic and compassionate and all that jazz, but he's no bleeding-heart liberal. At the beginning of the book, he lists all the reasons why he shouldn't get involved in this kind of thing. They include "Students all gangbangers," "Still angry about getting mugged in 1978," and, even less ambiguously, "Wish we could tilt LA County and shake it until everybody with a shaved head and tattoos falls into the ocean." Toward the end of the book, he attends the trial of the student he loves the most, listens to all the extenuating circumstances, and finds himself going to bed that night with a broken heart, just as he feared he would. However, his sadness is engendered "not because of what the legal system was doing to young people… I had to wrap my mind around the fact that someone I had grown so fond of, and who seemed so gentle, had been foolish enough to go to a movie theater carrying a loaded gun, violent enough to shoot three people with it—two of them in the back—and then callous enough to want to go to a movie afterwards."

I don't want to give the impression that *True Notebooks* is unreadable in its gray-grimness, or unpalatably preachy. It's consistently entertaining, and occasionally bleakly funny. "How about describing a time you helped someone?" Salzman suggests to a student who is struggling for a topic to write about.

"Mm… I never did anything that nice for anybody."

"It can be a small thing."

"Mm… it's gonna have to be real small, Mark."

This is one of those books where the characters learn and grow and change, and we've all read countless novels and seen countless films like that, and we know what to expect: redemption, right? But *True Notebooks* is real, so the characters learn and grow and change, and then get sentenced to thirty-plus years in prison, where god knows what fate awaits them. In the acknowledgments at the end of the book, Salzman thanks the students for making him decide to have children of his own. It might not be much when set against the suffering and pain both caused and experienced by the kids he teaches, but it's all we've got to work with, and I'm disproportionately glad he mentioned it: when I'd finished *True Notebooks,* Salzman's kids were all I had to keep me going. I'm enjoying *The Long Firm,* Jake Arnott's clever and vivid novel about London's gangland in the 1960s, but I think perhaps *True Notebooks* spoiled it for me a little. Gangland, gangs, guns, murder… none of it is as much fun as you might think.

Next month I'm going to read *David Copperfield,* the only major Dickens I haven't done yet. I'll probably still be reading it the month after, too, so if you want to take a break from this column, now would probably be the time to do it. I've been putting it off for a while, mostly because of the need to read loads of stuff that I can use to fill up these pages, but I'm really feeling the need for a bit of Dickensian nutrition. I don't know what I'll find to say about it, though, and I'm really hoping that Jose Antonio Reyes can help me out of a hole. Are thirty-yard thunderbolts better than Dickens at his best? I'll bet you can't wait to find out. ✶

MAY 2004

Anyone and everyone taking a writing class knows that the secret of good writing is to cut it back, pare it down, winnow, chop, hack, prune and trim, remove every superfluous word, compress, compress, compress. What's that chinking noise? It's the sound of the assiduous creative-writing student hitting bone. You can't read a review of, say, a Coetzee book without coming across the word "spare," used invariably with approval; I just Googled "J. M. Coetzee + spare" and got 907 hits, almost all of them different. "Coetzee's spare but multi-layered language," "detached in tone and spare in style," "layer upon layer of spare, exquisite sentences," "Coetzee's great gift—and it is a gift he extends to us—is in his spare and yet beautiful language," "spare and powerful language," "a chilling, spare book," "paradoxically both spare and richly textured," "spare, steely beauty." Get it? Spare is good.

Coetzee, of course, is a great novelist, so I don't think it's snarky to point out that he's not the funniest writer in the world. Actually, when you think about it, not many novels in the Spare tradition are terribly cheerful. Jokes you can usually pluck out whole, by the roots, so if you're doing some heavy-duty prose-weeding, they're the first things to go. And there's some stuff about the whole winnowing process that I just don't get. Why does it always stop when the work in question has been reduced to sixty or seventy thousand words—entirely coincidentally, I'm sure, the minimum length for a publishable novel? I'm sure you could get it down to twenty or thirty, if you tried hard enough. In fact, why stop at twenty or thirty? Why write at all? Why not just jot the plot and a couple of themes down on the back of an envelope and leave it at that? The truth is, there's nothing very utilitarian about fiction or its creation, and I suspect that people are desperate to make it sound like manly, back-breaking labor because it's such a wussy thing to do in the first place. The obsession with austerity is an attempt to compensate, to make writing resemble a real job, like farming, or logging. (It's also why people who work in advertising put in twenty-hour days.) Go on, young writers—treat yourself to a joke, or an adverb! Spoil yourself! Readers won't mind! Have you ever looked at the size of books in an airport bookstall? The truth is that people like superfluity. (And, conversely, the writers' writers, the pruners and the winnowers, tend to have to live off critical approval rather than royalty checks.)

Last month, I ended by saying that I was in need of some Dickensian nutrition, and maybe it's because I've been sucking on the bones of pared-down writing for too long. Where would *David Copperfield* be if Dickens had gone to writing classes? Probably about seventy minor characters short, is where. (Did you know that Dickens is estimated to have invented thirteen thousand characters? Thirteen thousand! The population of a small town! If you want to talk about books in terms of back-breaking labor, then maybe we should think about how hard it is to write a lot—long books, teeming with exuberance and energy and life and comedy. I'm sorry if that seems obvious, but it can't always be true that writing a couple of hundred pages is harder than writing a thousand.) At one point near the beginning of the book, David runs away, and ends up having to sell the clothes he's wearing for food and drink. It would be enough, maybe, to describe the physical hardship that ensued; but Dickens being Dickens, he finds a bit part for a real rogue of a secondhand clothes merchant, a really scary guy who smells of rum and who shouts things like "Oh, my lungs and liver" and "Goroo!" a lot.

As King Lear said—possibly when invited in to Iowa as a visiting speaker—"Reason not the need." There is no *need*: Dickens is having fun, and he extends the scene way beyond its function. Rereading it now, it seems almost to have been conceived as a retort to spareness, because the scary guy insists on paying David for his jacket in halfpenny installments over the course of an afternoon, and thus ends up sticking around for two whole pages. Could he have been cut? Absolutely he could have been cut. But there comes a point in the writing process when a novelist—any novelist, even a great one—has to accept that what he is doing is keeping one end of a book away from the other, filling up pages, in the hope that these pages will move, provoke, and entertain a reader.

Some random observations:

1) *David Copperfield* is Dickens's *Hamlet*. *Hamlet* is a play full of famous quotes; *Copperfield* is a novel full of famous characters. I hadn't read it before, partly because I was under the curious misapprehension that I could remember a BBC serialization that I was forced to watch when I was a child, and therefore would be robbed of the pleasures of the narrative. (It turns out that all I could remember was the phrase "Barkis is willing," and Barkis's willingness isn't really the book's point.) So I really had no idea that I was going to run into both Uriah Heep and Mr. Micawber, as well as Peggotty, Steerforth, Betsey Trotwood, Little Em'ly, Tommy Traddles and the rest. I'd presumed Dickens would keep at least a couple of those back for some of the other novels I haven't read—*The Pickwick Papers,* say, or *Barnaby Rudge*. But he's blown it now. That might be an error on his part. We shall see, eventually.

2) Why do people keep trying to make movie or TV adaptations of Dickens novels? In the first issue of this magazine, Jonathan Lethem asked us to reimagine the characters in *Dombey and Son* as animals, in order to grasp the essence of these characters, and it's true that only the central characters in a Dickens novel are human. Here's Quilp, in *The Old Curiosity Shop,* terrifying Kit's mother with "many extraordinary annoyances; such as hanging over from the side of the coach at the risk of his life, and staring in with his great goggle eyes…; dodging her in this way from one window to another; getting nimbly down whenever they changed horses and thrusting his head in at the window with a dismal squint…" And here's Uriah Heep: "hardly any eyebrows, and no eyelashes, and eyes of a red-brown, so unsheltered and unshaded, that I remember wondering how he went to sleep… high-shouldered and bony… a long, lank skeleton hand… his nostrils, which were thin and pointed, with sharp dints in them, had a singular and most uncomfortable

way of expanding and contracting themselves; that they seemed to twinkle instead of his eyes, which hardly ever twinkled at all."

So who would *you* cast as these two? If the right actors ever existed, I'm betting that they wouldn't be much fun to hang out with on set, what with having no social lives, or girlfriends, or prospects of working in anything else ever, apart from *Copperfield 2: Heep's Revenge*. And once these cartoon gremlins take corporeal form, they lose their point anyway. Memo to studios: a mix of CGI and live action is the only way forward. True, it would be expensive, and true, no one would ever want to pay to watch. But if you wish to do the great man justice—and I'm sure that's all you Hollywood execs think about, just as I'm sure you're all subscribers to this magazine—then it's got to be worth a shot.

3) In *The Old Curiosity Shop* I discovered that in the character of Dick Swiveller, Dickens provided P. G. Wodehouse with pretty much the whole of his oeuvre. In *David Copperfield,* David's bosses Spenlow and Jorkins are what must be the earliest fictional representations of good cop/bad cop.

4) I have complained in this column before about how everyone wants to spoil plots of classics for you. OK, I should have read *David Copperfield* before, and therefore deserve to be punished. But even the snootiest critic/publisher/whatever must presumably accept that we must all, at some point, read a book for the first time. I know that the only thing brainy people do with their lives is reread great works of fiction, but surely even James Wood and Harold Bloom read before they reread? (Maybe not. Maybe they've only ever reread, and that's what separates them from us. Hats off to them.) Anyway, the great David Gates gives away two or three major narrative developments in the *very first paragraph* of his introduction to my Modern Library edition (and I think I'm entitled to read the first paragraph, just to get a little context or biographical detail); I tried to check out the film versions on Amazon, and an Amazon reviewer pointlessly gave away another in a three-line review. That wouldn't have happened if I'd been looking for a Grisham adaptation.

5) At the end of last year, I was given a first edition *David Copperfield* as a prize, and I had this fantasy that I was going to sit in an armchair and read a few pages of it, and feel the power of the great man enter me at my fingertips. Well, I tried it, and nothing happened. Also, the print was really small, and I was scared of dropping it in the bath, absentmindedly putting a cigarette out on it, etc. I actually ended up reading four different copies of the book. An old college Penguin edition fell apart in my hands, so I bought a Modern Library edition to replace it. Then I lost the Modern Library copy, temporarily, and bought another cheap Penguin to replace it. It cost £1.50! That's only about ninety dollars! (That was my attempt at edgy au courant humour. I won't bother again.)

There was a moment, about a third of the way through, when I thought that *David Copperfield* might become my new favorite Dickens novel—which, seeing as I believe that Dickens is the greatest novelist who ever lived, would mean that I might be in the middle of the best book I'd ever read. That superlative way of thinking ceases to become very compelling as you get older, so the realization wasn't as electrifying as you might think. I could see the logic, in the same way that you can see the logic of those ontological arguments that the old philosophers used to trot out to prove that God exists—Dickens = best writer, *DC* = his best book, therefore *DC* = best book ever written—without feeling it. But, in the end, there was too much wrong. The young women, as usual, are weedy. Bodies start to pile up in uncomfortable proximity—there are four deaths, if you count drippy Dora's bloody dog, which I don't but Dickens does—between pages 714 and 740. And just when you want the book to wrap up, Dickens inserts a pointless and dull chapter about prison reform, twenty pages from the end. (He's against solitary confinement. Too good for 'em.)

What puts David Copperfield right up there with *Bleak House* and *Great Expectations,* however, is its sweet nature, and its surprising modernity. There's some metafictional stuff going on, for example: David grows up to be a novelist, and the full title of the book, according to Edgar Johnson's biography (not that I can find any evidence of this anywhere) is *The Personal History, Experience and Observations of David Copperfield the Younger of Blunderstone Rookery, which he never meant to be published on any account.* And there's a point to the metafictional stuff, too. The last refuge of the scoundrel-critic is any version of the sentence, "Ultimately, this book is about fiction itself/this film is about film itself." I have used the sentence myself, back in the days when I reviewed a lot of books, and it's bullshit: invariably all it means is that the film or novel has drawn attention to its own fictional state, which doesn't get us very far, and which is why the critic never tells us exactly what the novel has to say about fiction itself. (Next time you see the sentence, which will probably be some time in the next seven days if you read a lot of reviews, write to the critic and ask for elucidation.)

Anyway, David Copperfield's profession allows him these piercing little moments of regret and nostalgia; there's a lot about memory in this book, and in an autobiographical novel, memory and fiction get all tangled up. Dickens uses the tangle to his advantage, and I can't remember being so moved by one of his novels. The other thing that seems to me different about *David Copperfield* is the sophistication of a couple of the characters and relationships. Dickens isn't the most sophisticated of writers, and when he does attain complexity, it's because subplot is layered upon subplot, and character over character, until he can't help but get something going. But there's a startlingly contemporary admission of marital dissatisfaction in *Copperfield,* for example, an acknowledgment of lack and of an unspecified yearning that you'd associate more with Rabbit Angstrom than with someone who spends half the novel quaffing punch with Mr. Micawber. Dickens eventually takes the Victorian way out of the twentieth-century malaise, but even so… Making notes for this column, I find that I wrote "He's from another planet"; "Was he a Martian?" David Gates asks in the introduction. And to think that some people don't rate him! To think that some people have described him as "the worst writer to plague the English language"! Yeah, well. You can believe them or you can side with Tolstoy, Peter Ackroyd, and David Gates. And me. Your choice.

For the first time since I've been writing this column, the completion of a book has left me feeling bereft: I miss them all. Let's face it, usually you're just happy as hell to have chalked another one up on the board, but this last month I've been living in this hyper-real world, full of memorable, brilliantly eccentric people, and laughs (I hope you know how funny Dickens is), and proper bendy stories you want to follow. I suspect that it'll be difficult to read a pared-down, stripped-back, skin-and-bones novel for a while. ✶

JUNE 2004

The Polysyllabic Spree—the ninety-nine young and menacingly serene people who run the *Believer*—recently took their regular columnists out for what they promised would be a riotous and orgiastic night on the town. Now, I have to confess that I've never actually seen a copy of this magazine, due to an ongoing dispute with the Spree (I think that as a contributor I should be entitled to a free copy, but they are insisting that I take out a ten-year subscription—does that sound right to you?), so I was completely unaware that there is only one other regular columnist, the Croatian sex lady, and she didn't show. I suspect that she'd been given a tip-off, probably because she's a woman (the Spree hold men responsible for the death of Virginia Woolf) and stayed at home. It shouldn't have made much difference, though, because you can have fun with a hundred people, right?

Wrong. The Spree's idea of a good time was to book tickets for a literary event—a reading given by all the nominees for the National Book Critics' Circle Awards—and sit there for two and a half hours. Actually, that's not quite true: they didn't sit there. Such is their unquenchable passion for the written word that they were too excited to sit. They stood, and they wept, and they hugged each other, and occasionally they even danced—to the poetry recitals, and some of the more up-tempo biography nominees. In England we don't often dance at dances, let alone readings, so I didn't know where to look. Needless to say, drink, drugs, food, and sex played no part in the festivities. But who needs any of that when you've got literature?

I did, however, discover a couple of books as a result of the evening: Tony Hoagland's *What Narcissism Means to Me,* which didn't win the poetry award, and Adrian Nicole LeBlanc's *Random Family,* which didn't win the nonfiction award. I haven't read the books that did win, and therefore cannot comment on the judges' inexplicable decisions, but they must be pretty good, because Hoagland's poems and LeBlanc's study of life in the Bronx were exceptional.

Middle-class people—especially young middle-class people—spend an awful lot of time and energy attempting to familiarize themselves with what's going down on the street. *Random Family* is a one-stop shop: it tells you everything you need to know, and may even stop you from hankering after a gun or a crack habit as a quick way out of the graduate-school ghetto. And yes, I know that all reality is mediated, and so on and so forth, but this book does a pretty good job of convincing you that it knows whereof it speaks.

Random Family is about two women, Coco and Jessica; LeBlanc's story, which took her ten years to write and research, begins when they're in their mid-teens, and follows them through the next couple of decades. Despite the simplicity of the setup, it's not always an easy narrative to follow. If LeBlanc were a novelist, you'd have to observe that she's screwed up by overpopulating her book, but Coco and Jessica and the Bronx don't give her an awful lot of choice, because *Random Family* is partly about overpopulation. Coco and Jessica have so many babies, by so many fathers, and their children have so many half-siblings, that at times it's impossible to keep the names straight. By the time the two women are in their early thirties, they have given birth to Mercedes, Nikki, Nautica, Pearl, LaMonte, Serena, Brittany, Stephany, Michael, and Matthew, by Cesar, Torres, Puma (or maybe Victor), Willy (or maybe Puma), Kodak, Wishman, and Frankie. This is a book awash with sperm (Jessica even manages to conceive twins while in prison, after an affair with a guard), and at one stage I was wondering whether it was medically possible for a man to become pregnant through reading it. I think I'm probably too old.

The combination of LeBlanc's scrupulous attention to quotidian detail and her absolute refusal to judge is weirdly reminiscent of Peter Guralnick's approach to Elvis in his monumental two-volume biography. Those of you who read the Elvis books will know that though Presley's baffling, infuriating last decade gave Guralnick plenty of opportunity to leap in and tell you what he thinks, he never once does so. LeBlanc's stern neutrality is generous and important: she hectors nobody, and the space she leaves us allows us to think properly, to recognize for ourselves all the millions of complications that shape these lives.

There are many, many things, a *zillion* things, that make my experiences different from those of Coco and Jessica. But it was remembering my first pregnancy scare that helped me to fully understand the stupidity and purposelessness of the usual conservative rants about responsibility and fecklessness and blah blah blah. It was the summer before I went to college, and my girlfriend's period was late, and I spent two utterly miserable weeks convinced that my life was over. I'd have to get, like, an office job, and I'd miss out on three years pissing around at university, and my brilliant career as a... as a something or other would be over before it had even begun. We'd used birth control, of course, because failing to do so would cost us everything, including a very great deal of money, but we were still terrified: I would just as soon have gone to prison as started a family. What *Random Family* explains, movingly and convincingly and at necessary length, is that the future as Coco and Jessica and the fathers of their children see it really isn't worth the price of a condom, and they're right. I eventually became a father for the first time around the same age that Jessica became a grandmother.

As I hadn't noticed the publication of *Random Family*, I caught up with the reviews online. They were for the most part terrific, although one or two people wondered aloud whether LeBlanc's presence might not have affected behavior and outcome. (Yeah, right. I can see how that might work for an afternoon, but a whole decade? Stick a writer in a corner of the room and watch the combined forces of international economics, the criminal justice system, and the drug trade wither before her pitiless gaze.) "I believe I had far less effect than anybody would imagine," LeBlanc said in an interview, with what I like to imagine as wry understatement. I did come across this, however, the extraordinary conclusion to a review in the *Guardian* (UK):

It is only by accident, in the acknowledgements, that the book finally confronts the reader with the "American experience of class injustice" that is ostensibly its subject. So many institutions, so many funds and fellowships, retreat centers and universities, publishers, mentors, editors, friends, formed a net to support this one writer. Nothing comparable exists to hold up the countless Cocos and Jessicas…

But the tougher question is why the stories of poor people—and not just any poor people but those acquainted with chaos and crime, those the overclass likes to call the underclass—are such valuable raw material, creating a frisson among the literary set and the buyers of books? Why are their lives and private griefs currency for just about anyone but themselves?

First of all: "by accident"? "BY ACCIDENT"? Those two words, so coolly patronizing and yet, paradoxically, so dim, must have made LeBlanc want to buy a gun. And I think a decent lawyer could have got her off, in the unfortunate event of a shooting. She spends ten years writing a book, and a reviewer in a national newspaper doesn't even notice what it's about. (It's about the American experience of class injustice, among other things.) Secondly: presumably the extension of the argument about grants and fellowships and editors is that they are only appropriate for biographies of bloody, I don't know, Vanessa Bell; I doubt whether "the support net" has ever been put to better social use.

And lastly: if you get to the end of *Random Family* and conclude that it was written to create "a frisson," then, I'm sorry, but you should be compelled to have your literacy surgically removed, without anesthetic. The lives of Coco and Jessica are "valuable raw material" because people who read books—quite often people who are very quick to judge, quite often people who make or influence social policy—don't know anyone like them, and certainly have no idea how or sometimes even why they live; until we all begin to comprehend, then nothing can even begin to change. Oh, and there's no evidence to suggest that Coco and Jessica resented being used in this way; there is plenty of evidence to suggest that they got it. But what would they know, right?

It's not humorless, either, although of necessity the humor tends to be a little bleak. When Coco is asked, as part of her application, for an essay entitled "Why

I Want To Live in Public Housing," she writes simply, "Because I'm homeless." And a description of the office Christmas party thrown by Jessica's major-duty drug-dealing boyfriend Boy George is hilarious, if you're able to laugh at the magnitude of your misapprehensions concerning the wages of sin. (The party took place on a yacht. There were 121 guests, who ate steak tartare and drank twelve grand's worth of Moët, and who won Hawaiian trips and Mitsubishis in the raffle. The Jungle Brothers, Loose Touch, and Big Daddy Kane performed. Are you listening, Spree?)

George is banged up in the end, of course, so mostly Jessica and Coco are eating rice and beans, when they're eating at all, and moving from one rat-infested dump to the next. Luckily we don't have poverty in England, because Tony Blair eradicated it shortly after he came to power in 1997. (Note to *Guardian* reviewer—that was a joke.) But American people should really read this book. That's "should" as in, It's really good, and "should" as in, You're a bad person if you don't.

I warned you that this was going to be a nonfiction month. I started three novels, all of them warmly recommended by friends or newspapers, and I came to the rather brilliant conclusion that not one of them was *David Copperfield,* the last novel I read, and the completion of which has left a devastating hole in my life. So it seemed like a good time to find out about Coco and Jessica and Bobby Fischer, real people I knew nothing about. *Bobby Fischer Goes to War* isn't the most elegantly written book I've ever read, but the story it tells is so compelling—so hilarious, so nutty, so resonant—that you forgive it its prose trespasses.

When Fischer played Spassky in Reykjavik in 1972 I was fifteen, and not yet worrying about whether anyone was pregnant. You heard about chess all the time that summer, on the TV and on the radio, and I presumed that you always heard about chess in the year of a World Chess Championship, that I'd simply been too young to notice the previous tournament. That happened all the time when you were in your early teens: things that only rolled around every few years, like elections and Olympics, suddenly assumed a magnitude you'd never known they possessed, simply because you were more media-aware. The truth in this case was, of course, that no one had ever talked about chess before, and no one ever would again, really. Everyone was talking about Fischer: Fischer and his refusal to play, Fischer and his demands for more money (he just about bankrupted an entire country by demanding a bigger and bigger chunk of the purse, and then refusing to allow the Icelanders to recoup it through TV and film coverage), Fischer and his forfeit of the second game, Fischer and his absence from the opening ceremony... You could make an absolutely gripping film of Reykjavik '72 which would end with the very first move of the very first match, and which would be about pretty much everything.

Tony Hoagland is the sort of poet you dream of finding but almost never do. His work is relaxed, deceptively easy on the eye and ear, and it has jokes and unexpected little bursts of melancholic resonance. Plus, I pretty much understand all of it, and yet it's clever—as you almost certainly know, contemporary poetry is a kind of Reykjavik, a place where accessibility and intelligence have been fighting a Cold War by proxy for the last half-century. If something doesn't give you even a shot at comprehension in the first couple of readings, then my motto is "Fuck it," but I never swore once. They can use that as a blurb, if they want. They should. Who wouldn't buy a poetry book that said "I never swore once" on the cover? Everyone would know what it meant. And isn't *What Narcissism Means to Me* a great title?

I cheated a little with *What Narcissism Means to Me*—I read it last month, immediately after my night on the town with the Spree. But I wanted this clean *Copperfield* line in my last column, and anyway I was worried that I'd be short of stuff this month, not least because it's been a big football month. Arsenal lost the Champions League quarterfinal to Chelsea, lost the FA Cup semi to Man Utd, and then, just this last weekend, won the Championship. (The two losses were in knock-out competitions. The Championship is what counts, really. That's what we're all telling ourselves here in Highbury.) So on Sunday night, when I should have been reading stuff, I was in a pub called the Bailey, as has become traditional on Championship nights, standing on a chair and singing a comical song about Victoria Beckham. To be honest, I thought if I threw in some poetry, you might like me more. I thought I might even like myself more. Anyway, the standing on the chair and singing wasn't as much fun as the consumption of contemporary literature, obviously, but, you know. It was still pretty good. ✶

JULY 2004

If you wanted to draw a family tree of everything I read and bought this month—and you never know, it could be fun, if you're a writer, say, or a student, and there are several large holes in your day—you'd have to put *McSweeney's* 13 and Pete Dexter's novel *Train* right at the top.[2] They're the Adam and Eve here, or they would be if Adam and Eve had been hermaphrodites, each able to give birth independently of the other. *McSweeney's* 13 and *Train* never

---

1. I bought so many books this month it's obscene, and I'm not owning up to them all: this is a selection. And to be honest, I've been economical with the truth for months now. I keep finding books that I bought, didn't read, and didn't list.

2. [We do indeed pay Nick Hornby to write his monthly column, but we didn't pay him to mention *McSweeney's* 13. —Ed.]

actually mated to produce a beautiful synthesis of the two; and nor did any of the other books actually get together, either. So it would be a pretty linear family tree, to be honest: one straight line coming out of *McSweeney's* 13, because *McSweeney's* begat a bunch of graphic novels (*McSweeney's* 13, edited by Chris Ware, is a comics issue, if you're not from 'round these parts), and another straight line coming out of *Train,* which leads to a bunch of nonfiction books, for reasons I will come to later. *Train* didn't directly beget anything, although it did plant some seeds. (I know what you're thinking. You're thinking, Well, if *Train* and *McSweeney's* 13 never actually mated, and if *Train* never directly begat anything, then how good is this whole family-tree thing? And my answer is, Oh, it's good. Trust me. I have a writer's instinct.) Anyway, if you do decide to draw the family tree, the good news is that it's easy; the bad news is that it's boring, pointless, and arguably makes no sense. Up to you.

Pete Dexter's *Train* was carefully chosen to reintroduce me to the world of fiction, a world I have been frightened of visiting ever since I finished *David Copperfield* a couple of months back. I've read Dexter before—*The Paperboy* is a terrific novel—and the first couple of chapters of *Train* are engrossing, complicated, fresh, and real, and I really thought I was back on the fictional horse. But then, in the third chapter, there is an episode of horrific violence, graphically rendered, and suddenly I was no longer under the skin of the book, the way I had been; I was on the outside looking in. What happens is that in the process of being raped, the central female character gets her nipple sliced off, and it really upset me. I mean, I know I was supposed to get upset. But I was bothered way beyond function. I was bothered to the extent that I struck up a conversation with the author at periodic intervals thereafter. "Did the nipple really have to go, Pete? Explain to me why. Couldn't it have just… nearly gone? Or maybe you could have left it alone altogether? I mean, come on, man. Her husband has just been brutally murdered. She's been raped. We get the picture. Leave the nipple alone."

I am, I think, a relatively passive reader, when it comes to fiction. If a novelist tells me that something happened, then I tend to believe him, as a rule. In his memoir *Experience,* Martin Amis recalls his father, Kingsley, saying that he found Virginia Woolf's fictional world "wholly contrived: when reading her he found that he kept interpolating hostile negatives, murmuring 'Oh no she didn't' or 'Oh no he hadn't' or 'Oh no it wasn't' after each and every authorial proposition"; I only do that when I'm reading something laughably bad (although after reading that passage in *Experience*, I remember it took me a while to shake off Kingsley's approach to the novel). But in the nipple-slicing incident in *Train*, I thought I could detect Dexter's thumb on the scale, to use a brilliant Martin Amis phrase from elsewhere in *Experience*. It seemed to me as though poor Norah lost her nipple through a worldview rather than through a narrative inevitability; and despite all the great storytelling and the muscular, grave prose, and the richness and resonance of the setup (Train is a golf caddy in 1950s L.A., and the novel is mostly about race) I just sort of lost my grip on the book. Also, someone gets shot dead at the end, and I wasn't altogether sure why. That's a sure sign that you haven't been paying the right kind of attention. It should always be clear why someone gets shot. If I ever shoot you, I promise you there will be a really good explanation, one you will grasp immediately, should you live.

While I was in the middle of *Train*, I went browsing in a remainder bookshop, and came across a copy of Frank Kermode's memoir *Not Entitled*. I knew of Kermode's work as a critic, but I didn't know he'd written a memoir, some of which is about his childhood on the Isle of Man, and when I saw it, I was seized by a need to own it. This need was entirely created by poor Norah in *Train*. There would be no nipple-slicing in *Not Entitled*, I was sure of it. I even started to read the thing in a cab on the way home, and although I gave up pretty quickly (it probably went too far the other way—it's a delicate balance I'm trying to strike here), it was very restorative.

I bought Claire Tomalin's gripping, informative *The Invisible Woman* at the Dickens Museum in Doughty Street, London, which is full of all sorts of cool stuff: marked-up reading copies which say things like "SIGH here," letters, the original partwork editions of the novels, and so on. The thing is, I really want to read a Dickens biography, but they're all too long: Ackroyd's is a frankly hilarious 1,140 pages, excluding notes and postscript. (It has a great blurb on the front, the Ackroyd. "An essential book for anyone who has ever loved *or read* Dickens," says P. D. James [my italics]. Can you imagine? You flog your way through *Great Expectations* at school, hate it, and then find you've got to read a thousand pages of biography! What a pisser!) So both the museum visit and the Tomalin book—about his affair with the actress Nelly Ternan—were my ways of fulfilling a need to find out more about the great man without killing myself.

Here's something I found out in *The Invisible Woman*: the son of Charles Dickens's mistress died during my lifetime. He wasn't Dickens's son, but even so: I could have met a guy who said, "Hey, my mum slept with Dickens." I wouldn't have understood what he meant, because I was only two, and as Tomalin makes clear, he wouldn't have wanted to own up anyway, because he was traumatized by what he found out about his mother's past. It's still weird, though, I think, to see how decades—centuries—can be eaten up like that.

Ackroyd, by the way, disputes that Ternan and Dickens ever had an affair. He concedes that Chas set her up in a couple of houses, one in France, and disappeared for long stretches of time in order to visit her, but he won't accept that Dickens was an adulterer: that sort of explanation might work for an ordinary man, he says, but Dickens "was not 'ordinary' in any sense." *The Invisible Woman* is such a formidable work of scholarship, however, that it leaves very little room for doubt. Indeed, Claire Tomalin is so consumed by her research, so much the biographer, that she actually takes Dickens to task for destroying evidence of his relationship with Nelly Ternan. "Dickens himself would not have welcomed our curiosity," she says. "He would have been happier to have every letter he ever wrote dealt with as Nelly... dealt with the bundles of twelve years' intimate correspondence. [She destroyed it all.] He was wrong by any standards."

Don't you love that last sentence? The message is clear: if you're a writer whose work will interest future generations, and you're screwing around, don't delete those emails, because Claire Tomalin and her colleagues are going to need them. Zadie Smith and Michael Chabon and the rest of you, watch out. (I'm not implying, of course, that either of you is screwing around, and I'm sorry if you made that inference. It was supposed to be a compliment. It just came out wrong. Forget it, OK? And sue the Spree, not me. It was their sloppy editing.)

This Is Serbia Calling, Matthew Collin's book about the Belgrade radio station B92 and the role it played in resisting Milosevic, has been lying around my house for a while. But when my post–*McSweeney's* 13 research into comic books led me to conclude that I should buy, among other things, Joe Sacco's *Safe Area Gorazde,* I wanted to do a little extra reading on the Yugoslavian wars, and Collin's book is perfect: it gives you a top-notch potted history, as well as an enthralling and humbling story about very brave young people refusing to be cowed by a brutal regime. It's pretty funny, too, in places. If you have a taste for that hopelessly bleak Eastern European humor, then the Serbian dissenter of the 1990s is your sort of guy. You've got warring nationalist groups, and an inflation rate, in January '94, of 313,563,558 percent (that's on the steep side, for those of you with no head for economics) which resulted in a loaf of bread costing 4,000,000,000 dinars. You've got power cuts, rigged elections, a government too busy committing genocide to worry about the niceties of free speech, and, eventually, NATO bombs. There are good jokes to be made, by those with the stomach for them. "The one good thing about no electricity," one cynic remarked during the power failures, "is that there's no television telling us we've got electricity." *This Is Serbia Calling* is essential reading if you've ever doubted the power or the value of culture, of music, books, films, theater; it also makes a fantastic case for Sonic Youth and anyone else who makes loud, weird noises. When your world is falling round about your ears, Tina Turner isn't going to do it for you.

Y: The Last Man is a comic-book series about a world run by women, after every man but one has been wiped out by a mysterious plague. It's a great premise, and full of smart ideas: the Democrats are running the country, because the only Republican women are Republican wives; Israel is cleaning up in the Middle East, because they have the highest proportion of trained female combat soldiers. It's strange, reading a comic—a proper comic, not a graphic novel—in which a woman says "You can fuck my tits if you want" (and I can only apologize, not only for repeating the expression, but for the number of references to breasts in this month's column. I'm pretty sure it's a coincidence, although we should, I suppose, recognize the possibility that it marks the beginning of a pathetic middle-aged obsession). Is that what happens in comics now? Is this the sort of stuff your ten-year-old boy is reading? Crikey. When I was ten, the only word I'd have understood in the whole sentence would have been "you," although not necessarily in this context. Daniel Clowes's *David*

Boring—yeah, yeah, late again—is partly about large bottoms, but as one of the reviews quoted on the back called the book "perverse and fetishistic," I'd have wanted my money back if it hadn't been. It's also clever, and the product of a genuinely odd imagination.

There's no rule that says one's reading has to be tonally consistent. I can't help but feel, however, that my reading has been all over the place this month. *The Invisible Woman* and *Y: The Last Man* were opposites in just about every way you can imagine; they even had opposite titles. A woman you can't see versus a guy whose mere existence attracts the world's attention. Does this matter? I suspect it might. I was once asked to DJ at a *New Yorker* party, and the guy who was looking after me (in other words, the guy who was actually playing the records) wouldn't let me choose the music I wanted because he said I wasn't paying enough attention to the beats per minute: according to him, you can't have a differential of more than, I don't know, twenty bpm between records. At the time, I thought this was a stupid idea, but there is a possibility that it might apply to reading. *The Invisible Woman* is pacy and engrossing, but it's no graphic novel, and reading Tomalin's book after *The Last Man* was like playing John Lee Hooker after the Chemical Brothers—in my opinion, John Lee Hooker is the greater artist, but he's in no hurry, is he? Next month, I might try starting with the literary equivalent of a smoocher, and move on to something a bit quicker. And I promise that if there are any breasts, I won't mention them. In fact, I won't even look at them. ✶

AUGUST 2004

Shortly after I submitted my copy for last month's column, my third son was born. I mention his arrival not because I'm after your good wishes or your sympathy, but because reading is a domestic activity, and is therefore susceptible to any changes in the domestic environment. And though it's true that the baby is responsible for everything I read this month, just about, he's been subtle about it: he hasn't made me any more moronic than I was before, and he certainly hasn't prevented me from reading. He could argue, in fact, that he has actually encouraged reading in our household, through his insistence on the increased consciousness of his parents. (Hey—if you lot are all so brainy and so serious about books, how come you're still using contraception?)

Shortly after the birth of a son, I panic that I will never be able to visit a bookshop again, and that therefore any opportunity I have to buy printed matter should be exploited immediately. Jesse (and yes, the T. J. Stiles bio was bought as a tribute) was born shortly before 7 a.m.; three or four hours later I was in a newsagents', and I saw a small selection of best-selling paperbacks. There wasn't an awful lot there that I wanted, to be honest; but because of the consumer fear, something had to be bought, right there and then, just in case, and I vaguely remembered reading something good about Dennis Lehane's *Mystic River*. Well, the shop didn't have a copy of *Mystic River*, but they did have another Dennis Lehane book, *Prayers for Rain*: that would have to do. Never mind that, as regular readers of this column know, I have over the last few months bought several hundred books I haven't yet read. And never mind that, as it turned out, I found myself passing a bookshop the very next day, and the day after that (because what else is there to do with a new baby, other than mooch around bookshops with him?), and was thus able to buy *Mystic River*. I didn't know for sure I'd ever go to a bookshop again; and if I never went to a bookshop again, how long were those several hundred books going to last me? Nine or ten years at the most. No, I needed that copy of *Prayers for Rain*, just to be on the safe side.

And then, when the baby was a couple of weeks old, I became convinced that I was turning into a vegetable, and so took urgent corrective action: I bought and read, in its entirety, Jonathan Coe's five-hundred page biography of B. S. Johnson, an obscure experimental novelist—again, just to be on the safe side, just to prove I still could, even though I never did. I'm hoping that the essential anti-vegetative nutrients and minerals I ingested will last me for a while, that they won't be expelled from the brain via snot or saliva, because I'm not sure when I will next get the chance to read a few hundred pages about a difficult writer I've never read. It almost certainly won't be for a couple of months.

They actually make a very nice theoretical contrast, Johnson and Dennis Lehane. Johnson thought that our need for narrative, our desire to find out what happens next, was "primitive" and "vulgar," and if you took that vulgarity out of *Prayers for Rain*, there wouldn't be an awful lot left. *Prayers for Rain* is "a Kenzie and Gennaro novel," and if I'd spotted those words on the cover, I probably wouldn't have read it. I appreciate that I'm in a minority here, but I just don't get the appeal of the reappearing hero. I don't get Kay Scarpetta, or James Bond, or Hercule Poirot; I don't even get Sherlock Holmes. My problem is that, when I'm reading a novel, I have a need—a childish need, B. S. Johnson would argue—to believe that the events described therein are definitive, that they really matter to the characters. In other words, if 1987 turned out to be a real bitch of a year for Winston Smith, then I don't want to be wasting my time reading about what happened to him back in '84. The least one can ask, really, is that fictional characters should be able to remember the stuff that's happened to them, but I get the impression that Kenzie and Gennaro would struggle to distinguish the psycho killer they're tracking down in *Prayers for Rain* from the psycho killers they've tracked down in other books.

There is a rather dispiriting moment in *Prayers for Rain* that seems to confirm this suspicion. Angie Gennaro, who is involved both professionally and romantically with Patrick Kenzie, asks whether she can shave off his stubble—stubble that he has grown to cover scars. "I considered it," Kenzie tells us. "Three years with protective facial hair. Three years hiding the damage delivered on the worst night of my life…" Hang on a moment. The worst night of your life was *three years ago*? So what am I reading about now? The fourth-worst night of your life? Sometimes, when you walk into a pub in the center of town mid-evening, you get the feeling that you've missed the moment: all the after-work drinkers have gone home, and the late-night drinkers haven't arrived, and there are empty glasses lying around (and the ashtrays are full, if you're drinking in a civilized country), and you didn't make any of the mess… Well, that's kind of how I felt reading *Prayers for Rain*.

I liked Lehane's writing, though. It's humane, and humorous at the right moments, and he has a penchant for quirky cultural references: I hadn't expected a discussion about David Denby's film criticism, for example. (On the other hand: would someone who reads Denby accuse someone who uses the word "finite" of showing off?) I was more than happy to plough straight on into the next one. And the next one was absolutely fantastic.

Why hasn't anyone ever told me that *Mystic River* is right up there with *Presumed Innocent* and *Red Dragon*? Because I don't know the right kind of people, that's why. In the last three weeks, about five different people have told me that Alan Hollinghurst's *The Line of Beauty* is a work of genius, and I'm sure it is; I intend to read it soonest. (Luckily, I happened to be passing a bookshop with the baby, and I was able to pick up a copy.) I'm equally sure, however, that I won't walk into a lamp-post while reading it, like I did with *Presumed Innocent* all those years ago; you don't walk into lamp-posts when you're reading literary novels, do you? How are we supposed to find out about landmark thrillers like *Mystic River*? Anyway, if you haven't seen the movie (and the same goes for *Presumed Innocent* and *Red Dragon*) then take *Mystic River* with you next time you get on a plane, or a holiday, or a toilet, or into a bath, or a bed. Onto or into anything.

Years and years ago, I read a great interview with Jam and Lewis, the R&B producers, in which they described what it was like to be members of Prince's band. They'd sit down, and Prince would tell them what he wanted them to play, and they'd explain that they couldn't—they weren't quick enough, or good enough. And Prince would push them and push them until they mastered it, and then, just when they were feeling pleased with themselves for accomplishing something they didn't know they had the capacity for, he'd tell them the dance steps he needed to accompany the music.

This story has stuck with me, I think, because it seems like an encapsulation of the very best and most exciting kind of creative process, and from the outside, the craft involved in the creation of *Mystic River* looks as though it must have involved the same stretch. Lehane has done everything that a literary novelist is supposed to be able to do (this is a novel about grief, a community, the childhood ties that bind); the intensely satisfying whodunit element is the equivalent of the dance step on top. Indeed, Lehane has ended up making it look so effortless that no one I've ever met seems to have noticed he's done anything much at all. But then, the lesson of literature over the last eighty-odd years is the old math teacher's admonishment: "SHOW YOUR WORKINGS!" Otherwise, how is anyone to know that there are any?

In *Prayers for Rain*, Lehane piles complication upon complication in order to keep his detectives guessing, and there is a certain readerly pleasure to be had from that, of course; but it just seems like a more routine pleasure, compared to what he does in *Mystic River*. There, Lehane peers into the deep, dark hole that the murder of a young girl leaves in various lives, and tries to make sense of everything revealed therein; everything seems organic, nothing—or almost nothing, anyway—feels contrived. I'm happy to have friends who recommend Alan Hollinghurst, really I am. They're all nice, bright people. I just wish I had friends who could recommend books like *Mystic River*, too. Are you that person? Do you have any vacancies for a pal? If you can't be bothered with a full-on friendship, with all the tearful, drunken late-night phone calls and bitter accusations and occasional acts of violence thus entailed (the violence is always immediately followed by an apology, I hasten to add), then maybe you could just tell me the titles of the books.

At the time of writing, *Like a Fiery Elephant,* Jonathan Coe's brilliant biography of B. S. Johnson, doesn't have a U.S. publisher, which seems absurd. Your guys seem to have been frightened off by Johnson's obscurity, but we've never heard of him, either; the book works partly because its author anticipates our ignorance. It also works because Jonathan Coe, probably the best English novelist of his generation (my generation, as bad luck would have it), has been imaginative and interrogative about the form and shape of the book, and because it's a book about writing, perhaps more than anything else. Johnson may have been a 1960s experimentalist who hung out with Beckett and cut holes in his books, but he was as egocentric and arrogant and bitter and money-obsessed as the rest of us. Johnson was a depressive who eventually killed himself; his suicide note read:

> This is my last
> word.

But he was a great comic character, too, almost Dickensian in his appetites and his propensity for pomposity. Whenever he wrote to complain to publishers, or agents, or even printers—and he complained a lot, not least because he got through a large number of publishers, agents, and printers—he was never backwards in coming forwards, as we say here, and he included the same self-promoting line again and again. "In reviewing my novel *Albert Angelo,* the Sunday *Times* described me as 'one of the best writers we've got,' and the Irish *Times* called the book 'a masterpiece' and put me in the same class as Joyce and Beckett," he wrote to Allen Lane, the founder of Penguin, demanding to know why he wasn't interested in paperback rights. "The Sunday *Times* called me 'one of the best writers we've got,' and the Irish Times called the book a masterpiece and put me in the same class as James Joyce and Samuel Beckett," he wrote to his foreign rights agent, demanding to know why there had been no Italian publication of his first novel. "You ignorant unliterary Americans make me puke," he wrote to Thomas Wallace of Holt, Rhinehart and Winston, Inc. after Wallace had turned him down. (Maybe Coe should write a version of the same letter, if you ignorant unliterary Americans still refuse to publish his book.) "For your information, *Albert Angelo* was reviewed by the Sunday *Times* here as by 'one of the best writers we've got,' and the Irish *Times* called the book a masterpiece and put me in the same class as Joyce and Beckett." And then, finally and gloriously:

> …The Sunday *Times* called me 'one of the best writers we've got,' and the Irish *Times* called the book a masterpiece, and compared me with Joyce and Beckett.
>
> However, it seems that I am to be denied the opportunity of a most profound and enormous experience: of being present with my wife Virginia when our first child is born at your hospital on or about July 24th…

This last letter was to the Chief Obstetrician of St. Bartholomew's Hospital in London, after Johnson had discovered that it was not the hospital's policy to allow fathers to attend a birth. It's the "However" kicking off the second paragraph that's such a brilliant touch, drawing attention as it does to the absurdity of the contradiction. "I can understand you keeping out the riff-raff, your Flemings and your Amises and the rest of the what-happened-next brigade," it implies. "But surely you'll make an exception for a genius?" In the end, it's just another variation on "Don't you know who I am?"—which in Johnson's case was an even more unfortunate question than it normally is. Nobody knew then, and nobody knows now.

Johnson had nothing but contempt for the enduring influence of Dickens and the Victorian novel; strange, then, that in the end he should remind one of nobody so much as the utilitarian school inspector in the opening scene of *Hard Times*. Here's the school inspector: "I'll explain to you… why you wouldn't paper a room with representations of horses. Do you ever see horses walking up and down the sides of rooms in reality—in fact?… Why, then, you are not to see anywhere what you don't see in fact; you are not to have anywhere what you don't have in fact. What is called Taste is only another name for Fact." And here's Johnson: "Life does not tell stories. Life is chaotic, fluid, random; it leaves myriads of ends untied, untidily. Writers can extract a story from life only by strict, close selection, and this must mean falsification. Telling stories really is telling lies." Like communists and fascists, Johnson and the dismal inspector wander off in opposite directions, only to discover that the world is round. I'm glad that they both lost the cultural Cold War: there's room for them all in our world, but there's no room for *Mystic River* in theirs. And what kind of world would that be? ✶

SEPTEMBER 2004

BOOKS BOUGHT:

* ✭ *20,000 Streets Under the Sky*—Patrick Hamilton
* ✭ Unnamed Literary Novel—Anonymous
* ✭ *The Letters of Charles Dickens, Vol. 1*
* ✭ *Through a Glass Darkly: The Life of Patrick Hamilton*—Nigel Jones

BOOKS READ:

* ✭ *The Midnight Bell*—Patrick Hamilton
* ✭ *Blockbuster*—Tom Shone
* ✭ *We're in Trouble*—Chris Coake
* ✭ Literary novel (unfinished)
* ✭ Biography (unfinished)

Twelve months! A whole year! I don't think I've ever held down a job for this long. And I have to say that when I first met the Polysyllabic Spree, the eighty-four chillingly ecstatic young men and women who run this magazine, I really couldn't imagine contributing one column, let alone a dozen. The Spree all live together in Believer Towers, high up in the hills somewhere; they spend their days reading Montaigne's essays aloud to each other (and laughing ostentatiously at the funny bits), shooting at people who own TV sets, and mourning the deaths of every single writer since the Gawain-Poet, in chronological order. When I first met them, they'd got up to Gerard Manley Hopkins. (They seemed particularly cut up about him. It may have been the Jesuit thing, kindred spirits and all that.) I was impressed by their seriousness and their progressive sexual relationships, but they really didn't seem like my kind of people.

And yet here we are, still. I'm beginning to see through the white robes to the people beneath, as it were, and they're really not so bad, once you get past the incense, the vegan food, and the communal showers. They've definitely taught me things: they've taught me, for example, that there is very little point in persisting with a book that isn't working for me, and even less point in writing about it. In snarky old England, we're used to working the other way around—we only finish books that aren't working for us, and those are definitely the only ones we write about. Anyway, as a consequence, my reading has become more focused and less chancy, and I no longer choose novels that I know in advance will make me groan, snort, and guffaw.

I still make mistakes, though, despite the four-hundred-page manual they make you read before you can contribute to this magazine, and I made two in the last four weeks. The biography I abandoned was of a major cultural figure of the twentieth century—he died less than forty years ago—so when you see, in the opening chapter, the parentheses "(1782–1860)"after a name, it's really only natural that you become a little disheartened: you're a long, long way from the action. I made it through to the subject's birth, but then got irritated by a long-winded story about a prank he played on a little girl when he was seven. I had always suspected, even before I knew anything about him, that this major cultural figure was once a small boy, so the confirmation was superfluous. And the prank was so banal that he could just as easily have grown up to be Hemingway, or Phil Silvers, or any other midcentury colossus. It wasn't, like, a revealingly or quintessentially ____esque prank. At that point I threw the book down in disgust. It went straight through the bedroom floor, only just missing a small child. Please, biographers. Please, please, please. Have mercy. Select for us. We have jobs, kids, DVD players, season tickets. But that doesn't mean we don't want to know about stuff.

My other mistake was a literary first novel, and I've probably broken every rule in the Spree manual just by saying that much. I took every precaution, I promise: I was reading a paperback that came garlanded with superlative reviews, and there were a couple of recommendations involved, although I can see now that they came from untrustworthy sources. I ignored the most boring opening sentence I have ever read in my life and ploughed on, prepared to forgive and forget; I got halfway through before its quietness and its lack of truth started to get me down. I don't mind nothing happening in a book, but nothing happening in a phony way—characters saying things people never say, doing jobs that don't fit, the whole works—is simply asking too much of a reader. Something happening in a phony way must beat nothing happening in a phony way every time, right? I mean, you could prove that, mathematically, in an equation, and you can't often apply science to literature.

Here's Tom Shone writing about Spielberg's *Jaws* in his book *Blockbuster*:

> What stays with you, even today, are less the movie's big action moments than the crowning gags, light as air, with which Spielberg gilds his action—Dreyfuss crushing his Styrofoam cup, in response to Quint's crushing of his beercan, or Brody's son copying his finger-steepling at the dinner table…
>
> To get anything resembling such fillets of improvised characterisation, you normally had to watch something far more boring—some chamber piece about marital disintegration by John Cassavetes, say—and yet here were such things, popping up in a movie starring a scary rubber shark. It was nothing short of revolutionary: you could have finger steepling and scary rubber sharks *in the same movie*. This seemed like important information. Why had no one told us this before?

If this column has anything like an aesthetic, it's there: you can get finger-steepling and sharks in the same book. And you really need the shark part, because a whole novel about finger steepling—and that's a fair synopsis of both the Abandoned Literary Novel and several thousand others like it—can be on the sleepy side. You don't have to have a shark, of course; the shark could be replaced by a plot, or, say, thirty decent jokes.

Tom Shone is a friend, and I've known him for ages—he's younger than me, but I'm pretty sure he was the first person ever to phone me up and ask me to write something for him, when he was the literary editor of a now-defunct newspaper in London. That doesn't mean I owe him anything, and it certainly doesn't mean I have to be nice about his book. He gave me something like one hundred and fifty quid for a thousand-word piece, so he probably still owes me. In England, writers are never nice about their friends' books: I read out a terrific sentence from *Blockbuster* with the express purpose of making a mutual friend groan with horrified envy, and it worked a treat.

With a heavy heart, then, I must tell you that *Blockbuster* is compelling, witty, authoritative, and very, very smart. Subtitled *How Hollywood Learned to Stop Worrying and Love the Summer,* it's an alternative view of the film universe to that expounded in *Easy Riders, Raging Bulls*; where Peter Biskind believes that Spielberg and Lucas murdered movies, Shone takes the view that they breathed a whole new life into them. "It seems worth pointing out: the art of popular cinema was about to get, at a rough estimate, a bazillion times better." He's not philistine about it—he doesn't think that blockbusters have got better and better with each successive summer, for example, and he despairs in all the right places.

Indeed, he manages to put his finger on something that had always troubled my populist soul: he explains why breaking all box-office records has become a meaningless feat, almost certainly indicative of lack of quality rather than the opposite, over the last few years. *Raiders of the Lost Ark* took $8 million in its opening weekend, but then went on to make $209 million. By contrast, the big movies of 2001—*AI, Jurassic Park III, Pearl Harbor, The Mummy Returns, Planet of the Apes*—all opened big, and then disappeared fast. "By the time we've all seen that it sucked, it's a hit. The dollar value of our bum on seat has never been greater, but what it signifies has never meant less."

There is, in the end, something untrustworthy about the film critics who have sat in an audience spellbound by *Close Encounters of the Third Kind* and then gone on to slag it off at some stage in their careers. There's certainly something untrustworthy about them as critics, and I would argue that there is something untrustworthy about them as people: what was it that prevented them from responding in the way we all responded, those of us who were old enough to go to a cinema in 1977? What bit of them is missing? *Star Wars, Raiders, ET, Close Encounters*, and the rest clearly worked for discriminating cinema audiences; Tom Shone demonstrates that all his bits are where they should be by writing with acuity and enthusiasm about how and why they worked. This may be a strange thing to say about a book that embraces the evil Hollywood empire so warmly, but *Blockbuster* is weirdly humane: it prizes entertainment over boredom, and audiences over critics, and yet it's a work of great critical intelligence. It wouldn't kill me, I suppose, to say I'm proud of the boy.

I know Chris Coake, too. I taught him for a week, a couple of years ago—by which I mean that I read a couple of his stories, scratched my head while trying to think of some way they could be improved, gave up the unequal struggle, and told him they were terrific. I would like to claim that I discovered him, but you can't really discover writers like this: the quality of the work is so blindingly obvious that he was never going to labor in obscurity for any length of time, and the manuscript he sent me has already been bought by Harcourt Brace in the United States, Penguin in the UK, Guanda in Italy, and so on. You won't be able to read his book until next year, but when you see the reviews, you'll be reminded that you heard about it here first—which is, after all, how you usually hear about most things, apart from sports results.

We're in Trouble is, for the most part, a book about death—quite often, about how death affects the young. "In the Event" takes place over the course of a few hours: it begins in the early morning, just after a car crash that has killed the parents of a three-year-old boy, and ends shortly before the boy wakes up to face his terrible new world. In between times, the child's youthful and unto-gether godfather, who will raise the child, has a very long and very dark night of the soul. In the collection's title story, death casts a shadow over three relation-ships, at various stages of maturity, and with increasing directness. Sometimes, when you're reading the stories, you forget to breathe, which probably means that you read them with more speed than the writer intended. Are they literary? They're beautifully written, and they have bottom, but they're never dull, and they all contain striking and dramatic narrative ideas. And Coake never draws attention to his own art and language; he wants you to look at his people, not listen to his voice. So they're literary in the sense that they're serious, and will probably be nominated for prizes, but they're unliterary in the sense that they could end up mattering to people.

Patrick Hamilton, who died in 1962, is my new best friend. I read his most famous book, *Hangover Square,* a couple of months back; now a trilogy of novels, collectively entitled *20,000 Streets Under the Sky,* has just been repub-lished here in the UK, and the first of them, *The Midnight Bell,* seemed to me to be every bit as good as *Hangover Square.* Usually, books have gone out of print for a reason, and that reason is they're no good, or, at least, of very marginal interest. (Yeah, yeah, your favorite book of all time is currently out of print, and it's a scandal. But I'll bet you any money you like it's not as good as *The Catcher in the Rye,* or *The Power and the Glory,* or anything else still available that was written in the same year.) Hamilton's books aren't arcane, or difficult, although they're dated in the sense that the culture which produced them has changed beyond recognition. Tonally, though, they're surprisingly modern: they're gritty, real, tough, and sardonic, and they deal with dissipation. And we love a bit of dissipation, don't we? We're always reading books about that. Or at least, someone's always writing one. Hamilton's version, admittedly, isn't very glamorous—people sit in pubs and get pissed. But if you were looking to fly from Dickens to Martin Amis with just one overnight stop, then Hamilton is your man. Or your airport, or whatever.

Doris Lessing called him "a marvellous novelist who's grossly neglected," and she felt that he suffered through not belonging to the 1930s Isherwood clique. She also thought, in 1968, that "his novels are true now. You can go into any pub and see it going on." This, however, is certainly no longer the case—our pub culture here in London is dying. Pubs aren't pubs any more—not, at least, in the metropolitan center. They're discos, or sports bars, or gastropubs, and the working- and lower-middle-class men that Hamilton writes about with such appalled and amused fascination don't go anywhere near them. That needn't bother you, however. You're all smart enough to see that the author's central theme—men are vile and stupid, women are vile and manipulative—is as meaningful today as it ever was. I have only just started to read Nigel Jones's biography, but I suspect that Hamilton wasn't the happiest of chaps.

Thank you, dear reader, for your time over these last twelve months, if you have given any. And if you haven't, then thank you for not complaining in large enough numbers to get me slung out. I reckon I've read at least a dozen wonderful books since I began this column. I've read *Hangover Square, How to Breathe Underwater, David Copperfield, The Fortress of Solitude, George and Sam, True Notebooks, Random Family,* Ian Hamilton's Lowell biography, *The Sirens of Titan, Mystic River, Clockers, Moneyball...* And there'll be the same number this coming year, too. More, if I read faster. What have you done twelve times over the last year that was so great, apart from reading books? Fibber. ✷

OCTOBER 2004

BOOKS BOUGHT:

* ★ *Chekov: A Life in Letters*
* ★ *Dylan Thomas: The Collected Letters*
* ★ *The Letters of Kingsley Amis*
* ★ *Soldiers of Salamis*—Javier Cercas
* ★ *Timoleon Vieta Come Home*—Dan Rhodes
* ★ *The Wisdom of Crowds*—James Surowiecki
* ★ *Liars and Saints*—Maile Meloy
* ★ *Stasiland: Stories from behind the Berlin Wall*—Anna Funder
* ★ *Seven Types of Ambiguity*—Elliot Perlman

BOOKS READ:

* ★ *How I Live Now*—Meg Rosoff
* ★ *Liars and Saints*—Maile Meloy
* ★ *Through a Glass Darkly: Life of Patrick Hamilton*—Nigel Jones
* ★ *Father and Son*—Edmund Gosse
* ★ *The Siege of Pleasure*—Patrick Hamilton
* ★ *So Many Books*—Gabriel Zaid

Sex with cousins: are you for or against? I only ask because the first two books I read this month, Maile Meloy's *Liars and Saints* and Meg Rosoff's *How I Live Now,* answer the question with a resounding affirmative. (It's a long story, but in *Liars and Saints,* the couple in question is under the impression that they're actually uncle and niece, rather than cousins—and even that doesn't stop 'em! Crikey!) People are always plighting their troth to and/or screwing their cousins in Hardy and Austen, but I'd always presumed that this was because of no watercoolers, or speed-dating, or college dances; what is so dispiriting about *Liars and Saints* and *How I Live Now* is that they are set in the present, or even in the near-future, in the case of the latter book. No offense to my cousins—or, indeed, to *Believer* readers who prefer to keep things in the family—but is that really all we have to look forward to?

I know that when it comes to subconscious sexual deviation there's no such thing as coincidence, but I swear I haven't been scouring the bookshops for novels about the acceptable face of incest. I picked up *Liars and Saints* because it's been blurbed by both Helen Fielding and Philip Roth, and though I enjoyed the book, that conjunction set up an expectation that couldn't ever be fulfilled: sometimes blurbs can be too successful. I was hoping for something bubbly and yet achingly world-weary, something diverting and yet full of lacerating and unforgettable insights about the human condition, something that was fun while being at the same time no fun at all, in a bracing sort of a way, something that cheered me up while making me want to hang myself. In short, I wanted Roth and Fielding to have cowritten the book, and poor Maile Meloy couldn't deliver. *Liars and Saints* is a fresh, sweet-natured first novel, but it's no Nathan Zuckerman's *Diary*. (Cigarettes—23, attacks of *Weltschmerz*—141, etc.)

How I Live Now has had amazing reviews here in England—someone moderately sensible called it "a classic"—and although that might sometimes be enough to persuade me to shell out (cf. *Seven Types of Ambiguity*, which has received similar press), normally that wouldn't be enough to persuade me to read the thing. Rosoff's book, however, is delightfully short, and aimed at teenagers, and the publishers sent me a copy, so you can see the thinking here: knock off a classic in a day or so, at no personal expense, and bulk this column out a little. And that's pretty much how things worked out.

I'm not sure that *How We Live Now* is a classic, though, even if a book can achieve that kind of status in the month of its publication. It's set in a war-torn England a few years from now, and though the love affair between the cousins has a dreamy intensity, and Rosoff's teenage voice is strong and true, her war is a little shoddy, if you ask me. London has been occupied, but by whom no one, not even the adults, seems quite sure: it could be the French, it could be the Chinese. What sort of war is that? Rosoff is aiming for a fog of half-truth and rumor, the sort of fog that most teenagers live in most of the time, and yet one is given the impression that not even Seymour Hersh would be able to shed much light on the matter of who invaded Britain and why.

I've been meaning to read Edmund Gosse's *Father and Son* for about ten years; the only thing that was stopping me from reading it was the suspicion that it might be unreadable—miserable and dreary and impossibly remote. First published (anonymously) in 1907, *Father and Son* describes Edmund's relationship with his father, Philip, a marine biologist of some distinction who was also a member of the Plymouth Brethren, and whose fierce, joyless evangelism crippled his son's childhood. In fact, *Father and Son* is a sort of Victorian *This Boy's Life*: it's inevitably, unavoidably painful, but it's also tender and wry. OK, sometimes it reads like that Monty Python sketch about the Yorkshiremen, constantly trying to trump each other's stories of deprivation ("You lived in a hole in the road? You were lucky."): when Gosse's mother was dying of cancer, and too sick to travel from one London borough to another for the hopeless last-chance quack treatment she was trying, she and her young son stayed in a grim boarding house in Pimlico, where Edmund was allowed to entertain her by reading from religious tracts. His pathetic treat, at the end of the day, was to read her a hymn—in the Gosse family, that was what passed for fun.

My first book, *Fever Pitch,* was a memoir, and I own a copy of *Father and Son* because some clever-dick reviewer somewhere compared the two. (I seem to remember that the comparison did me no favors, before you accuse me of showing off. Someone must have been dissed, and I can't imagine it was Gosse.) My young life was blighted by my devotion to Arsenal Football Club, a team so dour and joyless during the late sixties and seventies that they would have been rather intimidated by the comparative exuberance and joie de vivre of the Plymouth Brethren. It's always weird, though, for a writer to spot the same impulses and ambitions in another, especially when the two are separated by history, culture, environment, belief, and just about anything else you can think of, and I identified absolutely with more or less every page in Gosse's book. I had hoped, when I wrote mine, that even if I were to allow myself the indulgence of writing in detail about 1960s League Cup finals, people might be prepared to put up with it if they thought there was something else going on as well; Gosse's football-sized hole was created by religion, and filled by marine biology, so he was, in effect, both damaged and repaired by his father's twin obsessions. (His father, meanwhile, was almost split in two by them—Darwin's theories were more devastating for the evangelical naturalist than for just about anyone else in the country.) *Father and Son* is an acknowledged classic, so I had expected it to be good, but I hadn't expected it to be lovable, or modern, nor had I expected it to speak to me. *How I Live Now,* by contrast, felt as if it was talking to everyone else but me—I was watching from the wings as its author addressed the multitudes. Maybe that's why you have to give books time to live before you decide that they're never going to die. You have to wait and see whether anyone in that multitude is really listening.

Every time I read a biography of a novelist, I discover that the novels in question are autobiographical to an almost horrifying degree. In Blake Bailey's book about Richard Yates, for example, we learn that Yates fictionalized his mother by changing her name from Dookie to Pookie (or perhaps from Pookie to Dookie, I can't remember now). In Nigel Jones's *Through a Glass Darkly* we learn that, like Bob in *The Midnight Bell,* Patrick Hamilton had a disastrous crush on a prostitute, and that, like Bone in *Hangover Square,* his obsession with a young actress (Geraldine Fitzgerald, who appeared in *Wuthering Heights* alongside Laurence Olivier and Merle Oberon) was deranged, although he stopped short of murdering her. And, of course, like all of his characters, Hamilton was a drunk. I'm sure that a biography of Tolkien would reveal that *The Lord of the Rings* was autobiographical, too—that Tolkien actually fell down a hole and found a place called Central Earth, where there were a whole bunch of Bobbits. Some people—critics, mostly—would argue that this diminishes the achievement somehow, but it's the writing that's hard, not the invention.

See, some of us just don't come from the right kind of background to be the subject of a literary biography. Hamilton's father was left a hundred thousand pounds in 1884, and pissed it all away during a lifetime of utter indolence and dissolution; his first wife was a prostitute whom Hamilton Sr. imagined he could save from the streets, but the marriage didn't work out. 'Snot fair! Why didn't my dad ever have a thing with prostitutes? (Note to *Believer* fact-checker: I'll give you his number, but I'm not making the call. He's pretty grouchy at the best of times.)

Jenny, the prostitute in *The Midnight Bell,* takes center stage in *The Siege of Pleasure,* the second novel in the *20,000 Streets Under the Sky* trilogy. Hamilton was a Marxist for much of his life, and though he ended up voting conservative, as so many English Marxists did, in his case it was because the Tories hated the Labor Party as much as he did, which at least shows a warped kind of ideological consistency. *The Siege of Pleasure* is in part a careful, convincing analysis of the economic and social pressures that forced Jenny onto the streets and out of her life below stairs. It's more fun than this sounds, because Hamilton, who wrote the play *Rope,* which Hitchcock later filmed, loves his ominous narratives. He's a sort of urban Hardy: everyone is doomed, right from the first page. Hamilton isolates Jenny's plight to an evening spent boozing with a tarty friend; she gets plastered, wakes up late in the house of a man she doesn't know, and fails to turn up at her new job, skivvying for a comically incapable trio of old people. It's sad, but Hamilton's laconic narrative voice is always a joy to read, and as a social historian, Hamilton is unbeatable. Who knew that you could get waiter service in pubs in the 1920s? And plates of biscuits? Biscuits! What sort of biscuits? Hamilton doesn't say.

In *So Many Books,* Gabriel Zaid attempts to grapple with the question that seems constantly to arise in this column, namely, Why bloody bother? Why bother reading the bastards, and why bother writing them? I'm not sure he gets a lot further than I've ever managed, but there are some great stats here: Zaid estimates, for example, that it would take us fifteen years simply to read a list of all the books ever published. ("Author and title"—he's very precise. You can, presumably, add on another seven or eight years if you want to know the names of the publishers.) I think he intends to make us despair, but I was actually rather heartened: not only can I now see that it's possible—I'd be finished some time in my early sixties—but I'm seriously tempted. A good chunk of coming across as educated, after all, is just a matter of knowing who wrote what: someone mentions Patrick Hamilton, and you nod sagely and say, *Hangover Square,* and that's usually enough. If I read the list, something might stick in the memory, because God knows that the books themselves don't.

Zaid's finest moment, however, comes in his second paragraph, when he says that "the truly cultured are capable of owning thousands of unread books without losing their composure or their desire for more."

That's me! And you, probably! That's us! "Thousands of unread books"!

"Truly cultured"! Look at this month's list: Chekhov's letters, Amis's letters, Dylan Thomas's letters… What are the chances of getting through that lot? I've started on the Chekhov, but the Amis and the Dylan Thomas have been put straight into their permanent home on the shelves, rather than onto any sort of temporary pending pile. The Dylan Thomas I saw remaindered for fifteen quid (down from fifty) just after I'd read a terrific review of a new Thomas biography in the *New Yorker*; the Amis letters were a fiver. But as I was finding a home for them in the Arts and Lit nonfiction section (I personally find that for domestic purposes, the Trivial Pursuit system works better than Dewey), I suddenly had a little epiphany: all the books we own, both read and unread, are the fullest expression of self we have at our disposal. My music is me, too, of course—but as I only really like rock and roll and its mutations, huge chunks of me—my rarely examined operatic streak, for example—are unrepresented in my CD collection. And I don't have the wall space or the money for all the art I would want, and my house is a shabby mess, ruined by children… But with each passing year, and with each whimsical purchase, our libraries become more and more able to articulate who we are, whether we read the books or not. Maybe that's not worth the thirty-odd quid I blew on those collections of letters, admittedly, but it's got to be worth something, right? ✱

NOVEMBER 2004

I have been meaning to read a book about cricket for awhile, with the sole intention of annoying you all. I even toyed with the idea of reading only cricket books this entire month, but then I realized that this would make it too easy for you to skip the whole column; this way, you have to wade through the cricket to get to the Chekhov and the Roddy Doyle. I'm presuming here that very few of you have ever seen a cricket match, and if you have, you are almost certain to have been both mystified and stupefied: this, after all, is a game which, in its purest form (there are all sorts of cheap-thrills bastardized versions now), lasts for five days and very frequently ends in a tie: five days is not quite long enough to get through everything that needs doing in a cricket match, especially as you can't play in the rain.

The funny thing is that we actually do like cricket here in England—it's not some hey-nonny-no phony heritage thing, like Morris dancing (horrific bearded men with sticks and bells), or cream teas. Thirty or forty years ago it was our equivalent of baseball, an all-consuming summer sport that drove football off the back pages of newspapers completely for three months; now

Beckham and the rest of them get the headlines even when they're lying on Caribbean beaches. But big international matches still sell out, and every now and again the England team starts winning, and we renew our interest.

Ed Smith reminds traditionalists of a time when cricketers were divided into two camps, "Gentlemen" and "Players"; the former were private-school boys and university graduates from upper-middle-class backgrounds, the latter horny-handed professionals who weren't even allowed to share a dressing room with their social betters. Smith is a Cambridge graduate who reviews fiction for one of the broadsheet newspapers. He's also good-looking, well-spoken, articulate, and he has played for England, so perhaps not surprisingly, *On and Off the Field*, his diary of a season, attracted a fair bit of attention, all of it, as far as I can tell, admiring. Where's the fairness in that? You'd think that if critics had any use at all, it would be to give our golden boys and girls a fearsome bashing, but of course you can't even rely on them for that.

To be fair to the critics, Smith didn't give them much ammunition: *On and Off the Field* is terrific, exactly the sort of book you want from a professional sportsman but you never get: it's self-analytical (even if, after the self-analysis, he attributes some of his early-season failure to sheer bad luck), wry, and honest. The sports memoir is such a debased form—George Best, the biggest football star of the sixties and seventies, has "written" five autobiographies to date, and he hasn't kicked a ball for thirty-odd years—but *On and Off the Field* is different: the photo on the back depicts Smith slumped against a wall, the very epitome of defeated misery. Defeated misery is what all sport is about, eventually, if you follow the story for long enough; all sportsmen know this, but Smith is one of the very few capable not only of recognizing this bitter truth, but acknowledging it in print. I know you're not going to read it. But let's say I've read it on your behalf, and we've all enjoyed it.

To my surprise, I managed to read, in its entirety, one of the many books of collected letters I inexplicably bought last month. Why I read it, however, is almost as mysterious as why I bought it in the first place; or rather, I'm not sure why I felt I had to read every word of every letter. After a little while, you get the pattern: letters to his feckless brothers tend to be fiercely admonitory (and therefore fun); letters to his mother and sister tend to be purely domestic, functional, and a little on the dull side ("Tell Arseny to water the birch tree once a week, and the eucalyptus"); letters to his wife, Olga Knipper, are embarrassingly slushy, and the letters he wrote to Alexey Suvorin, his publisher, are the letters I was hoping for when I started the book: they're the ones where you're most likely to find something about writing. I should have stuck to the Suvorin letters, but you get addicted to the (mostly sleepy) rhythms of Chekhov's quotidian life.

Chekhov, as you probably know (I don't know why, but I always think of you lot knowing everything, pretty much, apart from the rules of cricket) started life as a hack, a journalist who wrote short comic articles for various Russian periodicals while training and then practicing as a doctor. And then, in 1886, when he was just beginning to take his writing more seriously, he received the sort of letter most young writers can only dream of getting. Dmitry Grigorovich, a respected older novelist, wrote out of the blue to tell him he was a genius, and he should stop pissing around.

I know from personal experience that these letters have a galvanizing effect at first. But once you've had twenty or thirty of them, you start to chuck them straight into the bin once you've checked out the signature. I had a rule that I'd only take any notice if the correspondent had a Pulitzer or a Nobel; if you get involved with every two-bit literary legend who wants to be your friend, you'd never get any work done. Some of them can be a real pain. (Salinger? Reclusive? Yeah, I wish.) Anyway, Chekhov's reply to Grigorovich is every bit as humbled, as sweetly thunderstruck, as you'd want it to be.

"Everyone has seen a *Cherry Orchard* or an *Uncle Vanya*, while very few have even heard of 'The Wife' or 'In the Ravine,'" says Janet Malcolm in her short, moving, clever book *Reading Chekhov*. Perhaps this isn't the right time to talk about what "everyone" means here, although one is entitled to stop and wonder at the world in which our men and women of letters live—not "everyone" has seen a football match or an episode of *Seinfeld,* let alone a nineteenth-century Russian play. But she's right, of course, to point out that his stories languish in relative obscurity. In his introduction to the *Essential Tales,* Richard Ford writes about tackling the stories before he was old enough to realize that their plainness was deceptive, and though I hate that "writers' writer" stuff (after a lifetime of reading, I can officially confirm that readers' writers beat writers' writers every time), I can see what he means. When you're young and pretentious, you want your Greats to come with bells on, otherwise you can't see what the fuss is about, and there are no bells in those stories.

What's remarkable about the letters is that the drama hardly comes up at all. Every now and again, Chekhov tells someone that he's just written a rubbish new play, or that he's hopeless at the craft. "Reading through my newly born play convinces me more than ever that I'm not a playwright," he says when writing to Suvorin about *The Seagull*; *Three Sisters* is "boring, sluggish and awkward." He'd have been staggered at the way things have turned out. His working life was about prose—and money. He tells just about anyone who'll listen how much he got for this, and how much they could get for that.

The letters are full of useful advice—advice that holds good even now. "Sleeping with a whore, breathing right in her mouth, endlessly listening to her pissing… where's the sense in that? Civilized people don't simply obey their baser instincts. They demand more from a woman than bed, horse sweat and the sound of pissing." He's right, of course. There's no sense in that, at all. But that pissing sound is sort of addictive after a few years, isn't it? If you haven't even started listening to it, then I can only urge you never to do so.

Apart from the peculiar obsession with the sound of pissing, there's a modern writing life described here. There's the money thing, of course, but there's also gossip, and endless charitable activity, and fame (Chekhov was recognized everywhere he went). He's also the only genius I've come across who had no recognition of, or interest in, the immensity of his own talent.

As a special bonus, you also get some of those bad biopic comedy moments thrown in. "I went to see Lev Tolstoy the day before yesterday," he writes to Gorky. "He was full of praise for you, and said you were a 'splendid writer.' He likes your 'The Fair' and 'In The Steppe,' but not 'Malva.'" You just know that there's only three words in this letter Gorky would have registered, and that he spent the rest of the day too depressed to get out of bed.

This month, my bookshelves functioned exactly as they are supposed to. I'd just finished the Chekhov and dimly remembered buying Janet Malcom's book when it was first published. And then I found it, and read it. And enjoyed it. You forget that the very best literary critics are capable of being very clever about people and life, as well as books: there's a brilliant passage here where Malcolm, who is travelling around Russia visiting Chekhov's houses, links her feelings over the return of a lost bag to her feelings about travel: "[Our homes] are where the action is; they are where the riches of experience are distributed... Only when faced with one of the inevitable minor hardships of travel do we break out of the trance of tourism and once again feel the sharp savor of the real." I can't understand, though, why she thinks that the letters between Chekhov and Olga Knipper "make wonderful reading." I've only read Chekhov's side, but she seems to have reduced the man to mush: "My little doggie," "my dear little dog," "my darling doggie," "Oh, doggie, doggie," "my little dog," "little ginger-haired doggie," "my coltish little doggie," "my lovely little mongrel doggie," "my darling, my perch," "my squiggly one," "dearest little colt," "my incomparable little horse," "my dearest chaffinch"... For god's sake, pull yourself together, man! You're a major cultural figure!

Knipper and Chekhov were together only rarely in their short marriage (she was acting in St. Petersburg, he was trying to keep warm in Yalta) and Malcolm seems to suggest rather sadly that famous men and women with more conventional relationships rob biographers of future source material, because they have no reason to write to each other. On the evidence here, all couples should be compelled by law to spend twenty-four hours a day together, three hundred and sixty-five days a year, just in case either partner is tempted to call the other a chaffinch, or a perch, or an aardvark, in writing.

Malcolm, however, is one of those people so sweetly devoted to her subject that she won't recognize flaws as flaws, but as strengths—or, at least, as *characteristics*. There's this pedestal—I don't know anyone who's even seen it, but it's there—and once you're up on it, people stop telling you that you can't do this, or you're useless at that, and start wondering why you have allowed something that *looks* like uselessness to appear in your work. Christopher Ricks did it in his recent book *Dylan's Visions of Sin*: he becomes very troubled by a ropy rhyme ("rob them"/"problem") in "Positively Fourth Street," and then nags at it until the ropy rhyme becomes yet another example of Bob's genius: "It must be granted that if these lines induce queasiness, they do make a point of saying 'No,

I do not feel that good.' So an unsettling rhyme such as *problem/rob them* might rightly be hard to stomach..." The notion that Dylan might have just thought, "Oh, fuck it, that'll do" never crosses Ricks's mind for a moment.

Malcolm does her own, perhaps more self-aware version of this when talking about the troublingly "abrupt" and "unmotivated" changes of character in Chekhov's stories: "after enough time goes by, a great writer's innovations stop looking like mistakes." See, I'm at that early stage, where everything still looks like a mistake, so I would have liked Ms. Malcolm to be a little more precise with the figures here. What's "enough time"? Just, you know, roughly? Are we talking six months? Two years? I don't really want to have to wait much longer than that.

I've known Roddy Doyle for a while now. I read him before I met him, and the Barrytown trilogy was an important source of inspiration for me when I was starting out: who knew that books written with such warmth and simplicity could be so complex and intelligent? On this side of the Atlantic, at least, Doyle single-handedly redefined what we mean by "literary" fiction. *Oh, Play That Thing* is the second part of the trilogy that began with *A Star Called Henry*; it's set in the United States during the twenties and thirties, and features Louis Armstrong as a central character, so I've been reading it while listening to *Hot Fives and Sevens* on my iPod.

Reading reviews and interviews with him over the last few weeks, one is reminded that there's nothing critics like less than a writer producing something that he hasn't done before—apart, that is, from a writer producing more of the same. One reviewer complained that Doyle used to write short books, and now they've gone fat; another that he used to write books set in Dublin, and he should have kept them there; another that he used to write with a child's-eye view, and now he's writing about adults. All of these criticisms, of course, could have been based on the catalogue copy, rather than on the book itself—a two-line synopsis and information about the number of pages would have received exactly the same treatment. You're half-expecting someone to point out that back in the day he used to write books that sold for a tenner, and now they've gone up to seventeen quid.

What he's doing, of course, is the only thing a writer can do: he's writing the books that he wants, in the way he wants to. He wants to write about different things, and to add something to the natural talent that produced those early books. I wouldn't want to read anyone who did anything else—apart from P. G. Wodehouse, who did exactly the same thing hundreds of times over. So where does that leave us? Pretty much back where we started, I suppose. That's the beauty of this column, even if I do say it myself. ✶

NICK HORNBY'S PREFACE TO THE SECOND COLUMN COLLECTION, *HOUSEKEEPING VS. THE DIRT* (2006)

I began writing this column in the summer of 2003. It seemed to me that what I had chosen to read in the preceding few weeks contained a narrative, of sorts—that one book led to another, and thus themes and patterns emerged, patterns that might be worth looking at. And, of course, that was pretty much the last time my reading had any kind of logic or shape to it. Ever since then my choice of books has been haphazard, whimsical, and entirely shapeless.

It still seemed like a fun thing to do, though, writing about reading, as opposed to writing about individual books. At the beginning of my writing career I reviewed a lot of fiction, but I had to pretend, as reviewers do, that I had read the books outside of space, time, and self—in other words, I had to pretend that I hadn't read them when I was tired and grumpy, or drunk, that I wasn't envious of the author, that I had no agenda, no personal aesthetic or personal taste or personal problems, that I hadn't read other reviews of the same book already, that I didn't know who the author's friends and enemies were, that I wasn't trying to place a book with the same publisher, that I hadn't been bought lunch by the book's doe-eyed publicist. Most of all I had to pretend that I hadn't written the review because I was urgently in need of a couple hundred quid. Being paid to read a book and then write about it creates a dynamic which compromises the reviewer in all kinds of ways, very few of them helpful.

So this column was going to be different. Yes, I would be paid for it, but I would be paid to write about what I would have done anyway, which was read the books I wanted to read. And if I felt that mood, morale, concentration levels, weather, or family history had affected my relationship with a book, I could and would say so. Inevitably, however, the knowledge that I had to write something for the *Believer* at the end of each month changed my reading habits profoundly. For a start, I probably read more books than I might otherwise have done. I suspect that I used to take a longer break between books, a couple of days, maybe, during which time I'd carry a copy of the *New Yorker* or *Mojo* around with me, but now I push on with the next book, scared I won't have enough to write about (or that I'll look bad, unbookish and unworthy of the space in a publication as smart as the *Believer*). Magazines have been the real casualties of this regime (although the *Economist* has survived, partly to replace the newspapers I'm not reading.)

It was the very nature of the *Believer* itself, however, that really shook up my reading, hopefully forever. The magazine, which is five months older than the column, is a broad church, and all sorts of writers (and artists, and film-makers, and other creative types) are welcome to stand in the pulpit and preach, but it has one commandment: THOU SHALT NOT SLAG ANYONE OFF. As I understand it, the founders of the magazine wanted one place, one tiny corner of the world, in which writers could be sure that they weren't going to get a kicking; predictably and depressingly, this ambition was mocked mercilessly, mostly by those critics whose children would go hungry if their parents weren't able to abuse authors whose books they didn't much like.

I understood and supported the magazine's stance, which seemed admirable and entirely unproblematic to me—until I had to write about the books I'd read which I hadn't much liked. The first couple of times this happened, earnest discussions took place with the magazine's editors, who felt that I'd crossed a line, and I either rewrote the offending passages so that I struck a more conciliatory tone, or the offending books and writers became anonymous. I didn't mind in the least, and in any case it gave me the opportunity to mock the *Believer*'s ambition mercilessly. (For the record: there is no Polysyllabic Spree. I deal with Vendela Vida and Andrew Leland, co-editor and managing editor of the *Believer,* respectively, and they are neither humorless nor evangelical. They even watch television, I think.)

The *Believer*'s ethos did, however, make me think about what and why I read. I didn't want to keep rewriting offending passages in my columns, and I certainly didn't want to keep using the phrases *Anonymous writer* or *Unnameable novel.* So what to do? My solution was to try to choose books I knew I would like. I'm not sure this idea is as blindingly obvious as it seems. We often read books that we think we ought to read, or that we think we ought to have read, or that other people think we should read (I'm always coming across people who have a mental, sometimes even an actual, list of the books they think they should have read by the time they turn forty, fifty, or dead); I'm sure I'm not the only one who harrumphs his way through a highly praised novel, astonished but actually rather pleased that so many people have got it so wrong. As a consequence, the first thing to be cut from my reading diet was contemporary literary fiction. This seems to me to be the highest-risk category—or the highest risk for me, at any rate, given my tastes.

I am not particularly interested in language. Or rather, I am interested in what language can do for me, and I spend many hours each day trying to ensure that my prose is as simple as it can possibly be. But I do not wish to produce prose that draws attention to itself, rather than the world it describes, and I certainly don't have the patience to read it. (I suspect that I'm not alone here. That kind of writing tends to be admired by critics more than by book buyers, if the best-seller lists can be admitted as evidence: the literary novels that have reached a mass audience over the last decade or so usually ask readers to look through a relatively clear pane of glass at their characters.) I am not attempting to argue that the books I like are "better" than most opaquely written novels; I am simply pointing out my own tastes and limitations as a reader. To put it crudely, I get bored, and when I get bored I tend to get tetchy. It has proved surprisingly easy to eliminate boredom from my reading life.

And boredom, let's face it, is a problem that many of us have come to associate with books. It's one of the reasons why we choose to do almost anything else rather than read; very few of us pick up a book after the children are in bed and the dinner has been made and the dirty dishes cleared away. We'd rather turn on the television. Some evenings we'd rather go to all the trouble of getting into a car and driving to a cinema, or waiting for a bus that might take us somewhere near one. This is partly because reading appears to be more effortful than watching TV, and usually it is, although if you choose to watch one of the HBO series, such as *The Sopranos* or *The Wire,* then it's a close-run thing, because the plotting in these programs, the speed and complexity of the dialogue, are as demanding as a lot of the very best fiction.

One of the problems, it seems to me, is that we have got it into our heads that books should be hard work, and that unless they're hard work, they're not doing us any good. I recently had conversations with two friends, both of whom were reading a very long political biography that had appeared in many of 2005's "Books of the Year" lists. They were struggling. Both of these people are parents—they each, coincidentally, have three children—and both have demanding full-time jobs. And each night, in the few minutes they allowed themselves to read before sleep, they plowed gamely through a few paragraphs about the (very) early years of a major twentieth-century world figure. At the rate of progress they were describing, it would take them many, many months before they finished the book, possibly even decades. (One of them told me that he'd put it down for a couple of weeks, and on picking it up again was extremely excited to see that the bookmark was much deeper into the book than he'd dared hope. He then realized that one of his kids had dropped it and put the bookmark back in the wrong place. He was crushed.) The truth is, of course, that neither of them will ever finish it—or at least, not in this phase of their lives. In the process, though, they will have reinforced a learned association of books with struggle.

I am not trying to say that the book itself was the cause of this anguish. I can imagine other people racing through it, and I can certainly imagine these two people racing through books that others might find equally daunting. It seems clear to me, though, that the combination of that book with these readers at this stage in their lives is not a happy one. If reading books is to survive as a leisure activity—and there are statistics which show that this is by no means assured—then we have to promote the joys of reading rather than the (dubious) benefits. I would never attempt to dissuade anyone from reading a book. But please, if you're reading a book that's killing you, put it down and read something else, just as you would reach for the remote if you weren't enjoying a TV program. Your failure to enjoy a highly rated novel doesn't mean you're dim—you may find that Graham Greene is more to your taste, or Stephen Hawking, or Iris Murdoch, or Ian Rankin. Dickens, Stephen King, whoever. It doesn't matter. All I know is that you can get very little from a book that is making you weep with the effort of reading it. You won't remember it, and you'll learn nothing from it, and you'll be less likely to choose a book over *Big Brother* next time you have a choice.

"If reading is a workout for the mind, then Britain must be buzzing with intellectual energy," said one sarcastic columnist in the *Guardian*. "Train stations have shops packed with enough words to keep even the most muscular brain engaged for weeks. Indeed, the carriages are full of people exercising their intellects the full length of their journeys. Yet somehow, the fact that millions daily devour thousands of words from *Hello,* the *Sun, The Da Vinci Code, Nuts,* and so on does not inspire the hope that the average cerebrum is in excellent health. It's not just that you read, it's what you read that counts." This sort of thin—and it's a regrettably common sneer in our broadsheet newspapers—must drive school librarians, publishers, and literacy campaigners nuts. In Britain, more than twelve million adults have a reading age of thirteen or under, and yet some clever-dick journalist still insists on telling us that unless we're reading something proper, then we might as well not bother at all.

But what's proper? Whose books will make us more intelligent? Not mine, that's for sure. But has Ian McEwan got the right stuff? Julian Barnes? Jane Austen, Zadie Smith, E. M. Forster? Hardy or Dickens? Those Dickens readers who famously waited on the dockside in New York for news of Little Nell— were they hoping to be educated? Dickens is Literary now, of course, because the books are old. But his work has survived not because he makes you think, but because he makes you feel, and he makes you laugh, and you need to know what is going to happen to his characters. I have on my desk here a James Lee Burke novel, a thriller in the Dave Robicheaux series, which sports on its covers ringing endorsements from the *Literary Review,* the *Guardian,* and the *Independent* on Sunday, so there's a possibility that somebody who writes for a broadsheet might approve… Any chance of this giving my gray matter a workout? How much of a stretch is it for a nuclear physicist to read a book on nuclear physics? How much cleverer will we be if we read *Of Mice and Men,* Steinbeck's beautiful, simple novella? Or Tobias Wolff's brilliant *This Boy's Life,* or *Lucky Jim,* or *To Kill a Mockingbird*? Enormous intelligence has gone into the creation of all these books, just as it has into the creation of the iPod, but intelligence is not transferable. It's there to serve a purpose.

But there it is. It's set in stone, apparently: books must be hard work; otherwise they're a waste of time. And so we grind our way through serious, and sometimes seriously dull, novels, or enormous biographies of political figures, and every time we do so, books come to seem a little more like a duty, and *Pop Idol* starts to look a little more attractive. Please, please, put it down.

And please, please stop patronizing those who are reading a book—*The Da Vinci Code,* maybe—because they are enjoying it. For a start, none of us knows what kind of an effort this represents for the individual reader. It could be his or her first full-length adult novel; it might be the book that finally reveals the purpose and joy of reading to someone who has hitherto been mystified by the attraction books exert on others. And anyway, reading for enjoyment is what we should all be doing. I don't mean we should all be reading chick lit or thrillers (although if that's what you want to read, it's fine by me, because here's something else no one will ever tell you: if you don't read the classics, or the novel that won this year's Booker Prize, then nothing bad will happen to you; more importantly, nothing good will happen to you if you do); I simply mean that turning pages should not be like walking through thick mud. The whole purpose of books is that we read them, and if you find you can't, it might not be your inadequacy that's to blame. "Good" books can be pretty awful sometimes.

The regrettable thing about the culture war we still, after all these years, seem to be fighting is that it divides books into two camps: the trashy and the worthwhile. No one who is paid to talk about books for a living seems to be able to convey the message that this isn't how it works, that "good" books can provide every bit as much pleasure as "trashy" ones. Why worry about that if there's no difference anyway? Because it gives you more choice. You may not have to read about conspiracies, or the romantic tribulations of thirtysomething women, in order to be entertained. You may find that you're enthralled by Antony Beevor's *Stalingrad,* or Donna Tartt's *The Secret History,* or *Great Expectations.* Read anything, as long as you can't wait to pick it up again.

I'm a reader for lots of reasons. On the whole, I tend to hang out with readers, and I'm scared they wouldn't want to hang out with me if I stopped. (They're interesting people, and they know a lot of interesting things, and I'd miss them.) I'm a writer, and I need to read, for inspiration and education and because

I want to get better, and only books can teach me how. Sometimes, yes, I read to find things out—as I get older, I feel my ignorance weighing more heavily on me. I want to know what it's like to be him or her, to live there or then. I love the detail about the workings of the human heart and mind that only fiction can provide—film can't get in close enough. But the most important reason of all, I think, is this. When I was nine years old, I spent a few unhappy months in a church choir (my mum's idea, not mine). And two or three times a week, I had to sit through the sermon, delivered by an insufferable old windbag of a vicar. I thought it would kill me—that I would, quite literally, die of boredom. The only thing we were allowed for diversion was the hymnbook, and I even ended up reading it, sometimes. Books and comics had never seemed so necessary; even though I'd always enjoyed reading before then, I'd never understood it to be so desperately important for my sanity. I've never, ever gone anywhere without a book or a magazine since. It's taken me all this time to learn that it doesn't have to be a boring one, whatever the reviews pages and our cultural commentators tell me; and it took the Polysyllabic Spree, of all people, to teach me.

Please, please: put it down. You'll never finish it. Start something else. ✴

FEBRUARY 2005

BOOKS BOUGHT:

* *The Men Who Stare At Goats*—Jon Ronson
* *I Am Charlotte Simmons*—Tom Wolfe
* *Devil in the Details: Scenes from an Obsessive Girlhood*—Jennifer Traig
* *Palace Walk*—Naguib Mahfouz
* *Just Enough Liebling*—edited by David Remnick

BOOKS READ:

* *The Plot Against America*—Philip Roth
* *Father Joe: The Man Who Saved My Soul*—Tony Hendra
* *Chronicles: Volume One*—Bob Dylan
* *Little Children*—Tom Perrotta
* *Soldiers of Salamis*—Javier Cercas
* *The Book of Shadows*—Don Paterson

The story so far: I have been writing a column in this magazine for the last fifteen months. And though I have had frequent battles with the Polysyllabic Spree—the fifty-five disturbingly rapturous and rapturously disturbing young men and women who edit the *Believer*—I honestly thought that things had got better recently. We seemed to have come to some kind of understanding, a truce. True, we still have our differences of opinion: they have never really approved of me reading anything about sport, and nor do they like me referring to books wherein people eat meat or farmed fish. (There are a whole host of other rules too ridiculous to mention—for example, you try finding "novels which express no negative and/or strong emotion, either directly or indirectly"—but I won't go into them here.) Anyway, I was stupid enough to try to accommodate their whims, and you can't negotiate with moral terrorists. In my last column, I wrote a little about cricket, and I made a slightly off-color joke about Chekhov, and that was it: I was banned from the magazine, sine die, which is why my column was mysteriously absent from the last issue and replaced by a whole load of pictures. Pictures! This is how they announce my death! It's like a kind of happy-clappy North Korea round here.

I have no idea whether you'll ever get to read these words, but my plan is this: not all the fifty-five members of the Spree are equally sharp, frankly speaking, and they've got this pretty dozy woman on sentry duty down at the *Believer* presses. (Sweet girl, loves her books, but you wouldn't want her doing the Harold Bloom interview, if you know what I mean.) Anyway, we went out a couple of times, and I've told her that I've got the original, unedited, 600-page manuscript of *Jonathan Livingston Seagull,* her favorite novel. I've also told her she can have it if she leaves me unsupervised for thirty minutes while I work out a way of getting "Stuff I've Been Reading" into the magazine. If you're reading these words, you'll know it all came off. This is guerrilla column-writing, man. We're in uncharted territory here.

They couldn't have picked a worse time to ban me, because I read my ass off last month. *Gravity's Rainbow, Daniel Deronda,* Barthes's *S/Z,* an enormous biography of some poet or another that was lying around… It was insane, what I got through. And it was all for nothing. This month I read what I wanted to read, rather than what I thought the Spree might want me to read, and there was nothing I wanted to read more than *Chronicles* and *The Plot Against America.*

I'm not a Dylanologist—to me he's your common-or-garden great artist, prone to the same peaks and troughs as anyone else and with nothing of any interest in his trash can. Even so, when I first heard about a forthcoming Dylan autobiography, I still found it hard to imagine what it would look like. Would it have a corny title—*My Back Pages,* say, or *The Times, They Have A-Changed?* Would it have photos with captions written by the author? You know the sort of thing: "The eyeliner years. What was *that* all about?!!?" Or, "Mary Tyler Moore and I, Malibu, 1973. Not many people know that our break-up inspired *Blood On The Tracks.*" Would he come clean about who those Five Believers really were, and what was so obvious about them? Even if you don't have much time for the myth of Dylan, it's still hard to imagine that he'd ever be able to make himself prosaic enough to write autobiographical prose.

Chronicles ends up managing to inform without damaging the mystique, which is some feat. In fact, after reading the book, you end up realizing that Dylan isn't willfully obtuse or artful in any way—it's just who he is and how his mind works. And this realization in turn has the effect of contextualizing his genius—maybe even diminishing it, if you had a lot invested in his genius being the product of superhuman effort. He thinks in apocalyptic metaphors and ellipses, and clearly sees jokers and thieves and five (or more) believers everywhere he looks, so writing about them is, as far as he is concerned, no big deal. Here he is describing the difference a change in his technique made to him: "It was like parts of my psyche were being communicated to by angels. There was a big fire in the fireplace and the wind was making it roar. The veil had lifted. A tornado had come into the place at Christmastime, pushed all the fake Santa Clauses aside and swept away the rubble…" The boy can't help it. (My favorite little enigmatic moment comes when Dylan tells us how he arrived at his new surname, an anecdote that includes a reference to "unexpectedly" coming across a book of Dylan Thomas's poems. Where did the element of surprise come in, do you think? Did it land on his head? Did he find it under his pillow one morning?)

What's so impressive about *Chronicles* is the seriousness with which Dylan has approached the task of explaining what it's like to be him and how he got to be that way. He doesn't do that by telling you about his childhood or about the bath he was running when he started humming "Mr. Tambourine Man" to himself for the first time; *Chronicles* is non-linear and concentrates on tiny moments in a momentous life—an afternoon in a friend's apartment in New York in 1961, a couple of days in New Orleans in 1989, recording *Oh Mercy* with Daniel Lanois. But he uses these moments like torches, to throw light backwards and forwards, and by the end of the book he has illuminated great swathes of his interior life—the very part one had no real hope of ever being able to see.

And *Chronicles* is a lot humbler than anyone might have anticipated, because it's about wolfing down other people's stuff as much as it's about spewing out your own. Here is a random selection of names taken from the second chapter: The Kingston Trio, Roy Orbison, George Jones, Greil Marcus, Tacitus, Pericles, Thucydides, Gogol, Dante, Ovid, Dickens, Rousseau, Faulkner, Leopardi, Freud,

Pushkin, Robert Graves, Clausewitz, Balzac, Miles Davis, Dizzy Gillespie, Leadbelly, Judy Garland, Hank Williams, Woody Guthrie... Many of the writers on this list were apparently encountered for the first time on a bookshelf in that NYC apartment. I have no idea whether the shelf, or the apartment, or even the friend actually existed, or whether it's all an extended metaphor; and nor do I care, because this is a beautiful, remarkable book, better than anyone had any right to expect, and one of the best and most scrupulous I can remember reading about the process of creativity. You don't even have to love the guy to get something out of it; you just have to love people who create any art at all.

For a brief moment, as I put down *Chronicles* and picked up *The Plot Against America,* neither of them published for longer than a fortnight, I felt like some kind of mythical reader, dutifully plowing through the "new and noteworthy" list. I knew almost enough about what's *au courant* to throw one of those dinner parties that the newspaper columnists in England are always sneering at. They're invariably referred to as "Islington dinner parties" in the English press, because that's where the "liberal intelligentsia"—aka the "chattering classes"— are supposed to live, and where they talk about the new Roth and eat foccacia, which is a type of bread that the "chattering classes" really, really like, apparently. Well, I live in Islington (there's no entrance exam, obviously), and I've never been to a dinner party like that, and this could have been my moment to start a salon. I could have bought that bread and said to people, "Have you read the new Roth?" as they were taking off their coats. And they'd have gone, like, "What the fuck?" if they were my friends, or "Yes, isn't it marvelous?," if they were people I didn't know. Anyway, it's too late now. The books have been out for ages. It's too late for the dinner party, and it's too late even to impress readers of this column. The Spree took care of that with their pictures. This was the one chance I had to show off, and they ruined it, like they ruin everything.

What's even more galling is that I had something to say about *The Plot Against America,* and that almost never happens. The truest and wisest words ever written about reviewing were spoken by Sarah Vowell in her book *Take the Cannoli.* Asked by a magazine to review a Tom Waits album, she concludes that she "quite likes the ballads," and writes that down; now all she needs is another eight-hundred-odd words restating this one blinding aperçu. That's pretty much how I feel about a lot of things I read and hear, so the realization that I actually had a point to make about Roth's novel came as something of a shock to me. You'll have heard my point a million times by now, but tough—I don't have them often enough to just let them float off.

Actually, if I put it this way, my point will have the virtue of novelty and freshness: in my humble and partial opinion, my brother-in-law's alternative-history novel *Fatherland* was more successful as a work of fiction. (You've never heard anyone say that, right? Because even if you've heard someone compare Roth's book to *Fatherland,* they won't have begun the sentence with "My brother-in-law..." My brother could have said it, but I'll bet you any money you like, he hasn't read the Roth. He probably lied about having read *Fatherland,* come to think of it.) *The Plot Against America* is a brilliant, brilliantly-argued, and chilling thesis about America in the twentieth century, but I'm not sure it works as a novel, simply because one is constantly reminded that it is a novel— and not in a fun, postmodern way, but in a strange, slightly distracting way. As you will know, *The Plot Against America* is about what happened to the U.S. after the fascist-sympathizer Charles Lindbergh won the 1940 presidential election, but for large chunks of the book, this is *precisely* what it's about: the alternative history drives the narrative, and as a consequence, you find yourself wondering why we're being told these things. Because if Lindbergh became U.S. president in 1940—and this book asks us to believe that he did, asks us to inhabit a world wherein this was a part of our history—then surely we know it all already? Surely we know about the rampant anti-semitism and the ensuing riots, the heroic role that Mayor LaGuardia played, and Lindbergh's eventual fate? We read on, of course, because we don't know, and we want to know; but it's an uncomfortable compulsion, working as it does against the novel's easy naturalism. When Roth writes, for example, that "the November election hadn't even been close... Lindbergh got 57 percent of the popular vote," the only thing the sentence is doing is providing us with information we don't have; yet at the same time, we are invited to imagine that we do have it—in which case, why are we being given it again?

In *Fatherland,* my brother-in-law—Harris, as I suppose I should call him here—takes the view that in an alternative-history novel, he must imagine not only the alternative history, but the historical consciousness of his reader; in other words, the alternative history belongs in the background, and the information we need to understand what has taken place (in *Fatherland*, the Nazis have won WWII) is given out piecemeal, obliquely, while the author gets on with his thriller plot. Roth chooses to place his what-if at the center of his book, and so *The Plot Against America* ends up feeling like an extended essay.

The thing is, I don't even know if I care. Did any of this really spoil my enjoyment of *The Plot Against America*? Answer: no. I could see it, but I didn't feel it. Who wouldn't want to read an extended essay by Philip Roth? It's only on the books pages of newspapers that perceived flaws of this kind inhibit enjoyment, and that's because book reviewers are not allowed to say "I quite like the ballads."

I now see that just about everything I read was relatively new: Tom Perrotta's absorbing and brave satire *Little Children,* Tony Hendra's mostly lovable *Father Joe… Soldiers of Salamis* is, I think, the first translated novel I've read since I began this column. Is that shameful? I suppose so, but once again, I don't feel it. When you're as ill-read as I am, routinely ignoring the literature of the entire non-English-speaking world seems like a minor infraction.

In Scottish poet Don Paterson's clever, funny, and maddeningly addictive new book of epigrams, *The Book of Shadows,* he writes that "nearly all translators of poetry… fail to understand the poem's incarnation in its tongue is *all there is of it,* as a painting is its paint." I suppose this can't be true for novels, but there is always the sense that you're missing something. *Soldiers of Salamis* is moving and informative and worthwhile and well-translated and blah blah, and on just about every page I felt as though I were listening to a radio that hadn't quite been tuned in properly. You don't need to write in to express your disgust and disappointment. I'm disappointed enough in myself.

The Book of Shadows, though, came through loud and clear—FM through Linn speakers. Thought for the day: "Anal sex has one serious advantage: there are few cinematic precedents that instruct either party how they should *look.*" Your bathroom needs this book badly. ✶

MARCH 2005

BOOKS BOUGHT:

* ✶ *Case Histories*—Kate Atkinson
* ✶ *The Crocodile Bird*—Ruth Rendell
* ✶ *The Spy Who Came in from the Cold*—John le Carré
* ✶ *Another Bullshit Night in Suck City*—Nick Flynn
* ✶ *Help Us to Divorce*—Amos Oz

BOOKS READ:

* ✶ *The Man on the Moon*—Simon Bartram
* ✶ *Every Secret Thing*—Laura Lippman
* ✶ *Help Us to Divorce*—Amos Oz
* ✶ *Assassination Vacation*—Sarah Vowell
* ✶ *Early Bird*—Rodney Rothman

So this last month was, as I believe you people say, a bust. I had high hopes for it, too; it was Christmastime in England, and I was intending to do a little holiday comfort reading—*David Copperfield* and a couple of John Buchan novels, say, while sipping an eggnog and… wait a minute! I only just read *David Copperfield*! What the hell's going on here?

Aha. I see what's happened. In hoping to save myself some time by copying out the sentence that began this column a year ago, I neglected to change anything at all. If I'd substituted *Barnaby Rudge* for *David Copperfield,* say, I might have got away with it, but I couldn't be bothered, and now I'm paying the price. A few months ago—back in the days when the Polysyllabic Spree used to tell me, repeatedly and cruelly, that they had commissioned research showing I had zero readers—I could have got away with repeating whole columns. But then, gloriously and unexpectedly, a reader wrote in ["Dear the Believer," November, 2004] and the Spree had to eat their weasel words. My reader's name is Caroline, and she actually plowed through *Copperfield* at my suggestion, and I love her with all my heart. I think it's time to throw the question back at the Spree: so how many readers do you have, then?

Anyway, Caroline also responded to my recent plea for a list of thrillers that might make me walk into lampposts, which is how come I read Laura Lippman's *Every Secret Thing*. I really liked it, although at the risk of alienating my reader at a very early stage in our relationship, I have to say that it didn't make me walk into a lamppost. I'm not sure that it's intended to be that propulsive: it's gripping in a quiet, thoughtful way, and the motor it's powered with equips the author to putter around the inside of her characters' damaged minds, rather than to smash her reader headlong into an inert object. On Lippman's thoughtful and engaging website—and there are two adjectives you don't see attached to that particular noun very often—a reviewer compares *Every Secret Thing* to a Patricia Highsmith novel, and the comparison made sense to me: like Lippman, Highsmith wants to mess with your head without actually fracturing your skull. *Every Secret Thing* is an American-cheeseburger version of Highsmith's bloody filet mignon, and that suited me fine.

Like many parents, I no longer have a lot of desire to read books in which children are harmed. My imagination is deficient and puny in every area except this one, where it works unstoppably for eighteen or twenty hours a day; I really don't need any help from no thriller. *Every Secret Thing* opens with the release from prison of two girls jailed for the death of a baby, and no sooner are they freed than another child disappears. "It's not incidental that a childless woman wrote *Every Secret Thing*, and I was *very* worried about how readers would react," Lippman said in an interview with the crime writer Jeff Abbott, but I suspect that it's precisely *because* Lippman is childless that she doesn't allow her novel to be pulled out of shape by the narrative events within it. I recently saw *Jaws* again, for the first time since it was in the cinema, and I'd forgotten that a small boy is one of the shark's first victims; what's striking about the movie now is that the boy is chomped and then pretty much forgotten about. In the last thirty years, we've sentimentalized kids and childhood to the extent that if *Jaws* were made now, it would have to be about the boy's death in some way, and it would be the shark that got forgotten about. *Every Secret Thing* is suitably grave in all the right places, but it's not hysterical, and it's also morally complicated in ways that one might not have expected: the mother who lost a child in the original crime is unattractively vengeful, for example, and it's her bitterness that is allowed to drive some of Lippman's narrative. My reader, huh? She shoots, she scores.

Assassination Vacation is the first of the inevitable *Incredibles* cash-ins— Sarah Vowell, as some of you may know, provided the voice of Violet Incredible, and has chosen to exploit the new part of her fame by writing a book about the murders of Presidents Lincoln, Garfield and McKinley. See, I don't know how good an idea this is, from the cash-in angle. Obviously I'm over here in London, and I can't really judge the appetite for fascinating facts about the Garfield presidency among America's pre-teens, but I reckon Vowell might have done better with something more contemporary—a book about the Fair Deal, say, or an analysis of what actually happened at Yalta.

I should own up here and say that Sarah Vowell used to be a friend, back in the days when she still spoke to people who weren't sufficiently famous to warrant animation. She even knows some of the Spree, although obviously she's been cast out into the wilderness since she started bathing in asses' milk etc. Anyway, I make a walk-on appearance in *Assassination Vacation*—I am, enigmatically, a smoker from London called Nick—and Vowell writes of the four hours we spent sitting on a bench in a cold Gramercy Park staring at a statue of John Wilkes Booth's brother. (This was her idea of a good time, not mine.)

Being reminded of that day made me realize how much I will miss her, because, incredibly, ha ha, she made those four hours actually interesting. Did you know that John Wilkes came from this prestigious acting family, a sort of nineteenth-century Baldwin clan? Hence the Booth Theatre in NYC, and hence the statue in the park? There's loads more of this sort of stuff in *Assassination Vacation*: she trawls round museums examining bullets and brains and bits of Lincoln's skull, and hangs out in mausoleums, and generally tracks down all sorts of weird, and weirdly resonant, artefacts and anecdotes. If any other of my friends had told me that they were writing a book on this subject, I'd probably have moved house just so that they wouldn't have had a mailing address for the advance copy. But Vowell's mind is so singular, and her prose is so easy, and her instinct for what we might want to know so true, that I was actually looking forward to this book, and I wasn't disappointed. It's sad, because she does such a good job of bringing these people back to life before bumping them off again, and it's witty, of course (Garfield's assassin Charles Guiteau was a hoot, if you overlook the murderous bit), and, in the current political climate, it's oddly necessary—not least because it helps you to remember that all presidencies and all historical eras end. I hope her new friends, Angelina and Drew and Buzz and Woody and the rest, value Sarah Vowell as much as we all did.

Those of you who like to imagine that the literary world is a vast conspiracy run by a tiny yet elite cabal will not be surprised to learn that I read Rodney Rothman's book because Sarah recommended it, and she happened to have an advance copy because Rothman is a friend of hers. So, to recap: a friend of mine who's just written a book which I read and loved and have written about gives me a book by a friend of hers which she loved, so I read it and then I write about it. See how it works? Oh, you've got no chance if you have no connection with One of Us. Tom Wolfe, Patricia Cornwell, Ian McEwan, Michael Frayn, Anne Rivers Siddons… You're doomed to poverty and obscurity, all of you. Anyway, Rothman's book is the story of how he went to live in a retirement community in Florida for a few months, and it's very sweet and very funny. If you're wondering why a man in his late twenties went to live in a retirement community in Florida, then I can provide alternative explanations. Rothman's explanation is that he wanted to practice being old, which is a good one; mine is that he had a terrific idea for a nonfiction book, which in some ways is even better, even if it's not the sort of thing you're allowed to own up to. Travel writers don't have to give some bullshit reason why they put on their kayaks and climb mountains—they do it because that's what they do, and the idea of voluntarily choosing to eat at 5 p.m. and play shuffleboard for half a year simply because there might be some good jokes in it is, I would argue, both heroic and entirely laudable.

In *Early Bird,* Rothman discovers that he's hopeless at both shuffleboard and bingo, and that it's perfectly possible to find septuagenarians sexually attractive. He gets his ass kicked at softball by a bunch of tough old geezers, and he tries to resuscitate the career of a smutty ninety-three-year-old stand-up comic with the catchphrase "But what the hell, my legs still spread." There are very few jokes about Alzheimer's and prune juice, and lots of stereotype-defying diversions. And Rothman allows the sadness that must, of course, attach itself to the end of our lives to seep through slowly, surely and entirely without sentiment.

So this last month was, as I believe you people say... oh. Right. Sorry. What I'm trying to say here is that, once again, I didn't read as much as I'd hoped over the festive season, and one of the chief reasons for that was a book. This book is called *The Man on the Moon,* and I bought it for my two-year-old son for Christmas, and I swear that I've read it to him fifty or sixty times over the last couple of weeks. Let's say that it's, what, two thousand words long? So that's one-hundred-and-twenty-thousand-odd words—longer than the Alan Hollinghurst novel I still haven't read. And given I haven't got many other books to tell you about, I am reduced to discussing the salient points of this one, which has, after all, defined my reading month.

I bought *The Man on the Moon* after reading a review of it in a newspaper. I don't normally read reviews of children's books, mostly because I can't be bothered, and because kids—my kids, anyway—are not interested in what the *Guardian* thinks they might enjoy. One of my two-year-old's favorite pieces of nighttime reading, for example, is the promotional flyer advertising the *Incredibles* that I was sent (I don't wish to show off, but I know one of the stars of the film personally), a flyer outlining some of the marketing plans for the film. If you end up having to read that out loud every night, you soon give up on the idea of seeking out improving literature sanctioned by the liberal broad-sheets. I had a hunch, however, that what with the Buzz Lightyear obsession and the insistence on what he calls Buzz Rocket pajamas, he might enjoy a picture book about an astronaut who commutes to the moon every day to tidy it up. I dutifully sought the book out—and it wasn't easy to find, you know, just before Christmas—only to be repaid with a soul-crushing enthusiasm, when I would have infinitely preferred a polite, mild, and temporary interest. Needless to say, I won't be taking that sort of trouble again.

After his busy day on the moon, Bob the astronaut, we're told, has a nice hot bath, because working on the moon can make you pretty "grubby." And as my son doesn't know the word "grubby," I substitute the word "dirty," when I remember. Except I don't always remember, at which point he interrupts—somewhat tetchily—with the exhortation "Do 'dirty!'" And I'll tell you, that's a pretty disconcerting phrase coming from the mouth of a two-year-old, especially when it's aimed at his father. He says it to his mum, too, but I find that more acceptable. She's a very attractive woman.

Amos Oz's *Help Us to Divorce* isn't really a book—it's two little essays published between tiny soft covers. But as you can see, I'm desperate, so I have to include it here. Luckily, it's also completely brilliant: the first essay, "Between Right and Right," is a clear-eyed, calm, bleakly optimistic view of the Palestinian crisis, so sensible and yet so smart. "The Palestinians want the land they call Palestine. They have very strong reasons to want it. The Israeli Jews want exactly the same land for exactly the same reasons, which provides for a perfect understanding between the parties, and for a terrible tragedy," says Oz, in response to repeated invitations from well-meaning bodies convinced that the whole conflict could be solved if only the relevant parties got to know each other better. I wanted Oz's pamphlet to provide me with quick and easy mental nutrition at a distressingly mindless time of year; it worked a treat. He kicked Bob the astronaut's ass right into orbit. ✶

APRIL 2005

A few years ago, I was having my head shaved in a local barbers' when the guy doing the shaving turned to the young woman working next to him and said, "This bloke's famous."

I winced. This wasn't going to end well, I could tell. Any fame that you can achieve as an author isn't what most people regard as real fame, or even fake fame. It's not just that nobody recognizes you; most people have never heard of you, either. It's that anonymous sort of fame.

The young woman looked at me and shrugged.

"Yeah," said the barber. "He's a famous writer."

"Well, I've never heard of him," said the young woman.

"I never even told you his name," said the barber.

The young woman shrugged again.

"Yeah, well," said the barber. "You've never heard of any writers, have you?"

The young woman blushed. I was dying. How long did it take to shave a head, anyway?

"Name one author. Name one author ever."

I didn't intercede on the poor girl's behalf because it didn't seem to be that hard a question, and I thought she'd come through. I was wrong. There was a long pause, and eventually she said, "Ednit."

"Ednit?" said her boss. "Ednit? Who the fuck's Ednit?"

"Well, what's her name, then?"

"Who?"

"Ednit."

Eventually, after another two or three excruciating minutes, we discovered that 'Ednit' was Enid Blyton, the enormously popular English children's author of the 1940s and 1950s. In other words, the young woman had been unable to name any writer in the history of the world—not Shakespeare, not Dickens, not even Michel Houellebecq. And she's not alone. A survey conducted by WHSmith in 2000 found that 43 percent of adults questioned were unable to name a favorite book, and 45 percent failed to come up with a favorite author. (This could be because those questioned were unable to decide between Roth and Bellow, but let's presume not.) Forty percent of Britons and 43 percent of Americans never read any books at all, of any kind. Over the past twenty years, the proportion of Americans aged 18–34 who read literature (and literature is defined as poems, plays, or narrative fiction) has fallen by 28 percent. The 18–34 age group, incidentally, used to be the one most likely to read a novel; it has now become the least likely.

And meanwhile, the world of books seems to be getting more bookish. Anita Brookner's new novel is about a novelist. David Lodge and Colm Toíbín wrote novels about Henry James. In *The Line of Beauty,* Alan Hollinghurst wrote about a guy writing a thesis on Henry James. And in Ian McEwan's *Saturday,* the central character's father-in-law and daughter are both serious published poets and past winners of Oxford University's Newdigate Prize for under-graduate poetry. And though nobody should ever tell a writer what to write about… Actually, forget that. Maybe somebody should. I have called for quotas in these pages before—I would have been great on some Politburo cultural committee—and I must call for them again. Nobody listens anyway. Sort it out, guys! You can't all write literature about literature! One book a year, maybe, between you—but all of the above titles were published in the last six months.

There are, I think, two reasons to be a little queasy about this trend. The first is, quite simply, that it excludes readers; the woman in the barbers' is not the only one who wouldn't want to read about the Newdigate Prize. And yes, maybe great art shouldn't be afraid of being elitist, but there's plenty of great art that isn't, and I don't want bright people who don't happen to have a degree in literature to give up on the contemporary novel; I want them to believe there's a point to it all, that fiction has a purpose visible to anyone capable of reading a book intended for grown-ups. Taken as a group, these novels seem to raise the white flag: We give in! It's hopeless! We don't know what those people out there want! Pull up the drawbridge!

And the second cause for concern is that writing exclusively about highly articulate people... Well, isn't it cheating a little? McEwan's hero, Henry Perowne, the father and son-in-law of the poets, is a neurosurgeon, and his wife is a corporate lawyer; like many highly educated middle-class people, they have access to and a facility with language, a facility that enables them to speak very directly and lucidly about their lives (Perowne is "an habitual observer of his own moods"), and there's a sense in which McEwan is wasted on them. They don't need his help. What I've always loved about fiction is its ability to be smart about people who aren't themselves smart, or at least don't necessarily have the resources to describe their own emotional states. That was the way Twain was smart, and Dickens; and that is surely one of the reasons why Roddy Doyle is adored by all sorts of people, many of whom are infrequent book-buyers. It seems to me to be a more remarkable gift than the ability to let extremely literate people say extremely literate things.

It goes without saying that *Saturday* is a very good novel. It's humane and wise and gripping, just like *Atonement* and *Black Dogs* and just about everything McEwan has written. Set entirely on the day of the anti-war march in February 2003, it's about pretty much everything—family, uxoriousness, contemporary paranoia, the value of literature, liberalism, the workings of the human brain— and readers of this magazine will find much with which they identify. I spent too much time wondering about Henry Perowne's age, however. McEwan tells us that he's forty-eight years old, and though of course it's possible and plausible for a forty-eight-year-old man to have a daughter in her early twenties, it's by no means typical of highly qualified professional people who must have spent a good deal of their twenties studying; at the end of the book, (SKIP TO THE NEXT SENTENCE IF YOU DON'T WANT TO KNOW) Perowne learns that he is about to become a grandfather, and this too bucks a few demographic trends. I belong to Henry Perowne's generation, and my friends typically have kids who are now in their early-to-mid-teens. On top of that, I'm not sure that I am as consumed by thoughts of my own mortality as Perowne, although to be fair I'm a lot dimmer than he is, and as a consequence it may take me longer to get there. McEwan himself is fifty-six, and it felt to me like Perowne might have been, too. It doesn't matter much, of course, but the author's decision perhaps inevitably invites attempts at psychoanalysis.

It made me sad, thinking back to the day of the anti-war march. All that hope! All that confidence! And now it's dwindled to nothing! I should explain that Arsenal beat Man Utd two–nil that afternoon in an FA Cup match—my passionate opposition to the war was conquered by my passionate desire to watch the TV—and it looked as though we would beat them forever. In fact, we haven't beaten them since, and I finished *Saturday* in the very week that they thumped us 4-2 at Highbury to end all championship aspirations for the season.

Usually, when I read a novel I'm enjoying, I just lie there with my mouth open, occasionally muttering things like, "Oh, no! Don't go in there!" or, "You could still get back together, right? You love each other." But both *Saturday* and Kate Atkinson's novel *Case Histories* contain detailed descriptions of places where I used to live and work, and as a consequence there were moments when I forgot to maintain even that level of critical engagement. Whenever Kate Atkinson mentioned Parkside, a street in Cambridge, I exclaimed—out loud, the first few dozen times, and internally thereafter—"Parkside!" (I used to teach at Parkside Community College, you see, so that was weird.) And then whenever Ian McEwan mentioned Warren Street, or the Indian restaurants on Cleveland Street, the same thing happened: "Ha! Warren Street!" Or, "Ha! The Indian restaurants!" And if someone was in the room with me while I was reading, I'd say, "This book's set around Warren Street! Where I used to live!" (It's not a residential area, you see, so that was weird, too.) It felt entirely right that I should read these books back-to-back, and then I was sent a copy of John Harris's *So Now Who Do We Vote For?*, and I felt for a moment as though certain books were stalking me or something. Until someone writes a book called *I Know Where You Put Your House Keys Last Night*, I can't imagine a title more perfectly designed to capture my attention.

I am sorry if the following lesson in UK politics is redundant, but I'm going to give it anyway: our Democrats are already in office. We voted the right way in 1997, and we have had a Labour government ever since, and at the time of writing it is absolutely certain that we will have one for the next five years: there will be an election some time in 2005, and Blair will walk it. As you may have noticed, the only problem is that the Labour government turned out not to be a Labour government at all. It's not just that Blair helped to bomb Iraq; he's also introducing the profit motive into our once-glorious National Health Service, and allowing some pretty dodgy people to invest in the education of our children. Sir Peter Vardy, an evangelical Christian car-dealer, wants creationism taught alongside theories of evolution, and in return for two million pounds per new school he can do pretty much whatever he wants. He already controls a couple of schools in the North of England.

I waited for this government all my voting life, and Harris's title perfectly captures the disillusionment of several generations of people who thought that when the Tories went, all would be right with the world. Disappointingly, Harris tells me that I should carry on doing what I've been doing: my local MP (and we don't elect leaders, just local representatives of political parties) has voted against everything I would want him to vote against, so it seems unfair to castigate him for Blair's crimes and misdemeanors. I wanted to be told that the Liberal Democrats, our third party, or the Greens, or the vaguely nutty Respect Coalition were viable alternatives, but they're not, so we're stuffed. *So Now Who Do We Vote For?* is a useful and impassioned book nevertheless; it's a brave book, too—nobody wants to write anything that will self-destruct at a given point in its publication year, and I don't think he's going to pick up many foreign sales, either. John Harris, we salute you.

Another Bullshit Night in Suck City wasn't one of the stalker books, but after a couple of recommendations, I wanted to read it anyway. Nick Flynn's dark, delirious memoir describes his father's journey from employment, marriage, and a putative writing career to vagrancy and alcoholism. (The ambition to write, incidentally, is never abandoned, which might give a few of us pause for thought.) Nick loses touch with his dad; lives, not entirely companionably, with a few demons of his own; and then ends up working in a homeless shelter. And guess who turns up? One image in *Another Bullshit Night in Suck City*, of a homeless man sitting in the street in an armchair, watching a TV he has managed to hook up to a street lamp, is reminiscent of Beckett; readers will find themselves grateful that Flynn is a real writer, stonily indifferent to the opportunities for shameless manipulation such an experience might provide.

I bought Michael Frayn's *Towards the End of the Morning* from one of Amazon's "Marketplace Sellers" for 25p. I could have had it for 1p, but I was, perhaps understandably, deterred rather than attracted by the price: What can you get for a penny these days? Would I be able to read it, or would all the pages have been masticated by the previous owner's dog? It wasn't as if I was entirely reassured by the higher price, but a few days later, a perfectly-preserved, possibly unread 1970 paperback turned up in the post, sent by a lady in Scotland. Does anyone understand this Marketplace thing? Why does anyone want to sell a book for a penny? Or even twenty-five pennies? What's in it for anyone, apart from us? I'm still suspicious. It's a wonderful novel, though, urbane and funny and disarmingly gentle, and I might send the lady in Scotland some more money anyway. Or is that the scam? That's clever.

"If Frayn is about to step into anybody's shoes, they aren't Evelyn Waugh's, but Gogol's," says the blurb on the front of my thirty-five-year-old paperback. Is that how you sold books back then? And how would it have worked? As far as I can work out, the quote is a stern warning to fans of elegant English comic writing that this elegant English comic novel won't interest them in the slightest. It was a daring tactic, certainly; the penny copies lead one to suspect that it didn't quite come off. ✷

MAY 2005

Earlier today I was in a bookstore, and I picked up a new book about the migration patterns of the peregrine falcon. For a moment, I ached to buy it—or rather, I ached to be the kind of person who would buy it, read it, and learn something from it. I mean, obviously I could have bought it, but I could also have taken the fifteen pounds from my pocket and eaten it, right in the middle of Borders, and there seemed just as much point in the latter course of action as the former. (And before anyone gets on at me about Borders, I should point out that the last independent bookshop in Islington, home of the chattering literary classes, closed down a couple of weeks ago.)

I don't know what it was about, the peregrine falcon thing. That's some kind of bird, right? Well, I've only read one book about a bird before, Barry Hines's heartbreaking *A Kestrel for a Knave,* later retitled *Kes* to tie in with Ken Loach's film adaptation of that name. (You, dear reader, are much more likely to have read *Jonathan Livingston Seagull* than *Kes,* I suspect, and our respective tastes in bird books reveal something fundamental about our cultures. An Amazon reviewer describes *Jonathan Livingston Seagull* as "a charming allegory with a very pertinent message: DON'T ABANDON YOUR DREAMS." I would not be traducing the message of *Kes* if I were to summarize it thus: ABANDON YOUR DREAMS. In fact, "ABANDON YOUR DREAMS" is a pretty handy summary of the whole of contemporary English culture—of the country itself, even. It would be great to be you, sometimes. I mean, obviously our motto is more truthful than yours, and ultimately more useful, but there used to be great piles of *Kes* in every high-school stock room. You'd think they'd let us reach the age of sixteen or so before telling us that life is shit. I read Hines's book because it was a work of literature, however, not because it was a book about a bird. And maybe this book will turn out to be a work of literature, too, and a million people will tell me to read it, and it will win tons of prizes, and eventually I'll succumb, but by then, it will have lost the allure it seemed to have this afternoon when it promised to be the kind of book I don't usually open. I'm always reading works of bloody literature; I'm never reading about migration patterns.

This month, my taste in books seems to have soured on me: every book I pick up seems to be exactly the sort of book I always pick up. On the way home from the bookstore, as I was pondering the unexpectedly seductive lure of the peregrine falcon, I tried to name the book least likely to appeal to me that I have actually read all the way through, and I was struggling for an answer. Isn't that ridiculous? You'd have thought that there'd been something, somewhere—an apparently ill-advised dalliance with a book about mathematics or physics, say, or a history of some country that I didn't know anything about, but there's nothing. I read a biography of Margaret Thatcher's press secretary once, but my brother-in-law wrote it, so that doesn't really count. And I did struggle through Roy Jenkins's enormous *Gladstone,* which reduced me to tears of boredom on several occasions, but that was because I was judging a non-fiction prize. I would like my personal reading map to resemble a map of the British Empire circa 1900; I'd like people to look at it and think, How the hell did he end up right over there? As it is, I make only tiny little incursions into the territory of my own ignorance—every year, another classic novel conquered here, a couple of new literary biographies beaten down there. To be honest, I'm not sure that I can spare the troops for conquests further afield: they're needed to quell all the rebellions and escape attempts at home. But that's not the attitude. When you turn to these pages next month, I swear you'll be reading about peregrine falcons, or Robert the Bruce, or the combustion engine. I'm sorry that the four books I read these last few weeks seem to have brought all this on, because I loved them all. But look at them: a cute, sad literary novel, a couple of elegant true-crime stories, and a book about Dylan by one of America's cleverest cultural commentators—chips off the old block, every one of them. I can hardly claim to have pushed back any personal frontiers with any of these.

Recently the Polysyllabic Spree, the fifteen horrifically enthusiastic young men and women who control the minds of everyone who writes for this magazine, sent an emissary to London, and the young man in question handed me, without explanation, a copy of Philip Gourevitch's *A Cold Case*. I felt duty-bound to read it, not least because the Spree frequently chooses enigmatic methods of communication, and I presumed that the book would contain some kind of coded message. In fact, the purpose of the gift was straightforwardly cruel: the security tag was still attached to it, and as a consequence I was humiliated by store detectives whenever I tried to enter a shop with the book in my bag. I don't really know why the Spree wanted to do this to me. I suspect it's something to do with the recent discovery that I have one reader (a charming and extremely intelligent woman called Caroline—see the March issue) whereas there is still no evidence that they have any at all. I've tried not to be triumphalist, but even so, they haven't reacted with great magnanimity, I'm afraid.

A Cold Case is a short, simple, and engrossing account of a detective's attempt to solve a twenty-seven year-old double homicide—or rather, to find out whether the prime suspect is still alive. The detective's renewed interest in the case seems almost alarmingly whimsical (he happens to drive past a bar which reminds him of the night in question), but his rigor and probity are unquestionable, and one of the joys of the book is that its characters—upright, determined detective, psychotic but undeniably magnetic villain—seem to refer back to the older, simpler, and more dangerous New York City. In one of my favorite passages, Gourevitch reports verbatim the conversations he overhears in the office of a colorful lawyer with a lot of Italian-American clients:

> [*Enter Rocco, a burly man with a voice like a cement mixer*]
> RICHMAN: Your father and I grew up together… Your mother is a beautiful lady.
> ROCCO: She sure is…
> RICHMAN: Your uncle—the first time I had him, he was thirteen years old.

ROCCO: Yup.

RICHMAN: I represented Nicole when she killed her mother, when she cut her
mother's throat.

ROCCO: Yes, yes, I remember that.

The end of this exchange raises the alarming possibility of an alternative
version, wherein Rocco had forgotten all about Nicole cutting her mother's
throat. And though I do not wish to generalize about the people or person who
reads this magazine, I'm sure I speak for all of us when I say that we would have
retained at least the vaguest memory of an equivalent occasion in our own lives.

I was shamed into reading *In Cold Blood* at one of Violet Incredible's
London literary soirees. I think I may have mentioned before that I know Violet
Incredible of *The Incredibles* personally. Anyway, ever since the success of that
film, she has taken to gathering groups of writers around her, presumably in
the hope that she becomes more literary (and, let's face it, less animated) by
osmosis. I don't know why we all turn out. I suppose the truth is that we are
none of us as immune to the tawdry glitter of Hollywood as we like to pretend.
At the most recent of these events, most of the writers present suddenly started
enthusing about Truman Capote's 1965 nonfiction classic. And though it goes
without saying that I joined in, for fear of incurring Violet's disapproval, I've
never actually read the thing.

It makes a lot of sense reading it immediately after *A Cold Case,* and not
just because they belong in the same genre. Philip Gourevitch thanks David
Remnick in his acknowledgments, and Truman Capote thanks William Shawn;
this is *New Yorker* true crime, then and now (ish), and the comparison is
instructive. Capote's book is much wordier, and researched almost to within
an inch of its life, to the extent that one becomes acutely aware of the information that is being concealed from the reader. (If he knows *this* much, you keep
thinking, then he must know the rest, too. And of course anyone constructing
a narrative out of real events knows more than they're letting on, but it's not
helpful to be reminded so forcefully of the writer's omniscience.) Gourevitch's
book is short, understated, selective. And though *A Cold Case* doesn't quite
attain the heights that *In Cold Blood* reaches in its bravura, vertiginously tense,

unbearably ominous opening section, Gourevitch clearly reaps the benefits of Capote's groundbreaking work. *In Cold Blood* is one of the most influential books of the last fifty years, and as far as I can tell, just about every work of novelistic nonfiction published since the 1960s owes it something or another. But the trouble with influential books is that if you have absorbed the influence without ever reading the original, then it can sometimes be hard to appreciate the magnitude of its achievement. I loved *In Cold Blood*, but at the same time I could feel it slipping away from me as a Major Literary Experience—*A Cold Case* seemed to me simultaneously less ambitious and more sure-footed. I mean, I'm sure my impression is, you know, *wrong*. But what can I do?

I read Amanda Eyre Ward's lovely *How To Be Lost* after a warm recommendation from a friend, and it's got the mucus, as P. G. Wodehouse would and did say. ("The mucus" was to Wodehouse's way of thinking a desirable attribute, lest people think this is some kind of snotty snark.) *How To Be Lost* isn't one of those irritatingly perfect novels that people sometimes write; it has a slightly ungainly, gawky shape to it, and slightly more plot than it can swallow without giving itself heartburn. But it has that lovely tone that only American women writers seem to be able to achieve: melancholic, wry, apparently (but only apparently) artless, perched on the balls of its feet and ready to jump either towards humor or towards heartbreak, with no run-up and no effort. *How To Be Lost* has a great set-up, too. Narrator Caroline, a New Orleans barmaid with a drinking habit, has/had a sister who disappeared without trace when she was a little girl. Just as Caroline's family is about to declare Ellie dead, Caroline spots a photo in a magazine of a woman in a crowd whose face contains an unmistakeable trace of the child she knew, and she sets off to track the woman down. Good, no?

How To Be Lost is about all the usual stuff you read in literary novels: grief and families and disappointment and so on, and I was interested in what Ward had to say about all of these things. But as far as I was concerned, she'd earned the right to sound off because she'd lured me into her book with an intriguing narrative idea. It doesn't hurt, that's all I'm saying. The Kate Atkinson novel I read a few weeks back had a long-time absent little sister in it, too. But where *Case Histories* (and Atkinson is English) differs from *How To Be Lost* is… Are you going to read either of these? Perhaps you will. Well, remember the bird books, and choose accordingly.

The last book I read that contained the wealth and range of cultural references on show in Greil Marcus's *Like A Rolling Stone* was Bob Dylan's *Chronicles*. Those of you who've read Dylan's breathtakingly good memoir might remember that one of the many, many names (of writers, artists, historians, musicians) in there was that of Marcus himself, and there is no reason why Marcus shouldn't have helped Dylan to think about culture in the same way that he's helped many of us think about culture.

For the second time this month I found myself envying the advantages that being an American can bring, although on this occasion I envied only those who live and think in America; you can't envy those who live in America and don't think (although you could argue that those who don't think aren't really living anyway). One of the things that Marcus's book is about is the slipperiness of meaning in the U.S.; any major American artist, in any idiom, can change the way the country perceives itself. I'm not sure this is possible here in England, where our culture appears so monolithic, and our mouthiest cultural critics so insanely and maddeningly sure of what has value and what doesn't. If we have never produced a Dylan, it is partly because he would have been patronized back into obscurity: we know what art is, pal, and it's nothing you'd ever have heard on top 40 radio. I didn't always understand *Like a Rolling Stone* (and I can't for the life of me hear the things that Marcus can in the Pet Shop Boys' version of "Go West"), but my sporadic bafflement didn't matter to me in the least. Just to live in the world of this book, a world of intellectual excitement and curiosity and rocket-fuelled enthusiasm, was a treat.

STOP PRESS: Since I began this column, a friend has had an idea for a literary genre I'd never touch in a million years: SF/Fantasy, of the non-literary, nerdy-boys-on-websites variety. He's right, and already my heart is sinking in a gratifying way. Do I have to? I'm already wishing I'd shelled out for the peregrine falcon book. ✱

JUNE / JULY 2005

BOOKS BOUGHT:

* ★ *Little Scarlet*—Walter Mosley
* ★ *Out of the Silent Planet*—C. S. Lewis*
* ★ *Voyage to Venus*—C. S. Lewis*
* ★ *Maxton*—Gordon Brown*
* ★ *Nelson And His Captains*—Ludovic Kennedy*
* ★ *Excession*—Iain M. Banks

> * Don't worry. These books were bought for one pound or less at the Friends of Kenwood House Book Sale.

BOOKS READ:

* ★ *Excession*—Iain M. Banks (abandoned)
* ★ *The Men Who Stare at Goats*—Jon Ronson
* ★ *Adrian Mole and the Weapons of Mass Destruction*—Sue Townsend
* ★ *The Wonder Spot*—Melissa Bank
* ★ *Stuart: A Life Backwards*—Alexander Masters

The story so far: suddenly sick of my taste in books, I vowed in these pages last month to read something I wouldn't normally pick up. After much deliberation (and the bulk of the otherwise inexplicable Books Bought can be explained by this brief but actually rather exhilarating period), I decided that my friend Harry was right, and that in the normal course of events I'd never read an SF/Fantasy novel in a million years. Now read on, if you can be bothered.

Even buying Iain M. Banks's *Excession* was excruciating. Queuing up behind me at the cash desk was a very attractive young woman clutching some kind of groovy art magazine, and I felt obscurely compelled to tell her that the reason I was buying this purple book with a spacecraft on the cover was because of the *Believer,* and the *Believer* was every bit as groovy as her art magazine. In a rare moment of maturity, however, I resisted the compulsion. She could, I decided, think whatever the hell she wanted. It wasn't a relationship that was ever going to go anywhere anyway. I'm with someone, she's probably with someone, she was twenty-five years younger than me, and—let's face it—the *Believer* isn't as groovy as all that. If we had got together, that would have been only the first of many disappointing discoveries she'd make.

When I actually tried to read *Excession,* embarrassment was swiftly replaced by trauma. Iain M. Banks is a highly rated Scottish novelist who has written twenty-odd novels, half of them (the non-SF half) under the name Iain Banks, and though I'd never previously read him, everyone I know who is familiar with his work loves him. And nothing in the twenty-odd pages I managed of *Excession* was in any way bad; it's just that I didn't understand a word. I didn't even understand the blurb on the back of the book: "Two and a half millennia ago, the artifact appeared in a remote corner of space, beside a trillion-year-old dying sun from a different universe. It was a perfect black-body sphere, and it did nothing. Then it disappeared. Now it is back." This is clearly intended to entice us into the novel—that's what blurbs do, right? But this blurb just made me scared. An artifact—that's something you normally find in a museum, isn't it? Well, what's a museum exhibit doing floating around in space? So what if it did nothing? What are museum exhibits supposed to do? And this dying sun—how come it's switched universes? Can dying suns do that?

The urge to weep tears of frustration was already upon me even before I read the short prologue, which seemed to describe some kind of androgynous avatar visiting a woman who has been pregnant for forty years and who lives on her own in the tower of a giant spaceship. (Is this the artifact? Or the dying sun? Can a dying sun be a spaceship? Probably.) By the time I got to the first chapter, which is entitled "Outside Context Problem" and begins "(*CGU Grey Area* signal sequence file #n428857/119)," I was crying so hard that I could no longer see the page in front of my face, at which point I abandoned the entire ill-conceived experiment altogether. I haven't felt so stupid since I stopped attending physics lessons aged fourteen. "It's not *stupidity,*" my friend Harry said when I told him I'd had to pack it in. "Think of all the heavy metal fans who devour this stuff. You think you're dimmer than them?" I know that he was being rhetorical, but the answer is: Yes, I do. In fact, I'm now pretty sure that I've never really liked metal because I don't understand that properly, either. Maybe that's where I should start. I'll listen to Slayer or someone for a few years, until I've grasped what they're saying, and then I'll have another go at SF. In the meantime, I have come to terms with myself and my limitations, and the books I love have never seemed more attractive to me. Look at them: smart and funny novels, nonfiction books about military intelligence and homeless people... It's a balanced, healthy diet. I wasn't short of any vitamins. I was looking for the literary equivalent of grilled kangaroo, or chocolate-covered ants, not spinach, and as I am never drawn to the kangaroo section of a menu in a restaurant, it's hardly surprising that I couldn't swallow it in book form.

Stupidity has been the theme of the month. There's a lot of it in Jon Ronson's mind-boggling book about U.S. military intelligence, *The Men Who Stare at Goats*; plenty of people (although admittedly none any of us is likely to spend much time with) would describe the behavior of the tragic and berserk Stuart in Alexander Masters's brilliant book as stupid beyond belief. And Sue Townsend's comic anti-hero Adrian Mole, who by his own admission isn't too bright, has unwittingly contributed to the post-*Excession* debate I've been having with myself about my own intelligence.

Adrian Mole is one of the many cultural phenomena that has passed me by until now, but my friend Harry—yes, the same one, and no, I don't have any other friends, thank you for asking—suddenly declared Townsend's creation to be a work of comic genius, and insisted I should read *Adrian Mole and the Weapons of Mass Destruction* immediately. He pointed out helpfully that I'd understand quite a lot of it, too, and as I needed the boost in confidence, I decided to take his advice.

Adrian Mole, who famously began his fictional life aged thirteen and three-quarters, is now thirty-four, penniless, becalmed in an antiquarian bookshop, and devoted to our Prime Minister. One of the many unexpected pleasures of this book was the acerbity of its satire. There is real anger in here, particularly about the war in Iraq, and the way Townsend manages to accommodate her dismay within the tight confines of light comedy is a sort of object lesson in what can be done with mainstream fiction. There's a great running gag about Blair's ludicrous claim that Saddam could hit Cyprus with some of the nasty missiles at his disposal: Adrian Mole has booked a holiday on that very island, and spends much of the book trying to reclaim his deposit from the travel agent.

I do wish that comic writing took itself more seriously, though. I don't mean I want fewer jokes; I simply mean that the cumulative effect of those jokes would be funnier if they helped maintain the internal logic of the book. Mole has a blind friend, Nigel, to whom he reads books and newspapers, and at one point Nigel accuses him of not understanding much of what he's reading. "I had to admit that I didn't," Mole says, before, just a few pages later, making an admittedly inappropriate allusion to Antony Beevor's *Stalingrad*. It might seem pedantic to point out that anyone who's plowed their way through *Stalingrad* is probably capable of grasping the essence of a newspaper article (if not the opening of an Iain M. Banks novel)—just as it's probably literal-minded to wonder how an unattractive man with a spectacularly unenviable romantic history gets repeatedly lucky with an extremely attractive woman. But moments like this tend to wobble the character around a little bit, and I found myself having occasionally to recreate him in my head, almost from scratch. I'm sure that Mole has a fixed identity for those who have read the entire series, and he remains a fantastic, and fantastically English, comic creation: upright and self-righteous, bewildered, snobby, self-hating, provincial, and peculiarly lovable. We all are, here.

Jon Ronson's *The Men Who Stare at Goats* is one of the most disorienting books I have ever read. While reading it, I started feeling like the victim of one of the extremely peculiar mindfuck experiments that Ronson describes in his inimitable perplexed tones. Here's his thesis: after the rout in Vietnam, the U.S. military started investigating different ways to fight wars, and as a consequence co-opted several somewhat eccentric New Age thinkers and practitioners who, your generals felt, might point them toward a weaponless future, one full of warriors capable of neutralizing the enemy with a single glance. And the first half of the book is uproarious, as Ronson endeavors to discover, for example, whether the actress Kristy McNichol (who appeared in *The Love Boat 2* and the cheesy soft porn movie *Two Moon Junction*), had ever been called upon to help find Manuel Noriega. (A U.S. Sergeant called Lyn Buchanan, who was part of a secret unit engaged in a "supernatural war" against Noriega, had repeatedly written her name down while in a self-induced trance, and became convinced that the actress knew something.) Gradually Ronson builds a crazy-paving path that leads to Abu Ghraib, and both the book and its characters become darker and more disturbing.

You have probably read those stories of how people in Iraq and Afghanistan were tortured by having American pop music blasted at them day and night. And you have probably read or heard many of the jokes made as a consequence of these stories—people writing in to newspapers to say that if you have a teenager who listens to 50 Cent or Slipknot all day then you know how those Iraqi prisoners feel, etc. and so on. (Even the *Guardian* made lots of musical torture jokes for a while.) Ronson floats the intriguing notion that the jokes were an integral part of the strategy: in other words, if you can induce your citizens to laugh at torture, then outrage will be much harder to muster. Stupidity is, despite all appearances to the contrary, a complicated state of mind. Who's stupid, in the end—them or us?

This month's Book by a Friend was Melissa Bank's *The Wonder Spot,* and this paragraph must be parenthetical, because neither the novel nor the friend can be shoehorned into the stupid theme. It's been a long time since *The Girls' Guide to Hunting and Fishing,* and some of us—including the author herself— were wondering whether she'd ever get around to a second book. But she has, finally, and it's a lovely thing, sweet-natured, witty, lots of texture. It's hard to write, as Bank does here, about growing up, and about contemporary adult urban romance: It's such an apparently overpopulated corner of our world that she must have been tempted, at least for a moment, by artifacts and dying suns and women who are pregnant for decades. We need someone who's really, really good at that stuff, though, because it still matters to us, no matter how many millions of words are written on the subject. In fact—and once again in these pages I'm calling for Soviet-style intervention into the world of literature—it would be much easier for everyone if Melissa Bank and maybe two or three other people in the world were given an official government license, and you could no more appoint yourself as chronicler of contemporary adult urban romance than you could set yourself up as a neurosurgeon. In this Utopia,

Melissa Bank would be… well, you'll have to insert the name of your own top neurosurgeon here. I don't know any. Obviously. I'm too dim. Damn that Iain M. Banks. He's wrecked my confidence.

Here's an unlikely new subgenre: biographical studies of vagrants. Alexander Masters's *Stuart: A Life Backwards* is, after *Another Bullshit Night in Suck City*, the second one I've read recently, and if these two are as successful as they should be, then on top of everything else, down-and-outs may have to contend with the unwanted attentions of hungry nonfiction writers. At the moment, there's still plenty of room in the field for tonal contrast; where Nick Flynn's book about his homeless, alcoholic father was poetic, as deep and dark and languid as a river, *Stuart* is quick, bright, angry, funny, and sarcastic—Masters finds himself occasionally frustrated by Stuart's inexplicable and self-destructive urge to punch, stab, self-lacerate, incinerate and cause general mayhem. ("I headbutted the bloke," Stuart explains when Masters asks him what happened to a particular employer and job. "Excellent. Of course you did. Just the thing," Masters finds himself thinking.)

The story is told backwards at Stuart's suggestion, after he'd told Masters that his first draft was "bollocks boring"; he thinks the narrative structure will pep it up a little, turn it into something "like what Tom Clancy writes." It feels instead like a doomed search for hope and innocence; as Masters trudges back through three decades of illness and drug abuse and alcohol abuse and self-abuse and the shocking, sickening abuse perpetrated by Stuart's teachers and family members, he and we come to see that there never was any. This is an important and original book, and it doesn't even feel as though you should read it. You'll want to, however much good it's doing you.

I'm certain that I read five books all the way through in the last month, and yet I've written about only four of them. This means that I've forgotten about the other one completely, the first time that's happened since I began writing this column. I'm sorry, whoever you are, but I think you've got to take some of the blame. Your book was… well, it was good, obviously, because we are forced by the Polysyllabic Spree, the sixty-three white-robed literary maniacs who run this magazine, to describe every book as good. But clearly it could have been better. Try a joke next time, or maybe a plot. ✶

AUGUST 2005

BOOKS BOUGHT:

- ★ *Gilead*—Marilynne Robinson
- ★ *The Bullfighter Checks Her Makeup*—Susan Orlean
- ★ *Housekeeping*—Marilynne Robinson*
- ★ *You Are Here: Personal Geographies and Other Maps of the Imagination*
  —Katharine Harmon
- ★ *Babbitt*—Sinclair Lewis
- ★ *Between Silk and Cyanide*—Leo Marks
- ★ *Bartleby the Scrivener*—Herman Melville
- ★ *The Disappointment Artist*—Jonathan Lethem
- ★ *Wonderland*—Michael Bamberger

    *Bought twice—administrative error.

BOOKS READ:

- ★ *Gilead*—Marilynne Robinson
- ★ *Little Scarlett*—Walter Mosley
- ★ *Noblesse Oblige*—Nancy Mitford
- ★ *Spies*—Michael Frayn
- ★ *The Amateur Marriage*—Anne Tyler
- ★ *Penguin Special*—Jeremy Lewis
- ★ *Hard News*—Seth Mnookin
- ★ *Jane Austen: The Girl with the Magic Pen*—Gill Hornby

A few months ago, I heard a pompous twit on a radio program objecting, bitterly and at some length, to Martin Amis's *Money* being republished in the Penguin Modern Classic series. It couldn't possibly be a classic, said the pompous twit, because we need fifty years to judge whether a book is a classic or not. It seemed to me that the twit's argument could be summarized succinctly thus: "I don't like Martin Amis's *Money* very much," because nothing else made much sense. (Presumably we're not allowed to use the phrase "modern classic" about anything at all unless we wish to appear oxymoronic, even though in this context the word "classic" means, simply, "of the highest class." The pompous twit seemed to be laboring under the misapprehension that a "classic" book is somehow related to classical music, and therefore has to be a bit old and a bit posh before it qualifies.) Do you have Penguin Modern Classics in your country? Over here, they used to mean a lot to young and pretentious lovers of literature. My friends and I used to make sure we had a PMC, with its distinctive light green spine, about our persons at all times, as an indication both of our intellectual seriousness and of our desire/willingness to sleep with girls who also liked books. It never worked, of course, but we lived in hope. Anyway, *L'Étranger* was a Penguin Modern Classic; I probably read it in 1974, thirty-odd years after it was published. And when I was talking embarrassing rubbish about Sartre to fellow seventeen-year-olds, *La Nausee*—another light green 'un—had been around for less than forty years. If the pompous twit's fifty-year rule had been enforced when I was a teenager, I'd never have read either of them—we needed that green spine for validation—and as a consequence I'd be even more ill-educated than I am now.

Anyway, Marilynne Robinson's *Gilead* is clearly a modern classic, and it hasn't even been in print for five minutes. It's a beautiful, rich, unforgettable work of high seriousness, and you don't need to know that the book has already won the Pulitzer Prize to see that Robinson isn't messing around. I didn't even mind that it's essentially a book about Christianity, narrated by a Christian; in fact, for the first time I understood the point of Christianity—or at least, I understood how it might be used to assist thought. I am an atheist living in a godless country (7 percent of us attend church on a regular basis), so the version of Christianity I am exposed to most frequently is the evangelical U.S. version. We are a broad church here at the *Believer,* and I don't wish to alienate any of our subscribers who believe that gays will burn in hell for all eternity and so on, but your far-right evangelism has never struck me as being terribly conducive to thought—rather the opposite, if anything. I had to reread passages from *Gilead* several times—beautiful, luminous passages about grace, and debt, and baptism—before I half-understood them, however: there are complicated and striking ideas on every single page.

Gilead is narrated by a dying pastor, the Reverend John Ames, and takes the form of a long letter to his young son; the agony of impending loss informs every word of the book, although this agony has been distilled into a kind of wide-eyed and scrupulously unsentimental wonder at the beauty of the world. It's true that the book contains very little in the way of forward momentum, and one reads it rather as one might read a collection of poetry; it's only two hundred and fifty pages long, but it took me weeks to get through. (I kept worrying, in fact, about reading *Gilead* in the wrong way. I didn't want it to go by in dribs and drabs, but it seemed equally inappropriate to scoff something containing this amount of calories down in a few gulps.) This column has frequently suggested that a novel without forward momentum isn't really worth bothering with, but that theory, like so many others, turned out not to be worth the (admittedly very expensive) paper it was printed on: *Gilead* has turned me into a wiser and better person. In fact, I am writing these words in a theological college somewhere in England, where I will spend the next several years. I'll miss my kids, my partner, and my football team, but when God comes knocking, you don't shut the door in His face, do you? All this only goes to show that you never know how a novel's going to affect you.

We all of us know that the circumstances surrounding the reading of a book are probably every bit as important as the book itself, and I read *Gilead* at a weird time. I was on book tour in the UK, and I was sick of myself and of the sound of my own voice, and of appearing on daft radio shows, where I found that it was surprisingly easy to reduce my own intricately wrought novel to idiotic sound bites: if anyone were ever in need of the astonishing hush that Marilynne Robinson achieves in her book—how do you do that, in something crafted out of words?—it was I. Caveat emptor, but if you don't like it, then you have no soul.

So *Gilead* is one of the most striking novels I have ever read, and it won the Pulitzer Prize, and it's a modern classic, but it doesn't win the coveted "Stuff I've Been Reading" book-of-the-month award. It didn't even come close, incredibly. That honor goes to my sister Gill's *Jane Austen: The Girl with the Magic Pen,* a biography intended for children but strongly recommended to anyone of any age. If you want me to be definitive about it, then I would say that whereas *Gilead* is one of the best new novels I've read for years, Hornby's biography is undoubtedly the best book of all time. Strong words, I know, but: it's ninety pages long! It's about Jane Austen, who was great, right? I rest my case.

My sister's work is, however, quite clearly, underneath it all, both about and aimed at me. Listen to this: "Jane's eldest brother, James, was busy trotting out lofty verse, in a manner befitting the vicar he was soon to become… There was no doubt, they all said, who was the writer in the family—and James readily (and a little smugly) agreed!" I think we can all read the subtext here, can't we? James Austen = NH. Jane Austen = GH. (Weirdly, my sister didn't even know about my recent decision to become a man of the cloth when she wrote those lines.) And what about this? "Families are funny things, and often cannot see what is under their noses." Hey, no need to beat around the bush! Just come out and say what's on your mind, Oh Great One! As if Mum ever allowed me to forget that you were the really clever member of the family. As if Mum didn't always love you more than me anyway… Sorry. This probably isn't the most appropriate forum in which to air grievances of this kind, however justifiable. And in any case, if you're too dim to understand the book properly, to see it for what it really is—namely, a rage-fueled, ninety-page poison-pen letter to the author's brother—you'll find much to enjoy on the superficial level. She had to pretend at least that she was writing about Austen, and that stuff is great, lively, and informative. See? If I can be generous about your work, how come you can't bring yourself to… Sorry again. I'm just going out for a cigarette and a walk. I'll be right back.

A whole bunch of these books I read for work. You can't just go on the radio and say, "Buy my new novel. It's great." Oh, no. That's not how it works. You have to go on the radio and say, "Buy *his* new novel. It's great." And then, according to the publicity departments at my publishers, the listening public is so seduced by the sound of your voice that it ignores what you're actually telling them, and goes out to buy your book anyway. We have this show called *A Good Read*, on which a couple of guests talk with the show's presenter about a book they love, and I chose Michael Frayn's *Spies*, which is a wonderful, complicated, simple novel about childhood, suburbia, and the Second World War. My fellow guest chose Nancy Mitford's *Noblesse Oblige,* which was published in the 1950s, and discusses the upper classes and their use of language—they say "lavatory," we say "toilet," that kind of thing. My fellow guest wasn't so keen on *Spies,* which was kind of hilarious, considering that he'd just made us plough through all this stuff about "napkin" versus "serviette." I won't say any more about *Noblesse Oblige,* as otherwise the Polysyllabic Spree will ban me for yet another issue, and I'm spending more time out than in as it is.

Our host, meanwhile, chose Anne Tyler's *The Amateur Marriage,* and both the choice and the novel itself made me very happy. Anne Tyler is the person who first made me want to write: I picked up *Dinner at the Homesick Restaurant* in a bookshop, started to read it there and then, bought it, took it home, finished it, and suddenly I had an ambition, for about the first time in my life. I was worried that *The Amateur Marriage* was going to be a little schematic: Tyler tells the story of a relationship over the decades, and the early part of the book is perhaps too tidy. In the '50s, the couple are living out America's postwar suburban dream, in the '60s they're on the receiving end of the countercultural revolution, and so on. But the cumulative details of the marriage eventually sprawl all over the novel's straight, tight lines as if Tyler were creating a garden; as it turns out, in those first chapters, she's saying, "Just wait for spring—I know what I'm doing." And she does, of course. Before too long, *The Amateur Marriage* is teeming with life and artfully created mess, and when it's all over, you mourn both the passing of Tyler's creation and the approaching end of her characters' lives.

My ongoing disciplinary troubles with the Polysyllabic Spree, the four hundred and thirty white-robed and utterly psychotic young men and women who control both the *Believer* and the minds of everyone who contributes to it, mean that I have to cram two months' worth of reading into one column. (I no longer have any sense of where I'm going wrong, by the way. I've given up. I think I may have passed on some admittedly baseless gossip about the Gawain poet at the monthly editorial conference, and it didn't go down well, but who knows, really?) So, in brief: Jeremy Lewis's biography of Allen Lane, the founder of Penguin, is a tremendous piece of social history, which I have already written about in *Time Out.* (It was the same deal as with *Spies*—I recommend someone else's book, this time in print, and everyone rushes out to buy mine. See how it works? You've got to hand it to the people who think this stuff up.) And Walter Mosley's *Little Scarlett* comprehensively rubbishes yet another theory this column has previously and unwisely expounded—that crime novels in a series are always inferior to what I believe the trade calls "stand-alones." Easy Rawlins is one of probably scores of exceptions to the rule, possibly because one of Mosley's aims in the Rawlins books is to write about race in twentieth-century America. *Little Scarlett* is set in L.A. during the Watts riots of 1965, and you never get the sense that you're whiling away the time; the stakes are high, and both detective and book demonstrate a moral seriousness that you don't find in many literary novels, never mind generic thrillers.

Seth Mnookin is yet another member of Violet Incredible's literary set. So those of us who pretend we still know her since she went all Hollywood animated have dutifully read his book about Jayson Blair and the *New York Times,* even though the subject has nothing to do with us, for fear that we'll be cast into the darkness, far away from the warm glow of celebrity. Luckily, Mnookin's book is completely riveting: I doubt I'll read much else about U.S. newspaper culture, so it's just as well that this one is definitive. Mnookin's thoroughness—he explains with clarity and rigor how Blair and the *NYT* was an accident waiting to happen—could have resulted in desiccation, but it's actually pretty juicy in all the right places. None of the outrage Blair caused makes much sense to us in England—you can make up whatever you want here, and you'll never hear from a fact-checker or even an editor—so reading *Hard News* was like reading an Austen novel. You have to understand the context, the parameters of decency in an alien environment, to make any sense of it.

So I'm off on a book tour of the U.S. now, and I'm thinking of taking *Barnaby Rudge* with me. It'll last me the entire three weeks, and it's about the Gordon riots, apparently. I'll bet you can't wait for the next column. ✶

SEPTEMBER 2005

BOOKS BOUGHT:

* *The Diary of a Country Priest*—Georges Bernanos
* *A Complicated Kindness*—Miriam Toews
* *Blood Done Sign My Name*—Timothy B. Tyson
* *Over Tumbled Graves*—Jess Walter
* *Becoming Strangers*—Louise Dean

BOOKS READ:

* *Citizen Vince*—Jess Walter
* *A Complicated Kindness*—Miriam Toews

On my recent book tour of the U.S. I met a suspiciously large number of people who claimed to be *Believer* readers; some of the people who came to the signings even told me that they had read and enjoyed this column, although I can see that if you're standing in front of someone waiting for a signature, you might as well say something, even if what you end up saying is patently and laughably untrue. Anyway, having met and talked to some of you, I now realize that the descriptions I occasionally provide of the Polysyllabic Spree, the eighty horribly brainwashed young men and women who control this magazine (and who may in turn, I am beginning to realize, be controlled by someone else), have been misleading. There are some misconceptions out there, and I feel it's only fair, both to you and to the Spree, to clear a few things up.

Numbers. The Spree consists of sixty-four people. You can safely ignore any other figure you may come across, either here or in the national media. Sometimes I have inflated or deflated the numbers, for comic purposes—because the joke of saying, for example, forty or eighty when really it's sixty-four is always funny, right? Or it could have been funny, if people weren't so literal-minded. My recent conversations have left me with the feeling that this particular witticism, along with several others (see below), may have fallen flat.

Robes. The trademark, tell-tale Spree white robes are only worn in certain circumstances, namely during editorial meetings, major sporting events (as a protest against their existence) and morning "prayers," wherein the Spree shout out the names of literary figures. (I can't tell you how disconcerting it is to hear otherwise attractive and frequently naked young women yelling out "SYBILLE BEDFORD!" in a banshee wail.) I'm sorry if I have somehow given the impression that they wear white robes all the time. They don't. In fact, given the propensity for nudity up at Believer Towers, I wish they'd put them on more often.

Free copies of the *Believer.* A while back I remarked in passing that I didn't ever see this magazine because the Spree refused to send me free copies. I can't say too much about this, because, sadly, it's all *sub judice,* and my lawyers have told me to be careful about how I address the matter in print. In brief: I have discovered that the magazine and its new publishing venture is not, as I had been assured previously, a vanity publishing outfit, and that therefore I should not have been paying the company to have my columns and my book *The Polysyllabic Spree* published. In a desperate attempt to avoid having their asses sued off, the Spree have started lavishing subscriptions and T-shirts upon me. It won't do them any good. Things have gone too far.

Suspensions. Similarly, I have in the past complained bitterly about my suspension from these pages after having ignored one of the Spree's many unfathomable and apparently random edicts. The truth is that I haven't been suspended by the Spree nearly as often as I've claimed; I made some of those stories up, usually to excuse my own indolence and/or temporary disappearances, usually prompted by the investigations of the relentless Child Support Agency here in the UK.

I hope that's cleared a few things up and we can now all make a fresh start.

As you were probably beginning to suspect, the preceding nonsense was a crude attempt to deflect attention away from the dismal brevity of this month's Books Read list: for the first time since I began writing for this magazine, I have completely lost my appetite for books. I have half-read several, and intend to finish all of them, but at the moment I find it impossible to concentrate on what anyone has to say about more or less any subject. This seems, in part, to be something to do with my book tour—it's unfair, I know, but I seem to be sick of the sound of everyone's voice, not just my own. Plus, at the time of this writing, I live in a city which seems to be exploding about our ears, and this has done nothing at all for my interest in contemporary literature. It all seems a bit beside the point at the moment. I'm sure that's an error in my thinking, and that my unwillingness to engage with sensitive first novels about coming out on a sheep farm in North Dakota in the 1950s—I made this book up, by the way, and if you wrote it, I mean no offense—proves that the terrorists have won, to use the phrase that seems to end every sentence here at the moment. ("It means they've won" is applied indiscriminately to anyone's failure to do anything at all that they usually do. If you don't feel like getting on a tube or a bus, going into the center of the city, reading a book, getting drunk, or punching someone on the nose, it means you're a scaredy-cat, not British, etc.) Instead of reading, I play endless games of solitaire on my mobile phone, watch twenty-four-hour news channels, and try to find newspaper articles written by experts on fundamentalism assuring me that this will all be over by Tuesday. I haven't found any such reassurance yet. This morning I found myself moderately uplifted by a piece in the *Times* explaining that acetone peroxide, the explosive that London bombers favor, has a shelf-life of less than a week. It's cheap, though, and available in any half-decent hardware store, so it's not all good news.

Anyway, in this context it seems something of a miracle that I've finished any books at all. Jess Walter, a wonderful writer of whose existence I was previously unaware, sent me *Citizen Vince* in the hope that I might start a third list at the top of this page, a list entitled "Books Foisted Upon Me," so I was immediately intrigued by his novel; as a freelance reviewer I get sent a ton of books, but nobody to date has expressed an ambition to appear in a *Believer* list. If I hadn't actually gone and read the thing I might have been tempted.

The clincher for me was an enthusiastic blurb by the great Richard Russo, and he didn't let me down, because *Citizen Vince* is fast, tough, thoughtful, and funny. (Right at the beginning of the book there's a terrific scene involving an unwilling hooker and her unsatisfied customer, a scene culminating in an interesting philosophical debate about whether there's such a thing as half a blow job.) It's about a guy who's moved from New York City to Spokane, Washington, under the Witness Protection Program; he's going about his business of making doughnuts and committing petty fraud when it becomes apparent that a man who may or may not be connected to Vince's past wants to kill him. And this guy, the bad guy, he's really, *really* bad. He threatens to do something so vile to a small child that you can't read on until you've started breathing again.

Citizen Vince would have worked fine as "just" a thriller, but Walter has ambitions on top of that, because it's also about voting, believe it or not; Vince has been registered by the authorities, and for the first time in his life he has to decide who he wants as President. The book's set in 1980, so the choice is between Carter and Reagan, and Vince is paralyzed by it; this is hardly surprising, seeing as Walter suggests that the choice is between the America you ended up with, and another America, one that vanished when poor, decent, hopeless Jimmy was beaten. In a couple of bravura passages, Walter leaves his gangsters and petty crooks to fend for themselves while he enters the minds of the candidates themselves. I loved this novel. It came through my letter box just when I was beginning to think that I'd have to write "NONE!" under the heading Books Read; it seemed to know that what I needed was pace, warmth, humor, and an artfully disguised attempt to write about a world bigger than the one its characters live in.

Miriam Toews's lovely *A Complicated Kindness* is funny, too, but it's not overly bothered about pace, not least because it's partly about the torpor that comes from feeling defeated. Last month, I believe I threatened to get religion; I may even have said that I'd gone to live in a monastery, but before anyone at a reading asks me how I'm enjoying the monastic life, I should explain that this was another of those jokes where I say that something is so when it is in fact not so. (Maybe it's a cultural thing, these jokes falling flat? But then again, I don't make anyone laugh here either.) Anyway, *A Complicated Kindness* has further delayed my plans to turn my back on this vale of tears: Nomi Nickel, Miriam Toews's narrator, is a Mennonite, or at least she comes from a family of Mennonites, and she doesn't make it sound like too much fun.

Mennonites—and everyone's a Mennonite where Nomi lives—are against the things that make life bearable: sex, drugs, rock and roll, make-up, TV, smoking, and so on; Nomi Nickel, on the other hand, is for all of those things, wherein lies both the tension and the torpor. Nomi's sister Tash and her mother have already been driven out of town by the Mennonite powers-that-be, but Nomi has stayed behind to look after her father Ray, a man who spends a lot of time sitting on his lawn chair and staring into space; Nomi, meanwhile, bounces round the town off the diamond-hard disapproval she meets everywhere, getting into all the trouble she can, which isn't so much, in a town that doesn't even have a bus station—it was removed because the more rebellious spirits kept wanting to go places. One of the joys of the book, in fact, is the desperate ingenuity of its characters, looking for ways to express themselves in a culture that allows no self-expression. "That was around the time our Aunt Gonad asked Tash to burn her *Jesus Christ Superstar* soundtrack. Tash could do a hilariously sexy version of 'I Don't Know How to Love Him' where she basically worked herself into a complete fake orgasm during that big crescendo." You may think that you don't want to read about the problems of being brought up Mennonite, but the great thing about books is that you'll read anything that a good writer wants you to read. And the voice that Miriam Toews finds for her narrator is so true and so charming that you don't even mind spending a couple hundred pages in a town as joyless as Nomi's East Village.

I bought *A Complicated Kindness* in the Powell's bookstall at the Portland, Oregon, airport, after several fervent recommendations from the Powell's staff who looked after me at my signing. Did you know that you have the best bookshops in the world? I hope so. Over here in England, the home of literature ha-ha, we have only chain bookstores, staffed by people who for the most part come across as though they'd rather be selling anything else anywhere else; meanwhile you have access to booksellers who would regard their failure to sell you novels about Mennonites as a cause of deep personal shame. Please spend every last penny you have on books from independent bookstores, because otherwise you'll end up as sour and as semi-literate as the English.

I bought *The Diary of a Country Priest* in a fit of post-*Gilead* enthusiasm, although I have to say that at the moment, my chances of reading it, at least in this life, are slim. I was tempted, however, by the following review on the Amazon site:

This book has had an enormous impact on my life. Having had to read it as part of my French A level course (in French!) it left me psychologically scarred. Grinding through each passage was like torture, making me weep with frustration and leaving me with a long-burning and deep-felt resentment against my French teacher and the A level exam board. This resulted in a low grade for my French lit paper, which offset a decent language paper, resulting in a 'C' which wasn't good enough for my chosen university. So I had to switch from French to business studies, so changing the course of my life. To say I detest this book is an understatement.

You see the profound effect that literature can have on a life? Who says it's all a waste of time? If only I could produce one book that left someone with that kind of ferocious grievance. If you have read one of my books, you probably feel cheated out of however much money it might have cost you, and you'll certainly begrudge the time you wasted on it. But even at my most bullish and self-aggrandizing, I can't quite make myself believe that I've actually wrecked someone's life. Any documentary evidence to the contrary will be gratefully received. ✭

OCTOBER 2005

BOOKS BOUGHT:

  ✳ None

BOOKS READ:

  ✳ *Blood Done Sign My Name: A True Story*—Timothy B. Tyson
  ✳ *Candide*—Voltaire
  ✳ *Oh the Glory of It All*—Sean Wilsey

I want to take back some things I said last month. Or rather, I don't so much want to take them back as to modify my tone, which is a pretty poor show, considering that writing, especially writing a column, is all about tone: what I'm essentially saying is, don't read last month's column, because it was all wrong. I was way too defensive, I see now, about my relative lack of literary consumption (two books, for the benefit of those of you who are too busy busy busy to retain the minutiae of my reading life from one month to the next). Shamefully—oh, god, it's all coming back to me now—I tried to blame it on all sorts of things, including the London bombs, but the truth is that two books in a month isn't so bad. There are lots of people who don't get through two books a month. And anyway, what would happen if I had read no books? Obviously, I'd lose this job (although that's assuming one of the Spree noticed). But apart from that? What would happen if I read no books ever? Let's imagine someone who reads no books ever but polishes off every word of the *New Yorker,* the *Economist,* and their broadsheet newspaper of choice: well, this imaginary person would do more reading than me, because that's got to be a couple of hundred thousand words a week, and would also be a lot smarter than me, if you use that rather limited definition of smart which involves knowing stuff about stuff. The *New Yorker* has humor in it and also provides an introduction to contemporary fiction and poetry. So the only major food group not covered is starch: in other words, the classics. And what would happen if we never read the classics? There

NICK HORNBY

comes a point in life, it seems to me, where you have to decide whether you're a Person of Letters or merely someone who loves books, and I'm beginning to see that the book lovers have more fun. Persons of Letters have to read things like *Candide* or they're a few letters short of the whole alphabet; book lovers, meanwhile, can read whatever they fancy.

I picked up *Candide* because my publishers sent me a cute new edition, and though that in itself wouldn't have persuaded me, I flicked through it and discovered it was only ninety pages long. Ninety pages! Who knew, apart from all of you, and everybody else? A ninety-page classic is the Holy Grail of this column, and when the Holy Grail is pushed through your letter box, you don't put it on a shelf to gather dust. (Or maybe that's exactly what you'd do with the Holy Grail. Is it ornamental? Has anyone ever seen it?) Anyway, I have now read *Candide*. That's another one chalked off. And boy, does Voltaire really have it in for Leibnizian philosophy! Whoo-hoo! Now, there's a justification for reading *Candide* right there. Many of you will have been living, like Leibniz, in the deluded belief that all is for the best, in the best of all possible worlds (because you believe that God would have created nothing but the best), but I have read Voltaire, and I can now see that this is a preposterous notion that brings only despair. And it's not only Leibniz who comes in for a kicking, either. Oh, no. Corneille, the Jesuits, Racine, the Abbé Gauchat, Rousseau… Just about everyone you've ever wanted to see lampooned in a short novel gets what's coming to them. You lot are probably all familiar with the Abbé Gauchat, the Theatines, the Jansenists, and the literary criticism of Élie-Catherine Fréron, but I'm afraid I found myself flicking frantically between the text and the foot-notes at the end; I was unhappily reminded of the time I had to spend at school reading Alexander Pope's equally mordant attacks on poetasters and so forth. Literary types will tell you that underneath all the contemporary references, you will recognize yourselves and your world, but it's not true, of course. If it's this world you're after, the one we actually live in, you're better off with Irvine Welsh or Thomas Harris.

The trouble with *Candide* is that it's one of those books that we've all read, whether we've read it or not (cf. *Animal Farm, 1984, Gulliver's Travels, Lord of the Flies*). The meat was picked off it and thrown to the crowd in the eighteenth century, and… I'll abandon this metaphor here, because I suspect that it must inevitably conclude with digestive systems and the consumption of ancient excrement. The point is that we are familiar with silly old Dr. Pangloss, just as we know that some animals are more equal than others. Satires and allegories tend to have been decoded long before we ever get to them, which renders them somewhat redundant, it seems to me. *Panglossian* is the sort of word you might find from time to time in the *Economist* and the *New Yorker,* and in any case, if ever anyone lived in an age that had no need for a savage debunking of optimism, it is us. We believe that everything everywhere is awful, all the time. In fact, Voltaire was one of the people who first pointed it out, and he was so successful that we find ourselves in desperate need of a Pangloss in our lives. Bitter footnote: just after I'd finished my cute hardback, I found an old paperback copy on my shelves (unread, obviously): a hundred and thirty pages. Oh, the pain! I'd never have read—or paid, as you have to think of it in this case—three figures. I was tricked, swindled and cheated by my own publishers, who clearly scrunched everything up a bit to dupe the innocent and the ill read.

Book length, like time, is an abstract concept. Sean Wilsey's *Oh the Glory of It All* is a good four times the length of *Candide,* and I enjoyed it probably four times as much, even though all book logic suggests that the reverse might have been the case. I'm sure young Sean would be the first to admit that there's some sag around the middle, but like many of us, it's lovable even at its saggiest point. And also, you never once have to laugh at the pomposities of the French Academies of the eighteenth century, a prerequisite, I now understand, for any book. (In fact, publishers should use that as a blurb. "You never once have to laugh at the pomposities of the French Academies of the eighteenth century!" I'd buy any book that had that on the cover.)

Oh the Glory of It All is a memoir, as those of you who live in the Bay Area may already know; Wilsey was brought up in San Francisco by squillionaire socialites, although after his parents' divorce, the silver spoon wasn't as much use as he might have hoped: his mother devoted her time to saving the world, and dragged Sean off around the world to meet the Pope and various scary old-school Kremlin types; meanwhile his dad married a scary old-school step-mother who treated Wilsey like dirt. (Hey, Dede! You may be a bigshot in a little bit of San Francisco, but nobody has ever heard of you here in London! Or anywhere else! I'm sorry, but she got me so steamed up that I had to get back at her somehow.) He got chucked out of every school he attended, and ran away from a creepy establishment which didn't allow you to utter the names of rock bands out loud.

American lives seem, from this distance at least, very different from European lives. Look at this: Sean Wilsey's mother was the daughter of an itinerant preacher. She ran away to Dallas to be a model, an escape funded initially by the nickels from her uncle's jukeboxes and peanut machines. She was dragged off to California by her angry family, and while waitressing there she met a U.S. Air Force major who married her on a live national radio programme called *The Bride and Groom*. She split from the major, dated Frank Sinatra for a while, married a couple of other guys—one marriage lasted six months; the other, to the trial lawyer who defended Jack Ruby, lasted three weeks. She got a TV job and she had a fan club. And then she married Sean's dad. We don't do any of that here. We don't have itinerant preachers, or peanut machines, or Sinatra. We are born in, for example, Basingstoke, and then we either stay there, or we move to London. That's probably why we don't write many memoirs.

Timothy B. Tyson's *Blood Done Sign My Name* is a memoir, too, although it's not the peculiarities of his life that Tyson is writing about, but the point at which his experiences intersect with recent American history. Tyson was brought up in Oxford, North Carolina, where his father was the pastor of the Methodist church; in 1970, Robert Teel, the father of one of Tyson's friends, and a couple of other white thugs murdered a young black man, and after the contemptible trial, wherein everyone was found not guilty of everything, there was a race riot, and great chunks of Oxford got torched. Young Tim Tyson grew up to be a professor of Afro-American studies, and *Blood Done Sign My Name* is a perfect reflection of who he is now and where he came from: it's both memoir and social history, and it's riveting. Tyson has a deceptively folksy prose style that leads you to suspect that his book will in part be about the triumph of Civil Rights hope over bitter Southern experience, but it ends with a coda, a visit to a club in Greensboro, North Carolina, in 1992 to see Percy Sledge: Tyson's black friend is denied admission. Yes, 1992. Yes, Percy Sledge, the soul singer.

Blood Done Sign My Name is uncompromisingly tough minded, righteous, and instructive (there is a terrific section unraveling the taboo that surrounded black men sleeping with white women), and it's not about people singing "We Shall Overcome" and holding hands until black and white live together in perfect harmony. On the contrary, Tyson is very good on how the history of the Civil Rights movement is being rewritten daily until it begins to look like the triumph of liberal good sense over prejudice; nothing would have happened, he argues, without things being set on fire. "If you want to read only one book to understand the uniquely American struggle for racial equality and the swirls of emotion around it, this is it," says one of the reviews on the back of the book. Well, I have read only one book about the uniquely American struggle for racial equality, and this was it. But I will read another one one day soon: it would seem strange, and perhaps a little perverse, to allow a white man to provide my entire Civil Rights education. I mean no offense to the author of this memorable book, but he'd be the first to admit that Afro-Americans might have something of interest to say on the subject.

I moved house this month and have bought no books at all for the first time since I became a Believer. I have spent hour after hour finding homes for unread novels, biographies, memoirs, and collections of essays, poetry, and letters, and suddenly I can see as never before that we're fine for books at the moment, thanks very much. I came across quite a few of the things that have appeared in the Books Bought column at the top of these pages, and marvelled at my own lack of self-knowledge. When exactly was I going to read Michael B. Oren's no doubt excellent book about the Six-Day War? Or Dylan Thomas's letters? The ways in which a man can kid himself are many and various. Anyway, the football season has restarted, which always reduces book time. Arsenal bought only one player over the summer and sold their captain, so we've got a perilously thin squad, and Chelsea have spent squillions again, and... The truth is, I'm too worried to begin Hilary Spurling's apparently magnificent biography of Matisse (bought about five years ago, new, in hardback, because I couldn't wait). I won't even be able to think about picking it up until Wenger brings in a new central midfield player. And at the time of writing, there's no sign of that. ✻

NOVEMBER 2005

BOOKS BOUGHT:

* *A Little History of the World*—Ernst Gombrich
* *What Good Are the Arts?*—John Carey
* *What I Loved*—Siri Hustvedt
* *Death and the Penguin*—Andrey Kurkov

BOOKS READ:

* *The Trick of It*—Michael Frayn
* *Housekeeping*—Marilynne Robinson
* *Over Tumbled Graves*—Jess Walter
* Unnameable comedy thriller—Anonymous

On my copy of Michael Frayn's *The Trick of It*, there is a quote from Anthony Burgess that describes the novel as "one of the few books I have read in the last year that has provoked laughter." Initially, it's a blurb that works in just the way the publishers intended. Great, you think. Burgess must have read a lot of books; and both the quote itself and your knowledge of the great man suggest that he wouldn't have chuckled at many of them. So if *The Trick of It* wriggled its way through that forbidding exterior to the Burgess sense of humor, it must be absolutely hilarious, right? But then you start to wonder just how trustworthy Burgess would have been on the subject of comedy. What, for example, would have been his favorite bit of *Jackass: The Movie*? (Burgess died in 1993, so sadly we will never know.) What was his most cherished *Three Stooges* sketch? His favorite *Seinfeld* character? His top David Brent moment? And after careful contemplation, your confidence in his comic judgment starts to feel a little misplaced: there is a good chance, you suspect, that Anthony Burgess would have steadfastly refused even to smile at many of the things that have ever made you chortle uncontrollably.

Sometimes it feels as though we are being asked to imagine cultural judgments as a whole bunch of concentric circles. On the outside, we have the wrong ones, made by the people who read *The Da Vinci Code* and listen to Celine Dion; right at the center we have the correct ones, made by the snootier critics, very often people who have vowed never to laugh again until Aristophanes produces a follow-up to *The Frogs*. (I haven't read James Wood's collection of essays *The Irresponsible Self: Laughter and the Novel*, but I'm counting on Woody to provide a useful counterbalance to that sort of high moral seriousness. So I'm presuming that all the comic greats—P. G. Wodehouse, the Molesworth books, George and Weedon Grossmith, and so on—are present and correct between its covers.) The world is a lot more complicated than this diagram allows, of course, but sometimes it's easy to forget that the Frog people don't know everything. If I had to choose between a Celine Dion fan and Anthony Burgess for comedy recommendations, I would go with the person standing on the table singing "The Power of Love" every time. I'll bet Burgess read *Candide*—I had a bad experience with *Candide* only recently—with tears of mirth trickling down his face.

As you may have guessed by now, *The Trick of It* didn't make me laugh, so I'm feeling insecure. It's brilliant—witty, smart, readable, and engaging; but you know that bit in *Jackass: The Movie* when the guy takes a crap in the bathroom shop? Well, gags of that quality are conspicuously absent. I suspect that it wasn't Michael Frayn's intention to provide them, either; I raise the comparison only because when you see the word "funny" all over a paperback (Burgess was not alone in having his ribs tickled), it raises expectations to a possibly unrealistic level. *The Trick of It* is about the relationship between a young college professor and his area of expertise, a middle-aged woman novelist he refers to as JL. This relationship becomes complicated, although perhaps in some ways simplified, when he sleeps with her and then marries her: he thus becomes a part of his own research material, a chapter in her still unwritten biography. We have objected to novels about writers and writing in this column before, have we not? We are concerned that the preciousness to which these novels can be prone will alienate the last few readers left out there. But we have no complaints in this case, you and Michael Frayn will be delighted to hear. *The Trick of It* has a healthy resonance rather than a sickly insularity—anyone who has ever been a fan will recognize something in here—and if you've read Frayn's work then you will know how effortlessly clever he is, and thus you can imagine the fun he has with the hall of mirrors he has rigged up here.

I've been reading *Housekeeping* off and on since I finished Marilynne Robinson's second novel, *Gilead,* a while back, but I kept losing it and getting distracted, and in the end I put it down for a while because I was being disrespectful to a novel that people clearly love. I thought I knew what *Housekeeping* would be because I've seen Bill Forsyth's lovely film adaptation a couple of times; I thought it would be warm and quirky, like the movie, except with better prose. Indeed, during the floods in Louisiana I nearly stopped reading the book again, for the hundredth time, because there is a description of a flood right at the beginning of the book, and I was worried that warmth and quirkiness would jar, fight horribly with the scenes we were seeing on the news. So I wasn't prepared for what I actually got, which was this extraordinary, yearning mystical work about the dead and how they haunt the living; if books can work as music, then *Housekeeping* served as a soundtrack to the footage from New Orleans. The dead haunting the living, the core of the book… That was missing from the movie, as far as I remember. I'm not sure Bill Forsyth knew what to do about all the souls at the bottom of the lake, so he concentrated on his eccentric central characters, and how a small community finds this eccentricity hard to accommodate. It's a fine, slightly conventional theme, but now I've read the book, I can see that this is rather like making attractive ashtrays out of Kryptonite.

One of the souls at the bottom of the lake belongs to the mother of Ruth, the novel's teenage narrator, and of her sister Lucille; Helen drove into the lake, calmly and deliberately, when her daughters were young. Her father, the girls' grandfather, is down there somewhere too, along with the passengers on a train that came off the bridge that crosses the water. Ruth and Lucille never knew their father, so eventually their aunt Sylvie comes to live with them. She's not much of a mother figure, Sylvie. She sits in the dark surrounded by empty tin cans and old newspapers, and yearns to go back to traveling around on the railroads, but she stays anyway. Have you ever seen that great Stanley Spencer picture, *The Cookham Resurrection*? It depicts the dead coming alive again, sleepy and bewildered, in the small, pretty, and (otherwise) unremarkable Thameside village where Spencer lived. I'm sure that Robinson must have had the painting in some part of her extraordinary mind when she wrote *Housekeeping*. There is that same strange fusion of the humdrum and the visionary, and though Fingerbone, the bleak little town where the novel is set, clearly isn't as cute as Cookham, it still seems an unlikely location for waking dreams about a reunion of the living and all the people we have ever lost. ("Families should stay together," says Sylvie at the end of the book. "Otherwise things get out of control. My father, you know. I can't even remember what he was like, I mean when he was alive. But ever since, it's Papa here and Papa there, and dreams.")

It's quite clear to me now, having read her two novels, that Marilynne Robinson is one of America's greatest living writers, and certainly there's no one else like her. I think I am using that phrase literally: I have never come across a mind like this one, in literature or anywhere else, for that matter. Sometimes her singular seriousness, and her insistent concentration on the sad beauty of our mortality, make you laugh, in an Anthony Burgess kind of way. Pools and ponds and lakes "taste a bit of blood and hair," observes Ruth, with customary Robinsonian good cheer. "One cannot cup one's hand and drink from the rim of any lake without remembering that mothers have drowned in it, lifting their children toward the air, though they must have known as they did that soon enough the deluge would take all the children, too, even if their arms could have held them up." She may be a great writer, but you wouldn't want her on your camping holiday, would you? (I know, I know, that's a cheap joke, and I'm making the schoolboy error of confusing narrator and author; Marilynne Robinson almost certainly spends her camping holidays singing Beach Boys songs and trying to give everyone wedgies.)

We have, from time to time in these pages, expressed our impatience with a certain kind of literary fiction. (By "these pages," I mean the two I'm given. And by "we," I mean "I." The Spree would never express their impatience with literary fiction. In fact, "the duller the better" is engraved on the gates, in enormous letters, at Spree Castle.) To us, it can sometimes seem overwrought, pedestrian, po-faced, monotonous, out of touch; we would argue that literary fiction must take some of the blame for the novel's sad disappearance from the center of our culture. But sometimes, a book just can't help being literary; it can't do anything about its own complication, because its ideas defy simple expression. It took me forever to read *Housekeeping,* but it's not possible to read this short book quickly, because it comes fitted with its own speed bumps: the neo–Old Testament prose, exactly the right language for Robinson's heartbreaking, prophetic images. And I'm glad I wasn't able to race through it, too, because the time I spent with it means that it lives with me still.

I have always prized the accessible over the obscure, but after reading *Housekeeping* I can see that in some ways the easy, accessible novel is working at a disadvantage (not that *Housekeeping* is inaccessible, but it is deep, and dark and rich): it's possible to whiz through it without allowing it even to touch the sides, and a bit of side-touching has to happen if a book is going to be properly transformative. If you are so gripped by a book that you want to read it in the mythical single sitting, what chance has it got of making it all the way through the long march to your soul? It'll get flushed out by something else before it's even halfway there. The trouble is that most literary novels don't do anything but touch the sides. They stick to them like sludge, and in the end you have to get the garden hose out. (I have no idea what that might mean. But I had to escape from the metaphor somehow.)

Neither of the other books I read this month were sludgy, at least. I read and loved Jess Walter's *Citizen Vince* recently, so I wanted to check out one of his earlier books. Unlike *Citizen Vince, Over Tumbled Graves* belongs firmly within the crime genre, although it's not formulaic—it actually plays cleverly with the serial-killer formula. I enjoyed it a lot, but on the evidence of the recent book, Walter is a writer who is heading for territory that gives him more freedom than genre fiction allows. Under the *Believer* guidelines, the second novel must remain nameless because I hated it so much. I was recommended it by a friend with normally impeccable taste, and he's not alone—my paperback copy contains blurbs from a couple of clever literary figures who really should know better. Is the phrase "Deliciously politically incorrect" used with the same gay abandon in the U.S.? You come across it all the time here, and usually it means, quite simply, that a book or a movie or a TV program is racist and/or sexist and/or homophobic; there is a certain kind of cultural commentator who mysteriously associates these prejudices with a Golden Age during which we were allowed to do lots of things that we are not allowed to do now. (The truth is that there's no one stopping them from doing anything. What they really object to is being recognized as the antisocial pigs they really are.)

Anyway, this book is "deliciously politically incorrect." The narrator, who fancies himself as a cross between James Bond and Bertie Wooster, thinks it's funny to transpose the *r*s and *l*s in dialogue spoken by Chinese people, and has what he clearly regards as sound advice for women in the process of being raped: "lie quite still, try to enjoy it. The choice is a simple one: a brief and possibly not unpleasant invasion of one's physical privacy—or a painful bashing causing the loss of one's good looks and perhaps one's life." There may well have been men like this in the 1970s, when this book was written, but they were not clever men. It would have been torture to listen to them for two minutes at a bus stop, and you certainly don't want to hang around with them while they narrate a whole book. To compound the reader's misery, this narrator favors a jocular, florid circumlocution intended to invoke the spirit of Wodehouse, who is unwisely mentioned twice in the first fifty pages. I ended up hurling him across the room. At the time of writing, I haven't been able to confront the friend who recommended the book, but there will, I'm afraid, be bloodshed.

I really want to read every book I bought this month. That's true of every month, of course, and usually nothing happens, but this month I really *really* want to read the books I bought. I have just been to a wonderful literary festival in Iceland, where I spent time with Siri Hustvedt and Andrey Kurkov and lots of other interesting, companionable writers; and it's true that there is a slight possibility, judging from my track record, that either of these novels might fall off the bedside pile at some stage in the future, but surely they can see that the commitment is there? And the two works of nonfiction, by John Carey and Ernst Gombrich, have the most perfect titles imaginable: I desperately need to know what the uses of the arts are, and the great John Carey, who wrote the great *The Intellectuals and the Masses,* is undoubtedly the man to tell me, and thus make me feel better about the ways in which I waste my time. He may even tell me that I'm not wasting my time, as long as he manages to get solitaire and football under the arts umbrella. The title of Gombrich's book, meanwhile, cleverly isolates the precise area in which I am most ignorant. How did he know? ✳

FEBRUARY 2006

BOOKS BOUGHT:

* ✶ *Eminent Churchillians*—Andrew Roberts
* ✶ *The Holy Fox: A Biography of Lord Halifax*—Andrew Roberts
* ✶ *The Tender Bar: A Memoir*—J. R. Moehringer
* ✶ *The Brief and Frightening Reign of Phil*—George Saunders
* ✶ *Only in London*—Hanan Al-Shaykh
* ✶ *Traffics and Discoveries*—Rudyard Kipling
* ✶ *The Man Who Was Thursday: A Nightmare*—G. K. Chesterton
* ✶ *Ghosting: A Double Life*—Jennie Erdal
* ✶ *Untold Stories*—Alan Bennett
* ✶ *Selected Letters of Philip Larkin, 1940–1985*—Philip Larkin, ed. Anthony Thwaite
* ✶ *Scenes from Life*—William Cooper

BOOKS READ:

* ✶ *Selected Letters of Philip Larkin, 1940–1985*—Philip Larkin, ed. Anthony Thwaite
* ✶ *On Beauty*—Zadie Smith
* ✶ *Five Days in London, May 1940*—John Lukacs
* ✶ *All the King's Men*—Robert Penn Warren
* ✶ *Only in London*—Hanan Al-Shaykh
* ✶ *What Good Are the Arts?*—John Carey
* ✶ *The Man Who Was Thursday: A Nightmare*—G. K. Chesterton

If, as a recent survey in the UK suggested, most people buy books because they like to be *seen* reading rather than because they actually enjoy it, then I would suggest that you can't beat a collection of letters by an author—and if that author is a poet, then so much the better. The implication is clear: you know the poet's work inside out (indeed, what you're saying is that if you read his or her entire oeuvre one more time, then the lines would ring round and round in your head like a Kelly Clarkson tune), and you now need something else, something that might help to shed some light on some of the more obscure couplets.

So there I am, reading Larkin's letters every chance I get, and impressing the hell out of anyone who spots me doing so. (Never mind that I never go anywhere, and that therefore the only person likely to spot me doing so is my partner, who at the time I'm most likely to be reading Larkin's letters is very much a sleeping partner.) And what I'm actually reading is stuff like this: "Katherine Mansfield is a cunt." "I think this [poem] is really bloody cunting fucking good." "I have just made up a rhyme: After a particularly good game of rugger / A man called me a bugger / Merely because in a loose scrum / I had my cock up his bum." "Your letter found me last night when I came in off the piss: in point of fact I had spewed out of a train window and farted in the presence of ladies and generally misbehaved myself." And so on. In other words, you get to have your cake and eat it: you look like *un homme ou femme sérieux/sérieuse,* but you feel like a twelve-year-old who's somehow being allowed to read *Playboy* in an English lesson. And what you come to realize is that the lifestyle of a naughty twelve-year-old is enervating to the max, if you're a grown-up; indeed, there are quite a few thirteen-year-olds who would find great chunks of Larkin's correspondence embarrassingly puerile.

The irony is that I was drawn to Larkin's letters through that beautiful poem "Church Going," which makes a case for the value of churches long after organized religion has lost its appeal and its point: "And that much never can be obsolete / Since someone will forever be surprising / A hunger in himself to be more serious." This last line was quoted in an article I was reading in the *Economist,* of all places, and it struck a post-*Gilead* chord with me, so I reread a few of the poems and then decided that I'd like access to the prose version of the mind that created them. And yes, you can see where Larkin's hunger to become more serious came from; if I had a mouth like that, I'd have wanted to pay frequent visits to God's house, too. Larkin writes brilliantly and enthusiastically about his jazz records, and every now and again there's a peach of a letter about writing:

> Poetry (at any rate in my case) is like trying to remember a tune you've
> forgotten. All corrections are attempts to get nearer to the forgotten tune.
> A poem is written because the poet gets a sudden vision—lasting one second or
> less—and he attempts to express the whole of which the vision is a part.

And that's the sort of thing you want, surely, when you wade through a writer's letters. What you end up with, however, is a lot of stuff about farting and wanking. Every now and again you are reminded forcibly that the ability to write fiction or poetry is not necessarily indicative of a particularly refined intelligence, no matter what we'd like to believe; it's a freakish talent, like the ability to bend a ball into the top corner of the goal from a thirty-yard free kick, but no one's interested in reading Thierry Henry's collected letters—no literary critic, anyway. And Thierry would never call Katherine Mansfield a cunt, not least because he's a big fan of the early stories. Anyway, I have given up on Larkin for the moment. The rest of you: stick to the poems.

As nobody noticed, probably, I was barred from the *Believer* again last month, this time for quoting from one of Philip Larkin's letters, more or less accurately—what's a second-person pronoun between friends?—at an editorial meeting. The Polysyllabic Spree, the seventy-eight repellently evangelical young men and women who run the magazine, "couldn't hear the quotation marks," apparently, and anyway, as they pointed out (somewhat unnecessarily, I felt), I'm no Larkin. So I have a lot of ground to cover here—I have had several Major Reading Experiences over the last couple of months, and I've got to cram them all into a couple of measly pages, all because of those teenage white-robed prudes. Oh, it's not your problem. I'll just get on with it. I know I won't need to tell you anything about Zadie Smith's warm, moving, smart, and thoroughly enjoyable *On Beauty;* Hanan Al-Shaykh was one of the authors I met on a recent trip to Reykjavik, and her lovely novel *Only in London* was a perfect reflection of the woman: surprising, fun, thoughtful.

A disgruntled Barnesandnoble.com punter slams Robert Penn Warren's *All the King's Men:* "Oh well," says our critic in his one-star review. "At least it was better than the Odyssey." This means, presumably, that the Odyssey is a no-star book; you have to admire someone prepared to flout conventional literary wisdom so publicly. I personally don't agree, and for me the Odyssey still has the edge, but Warren's novel seems to have held up pretty well. It's overwritten, here and there—Warren can't see a sunny day without comparing it to a freckly girl wearing a polka-dot dress and new shoes, sitting on a fence clutching a strawberry lollipop and whistling—and at one point, apropos of almost nothing, there's a thirty-page story set during the Civil War which seems to belong to another book altogether. You could be forgiven for thinking that *All the King's Men* could have done with a little more editing, rather than a little less; but the edition I read is a new "restored" edition of the novel, containing a whole bunch of stuff—a hundred pages, apparently—that were omitted from the version originally published. A hundred pages! Oh, dear god. Those of us still prepared to pick up sixty-year-old Pulitzer Prize–winners should be rewarded, not horribly and unfairly punished.

You may well already have read *All the King's Men;* you will, therefore, be familiar with Willie Stark, Penn's central character, a demagogic Southern politician whose rise and demise deliberately recalls that of Huey Long. Me, I've just read a book about someone called Willie Talos—the name Warren originally wanted until he was talked out of it by his editor. I think the editor was right; as Joyce Carol Oates said in her *NYRB* piece about the restored edition, "'Talos' is a showy, pretentious, rather silly name in the 'Stephen Dedalus' tradition, while 'Willie Stark' is effective without being an outright nudge in the ribs." But even that, I don't think, is the point; the point is that Willie Stark is now the character's name, whatever the author intended all those years ago, and whichever name is better is a moot point. I feel as though I've just read a book about David Copperbottom or Holden Calderwood or Jay Gatsbergen. You can't mess around with that stuff, surely? These people exist independently of the books, now—I have, I now realize, seen countless references to Willie Stark in reviews and magazine articles, but as the book isn't widely known or read here in the UK, I had no idea that was who I was reading about until after I'd finished.

Talos was, apparently, the guardian of Crete, who threw boulders at people attempting to land on the island; he was also a mechanical man attendant on the Knight of Justice in Spenser's *Faerie Queene*. These are both very good reasons why Talos is a very bad name for a Southern American politician,

I would have thought, and I can imagine that a good editor would have made the same arguments. Noel Polk, who put this new edition together, is of the opinion that Warren was badly served by the editing process; in a reply to Joyce Carol Oates's piece, he claims that "many of us are interested in more than a good read," and that he knows, and Oates doesn't, "how often well-intentioned commercial editors have altered novels for the worse." If I were Robert Penn Warren's editor, I'd point to a Pulitzer Prize and sixty years in print as all the vindication I needed; we will never know whether Polk's version would ever have endured anywhere near as well. There is even the possibility, of course, that if Warren had had his way in 1947, there would have been no interest in any kind of edition in the twenty-first century. I can see that scholars might want to compare and contrast, but I notice on Amazon that the long 'un I read now has a movie tie-in cover. Caveat emptor.

I reread John Lukacs's little book on what turned out to be the biggest decision of the twentieth century—namely, Churchill's decision not to seek terms with Hitler in May 1940—because I found it on my bookshelf and realized that the only thing I could remember was Churchill deciding not to seek terms with Hitler in 1940. And I kind of knew that bit before I read it. So this time, I'm going to make a few notes that help make it all stick—it's great, having this column, because I keep the magazines, but I'd probably lose a notebook. Excuse me a moment. Norway defeat brings down Chamberlain; C becomes PM 5/10/1940. Early unpopularity of C in his own party—"blood, sweat, toil, and tears" speech didn't go down well—"gangsters" + "rogue elephant." Churchill v HALIFAX. Churchill and Lloyd George—wanted him in the Cabinet because LG admired Hitler, who might appoint him if and when… Dunkirk: feared max 50,000 evacuated—in the end over 338,000.

Thanks. That'll really help.

Lukacs's book is completely gripping, clear, and informative, and corroborates a theory I've been developing recently: the less there is to say about something, the more opaque the writing tends to be. In other words, you hardly ever come across an unreadable book on World War II, but pick up a book on, I don't know, the films of Russ Meyer, and you'll be rereading the same impossible sentence about poststructuralist auteurism three hundred times. People have to overcompensate, you see. And *Five Days in London* also helped give a context for Philip Larkin's early letters, too. Here's Larkin, in 1942: "If there is any new life in the world today, it is in Germany." "Germany will win this war like a dose of salts" (1940). "And I agree we don't deserve to win" (1942). Lukacs points out that there was a grudging admiration for Hitler's Germany in Britain: we were clapped-out, the old order, whereas Germany was thrusting, energetic, modern. And he also notes that it was the intellectuals—and I suppose Larkin must be categorized thus, despite the farting—who were most prone to defeatism. Ha! That's the Spree, right there. They're very brave when it comes to suspending innocent columnists. But you wait until someone (and my money is on the French) lands on the West Coast. You won't see them for dust.

And the coveted "Stuff I've Been Reading: Stuff That Stayed Read" award for the nonfiction book of 2005 goes to… John Carey, for *What Good Are the Arts?* It's rare, I think, for a writer, maybe for anyone, to feel that he's just read a book that absolutely expresses who he or she is, and what he or she believes, while at the same time recognizing that he or she could not have written any of it. But Carey's book—which in its first two chapters answers the questions "What is a work of art?" and "Is high art superior?"—is my new bible, replacing my previous bible, Carey's *The Intellectuals and the Masses.* I couldn't have written it because I—and I'm not alone, by any means—do not have Carey's breadth of reading, nor his calm, wry logic, which enables him to demolish the arguments of just about everyone who has ever talked tosh about objective aesthetic principles. And this group, it turns out, includes anyone who has ever talked about objective aesthetic principles, from Kant onwards. *What Good Are the Arts?* is a very wise book, and a very funny book, but beyond even these virtues, it's a very humane, inclusive, and empathetic book: as we all know, it's impossible to talk about "high" art without insulting the poor, or the young, or those without a university degree, or those who have no taste for, or interest in, Western culture. Carey's approach to the whole sorry mess is the only one that makes any sense. Indeed, while reading it, you become increasingly amazed at the muddle that apparently intelligent people have got themselves into when they attempt to define the importance of—and the superiority of—"high" culture.

Just after I'd finished it, and I was looking at the world through Carey's eyes, the winner of the 2005 Booker Prize claimed that at least his was a "proper" book—as if *Green Eggs and Ham* or *Bridget Jones's Diary* weren't proper books. And then, a few days later, the *Guardian*'s art correspondent launched an astonishing attack on the popular British artist Jack Vettriano: "Vettriano is not even an artist." (No, he's just someone who paints pictures and sells them. What do you call those people again?) "He just happens to be popular, with 'ordinary people'... I'm not arguing with you, I'm telling you... Some things about art are true, and some are false—all of which was easier to explain before we decided popularity was the litmus test of aesthetic achievement..."

Oh, man. That's got it all. This is not the time or the place to unravel the snobbery and the unexamined assumptions contained in those few lines; it's easier just to say that nothing about art is true, and nothing is false. And if that's scary, then I'm sorry, but you have to get over it and move on.

I read G. K. Chesterton's *The Man Who Was Thursday* because (*a*) I'd never read a word by Chesterton and (*b*) because I'd decided that from now on I'd only read stuff that John Carey recommends (in his useful little book *Pure Pleasure*). And it was pretty good, although I think that younger readers might get a little frustrated with the plotting. I don't want to give too much away. But say you were an *x*, and you believed that a group of seven people were all not *x*s but *y*s. And then you discovered that the first of these seven was actually an *x*, too. And then you found out the same thing about the second, and then the third. Wouldn't you start to get the idea? Yes, well. Anyway, I can't say anything else about it now other than that it's a novel that fundamentally believes in the decency and the wisdom of us all, and you don't find too many of those. John Carey has now made me buy a book by Kipling, and I didn't think anyone would ever manage that. ✶

MARCH 2006

BOOKS BOUGHT:

- ★ *Eustace and Hilda*—L. P. Hartley
- ★ *Hang-Ups*—Simon Schama
- ★ *Scenes from Metropolitan Life*—William Cooper

BOOKS READ:

- ★ *Scenes from Provincial Life*—William Cooper
- ★ *Scenes from Metropolitan Life*—William Cooper
- ★ *Death and the Penguin*—Andrey Kurkov
- ★ *Ghosting*—Jennie Erdal

So this last month was, as I believe you people say, a bust. I had high hopes for it, too; It was Christmastime in England, and I was intending to do a little holiday comfort reading—*David Copperfield* and a couple of John Buchan novels, say, while sipping an egg nog and…

Oh, what's the point? No one, I suppose, will remember that I began my March '05 column in this way. And if no one remembers me beginning my March '05 column in this way, then there is even less chance of them remembering that I began my March '04 column in this way, too. The tragedy is that I have come to think of those opening words as a tradition, and I was beginning to hope that you have come to value them as such. I even had a little fantasy that one of your popular entertainers—Stephen Sondheim, say, or Puff Diddle—might have set them to music, and at the beginning of March you all hold hands and sing a song called "It Was Christmastime in England," to mark the imminent arrival of spring. I am beginning to suspect, however, that this column is making only medium-sized inroads into the American consciousness. (I have had very little feedback from readers in Alabama, for example, and not much more from our Hawaiian subscribers.) I shall keep the tradition going, but more in hope than expectation. It's the New Year here in England,

and I'm sorry to say that, because of the apparent indifference of both Puff Diddle and Alabama (the whole state, rather than the band), I am entering 2006 on a somewhat self-doubting and ruminative note.

This last reading month really was a washout, though, for all the usual holiday reasons, so it was as well that, with incredible and atypical foresight, I held a couple of books back from the previous month, just to pad the column out a bit. I met Andrey Kurkov at the Reykjavik Literary Festival and loved the reading he gave from *Death and the Penguin*. (He also sat at the piano and sang a few jolly Ukrainian songs afterwards, thus infuriating one of the writers who had appeared on the same stage earlier in the evening: as I understood it, the Infuriated Writer seemed to think that Kurkov had wilfully and sacrilegiously punctured the solemnity of the occasion. You can see his point, I suppose. You can't mess around with readings by singing after them. The paying public might begin to expect fun at literary events, and then where would writers be? Up shit creek without a paddle, that's where.) I afterwards discovered that *Death and the Penguin* is one of those books that people love unreservedly. The eyes of the assistant in the bookshop lit up when I bought it, and all sorts of people have shown a frankly sickening devotion to the novel whenever I've mentioned it since.

I think I'd sort of presumed that the eponymous penguin was metaphorical, like both the squid and the whale in *The Squid and the Whale;* my antipathy to the animal kingdom is such that even animal metaphors tend to have a deterrent effect. (What kind of person thinks in animal metaphors? In this day and age?) Imagine my horror, then, when I learned during Kurkov's reading in Reykjavik that the penguin in *Death and the Penguin* is not like the squid or the whale, but, like, an actual penguin. The penguin really is a character, who—pull yourself together, man, *which*—has moods and feelings, and has an integral part in the story, and so on. And, as if the author actually wanted me to hate his novel, it's a cute penguin, too. "It will be a hard-hearted reader who is not touched by Viktor's relationship with his unusual pet," says one of the quotes on the back. (Why not just include a blurb saying "DON'T BUY THIS BOOK"?) And, of course, *Death and the Penguin* turns out to be fresh, funny, clever, incredibly soulful, and compelling, and the penguin turns out to be a triumphant creation. I might read only books about animals from now on.

Misha is effectively Viktor's flatmate; Viktor adopted it (I'm not giving in on the pronoun thing) when the failing local zoo was dishing out animals to whomever could afford to feed them, and as Viktor's girlfriend had recently moved out, he was feeling lonely. (Oh, stop it. It's not that sort of book.) Misha, however, turns out to be as depressed as Viktor, and it just sort of wanders about, and occasionally disappears off to its bedroom, like a homesick teenager on a foreign exchange program. Viktor, meanwhile, has recently started work as an obituarist: he's told to write and stockpile the obituaries of leading local figures, but the obits turn out to be needed earlier than anticipated, and Viktor eventually realizes that his work is somehow bringing about the untimely demise of his subjects.

It's a neat plot, but *Death and the Penguin* isn't a plotty book: Kurkov gives himself plenty of room to breathe (it's actually more of a long, rueful sigh) and that's pretty cool in and of itself. This is a literary novel—Kurkov loves his weltschmerz as much as the next guy—but he doesn't see why weltschmerz shouldn't come bundled up with a narrative that kicks a little bit of ass. Sometimes it seems as though everything in the arts (and I include sports in the arts) is about time and space—giving yourself room to move, finding the time to play... My copy of *Death and the Penguin* is two hundred and twenty-eight pages long, and yet it never seems overstuffed, or underpowered, and it manages to be about an awful lot, and it never ever forgets or overlooks gesture or detail. And I already said it was funny, didn't I? What more do you want? At that length, you couldn't even reasonably want less.

Jennie Erdal's *Ghosting* is a book about writing, so, you know, if you don't want to read it because you're a plumber or a chiropodist, then I quite understand. If I were you, I would resent the repeated implication, by publishers and books pages, that my profession is more interesting than yours. Unlike most books about writing, though, this one contains a narrative that is both genuinely gripping and eccentric. Jennie Erdal was employed by a flamboyant London publisher, the sort of man who is often described as "larger than life." (In other words, run for the hills! And don't look back!) She began as a translator, and then worked on a huge book of interviews this guy conducted with women; finally, she wrote two novels for him. They were his novels—his name, and his name alone, was on the title page—but according to Erdal, the author took only a passing interest in their conception and execution.

His first novel, he decides, will be both thrilling and very romantic: "It has to be a love story. People associate me with love…" When his amanuensis asks whether he has any notion of the characters who might populate this thrilling love story, he is precise and unequivocal: they must be "a man and a woman. Do you think I could write about poofters?"

So away Jennie Erdal goes, and writes a novel, and the flamboyant publisher publishes it, and it gets respectful reviews—partly because the flamboyant publisher is a respected figure, and partly, one suspects, because Erdal can clearly write. And, rather than breathe a huge sigh of relief, he decides to "write" another, although this one turns out to have a higher, tighter concept than the first: he wants it to be about two women, cousins born on the same day, who are so close that when one achieves orgasm, so does the other. Pretty good, you have to admit, and as Erdal seems, inexplicably, to have ignored the idea, it's still going begging.

Ghosting is a strange and rather wonderful book, and it makes you think about all sorts of things connected with writing and the notion of authorship. The truth is, however, that it's old news. Almost nobody writes their own books these days; indeed, to do so is seen as a mark of failure in literary circles. Of course, the young have no choice, and there are, apparently, a few renegades who insist on churning out word after word: the word on the literary street is that Michael Chabon wrote every word of *The Amazing Adventures of Kavalier and Clay,* for example, presumably out of some misguided and outdated notion of honesty. But the rest of us don't really bother. I have always used an old lady called Violet, who lives in a cottage in Cornwall, in the far west of England, and who is an absolute treasure. She's getting better, too.

For some reason, I found myself up a ladder in Strand Books in NYC a couple of months ago, looking to see whether they had any copies of old William Cooper novels. I know that Philip Larkin mentions him in his letters, but there may have been another nudge from somewhere, too. Whatever the motivation, I was led as if by magic to a beautiful 1961 Scribner hardback which cost me six dollars, and which contained Cooper's first and third novels, *Scenes from Provincial Life* and *Scenes from Married Life*, published in the U.S. as *Scenes from Life*.

I'd read them both before, twenty or more years ago, and I remembered them as being particularly important to me, although I wouldn't have been able to articulate why. Now I can see it: Joe Lunn, the hero of these books (and Cooper's thinly disguised alter ego) is, in the first book at least, a schoolteacher who has ambitions to make his living from writing, and that's exactly the situation I found myself in when my sister gave me the books as a Christmas present in what must have been '82 or '83, seeing as those were the only years I was in full-time gainful employment in a school. I don't think I managed to see the connection at the time. Really. I thought I'd been enjoying them for other reasons (they are incredibly enjoyable books). I thought I should own up to that, just to help you gauge the soundness of all the other literary judgments I make on these pages.

The reason that *Scenes from Metropolitan Life,* the second novel in the sequence, isn't included in the edition I bought is that it wasn't published until 1982, even though it was written in the 1950s; Cooper's work was so autobiographical that he was threatened with legal action by the real-life version of the young woman who is Joe's girlfriend in the first book and his mistress in the second. (Is that right? The thing is, she gets married in between the two, although he doesn't. Can you have a mistress if you're not married? Can you be a mistress if your lover isn't married? Is there a useful handbook you can look these things up in?) Publication of *Scenes from Metropolitan Life* was only possible after her death, and in the meantime Cooper's career had lost all the momentum it built up after the success of the first novel. All his books are out of print now.

Scenes from Provincial Life is a lovely novel, sweet-natured, and surprisingly frank about sexual relationships, considering the book is set in 1939: Joe has a weekend cottage which he shares with a friend, and where a lot of the book is set. Joe sleeps with Myrtle, the pious girlfriend, there; Joe's friend Tom uses it for trysts with his seventeen-year-old boyfriend Steve. See what I mean? Who knew anyone had sex in 1939, in a provincial town? Well, we all did, I suppose, but in Larkin's words, "sexual intercourse began / in 1963"—or at least, twentieth-century mainstream British artistic representations of it did—so it's weird to read what is effectively a Kingsley Amis–style comedy of sexual manners which also talks about Chamberlain at Munich.

If *Scenes from Metropolitan Life* is a little less successful, it's partly because all the characters are a little older, and a little sadder, and they take their jobs more seriously, and those jobs are a little more dull: Joe is a civil servant in the second book. He's still trying to make up his mind whether to marry Myrtle, but Myrtle's married already, to someone stationed in Palestine, and Cooper's insouciance doesn't really seem to take the sadness of any of that on board. (My pristine secondhand copy came from my Amazon Marketplace seller with Kingsley Amis's 1982 *Sunday Times* review tucked neatly into the dust jacket, by the way. Kingsley loved the first one but gave the second a reluctant thumbs-down.) I've just started the third, and Joe's nearly forty, still single, and still looking, and you're beginning to suspect that there might actually be something wrong with him that he's not owning up to. It's hard, trying to be funny about getting older. *Scenes from Provincial Life* can afford to be cute and fresh because the characters have so little at stake; but then we grow older, more tired, more cynical, more worried; and then we die. And where's the joke in that? Oh. Ha. I've just seen it. It's pretty good.

Happy March, dear *Believer* readers. I hope you have a fantastic ten months. ✶

APRIL 2006

"**C**haracter is fate." *Discuss with reference to Eustace Cherrington in* The Shrimp and the Anemone *and Nikki Sixx in* The Dirt.

(It occurred to me that with the exam season coming up, younger readers might actually prefer this format for the column. I don't know how many of you are studying L. P. Hartley's *The Shrimp and the Anemone* in conjunction with *The Dirt*—probably not many. But even if it's only a couple of hundred, I'll feel as though I've provided some kind of public service. Please feel free to lift as much of the following as you need.)

In many ways, Eustace Cherrington—the younger half of the brother-sister combo in Hartley's *Eustace and Hilda* trilogy—and Nikki Sixx, the Crüe's bass player, are very different people. Eustace is a young boy, and Nikki Sixx is a grown man; Eustace is English, middle-class, and fictional, and Nikki Sixx is working-class, American, and (according to the internet at least) a real person. *The Shrimp and the Anemone* is a very beautiful novel, full of delicate people and filigree observation, whereas *The Dirt* is possibly the ugliest book ever written. And yet Eustace and Nikki Sixx both, each in their own ways, somehow manage to disprove Heraclitus's maxim—or at any rate, they demand its modification.

Both Hartley's novel and the Crüe bio remind us it's not *character* but *constitution* that determine our destinies. Eustace is, let's face it, a weed and a wuss. He's got a weak heart, so he can't go out much, and when he eventually steels himself to take part in a paper chase with the delectable but destructive Nancy, he collapses with exhaustion and takes to his sickbed for months. Nikki Sixx, however, is made of sterner stuff. When he ODs on heroin in L.A. and nearly dies—a journalist phones one of his bandmates for an obituary—what does he do? He gets home, pulls a lump of heroin out of the medicine cabinet, and ODs again. Thus we can see that Nikki Sixx and Eustace Cherrington live the lives that their bodies allow them to live. Nothing really matters, apart from this. Why do some of us read a lot of books and watch a lot of TV instead of play in Mötley Crüe? Because we haven't got the stomachs for it. It's as simple as that.

It was a mistake, reading *The Dirt* straight after *The Shrimp and the Anemone*. (Is it just a coincidence, by the way, that whole shrimp/anemone/squid/whale combo? Because even though Hartley's sea creatures are little ones, unlike writer-director Noah Baumbach's monsters, they serve pretty much the same metaphorical function: the novel opens with a gruesome and symbolic battle to the death. Anyway, where's the meat? Can anyone think of a way to get a little artistic surf 'n' turf action going?) *The Dirt* shat and puked and pissed all over the memory of poor Eustace's defenseless introspection—indeed, so grotesque are the characters and narrative events described in the Mötley Crüe book that it's very difficult to see any ideal circumstance in which to read it. I certainly recommend not reading anything for a month before, because the strong flavors of Nikki, Tommy Lee, and the other two will overwhelm pretty much any other literary delicacy you may have consumed; and you probably won't want to read any fiction for a month afterward because it will be hard to see the point. There are moments in *The Dirt* that render any attempts to explain the intricate workings of the human heart redundant, because there are no intricate workings of the human heart, clearly. There are only naked groupies, and endless combinations of class-A drugs, and booze, and covers of "Smokin' in the Boys' Room." And what have you got to say about all that, Anita Brookner? No. I thought not. There is one moment in *The Dirt* so disturbingly repellent that it haunts me still, but I'm unsure whether to quote it or not, for obvious reasons. What I think I'll do is reproduce the offending line in tiny writing, and if you want to read it, you'll have to go and fetch a magnifying glass—that way, you have participated in your own corruption. I advise you not to bother. This, then, from the early days:

> We'd scrounge up enough money to buy an egg burrito from Noggles. Then we'd bite the end off and stick our dicks into the warm meat to cover up the smell of pussy, so that our girlfriends didn't know we were fucking anything stupid or drunk enough to get into Tommy's van.

I'm afraid I have various questions about this. In America, are showers not cheaper than egg burritos? Does Noggles itself (we don't even have the establishment here in England, let alone the Noggles-associated behavior) not have a washroom? And didn't the girlfriends ever wonder... actually, forget it. We've gone far enough. It could be, of course, that this episode is a fabrication, but without wishing to add to the contemporary furor about the falsification of real lives, I'd argue that this is of a whole new order: anyone depraved enough to imagine this is certainly depraved enough to do it.

So why read it at all? Well, I read it because my friend Erin gave it to me for Christmas, and she had taken quite a lot of trouble to track down a nice hardback copy. Why Erin thought this was an appropriate gift with which to commemorate the birth of our Lord I'm not sure; why she thought that it was an appropriate gift for me is even less clear and somewhat more troubling. Certain passages, it is true, were uncannily reminiscent of certain nights on my last book tour, especially the Midwest readings. I had hoped that what went on there was a secret between me and the women whose names began with the letters A through E (so many broken-hearted Felicitys!) at the signings in question, but clearly not.

And weirdly, *The Dirt* isn't a bad book. For a start, it's definitive, if you're looking for the definitive book on vile, abusive, misogynistic behavior: if there are any worse stories than this in rock and roll, they aren't worth telling, because the human mind would not be capable of comprehending them without the aid of expert gynecological and pharmaceutical assistance. It's very nicely put together, too. *The Dirt* is an oral biography in the tradition of *Please Kill Me,* and Neil Strauss, the Studs Terkel of hair metal, has a good ear for the band's self-delusions, idiocies, and fuck-ups. Strauss, one suspects, has class. (Wilkie Collins provides the book's epigraph, for example, and I'm guessing that this wasn't Tommy Lee's idea.) "I decided to have the name of the album, *Till Death Do Us Part,* carved into my arm," recalls the hapless John Corabi, who replaced singer Vince Neil for one unsuccessful album. "Soon afterward they changed the name of the album to just *Mötley Crüe.*" Unexpectedly, *The Dirt* contains real pain, too. None of these characters have childhoods that one might envy, and their adult lives seem every bit as bleak and as joyless—especially if you are cursed with a constitution that prevents anything more than an occasional night in the Bank of Friendship.

The real victim here, however, is *The Shrimp and the Anemone,* which never stood a chance. It was fantastic, too. I picked it up after my friend Wesley Stace, whose first novel *Misfortune* has been picking up a distressing amount of attention, recommended it. (Not personally, of course—he's beyond that now. He gave it a mention in a *Guardian* questionnaire.) I'm going to read the whole *Eustace and Hilda* trilogy, and I'll write about it more when I've finished. Suffice to say that after last month's entirely felicitous William Cooper experience, I'm happy with my run of lost mid-century minor classics. And just as, a while back, I vowed only to read things recommended by Professor John Carey, I am now determined only to read things blurbed by John Betjeman. He is quoted on the back of *Eustace and Hilda,* just as he is on *Scenes from Provincial Life,* and on Nigel Balchin's *Darkness Falls from the Air,* purchased this month after a tip-off. He was missing from the jacket of the Crüe book, which should have served as a warning. He clearly didn't like it much.

I was not able to heed my own advice and take time out after rubbing my nose in *The Dirt:* this column, as Nikki Sixx would say, is insatiable, a nymphomaniac, and I had to press on. I couldn't return to Hartley, for obvious reasons, so I went with Michael Connolly's clever serial killer—I needed the moral disgust that thriller writers cannot avoid when dealing with dismembered children, etc. There was one twist too many for me at the end, but other than that, *The Poet* did a difficult post-Crüe job well. I did end up thinking about how evolving technology makes things tough for contemporary crime-writers, though. *The Poet* was first published in 1996 and contains an unfortunate explanation of the concept of digital photography that even my mum would now find redundant; the novel ends with an enigma that DNA testing would render bathetically unenigmatic within seconds. Filmmakers hate setting movies in the recent past, that awkward time when things are neither "period" nor contemporary. The recent past just looks wrong. Characters have cell phones the size of bricks and listen to music on Discmen. The same principle applies here: at these moments, *The Poet* feels anachronistic. Surely people who know their way around a laptop can do a spot of DNA testing? But no. I now see why my thriller-writing brother-in-law has run off to ancient Rome and barricaded himself in. He's not daft.

Still trying to dispel the memory of the egg burrito, I picked up Andrew Smith's *Moondust,* a book about what happened to the astronauts who walked on the moon after they fell to earth, on the grounds that you wouldn't be able to see Nikki Sixx from space. (And even if you could, you wouldn't be able to see what he was doing.) I put it down again in order to read a proof copy of a terrific first novel, Joshua Ferris's *Then We Came to the End.* Young Ferris and I share a publisher, and *Then We Came to the End* came with a ringing endorsement from a colleague. She wasn't after a blurb—she just talked with infectious and intriguing enthusiasm about the book, and this enthusiasm is entirely understandable. This book is going to attract a lot of admiration when it comes out later this year. I'm glad I read it before everybody else, because I would otherwise have been deterred by the hype (and here "hype" is an envious and dismissive substitute for "praise," which how the word is usually used).

The author will, I suspect, become sick of descriptions of his novel, all of which will use the word "meets," or possibly the phrase "rewritten by." As *Then We Came to the End* has not been published yet, however, he is unlikely to be sick of them yet, so I can splurge. It's *The Office* meets Kafka. It's *Seinfeld* rewritten by Donald Barthelme. It's *Office Space* reimagined by Nicholson... Oh, that'll do. The book is written in the first-person plural (as in "we," for those who never got the hang of declining nouns), and I was reminded of Barthelme because of his two brilliant stories "Our Work and Why We Do It" and "Some of Us Had Been Threatening Our Friend Colby," neither of which is narrated in the first-person plural, but which, as you may have noticed, refer to "us" or "we" in the titles. So you could be forgiven for thinking that the resemblance is somewhat superficial. Barthelme, however, did have the very great gift of being able to make the mundane seem mysterious, and Ferris can do that when he wants to: his novel is set in an advertising office, and the rhythms and substance of a working day are slowly revealed to have the rhythms and substance of life itself. The novel, almost incidentally, feels utterly authentic in its depiction of office life—a rare achievement in fiction, seeing as most writers have never done a proper day's work in their lives—but the authenticity is not the point of it, because underneath the politicking and the sackings and the petty jealousies you can hear something else: the sound of our lives (that collective pronoun again) ticking away. And before I put you off, I should add that the novel is awfully funny, in both senses of the phrase. It's about cancer, totem poles, Emerson, and grief, among many other things, and you should preorder it now. It's our sort of book.

Oh, but what do any of these things matter? Is it really possible that Mötley Crüe have destroyed all the literature in the world, everything that came before them, and everything written since? I rather fear it is. Please don't go looking for that magnifying glass. Save yourself while there's still time. ⋆

MAY 2006

I have a bookshelf over my bed, which is where I put the Books Bought and others that I have a serious intention of reading one day. And inevitably, over time, some of these are pronounced dead, and taken gently and respectfully downstairs either to the living room shelves, if they are hardbacks, or the paperback bookcase immediately outside the bedroom door, where they are allowed to rest in peace. (Do we have a word for something that looked like a good idea once? I hope so.) I'm sure you all knew this, but in fact books never die—it's just that I am clearly not very good at finding a pulse. I have learned this from my two younger children, who have taken to pulling books off the shelves within their reach and dropping them on the floor. Obviously I try not to notice, because noticing might well entail bending down to pick them up. But when I have finally and reluctantly concluded that no one else is going to do it, the book or books in my hand frequently look great—great and unread—and they are thus returned to the bookshelf over the bed. It's a beautiful, if circular, system, something like the process of convectional rainfall: interest evaporates, and the books are reduced to so much hot air, so they rise, you know, sideways, or even downstairs, but then blah blah and they fall to the ground… something like, anyway, although perhaps not exactly like.

This is precisely how Michael Ondaatje's *Running in the Family* was recently rediscovered. It turns out that I own a beautiful little Bloomsbury Classics hardback, as attractive to a small child, clearly, as it was to me. Indeed it's so attractive that it wasn't even placed back on the bookshelf over the bed: I began reading it fresh off the floor, as if it weren't rainfall after all, but a ripe, juicy… enough with the inoperable imagery. *Running in the Family* is a fever dream of a book, delirious, saturated with color; it's a travel book, and a family history, and a memoir, and it's funny and unforgettable. Ondaatje grew up in Sri Lanka, then called Ceylon, and it would not be unkind to describe his father as nuts—now and again, dangerously so. He pretended to have gone to Cambridge University (he sailed to England, stayed in Cambridge for the requisite three years, read a lot, and hung out with students without ever bothering to enroll); he was banned from the Ceylon Railways after hijacking a train, knocking out his traveling companion, who happened to be the future Prime Minister of the country, and bringing the entire railway system to a standstill; he was a part-time alcoholic, prone to epic drinking bouts, who buried scores of bottles of gin in the back garden for emergencies.

Ondaatje helps us to float over all this emotional landscape so that it feels as if we were viewing it from a hot-air balloon on a perfect day; someone with a different temperament (or someone much younger, someone who still felt raw) could have written—and been forgiven for writing—something darker and more troubling. "I showed what you had written to someone and they laughed and said what a wonderful childhood we must have had, and I said it was a nightmare," says an unnamed sibling at the end of the book, which tells you pretty much all you need to know about the theory and practice of memoir: it ain't the meat, it's the motion. The passage describing the death of Lalla, Ondaatje's grandmother, who was swept away in a flood, is one of the most memorable accounts of someone's last moments that I can remember. I'm grateful to my children for all sorts of things, of course, things that will inevitably come to me immediately after I have finished this column and sent it off; but I'm extremely grateful that one of them dropped this wonderful book on the floor. Actually, that may well be it, in terms of what my sons have given me, which puts a different complexion on the experience. I loved *Running in the Family,* and I mean the author no disrespect. But it's not much to show for twelve years of fatherhood, really, is it?

I've been losing a lot of books recently, so I am glad that nature has been bountiful, whether that bounty takes the form of fruit or rain. I have no idea where I've put *Eustace and Hilda,* the L. P. Hartley trilogy I was reading and loving, and Andrew Smith's book about the Apollo astronauts, *Moondust,* which I started and stopped a while back, was missing for most of this month, and as a consequence I haven't quite finished it. (It turned up in a drawer.) Lots of people are reading it here at the moment—it's a Richard and Judy book, Richard and Judy being our equivalent of Oprah—which is both weird and great, because in many ways *Moondust* is an eccentric book, with a set of references (Bowie, Neil Young, Updike, Rufus Wainwright, Eric Hobsbawm) that perfectly reflect the author's interests without necessarily reflecting the tastes of a mass reading public.

Smith knows that his obsession with the moon landings is about something else, and he is particularly good at teasing out the personal and global meanings of the Apollo missions—hell, there are even a few cosmic meanings in there—without ever sounding mad or pretentious. The author argues that when Apollo died in 1972, the dreams of the '60s died with it (and David Bowie is quoted as saying that the '70s were the start of the twenty-first century, which means that the twentieth century, perhaps uniquely, contained only seven decades), and there's a nostalgia for what the future used to represent and no longer can, and there's all sorts of stuff about aging and ambition. Despite the astronauts' protestations to the contrary, it's clearly been a struggle, flying to the moon and back in your thirties and forties, and then having to live out the rest of your life earthbound.

There's something in *Moondust* that I'd never thought about before, and it's haunted me ever since I read it. I had always felt rather sorry for Michael Collins, Richard Gordon, and the other four guys who flew all the way to the moon but then had to stay in the Command Module. I'd always had them down as close-but-no-cigar Pete Best types, doomed to be remembered for all time as unlucky. And yet their Apollo mission was surely every bit as extraordinary as those of the guys who got to put up flags and drive around in little golf buggies: forty-seven minutes of each lunar orbit that the Command Module took was spent on the far side of the moon, "out of sight and unreachable and utterly, utterly alone." The six Pete Bests were, as one NASA employee put it, the loneliest men "since Adam." Charles Lindbergh actually wrote to Collins, saying that walking on the moon was all very well, "but it seems to me that you had an experience of in some ways greater profundity." I find that it takes most of my courage simply to contemplate their pitch-black solitude. The closest I have ever come, I think, was last Christmas Day, when I walked round the corner to buy cigarettes and my whole neighborhood was utterly deserted. I'm not suggesting for a moment that my existential terror rivalled theirs, but it was a pretty creepy couple of minutes, and I was certainly glad to see the guy in the shop.

There are now nine people in the world who have walked on the moon, and unless something dramatic happens (and I'm talking about a governmental rethink rather than a cure for death), it won't be too long before there is none. That might not mean anything to a lot of you, because you are, I am led to understand, young people, and the moonwalks didn't happen in your lifetime. (How can you be old enough to read the *Believer* and not old enough to have seen Neil Armstrong live? What's happening to the world?) But it means a lot to me, and Andrew Smith, and when the Apollo missions, the future as we understood it, become history, then something will be lost from our psyches. But what do you care? Oh, go back to your hip-hop and your computer games and your promiscuity. (Or your virginity. I forget which one your generation is into at the moment.)

Kurt Vonnegut's *A Man Without a Country* was an oddly fitting companion to Smith's book, perhaps because the quirky humanist hope that one used to discern in Vonnegut's novels—several of which were written just as men were trying to get to the moon, and which frequently took an extraterrestrial view of our planet—is all but extinguished here. It's a charming, funny, wise little book, of course, because Vonnegut is incapable of writing anything that doesn't possess these qualities, but it's sad, too. Perhaps the questionable advantage of old age—Vonnegut is in his eighties now—is that you can see that hope is chimerical, and *A Man Without a Country* is devastatingly gloomy about the mess we have made of the world. I know he's right, but there is something in me, something callow and unrealistic (and something connected with the little boys who pull books off the shelves and drop them on the floor), that stops me from *feeling* that he's right. It has a very good smoking joke in it, though, this book. "Here's the news," says Vonnegut. "I am going to sue the Brown & Williamson Tobacco Company, manufacturers of Pall Mall cigarettes, for a billion bucks! Starting when I was only twelve years old, I have never chain-smoked anything but unfiltered Pall Malls. And for many years now, right on the package, Brown and Williamson have promised to kill me. But I am now eighty-two. Thanks a lot, you dirty rats."

It's been kind of a gloomy month, all in all, because Marjane Satrapi's two brilliant, heartbreaking graphic novels, *Persepolis: The Story of a Childhood* and *Persepolis 2: The Story of a Return,* aren't likely to lift the spirits, either. The story of Satrapi's childhood is also the story of the Iranian revolution, so she witnessed one violent and repressive regime replacing another; I got the same feeling I had while reading Jung Chang's *Wild Swans,* that the events described are so fantastical, so surreal and horrific, that they no longer seem to belong to the real world but to some metaphorical Orwellian dystopia. We know very little of the real world, though, those of us who live in the U.S. and Europe, just our small and relatively benign corner of it, and though we can see that the Guardians of the Revolution are human, just like us, it's pretty hard to find a way in to their humanity. Satrapi follows the trail of blood that leads from the over-throw of the Shah, through the fatuous and tragic war with Iraq, and on to the imprisonment, torture, and eventual murder of the leftists who helped bring about his downfall. And as the free-thinking daughter of left-leaning parents, Satrapi is able to use the small frames of her own life to create the bigger picture without contrivance or omission. (If the first book is slightly more successful than the second, it's because Satrapi spent some of the 1980s in Austria, so her personal and national histories take divergent paths.)

Satrapi draws in stark black-and-white blocks which bring to mind some of Eric Gill's woodcuts, and these blocks quickly begin to make perfect sense; in fact, it would be pretty hard not to draw post-revolutionary Iran without them—what with the beards and the robes and the veils, there was and still is a lot of black around. You know how bad things were for young Marjane and her mates? A poster of Kim Wilde comes to represent freedom, and who wants to live in a place where that's been allowed to happen? I know myself well enough to understand that I would never have read a prose memoir describing this life and these events—I wouldn't have wanted to live with this amount of fear and pain over days and weeks. I'm glad I understand more than I did, though, and these books, it seems to me, provide an object lesson in all that's good about graphic novels.

I picked up Bernard Levin's *The Pendulum Years,* about Britain in the '60s, because there's a little story in it that I'd always thought would make a good film, and I wanted to remind myself of the details. But then I remembered that the book contained one of my favorite pieces of comic writing, Levin's account of the Lady Chatterley trial, so I reread that, and a few of the other chapters. The piece on the Lady Chatterley trial made me laugh all over again, but it struck me this time that, even though Levin does a great job, it's not so much his writing that's funny as the trial itself; it's hard to go wrong with this material. For the benefit of young people: at the beginning of the 1960s, Penguin Books published Lawrence's *Lady Chatterley's Lover,* the first time it had been available to the general public since 1928, and the publishers were promptly prosecuted. Penguin won the ensuing court case, but not before some very English (and, it has to be said, extremely dim) lawyers argued, with unintentional comic élan, that the book had no literary merit, and therefore Penguin couldn't justify its obscene content. The law's notion of literary merit was both revealing and instructive—Mr. Griffith-Jones, for the prosecution, doubted, for example, that any book which contains a misquotation from the 24th Psalm could be said to be much good. "Do you not think that in a work of high literary merit… he might take the trouble to look it up?"

Mr. Griffith-Jones was also perturbed by Lawrence's repeated use of the words *womb* and *bowels,* taking the view that your absolutely top authors, your greats, if you will, would get the thesaurus out. "Then a little bit further down page 141, towards the bottom, at the end of the longish paragraph the two words 'womb' and 'bowels' appear again… Is that really what you call expert, artistic writing?" This really happened, honestly.

I was going to point out the bleeding obvious (as I prefer to do whenever possible, because it takes less effort, but fills up the space anyway)—I was going to say that a decade that began like this ended with man walking on the moon. Things aren't quite that cheerily progressive, though, are they? Because we're not landing men on the moon, or anywhere else in space—indeed, we no longer even possess the proper technology. There are plenty of people out there, however, who don't want us reading about wombs and bowels. Just ask Marjane Satrapi. ✶

JUNE / JULY 2006

BOOKS BOUGHT:

- ★ *Sons of Mississippi*—Paul Hendrickson
- ★ *Last Days of Summer*—Steve Kluger
- ★ *True Adventures with the King of Bluegrass*—Tom Piazza
- ★ *On Fire*—Larry Brown
- ★ *The Devil's Highway*—Luis Alberto Urrea
- ★ *Happiness*—Darrin M. McMahon
- ★ *The Mysterious Secret of the Valuable Treasure*—Jack Pendarvis

BOOKS READ:

- ★ *Into the Wild*—John Krakauer
- ★ *The Boy Who Fell From the Sky*—Ken Dornstein
- ★ *The March*—E. L. Doctorow
- ★ *Freakonomics*—Steven D. Levitt and Stephen J. Dubner

Last month I read Marjane Satrapi's two Persepolis books and Kurt Vonnegut's *A Man Without a Country,* and I seem to recall that I described the experience as somewhat gloomy. Ha! That was nothing! I didn't know I was born! I now see that the time I spent in Satrapi's horrific postrevolutionary Iran, and the time I gave over to Vonnegut telling us that the world is ending, were the happiest days of my life. The end of the world? Bring it on! With the honorable exception of *Freakonomics,* the most cheerful book I read this month was Jon Krakauer's *Into the Wild,* the story of how and why a young man walked into the Alaskan wilderness and starved (or perhaps poisoned) himself to death. *Into the Wild* wins the Smiley Award because it has a body count of one. Ken Dornstein's memoir *The Boy Who Fell from the Sky* begins and ends with the Lockerbie disaster in 1988, when a Pan Am plane blew up over a Scottish village, killing all 259 passengers, including the author's older brother David. And E. L. Doctorow's novel *The March* describes William Sherman's journey from Atlanta up to North Carolina, and just about everybody dies, some of them in ways that you don't want to spend a long time thinking about.

I was actually in North Carolina when I finished *The March*—this is something I like to do when I'm particularly enjoying a novel, despite the cost. (Did you know that there's no such planet as Titan? Vonnegut just made it up. They could have put that on the jacket, no? Oh well. You live and learn.) A couple of days later I passed the book on to one of my travelling companions, Dave Bielanko of the mighty band Marah, and he in return gave me the Krakauer book. It's what you do when you're on the road. Oh, yeah. There's a lot of, like, brotherhood and stuff. We were actually on the road between Memphis, Tennessee, and Oxford, Mississippi, a journey that takes approximately ninety minutes, and those forty-five minutes were the only chunk of road I experienced. But never mind! I was there, swapping books, and, you know, looking out of the window. (And Oxford, Mississippi, is yet another place in the U.S. that I want to move to. Everyone there is a writer, or a musician, or someone who hasn't yet bothered doing either thing but could if he or she wanted to. And the mayor runs the bookstore, and in Faulkner's house you can read the plot outline he wrote in pencil on the wall, and you can see the can of dog repellent he kept by his desk, and the sun shines a lot.)

It's a strange experience, reading Ken Dornstein's memoir immediately after I'd finished *Into the Wild*, because there were occasions when it seemed as though Dornstein and Krakauer were writing about the same young man. Here's Chris McCandless, the doomed explorer, at college: "During that final year in Atlanta, Chris had lived off campus in a monkish room furnished with little more than a thin mattress on the floor, milk crates and a table." And here's David Dornstein: "David's room was a classic writer's Spartan cell—a desk, a chair, a mattress on the floor, books stacked all around." Both David Dornstein and McCandless spend an awful lot of time underlining meaningful passages in classic literature; these passages will later be discovered by future biographers, and both of these young men seemed to presume that there would be future biographers, because they left hundreds of pages of notes. David Dornstein, who wanted passionately to write, frequently imagines that his future biographer will have to piece together his work from these notes (chillingly, more than once he imagines himself killed in a plane crash); McCandless refers to himself in the pseudonymous third person—he was "Alexander Supertramp." Both of them have a taste for a slightly affected mock-heroic voice. And both of them seem doomed.

David Dornstein wasn't doomed in the same way as Chris McCandless, of course. McCandless chose to walk almost entirely unequipped into deadly terrain in order to live out some half-baked neurotic Thoreau fantasy. David Dornstein simply got on a routine passenger flight from London to New York, but what is remarkable about Ken Dornstein's memoir is that his brother's tragic and ungovernable fate seems like an organic part of the story he's telling. Someone sent me a proof copy of *The Boy Who Fell Out of the Sky* a while back, and I didn't think I was going to read it, partly because I couldn't imagine how it could be a *book*. To put it crudely and brutally, my anticipated problem was all in the title: whatever David's story was, it would be ended by a random, senseless explosion. (I'd been afraid of exactly the same thing with my brother-in-law's novel *Pompeii*—how can you create a narrative arc when you're just going to dump a load of lava on people's heads?) I don't know whether it's tasteless to say that the end of his life makes sense, but that's the unlikely trick that his brother pulls off.

Creating narrative coherence out of awful accident is, I suppose, a textbook way of dealing with this sort of grief (and grief, of course, is mostly what this book is about). It's partly Dornstein's skill as a writer that makes the raw material seem tailor-made for the form he has chosen, but the lives examined here are also freakishly appropriate for this kind of examination. It's not just the notes that his brother left, the half-finished stories and abandoned novels and instructions to literary executors, the letter to David from his father that explains and explores the story of Daedalus and Icarus. Ken ends up married to David's college girlfriend, but before they get there the two of them have to work out, slowly and painfully, whether there's any more to their relationship than a shared loss. And David wanted Ken to become the writer he feared he would never be, so the very existence of *The Boy Who Fell Out of the Sky* provides another layer of complication. It's a compelling, sad, thoughtful book, and I'm glad I picked it up.

Sixty passengers killed in the Lockerbie bombing fell onto the roof and garden of one particular house in the town. (The woman who lived there, perhaps understandably, moved away.) We can't imagine horror on that scale intruding into our domestic lives, but in Doctorow's novel *The March* it happens all the time. A still, hot morning, everything in its place, and then suddenly the sound and soon the sight of an avenging army come to fuck up everything you own and hold dear, and then the flames, and quite often something worse on top. And of course one has every right to be troubled by everything being held dear Down There, but this needn't prevent a sense of wonder at the sheer scale and energy of the devastation. (One of the things I kept thinking as I read the novel was, How on earth did you manage to create a country out of this mess?) In Doctorow's novel, Sherman's march absorbs turncoat soldiers just trying to get through, and freed slaves, and bereft Southern widows, and cold-eyed surgeons; they're all eaten up and digested without a second thought. The violence, and violence of feeling, in this novel is on occasions so intense that it becomes kind of metaphysical, in the way that the violence in *King Lear* is metaphysical; the pitiful soldier with a spike protruding from his skull who has no memory of any kind, who lives every single second in the now, takes on an awful weight of meaning. And he ends up killing himself in the only way he can.

Lincoln turns up at the end of the book, as he has to, and in Chapel Hill, North Carolina, I bought a used copy of his letters and speeches. He must have been an annoying person to live with, no? Yes, there's the Gettysburg address. But there's also this letter to a young family friend: "I have scarcely felt greater pain in my life than on learning from Bob's letter, that you had failed to enter Harvard University… *I know not how to aid you…*" [itals mine]. Come on, Abe! Is that really true? You couldn't pick up the phone for a pal? You can take this "honest" stuff too far, you know.

It would be easy, if unfair, to parody the post-Gladwell school of essays (and it's not unfair to say that *The Tipping Point* and *Blink* both paved the way for *Freakonomics*). You take two dissimilar things, prove—to your own satisfaction, at least—that they are not only not dissimilar but in fact more or less indistinguishable, suddenly cut away to provide some historical context, and then explain what it all means to us in our daily lives. So it goes something like this:

On the face of it, World War II and Pamela Anderson's breasts would seem to have very little in common. And yet on closer examination, the differences seem actually much less interesting than the similarities. Just as World War II has to be seen in the context of the Great War that preceded it, it's not possible to think about Pammie's left breast without also thinking about her right. Pamela Anderson's breasts, like World War II, have both inspired reams of comment and analysis, and occupied an arguably disproportionate amount of the popular imagination (in a survey conducted by the American Bureau of Statistical Analysis, more than 67 percent of men aged between thirty-five and fifty admitted to thinking about both World War II and what Anderson has under her T-shirt "more than once a year"); both World War II and the Anderson chest are becoming less *au courant* than they were. There are other, newer wars to fight; there are other, younger breasts to look at. What does all this tell us about our status as humans in the early years of the twenty-first century? To find out, we have to go back to the day in 1529 when Sir Thomas More reluctantly replaced Cardinal Wolsey as Lord Chancellor in Henry VIII's court…

They're always fun to read (the real essays, I mean, not my parody, which was merely fun to write, and a waste of your time). They pep you up, make you feel smart but a little giddy, occasionally make you laugh. *Freakonomics* occasionally hits you a little too hard over the head with a sense of its own ingenuity. "Now for another unlikely question: what did crack cocaine have in common with nylon stockings?" (One of the things they shared, apparently, is that they were both addictive, although silk stockings were only "practically" addictive, which might explain why there are comparatively few silk stocking–related drive-by shootings.) The answer to the question of whether mankind is innately and universally corrupt "may lie in… bagels." (The dots here do not represent an ellipsis, but a kind of trumpeting noise.) Schoolteachers are like sumo wrestlers, real estate agents are like the Ku Klux Klan, and so on. I enjoyed the book, which is really a collection of statistical conjuring tricks, but I wasn't entirely sure of what it was about.

I don't think I have ever had so many books I wanted to read. I picked up a few things in U.S. bookstores; I was given a load of cool-looking books by interesting writers when I was in Mississippi and ordered one or two more (Larry Brown's *On Fire,* for example) when I came home. Meanwhile I still want to go back to L. P. Hartley's *Eustace and Hilda* trilogy, but Hartley seems too English at the moment. And I have a proof copy of the new Anne Tyler, and this young English writer David Peace has written a novel about 1974 as seen through the prism of Brian Clough's disastrous spell in charge at Leeds United. (Brian Clough was… Leeds United were… Oh, never mind.) So I'd better push on.

Except… a long time ago, I used to mention Arsenal, the football team I have supported for thirty-eight years, in these pages. Arsenal was occasionally called in to provide an excuse for why I hadn't read as much as I wanted to, but up until a month or so ago, they were rubbish, and I couldn't use them as an excuse for anything. They weren't even an excuse for a football team. Anyway, now they're—*we're*—good again. We have the semifinals of the Champions League coming up in a couple of weeks, for the first time in my life, and I can see books being moved onto the bench for the next few weeks. Ah, the old dilemma: books versus rubbish. (Or maybe, books versus stuff that can sometimes seem more fun than books.) It's good to have it back. ✶

AUGUST 2006

It's been an unsettling couple of months. It took me a while to get over the notion that I wanted to go and live in Oxford, Mississippi, after my recent visit there; and I'd only just become resigned to my lot here in north London when Arsenal, my football team, reached what we older fans still refer to as the European Cup Final. I've been watching Arsenal since 1968, and this was the first time they'd even got close, so the anticipation, followed by the crushing disappointment, pretty much destroyed all my appetite for books, if not for words: I probably sucked down a hundred thousand of the little bastards, as long as they formed themselves into previews of the game.

The Oxford thing was pretty serious for a while—although not, of course, as serious as the European Cup Final, which achieved a level of gravity that I have no wish to repeat in the time remaining to me on the planet. (Without going into too much detail, after early Arsenal domination, our keeper Jens Lehmann was calamitously sent off for a professional foul on Barcelona's Samuel Eto'o after fifteen minutes or so. Arsenal defended heroically, despite being a man down, and then amazingly and sensationally took the lead through Sol Campbell, who's had a miserable year both on and off the pitch, what with injuries, form, and the breakdown of his relationship with the designer Kelly Hoppen. Anyway, we held the lead for the best part of an hour, and then—after we'd missed good chances to go 2-0 up—fifteen minutes from the end we conceded an equalizer, followed shortly afterward by what turned out to be Barca's winner. Like I said, this isn't the time or the place to give you a minute-by-minute account of the game. Suffice it to say that the game was more draining for me than for any of the players, none of whom have been watching Arsenal since 1968.)

Sorry. Oxford. My plan was to get myself adopted by the poet Beth Ann Fennelly and her husband, the novelist Tom Franklin. They already have a young daughter, but I can look after myself, pretty much, and I was pretty sure that I could contribute to the household income even after sending money home to my own young family. It didn't happen, in the end—something about some papers that didn't come through, unless Tom and Beth Ann were just trying to let me down gently—but I still couldn't shake the notion that their life in Mississippi was an enviable one. Maybe it would get boring after a while, drinking coffee in the sunshine on the veranda outside Square Books and walking down the road to visit Faulkner's house, but surely not for a year or two?

In an attempt to compensate for the disappointment caused by the bungling bureaucrats, my reading was exclusively Southern for a couple of weeks, and I began with Beth Ann Fennelly's collection of poems, *Tender Hooks*. I met Beth Ann and her daughter on the aforementioned veranda, admittedly only briefly (Claire will one day find it bewildering to learn that on the basis of these few minutes, I had made concerted attempts to become her extremely big brother), but both of them seemed like the kind of people that one would like to know better. And then, as luck would have it, a few days later I read "Bite Me," the very first poem in the collection, in which Beth Ann describes her daughter's birth:

> And Lord did I push, for three more hours
> I pushed, I pushed so hard I shat,
> Pushed so hard blood vessels burst
> in my neck and in my chest, pushed so hard
> my asshole turned inside-out like a rosebud...

So I ended up feeling as though I knew them both better anyway—indeed, I can think of one or two of my stuffier compatriots who'd argue that I now know more than I need to know. (Is now the appropriate time, incidentally, to point out the main advantage of adoption?) If I had never met mother or daughter, then these lines would have made me wince, of course, but I doubt if they would have made me blush in quite the same way; maybe one should know poets either extremely well or not at all.

Tom Franklin's novel *Hell at the Breech*—which I haven't yet read—is set in 1890s Alabama, and is by all accounts gratifyingly bloody. So from the outside it looks as though they obey old-school gender rules 'round at the Fennelly/ Franklin place: the man writes about guns and mayhem, the lady writes about babies and home. But as the above excerpt indicates, it's not really like that at all. Yes, *Tender Hooks* is mostly about motherhood, but Fennelly's vision has more in common with Tarantino's than Martha Stewart's. One long, rich poem placed at the center of the collection, "Telling the Gospel Truth," puts the blood and sweat back into the Nativity, before moving on, cleverly and without contrivance, to contemplate the fatuity of poems that use "dinner knives to check for spinach in their teeth." Fennelly's poems aren't mannered, needless to say. They're plain, funny, and raw, and if you want to buy a present that isn't cute or dreamy for a new mother then *Tender Hooks* will hit the spot—and won't stop hitting it even though it's sore.

Larry Brown lived in Oxford before his untimely death in 1994. *On Fire* is a terse, no-bullshit little memoir about his life as a fireman and a hunter and a father and a writer (he did all of those things simultaneously), and though I know next to nothing about the last two occupations… Ah, now, you see, that's precisely it. It's not true that I know next to nothing about the last two occupations, of course. I know a reasonable amount about both of them, and I was making a silly little self-deprecating joke. (There I go again. Was it silly? Was it little? Probably not. It was probably a brilliant and important self-deprecating joke.) But what struck me about Brown's memoir is that, if you have experience of firefighting and hunting, self-deprecation is inappropriate and possibly even obstructive. It's not that Brown is self-aggrandizing in any way. He isn't. But in order to describe simply and clearly how you rescued someone from a burning building, you don't want to waste words on all the throat-clearing and the oh-it-was-nothings that many of us (especially many of us in England) have to go through before we're able to say anything at all. Before I read *On Fire,* I believed that self-deprecation was a matter of taste and personality, but now I can see that it's much more a function of experience—that old joke, the one about having a lot to be modest about, is unavoidable here. There is a very precise description of the self-deprecator and his mindset in *The Sixth Heaven,* the second part of L. P. Hartley's Eustace and Hilda trilogy (about which more later):

> Eustace had no idea in what guise he wanted to appear to his listener—he tried to confine himself to the facts, but the facts must seem such small beer to her, with her totally different range of experience. He tried to make them sound more impressive than they were; then he was ashamed of himself, and adopted a lighter tone, with an ironical edge to it, as if he well knew that these things were mere nothings, the faintest pattering of rain-drops… But he thought she did not like this; once or twice she gently queried his estimate of events and pushed him back into the reality of his own feelings.

And that, of course, is the danger of self-deprecation: its avoidance of that reality. Larry Brown can confine himself to the facts, which actually aren't small beer (or certainly don't seem that way to those of us who experience no physical danger in the course of a normal working week); and as a consequence, the truth of any given situation is perhaps a lot easier to reach… Oh, there we are! Thank god! It was actually easier for him than it is for me! He had it cushy, with his diving into burning buildings and his, you know, his heavy equipment!

Still on my Southern kick, I read James Wilcox's gentle, rich, and atmospheric *Modern Baptists,* and *True Adventures with the King of Bluegrass,* Tom Piazza's little book (it was originally a magazine article) about Jimmy Martin, in which the backstage area of the Grand Ole Opry is rather charmingly revealed to be a kind of country music limbo, where Nashville musicians wander around, apparently forever, harmonizing and jamming with anyone they bump into. (The only bum notes are struck by Piazza's hero, who tries to pick a fight with anyone who still speaks to him.)

Baltimore isn't really in the South, I know, but when a new Anne Tyler novel is published, you have to kick whatever habit you've developed and pick it up. And then read it. *Digging to America* is, I think, my favorite of her recent books. It may be disconcerting for those of you reared on Bret Easton Ellis and Irvine Welsh to read a novel whose climactic scene deals with a parent's comical attempts to get her child to give up her pacifiers (or "binkies," as they are known within the family); I can imagine some critics complaining that Tyler ignores "the real world," wherever that might be—especially as Baltimore, where all her novels take place, is also the setting for *The Wire,* HBO's brilliant, violent series about drug dealers, their customers, and the police officers who have to deal with them. The best answer to this actually rather unreflective carping comes from John Updike, in his *New Yorker* review of bad boy Michel Houellebecq's new novel:

> But how honest, really, is a world picture that excludes the pleasures of
> parenting, the comforts of communal belonging, the exercise of daily curiosity,
> and the widely met moral responsibility to make the best of each stage of life,
> including the last?

Nicely put, John. (And if there's more where that came from, maybe it's time to have a go at something longer than a book review.) Neatly, his summary of Houellebecq's omissions serves as a perfect summary of some of the themes in *Digging to America,* although the emphasis on pleasures and comforts can't do justice to Tyler's complications and confusions. Perhaps no single novel can capture the variety of our lives; perhaps even Houellebecq and Anne Tyler between them can't get the job done. Perhaps we need to read a lot.

Ali Smith's brilliant *The Accidental* manages to capture more of our lives, including both the humdrum and the uncomfortable, than any novel has any right to do. The central narrative idea (stranger walks into a family holiday home) is basic, and the book is divided into three parts, "The Beginning," "The Middle," and "The End." And yet *The Accidental* is extremely sophisticated, very wise, wonderfully idiosyncratic, and occasionally very funny. (It says something about Ali Smith's comic powers that she can make you laugh simply by listing the schedule of UK History, a British cable channel.) Here's a little bit from the middle of the book, the section entitled "The Middle": "The people on the TV talk endlessly... They say the word *middle* a lot. Support among the middle class. No middle ground. Now to other news: more unrest in the Middle East. Magnus thinks about Amber's middle..." I should own up here and tell you that *The Accidental* is a literary novel; there's no point trying to hide this fact. But it's literary not because the author is attempting to be boring in the hope of getting on to the shortlist of a literary prize (and here in the UK, Smith's been on just about every shortlist there is) but because she can't figure out a different way of getting this particular job done, and the novel's experiments, its shifting points of view, and its playfulness with language seem absolutely necessary. I can't think of a single *Believer* reader who wouldn't like this book. And I know you all.

I read *The Shrimp and the Anenome,* the first part of L. P. Hartley's Eustace and Hilda trilogy, bloody ages ago. And then I lost the book, and then I went off on my Southern thing, and then it was way too slow to pick up in a European Cup Final month, and... to get to the point: I've now read *The Sixth Heaven,* the second part, and it was something of a disappointment after the first. *The Shrimp and the Anenome* is an extremely acute book about childhood because, well, it explores the reality of the feelings involved, even though these feelings belong to people not quite into their teens. Hartley (who wrote *The Go-Between* and hung out in country houses with Lady Ottoline Morrell and the like) never patronizes, and the rawness, the fear, and the cruelty of his young central characters chafes against their gentility in a way that stops the novel from being inert. In *The Sixth Heaven,* however, Eustace and Hilda are in their twenties, and inertia has taken hold—there is a lot more hanging out in country houses with posh people than I could stomach. *The Sixth Heaven,* indeed, might have become an Unnamed Literary Novel, as per the diktats of the Polysyllabic Spree, if Hartley didn't write so wonderfully well. I nearly gave up hundreds of times, but just as I was about to do so, along come another brilliant observation. Even so, the third novel, *Eustace and Hilda,* begins with a chapter entitled "Lady Nelly Expects a Visitor"; the first sentence reads thus: "Lady Nelly came out from the cool, porphyry-tinted twilight of St Marks into the strong white sunshine of the

Piazza." I fear it might be all over for me.

I have just consulted my Amazon Recommends list, just in case anything took my fancy, and the first five books were as follows:

1) *Fidgety Fish* by Ruth Galloway
2) *The Suicidal Mind* by Edwin S. Shneidman
3) *The Very Lazy Ladybird* by Isobel Finn, Jack Tickle (Illustrator)
4) *Clumsy Crab* by Ruth Galloway
5) *No Time to Say Goodbye: Surviving the Suicide of a Loved One* by Carla Fine

It will have to be *The Very Lazy Ladybird,* I think. I haven't got time for books about clumsy crabs in a World Cup month. ✷

SEPTEMBER 2006

BOOKS BOUGHT:
- ★ *Field Notes from a Catastrophe*—Elizabeth Kolbert
- ★ *The Case of Mr. Crump*—Ludwig Lewishon

BOOKS READ:
- ★ None

Y̲ou have probably noticed that we don't think much of scientists, here at Believer Towers. The Polysyllabic Spree, the eighty-seven white-robed and intimidatingly effete young men and women who edit this magazine, are convinced that the real work in our society is done by poets, novelists, animators, experimental filmmakers, drone-metal engineers, and the rest of the riff-raff who typically populate the pages of this magazine. I, however, am not so sure, which is why, after a great deal of agonized internal debate, I have decided to introduce a Scientist of the Month Award. As will become clear, this month's winner, Matthias Wittlinger of the University of Ulm, in Germany, is a worthy one, but I am very worried about several, if not all, of the months to come. I don't really know much about science, and my fear is that we'll end up giving the prize to the same old faces, month after month after month. A word in Marie Curie's ear: I hope you have plenty of room on your mantelpiece. Without giving anything away, you're going to need it.

According to the July 1 edition of the *Economist*, Matthias Wittlinger decided to investigate a long-held but never proven suspicion that what enables an ant to find his (or her) way home to the nest is an inbuilt pedometer—in other words, they count their steps. He tested this hypothesis in an ingenious way. First, he made the ants walk through a ten-meter tunnel to get food; he then made them walk back to their nests through a different ten-meter tunnel. But the fun really started once they'd got the hang of this. Wittlinger trimmed the legs of one group of ants, in order to shorten the stride pattern; another group was put on stilts made out of pig bristle, so that their steps became much bigger. The results were satisfying. The ants with little legs stopped about four meters short of the nest; the ants on stilts, meanwhile, overshot by fifteen feet. Anyone who thinks that someone other than Wittlinger is a more deserving recipient of the inaugural Stuff I've Been Reading Scientist of the Month Award is, to put it bluntly, an idiot. Science doesn't get any better than this.

I'm delighted for Matthias, of course, but I am also feeling a little rueful. For many years now, I've been trimming and lengthening ants' legs, mostly because the concentration and discipline involved has allowed me to forgo all sexual activity. (I have been using pieces of old guitar string for the stilts, and guitar string is funnier than pig bristle, because the ants kind of bounce along.) I wasn't, however, doing it in a particularly purposeful way—I had no idea that I could have been written about in the *Economist,* or that I could win prestigious awards. And anyway, I was making an elementary error: I was trimming and lengthening the legs of *the same ants*—and this, I see now, was completely and utterly pointless: three hours of microsurgery on each ant and they all ended up the same height anyway.

Cynics don't read the *Believer,* which is fortunate, because a cynic might say that the introduction of the Scientist of the Month award is a desperate attempt to draw attention away from the stark, sad entry under Books Read at the top of this page. And a clever cynic might wonder whether the absence of read books, and therefore the appearance of the award, have anything to do with the arrival of the World Cup, a football [*sic*] tournament that every four years consumes the inhabitants of every country in the world bar the U.S. The truth is that the World Cup *allowed* me to introduce the award. I'd been meaning to do it for years, but space had always prevented me from doing so. Now that I have no books to write about, I can fulfill what can be described, without exaggeration, as a lifelong dream.

I wish I had read some books this month, to be honest, and not just because I wouldn't have to drivel on about nothing for a couple of pages. It's not that I believe reading is more important than sport, but there have been moments during this last month when I knew, beyond any shadow of a doubt, that I was wasting my time and yet made no effort to turn off the TV and do something more constructive. Watching Ukraine v. Tunisia can in part be explained by my bet on Andrei Shevchenko to score during the game. (He did, after taking a dive to win a penalty that he himself took.) But I have no way of rationalizing my willingness to stick with Ukraine v. Switzerland, even after it was clear that it was going to be perhaps the most pointless and boring ninety minutes in the history, of not only soccer but of all human activity. Couldn't I have read something at some point during the second half? A couple of Dylan Thomas's letters, say? They were right there, on the bookshelf behind the sofa.

It wasn't a very good World Cup. The star players all underperformed; everybody was too scared of losing; there were too few goals, too many red and yellow cards; and there was way too much cheating and diving and shirtpulling. And yet the rhythm of a World Cup day is unimprovable, if you don't have a proper job. You wake up in the morning, do a little online betting, read the previews of the games in the newspaper, maybe watch the highlights program you recorded the previous night. The first game is at two, so just beforehand you are joined by other friends without proper jobs (some of whom won't leave until eleven that night); it finishes at four, when you repair to the garden, smoke, drink tea, and kick a ball about with any of your children who happen to be there. The second game finishes at seven, just in time for bed, bath, and story time, and I don't know about you, but we used the "live pause" feature on our digital system for the eight o'clock game—there was a heat wave in Europe, and my kids took a while to get to sleep. Food was ordered at halftime and delivered during the second half. Has there ever been a better way to live than this? Friends, football, takeaways, no work… One can only presume that if Robert Owen and those guys had waited a couple of hundred years for the invention of the World Cup, takeaway food, digital TV, and work-shy friends, there was no way any utopian experiment could have failed.

For maybe the first time in my life, however, I have begun to sympathize with Americans who find the game baffling and slow. The lack of goals has never bothered any football [*sic*] fan, but when it becomes clear that a team doesn't even *want* to score one, that they'd rather take their chances in a penalty shoot-out, then the lack of action ceases to become a matter of taste and starts to look like a fatal flaw in the tournament. If you're so scared of losing, don't enter! Stay home! Let Belgium and Lithuania play instead! Many teams played with one striker, playing all on his own against two or three defenders; England's striker Wayne Rooney became so frustrated by these odds that he attempted to even them out by stamping on the balls of one of the defenders looking after him.

We can be pretty sure that it hurts, having your testicles stamped on, but I understand that Americans have come to refer contemptuously to the more theatrical World Cup injuries as the "flop and bawl"—the implication being, I think, that these players are feigning their distress. First of all, you must understand that the rest of the world is more susceptible to pain than you. Our smoking, our poor diets, and our heightened sensitivities (to both literature and life) mean that even a slight push in the back can send excruciating agony coursing through our bodies. You, however, because of your all-meat diet and your status as a bullying superpower, feel nothing, either emotionally or physically, at any time. So you can sneer at our floppers and bawlers if you want, but what does that say about you? How can you ever understand a novel, if you don't understand pain?

And secondly, these players are terrible, awful cheats. It wasn't always like this. But ten or so years ago, those in charge of the game decided, laudably, that they wanted to encourage the more creative players, which meant penalizing the defenders whose job it was to stifle that creativity. Nobody foresaw what would happen as a result: that these creative players would spend more time trying to land their opponents with a yellow or red card than they would trying to score a goal. (A yellow card means that the recipient is frightened of making a tackle for the rest of the game; a red card means he can't take any further part. Either is useful for the opposing team, which means there's too much of an incentive to fake an injury at the moment.) In my book *Fever Pitch,* which was first published in 1992 (and you can take great literature out of the month, but you can't take it out of the man), I wrote that "for a match to be really, truly memorable… you require as many of the following features as possible," and the sixth requirement listed was for a member of the opposition to receive a red card. At that time, I'd maybe seen half a dozen sendings-off in my twenty-five-year life as a fan; in the last five years, I've probably seen five times that many. It's no fun any more, and it kills the game. I withdraw my earlier ruling.

The saddest moment for me in this World Cup was watching Thierry Henry, my role model and hero and the man that both my wife and I wish had fathered our children, clutching his face after receiving a blow on the chest. Et tu, Thierry? Anyway, flopping and bawling now occupies the same position in our sporting culture as steroids do in yours. Crying like a baby is obviously less harmful than performance-enhancing drugs, but a lot more annoying to the spectators.

I have always previously referred in these pages to the mother of my children as my "partner"; you may have noticed that she has now been downgraded to "wife," due to our marriage, two days before the World Cup final. This too has resulted in less reading than normal, what with all the suit fitting, seating plans, parties, and the actually rather distressing legal requirements for consummation. I have read a little, of course. I abandoned a sweet-natured but hopelessly overhyped novel halfway through, and I've nearly finished *Imperium,* my brother-in-law's forthcoming novel about Cicero, which I'll puff next month.

I've been buying books, too. At my eldest son's school fair I bought *The Case of Mr. Crump,* yet another Penguin classic I'd never heard of, because on the cover it had a blurb from Sigmund Freud. I bought Elizabeth Kolbert's *Field Notes from a Catastrophe,* about climate change, after reading the brilliant but terrifying series of articles in the *New Yorker* that form the basis for the book. I thought I was buying it because I wanted to be reminded that things like the World Cup and weddings don't really matter. But then I began to remember some of the details of the *New Yorker* pieces, and I changed my mind: if things are as bad as Kolbert suggests, then weddings and the World Cup are the only things that do matter. ✵

OCTOBER 2006

"What we need," one of those scary critics who write for the serious magazines said recently, "is more straight talking about bad books." Well, of course we do. It's hard to think of anything we need more, in fact. Because then, surely, people would stop reading bad books, and writers would stop writing them, and the only books that anyone read or wrote would be the ones that the scary critics in the serious magazines liked, and the world would be a happier place, unless you happen to enjoy reading the books that the scary critics don't like—in which case the world would be an unhappier place for you. Tough.

Weirdly, the scary critic was attempting to review a book she did like at the time, so you might have thought that she could have forgotten about bad books for a moment; these people, however, are so cross about everything that they can't ever forget about bad books, even when they're supposed to be thinking about good ones. They believe that if you stop thinking about bad books even for one second, they'll take over your house, like cockroaches. She got distracted mid-review by the *Believer,* and its decision—which was taken over three years ago—to try and play nice when talking about the arts; some people are beginning to come to terms with it now, not least because they can see that very few pages of the magazine are given over to reviews. (Do we have to do the straight talking even if we're interviewing someone? Wouldn't that be rude? And pointless, given that presumably we'd be interviewing someone whose work we didn't like?)

The scary woman is not a big fan of this column, which is sad, of course, but hardly a surprise. What's more disappointing to me is that she and I go way back, right to the time when we used to bump into each other on the North of England stand-up comedy circuit, and now we seem to have fallen out. People in Bootle still talk about her impression of the Fonz. Why did she want to throw all that merriment away and become a literary editor? To borrow an old line from the late, great Tommy Cooper: we used to laugh when she said she wanted to be a comedian. We're not laughing now.

I am unable, unfortunately, to do any straight talking about the books I've been reading, because they were all great. The one I enjoyed the least was Elizabeth Kolbert's *Field Notes From a Catastrophe,* and that's because she makes a very convincing argument that our planet will soon be uninhabitable. Usually, devastatingly depressing nonfiction gives you some kind of get-out: it couldn't happen here, it won't happen to me, it won't happen again. But this one really doesn't allow for much of that. Kolbert travels to Alaskan villages with permafrost experts to see how the permafrost is melting. (Hey, W. It's called *perma*frost. It's melting. Tell us again why there's nothing to worry about.) She visits Greenland with NASA scientists to watch the ice sheets disintegrating, listens to biologists describe how English butterflies are moving their natural habitats northwards, goes to Holland to look at the amphibious houses being built in preparation for the coming deluge. You couldn't wish for a cleaner or more concise explanation of the science—Kolbert's research is woven into her text like clues in the scariest thriller you'll ever read. There is no real debate about any of this in the scientific community, by the way. Oil companies and other interested parties occasionally try to start a debate by making claims that are clearly and criminally fallacious, on the grounds that we might believe there's an element of doubt, or that the truth lies somewhere in between, but really there's nothing to argue about. Climate change is happening now, and it will be devastating, unless unimaginably enormous steps are taken by everyone, immediately.

There is, I need hardly tell you, very little evidence that anyone in any position of authority in the U.S. is prepared to do what is desperately needed. Senator James Inhofe, the chairman of the Senate Committee on Environment and Public Works, believes that global warming is "the greatest hoax ever perpetrated on the American people"; White House official Philip Cooney "repeatedly edited government reports on climate change in order to make their findings seem less alarming," before quitting his job and going off to work for Exxon-Mobil.

I don't often have the urge to interview authors of nonfiction, because the book should, and invariably does, answer any questions I might have had on the subject. But I noticed in the author bio on the dust-jacket that Elizabeth Kolbert, like me, has three sons. Has she talked to them about this stuff? How does it affect her morale, her ability to provide the kind of positivity and sense of security that children need? The evidence suggests that our children will be living very different, and much less comfortable, lives than our own; they may well decide that there's not much point in having children themselves. You may not want to read a book as lowering as this one, but maybe that's one of the problems anyway, that we don't want to know. If you don't want to know, then you need to take your head out of your ass and read *Field Notes From a Catastrophe*. It's short, and it's rational and calm, and it's terrifying.

I picked up a manuscript of Tim Sandlin's novel *Jimi Hendrix Turns 80* just at the right time: not only is it funny, but it imagines a future, because that's where it's set. Sandlin's characters all live or work in Mission Pescadero, a retirement community in California, in the year 2023; almost all the old folk are pot-smoking, sexually incontinent hippies who have been sleeping with each other, and arguing with each other (quite often about the original line-up of Blue Cheer) for decades. The in-house band that plays covers at the Friday night sock hop is called Acid Reflux, which may well be the most perfect fictional band name I've ever come across.

The residents of Mission Pescadero, sick of being tranquillized and denied privileges by the authoritarian staff, stage a revolution and seize control, but *Jimi Hendrix Turns 80* is not the sort of satire that loses its soul in an attempt to crank up the pace, and nor does it waste its characters while wrapping up its narrative. And, of course, it would have been unreadable if it had attempted to patronize or poke fun at the old, or the ageing process, but it never does that. Sandlin can see that there is a kind of gruesome comedy in what happens to us, but the humor is never mean, and he loves his people too much not to understand that their grief and nostalgia and frustration is real. This clever novel slipped down easily, and provided real refreshment in this vicious, stupefying (and, Elizabeth Kolbert has taught me, probably sinister) London summer.

Imperium is the first novel in my brother-in-law's projected trilogy about Cicero. I wrote about his last novel, *Pompeii,* in this column, and was positive that I'd have been sacked by the time his next one came out, but here we are. I won't say too much about it, other than that I have the cleverest brother-in-law a man could wish for, and that having a clever brother-in-law is enormously and gratifyingly educative. He doesn't need any help from me, anyway.

OK, I will say this: Robert's Cicero is a proper, living, breathing politician, and therefore perhaps the best fictional portrayal of the breed I've come across. Usually, the narrative in novels about politics goes like this: earnest, committed and naïve young politician is made older and more cynical by the real world. Anyone who was ever at school or college with a politician, however, knows that this narrative only works as metaphor, because people who want to be politicians are never naïve. Those little bastards are sneaky and ambitious even when attempting to be elected as entertainments secretary. (We need our representatives in our respective parliaments, of course we do, but they are the least representative people you could ever come across.) Robert understands this, although he's a former political reporter, so he likes politicians more than I do, and as a result, Cicero is properly complicated: attractive, devious, passionate, ferociously energetic, pragmatic. This, surely, is how he was, and I suspect our own Prime Minister must have been very similar. Your President, however, is sui generis.

I've been waiting to see how Jess Walter followed up last year's brilliant

Citizen Vince, although I wish I'd had to wait a little longer—not because I thought his new book needed the extra time and care, but because he's not playing the game. Yes, it's perfectly possible to write a book every year—all you need to do is write five hundred words a day (less than a quarter of the length of this column) for about eight months. This, however, would only leave four months of the year for holidays, watching the World Cup, messing about on the internet, judging book prizes in exotic locales, and so on. So most authors keep to a much more leisurely schedule of a book every two or three years, while at the same time managing to give the impression to publishers that books are somehow bubbling away inside them, and that any attempt to force the pace of the bubbling process would be disastrous. It's a system that works well, provided that people like Walter don't work too hard. If the various writers' unions had any real teeth, he'd be getting a knock on the door in the middle of the night.

It doesn't help that *The Zero* is a dazzlingly ambitious novel, a sort of *Manchurian Candidate*-style satire of post-9/11 paranoia. Brian Remy is a policeman involved in the clear-up of an enormous structure that has been destroyed in some sort of horrific terrorist attack. To his bewilderment, he's taken off this job and put to work on an undercover counter-terrorist organization, a job he never fully understands—partly because the task itself is dizzyingly incomprehensible, and partly because Remy suffers from blackouts, or slippages out of consciousness, which means that he wakes up in the middle of scenes with no real awareness of how he got there, or what he's supposed to be doing.

This condition is a gift, for both writer and reader—we're as compelled and as thrillingly disoriented as he is—but where Walter really scores is in the marriage of form and content. Has there ever been a more confusing time in our recent history? You didn't have to be Brian Remy to feel that life immediately post 9/11 seemed to consist of discrete moments that refused to cohere into an unbroken narrative. And there were (and are still) pretty rich pickings for paranoiacs, too. Remy keeps stumbling into huge aircraft hangars filled with people poring over bits of charred paper, and one recognizes both the otherworldliness and plausibility of these scenes simultaneously. A couple of books ago, Walter was writing (very good) genre thrillers; now there's no telling where he's going to end up. I don't intend to miss a single step of his journey.

Last month I read nothing much at all, because of the World Cup, and this month I read a ton of stuff. I am usually able to convince myself that televised sport can provide everything literature offers and more, but my faith in my theory has been shaken a little by this control experiment. Who in the World Cup was offering the sophisticated, acutely observed analysis of the parent-child relationship to be found Alison Bechdel's extraordinary graphic novel *Fun Home,* for example? You could make an argument for Ghana, I suppose, in the earlier rounds, or Italy in the knock-out stages. But let's face it, your argument would be gibberish, and whoever you were arguing with would laugh at you.

Fun Home has had an enormous amount of praise ladled on it already, and those of us who love graphic novels will regret slightly the overt literariness of Bechdel's lovely book (there are riffs on Wilde, and *The Portrait of A Lady,* and Joyce)—not because it's unenjoyable or pretentious or unjustified, but because it is likely to encourage those who were previously dismissive of the form to decide that it is, after all, capable of intelligence. Never mind. We'll ignore them. *Fun Home* is still as good as the very best graphic novels, although it's a graphic memoir, rather than a novel, and as such can stand comparison with *The Liars' Club* or *This Boy's Life* or any of the best ones. Bechdel grew up in a fun(eral) home, and had a father who struggled with his homosexuality throughout his life, and despite these singularities, she has written (and drawn) a book whose truth is instantly recognizable to anyone who's ever had a complication in their youth or young adulthood. It's rich, and detailed, and clever even without the literary references.

Fun Home is, I think, a great book, yet someone, somewhere, won't like it, and will say so somewhere. If you want to do some "straight talking," do it about the environment, or choose some other subject where there's a demonstrable truth; Elizabeth Kolbert knows that there's enough hot air as it is. ✷

APRIL 2007

One thing I knew for sure before I started Claire Tomalin's biography of Thomas Hardy: I wouldn't be going back to the work. Hardy's prose is best consumed when you're young, and your endless craving for misery is left unsatisfied by a diet of the Smiths and incessant parental misunderstanding. When I was seventeen, the scene in *Jude the Obscure* where Jude's children hang themselves "becos they are meny" provided much-needed confirmation that adult life was going to be thrillingly, unimaginably, deliciously awful. Now I have too meny children myself, however, the appeal seems to have gone. I'm glad I have read Hardy's novels, and equally glad that I can go through the rest of my life without having to deal with his particular and peculiar gloom ever again.

I suppose there may be one or two people who pick up Tomalin's biography hoping to learn that the author of *Tess of the D'Urbervilles* and *Jude* turned into a cheerful sort of a chap once he'd put away his laptop for the night; these hopes, however, are dashed against the convincing evidence to the contrary. When Hardy's friend Henry Rider Haggard loses his ten-year-old son, Hardy wrote to console him thus: "I think the death of a child is never really to be regretted, when one reflects on what he has escaped." Every cloud, and all that... Those wise words could only have failed to help Haggard if he was completely mired in self-pity.

Hardy died in 1928, and one of the unexpected treats of Tomalin's biography is her depiction of this quintessentially rural Victorian writer living a metropolitan twentieth-century life. It's hard to believe that Hardy went to the cinema to see a film adaptation of one of his own novels, but he did; hard to believe, too, that he attended the wedding of Harold Macmillan, who was Britain's prime minister in the year that the Beatles' first album was released. What happened to Hardy after his death seemed weirdly appropriate: in a gruesome attempt to appease both those who wanted the old boy to stay in Wessex and those who wanted a flashy public funeral in London, Hardy was buried twice. His heart was cut out and buried in the churchyard at Stinsford where he'd always hoped he'd be laid to rest; what was left of him was cremated and placed in Westminster Abbey, where his pallbearers included Prime Minister Stanley Baldwin, A. E. Housman, Rudyard Kipling, George Bernard Shaw, J. M. Barrie, and Edmund Gosse. Hardy was a modern celebrity, but his characters inhabited a brutal, strange, preindustrial England.

Such is Tomalin's skill as a literary critic—and this is a book that restores your faith in literary criticism—that I did end up going back to the work, although it was the poetry, not the novels, that I read. The poems written immediately after the death of Hardy's first wife, Emma, are, as Tomalin points out, quite brilliant in their...

I think they've gone now. They never read on after the first couple of paragraphs, and I know they will approve of the Tomalin book, so I'm pretty sure they will leave me alone for a while, and I can tell you what's been going on here. Older readers of this magazine may recall that I had a regular column here, up until the autumn of 2006; you may have noticed that when I was removed, I was described as being "on sabbatical" or "on holiday," a euphemism, I can now reveal, for "being reeducated," which is itself a euphemism—and here the euphemisms must stop—for "being brainwashed."

The Polysyllabic Spree, the three hundred and sixty-five beautiful, vacant, scary young men and women who edit this magazine, have never really approved of me reading for fun, so after several warnings I was taken by force to the holding cells in the basement of their headquarters in the Appalachian Mountains and force-fed proper literature. It's a horrific place, as you can imagine; everywhere you can hear the screams of people who don't want to read *Gravity's Rainbow* very much because it's too long and too hard, or people who would rather watch *Elf* than that Godard film where people sit in wheelbarrows and read revolutionary poetry out loud. (I saw poor Amy Sedaris down there, by the way. I won't go into what they've actually done to her. Suffice to say that she won't be making any jokes for a while.)

Luckily, I have seen lots of films where "mad" people (i.e., people whose refusal to conform results in being labeled insane) resist all attempts by The Man to break them, and I have picked up a few tips. For example: I hid under my tongue all the Slovenian experimental novels without vowels they were trying to make me read, and spat them out later. I had a little cache of them hidden beneath my mattress, so if the worst came to the worst I could read them all at once and kill myself. Anyway, if you see me recommend a book that sounds incomprehensible, you'll know they are taking an interest in my activities again.

I have bought a lot of books and read a lot of books in the last few months, so this first postbrainwashing column is more in the nature of a representative selection than an actual diary. And in any case I have been told that there are certain books I have read recently, all novels, that I'm not allowed to talk about here. One beautiful, brilliant novel in particular, a novel that took me bloody ages to read but which repaid my effort many times over, was deemed unacceptable because its author apparently impregnated an important member of the Spree a while back (and some Spree members are more equal than others, obviously), and the Spree regard sex as being obstructive to the consumption of literature. What is the… What is the *point* of having a books column like this if you have to lie about what you've read?

In my tireless and entirely laudable attempts to teach myself more about the past, I have been working methodically through books about individual years, namely James Shapiro's *1599: A Year in the Life of William Shakespeare*, and Jonathan Mahler's *Ladies and Gentlemen, the Bronx Is Burning: 1977, Baseball, Politics, and the Battle for the Soul of a City*. And I read the actual books, too, not just the titles and subtitles. If I read two of these year-books a week, then I'm covering a century every year, and a millennium every decade. And how many millennia are worth bothering with, really? I'm pretty excited about this project. By 2017, I should know everything there is to know about everything.

Pedants might argue that there was more to 1599 than Shakespeare, and more to 1977 than Reggie Jackson signing for the Yankees, an event that provides the spine for Jonathan Mahler's book. But this, surely, shows a fundamental lack of faith in the writer. Mahler has had a good look at 1977, and decided it was about Reggie Jackson; if he'd thought there was anything going on in the rest of the world worth writing about, then he would have chosen something else instead.

Ladies and Gentlemen, the Bronx Is Burning is not just about Reggie Jackson, of course. That New York summer there was the blackout that resulted, almost instantaneously, in twelve hours of looting and burning over an area of thirty blocks; there was a colorful mayoral race between Bella Abzug, Abe Beame, Mario Cuomo, and Ed Koch; there was the Son of Sam, and Studio 54, and a World Series for the Yankees. In those few months, New York seemed to contain so much that you can believe, while reading this book, that while Mahler can't cover our planet, he has certainly touched on most of our major themes.

That phrase "the city itself emerges as the book's major character," or variants thereof, is usually the last desperate refuge of the critical scoundrel, but Mahler pretty much pulls off the trick of anthropomorphizing New York, and the face that emerges is almost unrecognizable; certainly there's been some major plastic surgery since the 1970s, and not all of us find the stretched skin and the absence of worry lines in SoHo and the Village attractive.

There's no doubt that New York is safer, less broke, and more functional than it was back then. But it's impossible to read about the city that *Ladies and Gentlemen, the Bronx Is Burning* portrays so thrillingly without a little ache for something funkier.

You know I said that you should view with suspicion any book I'm recommending that sounds dull? Well, James Shapiro's *1599* isn't one of them, honestly. It's a brilliant book, riveting, illuminating, and original (by which I mean, of course, that I haven't read much like it, in all my years of devouring Shakespeare biographies), full of stuff with which you want to amaze, enlighten, and educate your friends. 1599 was the year Shakespeare polished off *Henry V*, wrote *As You Like It*, and drafted *Hamlet*. (I was partly attracted to Shapiro's book because I'd had a similarly productive 2006—although, unlike Shakespeare, I'm more interested in quality than quantity, possibly because I've got one eye on posterity.) Shapiro places these plays in their context while trying to piece together, from all available sources, Shakespeare's movements, anxieties, and interests. Both *Julius Caesar* and *Henry V* are shown to be more about England's conflict with Ireland than we had any hope of understanding without Shapiro's expert illumination; the section on *Hamlet* contains a long, lucid, and unfussy explanation of how Montaigne and his essays resulted in Hamlet's soliloquies. I'd say that *1599* has to be the first port of call now for anyone teaching or studying any of these four plays, but if you're doing neither of those things, it doesn't matter. The only thing you have to care about to love this book is how and why things get written.

The "why" is relatively straightforward: Shakespeare wrote for money. He had a wife, a new theater, and a large theater company to support, and there was a frightening amount of competition from other companies. The "how" is more elusive, although Shapiro does such a wonderful job of accumulating sources and inspirations that you don't really notice the absence of the man himself, who remains something of a mystery.

Claire Tomalin and James Shapiro take different paths to their writers: there is scholarship in Tomalin's book, of course, but she is more interested in the psychology of her subject, and in exercising her acute, sensitive critical skills than she is in history. Both books, though, are exemplary in their ability to deepen one's understanding for and appreciation of the work, in their delight in being able to point out what's going on in the lines on the page. We're lucky to have both of these writers at the top of their game in the here and now.

Robert Altman's *Nashville* is one of my favorite films—or, at least, I think it is. I haven't seen it in a while, and the last time I did, I noticed the longueurs more than I ever had before. Maybe the best thing to do with favorite films and books is to leave them be: to achieve such an exalted position means that they entered your life at exactly the right time, in precisely the right place, and those conditions can never be re-created. Sometimes we want to revisit them in order to check whether they were really as good as we remember them being, but this has to be a suspect impulse, because what it presupposes is that we have more reason to trust our critical judgments as we get older, whereas I am beginning to believe that the reverse is true. I was eighteen when I saw *Nashville* for the first time, and I was electrified by its shifts in tone, its sudden bursts of feeling and meaning, its ambition, its occasional obscurity, even its pretensions. I don't think I'd ever seen an art movie before, and I certainly hadn't seen an art movie set in a world I recognized. So I came out of the cinema that night a slightly changed person, suddenly aware that there was a different way of doing things. None of that is going to happen again, but so what? And why mess with a good thing? Favorites should be left where they belong, buried somewhere deep in a past self.

Jan Stuart's *The Nashville Chronicles* is a loving account of the making of the film, and reading it was a good way of engaging with Altman's finest seven hours, or however long the thing was, without having to wreck it by watching it for a fourth or fifth time. And, in any case, *Nashville* is a film that relies on something other than script (which was thrown out of the window before shooting started) and conventional methods of filmmaking for its effects, so a book like this is especially valuable in helping us understand them. There was Altman's apparently haphazard casting—one actor was chosen when he came to another's house to give him guitar lessons, and Shelley Duvall was a student research-scientist before being co-opted into Altman's regular troupe. There was his famous *vérité* sound, which required the invention of a new recording system, and his reliance on improvisation, and his extraordinary handling of crowd scenes, which required all cast members to improvise at all times, just in case he should pick them out with the camera... Actually, there's no way this film can be no good. Forget everything I said! Revisit your favorites regularly!

It's nice to be back. ✶

MAY 2007

I have been listening to my iPod on "shuffle" recently, and, like everyone else who does this, I became convinced that my machine was exercising a will of its own. Why did it seem to play Big Star every third song? (All iPod users come to believe that their inanimate MP3 players have recondite but real musical tastes.) And how come, if you shuffle for long enough, the initial letters of the artists picked spell out the names of your children? Confused, as always, by this and most other matters, I remembered that an English magazine had extracted a book about the iPod in which the author had dealt with the very subject of the non-random shuffle. The book turned out to be Steven Levy's *The Perfect Thing*, a cute (of course) little (naturally) white (what else?) hardback history of the iPod—or at least, that is how it's billed. (The [British] subtitle of the book is "How the iPod became the defining object of the twenty-first century.") What the book is *actually* about, however—and maybe most books are these days—is my predilection for 1980s synth-pop.

I am not speaking metaphorically here. In an early chapter of the book, Mr. Levy describes, for reasons too complicated to explain, how a fellow writer was caught listening to "a pathetic Pet Shop Boys tune, the sort of thing Nick Hornby would listen to on a bad day." Now, I'm almost certain that this is supposed to be me, even though I don't recognize my own supposed musical tastes. (The Pet Shop Boys are a bit too groovy for my liking, and their songs don't have enough guitar on them.) I am relieved to hear, however, that I have good days and bad days, which at least opens up the possibility that on a good day I might be listening to something a little more au courant—Nirvana, say, or early Britney Spears.

Aren't people *rude*? It's something I don't think one can ever get used to, if you live a semipublic life—and writers, by definition, can never go any more than semipublic because not enough people are interested in what we do. It doesn't happen often—I don't seem to have cropped up in Orwell's essays, for example—but when it does, it's always a shock, seeing yourself in a book, listening to music you don't listen to (not, as Jerry Seinfeld said, that there's anything wrong with the Pet Shop Boys), put there by someone you have never met and who, therefore, knows nothing about you… And what has the band done to deserve this, to borrow one of their song titles? They were mentioned in my newspaper this morning, in a diary piece about their plans for a musical adaptation of Francis Wheen's brilliant biography of Marx; that, like so much they have done, sounds pretty cool to me. Unnerved, I skipped straight to his chapter about whether the shuffle feature is indeed random. It is, apparently.

The annoying thing about reading is that you can never get the job done. The other day I was in a bookstore flicking through a book called something like *1001 Books You Must Read Before You Die* (and, without naming names, you should be aware that the task set by the title is by definition impossible, because at least four hundred of the books suggested would kill you anyway), but reading begets reading—that's sort of the point of it, surely?—and anybody who never deviates from a set list of books is intellectually dead anyway. Look at the trouble Orwell's essays got me into. First of all there's his long and interesting consideration of Henry Miller's *Tropic of Cancer,* a novel that I must confess I had written off as dated smut; George has persuaded me otherwise, so I bought it. And then, while discussing the Orwell essays with a friend, I was introduced to Norman Lewis's astounding *Naples '44,* a book which, my venerable friend seemed to be suggesting, was at least a match for any of Orwell's nonfiction. (Oh, why be coy? My venerable friend was Stephen Frears, still best known, I like to think, as the director of *High Fidelity,* and an endless source of good book recommendations.)

I think he's right. The trouble with the Orwell essays is that they are mostly of no earthly use to anyone now—and this is perhaps the first book I've read since I started this column that I can't imagine any American of my acquaintance ploughing through. If you really feel you need to read several thousand words about English boys' weeklies of the 1930s, then I wouldn't try and stop you, but these pieces are mostly top-drawer journalism, Tom Wolfe, as it were, rather than Montaigne; Orwell is dissecting bodies that actually gave up the ghost eighty-odd years ago. This problem becomes particularly acute when he's dissecting bodies that gave up the ghost ninety or a hundred years ago. "In 1920, when I was about seventeen, I probably knew the whole of [A. E. Housman's] *A Shropshire Lad* by heart. I wonder how much impression *A Shropshire Lad* makes at this moment on a boy of the same age and more or less the same cast of mind? No doubt he has heard of it and even glanced into it; it might strike him as rather cheaply clever—probably that would be about all."

If you try and do Orwell the service of treating him as a contemporary writer, someone whose observations make as much sense to us now as they did in 1940, then that last sentence is merely hilarious—how many bright seventeen-year-old boys do you know who might have glanced into *A Shropshire Lad* and found it "cheaply clever"? So even when Orwell is talking about things that he knows haven't lasted, he is unable to anticipate their complete and utter disappearance from the cultural landscape. How was he to know that the average seventeen-year-old boy is more likely to have sampled his sister's kidney than Housman's poetry? It wasn't his fault. He couldn't see 50 Cent coming.

An essay titled "Bookshop Memories," about Orwell's experiences working in a secondhand bookstore, notes that the three best-selling authors were Ethel M. Dell, Warwick Deeping, and Jeffrey Farnol. "Dell's novels, of course, are read solely by women"—well, we all knew that—"but by women of all kinds and ages and not, as one might expect, merely by wistful spinsters and the fat wives of tobacconists." Ah, those were the days, when popular novelists were able to rely on the fat wives of tobacconists for half their income. Times are much harder (and leaner) now. Many is the time that I've wished I could tell the size-zero wives of tobacconists that I didn't want their rotten money, but I have had to button my lip, regrettably. I have a large family to support.

One of the most bewildering lines comes in "Inside the Whale," the long essay about the state of literature, first published in 1940, that begins with the appreciation of Henry Miller. "To say 'I accept' in an age like our own is to say that you accept concentration-camps, rubber truncheons, Hitler, Stalin, bombs, aeroplanes, tinned food, machine-guns, putsches, purges, slogans, Bedaux belts, gas-masks, submarines, spies, provocateurs, press-censorship, secret prisons, aspirins, Hollywood films, and political murders." Is it possible to accept, say, tinned food, Hollywood films, and aspirin without accepting Stalin and Hitler? I'm afraid I am one of those cowards who would have happily invaded Poland if it meant getting hold of a couple of pills to alleviate a hangover. And what was wrong with tinned food, that all those guys banged on about it so much? (Remember Betjeman's poem "Slough"? "Come, bombs, and blow to smith-ereens / Those air-conditioned, bright canteens / Tinned fruit, tinned meat, tinned milk, tinned beans / Tinned minds, tinned breath.") It's true, of course, that fresh fruit is better for you. But one would hope that, with the benefit of hindsight, Orwell, Betjeman, and the rest would concede that Belsen and the purges ranked higher up the list of the mid-twentieth century's horrors than a nice can of peaches. Mind you, when in fifty years' time, students examine the intellectual journalism of the early twenty-first century, they will probably find more about the vileness of bloggers and reality television than they will about the destruction of the planet.

There are some brilliant lines. How about this, from Orwell's essay on Dickens: "What people always demand of a popular novelist is that he shall write the same book over and over again, forgetting that a man who would write the same book twice could not even write it once." There's a great little essay called "Books v. Cigarettes," although some will find his conclusion (books) controversial. And of course his prose is beyond reproach, muscular, readable, accessible.

Naples '44, however, is something else altogether. Norman Lewis, who lived to be ninety-five and who published his last travel book in 2002, was an intelligence officer for the Allies; what he found when he was posted to Naples beggared belief. The Neapolitans were starving—they had eaten all the fish in the aquarium, and just about every weed by the roadside. An estimated 42,000 of the city's 150,000 women had turned to prostitution. And yet there is so much in this short diary other than sheer misery, so many tones and flavors. You might wish to point out that Lewis wasn't one of the starving, and so accessing flavors wasn't a problem for him, but the variety and richness and strangeness of life in what remains one of the maddest and most neurotic cities in the world clearly demanded his attention. This is a long-winded way of saying that this book is, at times, unbearably sad, but it is also very funny and weird too. There are the doctors who specialize in the surgical restoration of virginity (although before you book your flights, ladies, you should check that they're still working), and there are the biannual liquefactions and solidifications of the blood of saints, the relative speeds of which presage either prosperity or poverty for the city. Vesuvius erupts in the middle of all this; and of course, there's a war going on—a war which is occasionally reminiscent of the one Tobias Wolff described in *In Pharaoh's Army.* It allows for strange, pointless, occasionally idyllic trips out into the countryside, and the enemy is all around but invisible.

My favorite character, one who comes to symbolize the logic of Naples, is Lattarullo, one of the four thousand or so lawyers in Naples unable to make a living. Much of his income before the war came from acting as an "uncle from Rome," a job which involved turning up at Neapolitan funerals and acting as a dignified and sober out-of-towner, in direct contrast to the frenzied and grief-stricken native relatives. Paying for an uncle from Rome to turn up showed a touch of class. During the war, however, Lattarullo was denied even this modest supplement because Rome was occupied, and travel was impossible. So even though everyone knew Roman uncles came from Naples, the appearance of a Roman uncle at a Neapolitan funeral before the liberation of Rome would have punctured the illusion, like a boom mic visible in a movie. This is Orwell via

Lewis Carroll, and if I read a better couple of hundred pages of nonfiction this year, I'll be a happy man.

If, at the moment, you happen to be looking for a book that makes you feel good about sex, though, then I should warn you that this isn't the one. There are too many devout Catholic wives selling themselves for a tin of fruit, and way too many sexual diseases. William Kennedy's *Ironweed* is beautiful—haunted and haunting, thoughtful and visceral. But, like *Naples '44*, it is entirely without aphrodisiacal qualities. The people are too sick, and drunk, and cold, but they try it on anyway, sometimes just so they can get to sleep the night in a deserted car full of other bums. None of this matters so much to me anymore. By the time you read this I will have turned fifty, so I can't reasonably expect very much more in that department anyway. But you—you're young, some of you. I don't want you to feel bad about your bodies. Yes, you will die, and your bodies will decay and rot way before then anyway. But you shouldn't feel bad about that just yet. Actually, on second thought, the truth is that *Ironweed* is exactly the sort of book you should be reading when you're young, and still robust enough to slough it off. And it's a truly terrible book to be reading in the last few months of your forties. Is this really all that's left? ✶

JUNE / JULY 2007

This morning, while shaving, I listened to a reading from Anna Politkovskaya's *A Russian Diary* on BBC Radio 4. It was pretty extraordinary—brutal and brave (Politkovskaya, as I'm sure you know, was murdered, presumably because of her determination to bring some of her country's darkest wrongdoings into the light). And its depiction of a country where the state is so brazenly lawless is so bizarre that I couldn't help but think of fiction—specifically, a novel I had just abandoned by a senior, highly regarded literary figure. Politkovskaya's words reminded me that the reason I gave up on the novel was partly because I became frustrated with the deliberate imprecision of its language, its obfuscation, its unwillingness to give up its meaning quickly and easily. This, of course, is precisely what some people prize in a certain kind of fiction, and good luck to them. I can't say that this kind of ambiguity is my favorite thing, and it's certainly not what I look for first in a novel, but I know that I would have missed out on an awful lot of good stuff if I wasn't prepared to tolerate a little incomprehension and attendant exasperation every now and again. In this novel, however, I found myself feeling particularly impatient. "A perfect day begins in death, in the semblance of death, in deep surrender," the novelist (or his omniscient narrator) tells us. Does it? Not for me it doesn't, pal. Unless, of course, death here means "a good night's sleep." Or "a strong cup of coffee." Maybe that's it? "Death" = "a strong cup of coffee" and "the semblance of death" = some kind of coffee substitute, like a Frappuccino? Then why doesn't he say so? There is no mistaking what the word *death* means in Politkovskaya's diaries, and once again I found myself wondering whether the complication of language is in inverse proportion to the size of the subject under discussion. Politkovskaya is writing about the agonies of a nation plagued by corruption, terrorism, and despotism; the highly regarded literary figure is writing about some middle-class people who are bored of their marriage. My case rests.

The highly regarded literary figure recently quoted Irwin Shaw's observation that "the great machines of the world do not run on fidelity," in an attempt to explain his views on matrimony, and though this sounds pretty good when you first hear it, lofty and practical all at the same time, on further reflection it starts to fall apart. If we are going to judge things on their ability to power the great machines of the world, then we will have to agree that music, charity, tolerance, and bacon-flavored potato chips, to name only four things that we prize here at the *Believer*, are worse than useless.

It wasn't just the opacity of the prose that led me to abandon the novel, however; I didn't like the characters who populated it much, either. They were all languidly middle-class, and they drank good wine and talked about Sartre, and I didn't want to know anything about them. This is entirely unreasonable of me, I accept that, but prejudice has to be an important part of our decision-making process when it comes to reading, otherwise we would become overwhelmed. For months I have been refusing to read a novel that a couple of friends have been urging upon me, a novel that received wonderful reviews and got nominated for prestigious prizes. I'm sure it's great, but I know it's not for me: the author is posh—posh English, which is somehow worse than posh American, even—and he writes about posh people, and I have taken the view that life is too short to spend any time worrying about the travails of the English upper classes. If you had spent the last half century listening to the strangled vows and the unexamined and usually very dim assumptions that frequently emerge from the mouths of a certain kind of Englishman, you'd feel entitled to a little bit of inverted snobbery.

I'm not sure, then, quite how I was persuaded to read *In My Father's House*,

Miranda Seymour's memoir about her extraordinary father and his almost demented devotion to Thrumpton Hall, the stately home he came to inherit. George Seymour was a terrible snob, pathetically obsessed by the microscopic traces of blue blood that ran through his veins, comically observant of every single nonsensical English upper-class propriety—until he reached middle age, when he bought himself a motorbike and drove around England and Europe with a young man called Nick, with whom he shared a bedroom. Nick was replaced by Robbie, whom George called Tigger, after the A. A. Milne character; when Robbie shot himself in the head, a weeping George played the Disney song on a scratchy vinyl record at the funeral service. Actually, you can probably see why I was persuaded to read it: it's a terrific story, and Miranda Seymour is too good a writer not to recognize its peculiarities and its worth. Also, the same people who have been telling me to read the posh novel told me to read the posh memoir, and I felt that a further refusal would have indicated some kind of Trotskyite militancy that I really don't feel. It's more a mild distaste than a deeply entrenched worldview.

Miranda Seymour owns up to having inherited her father's snobbery, which meant that I was immediately put on the alert, ready to abandon the book and condemn the author to the legions of the unnameable, but there is nothing much here to send one to the barricades. There is one strange moment, however, a couple of sentences that I read and re-read in order to check that I wasn't missing the irony. When Seymour goes to visit some of her father's wartime friends to gather their recollections, she finds herself resenting what she perceives as their feelings of superiority; they saw active service and George Seymour didn't, and the daughter is defensive on the father's behalf. "I've plenty of reason to hate my father, but his achievement matches theirs. They've no cause to be disdainful. They fought for their country; he gave his life to save a house."

Where does one begin with this? Perhaps one should simply point out that George died in his bed (a bed within a bedroom within one of Britain's loveliest houses) at the age of seventy-one, so the expression "he gave his life" does not have the conventional meaning here; a more exact rendering would be something like "he put aside an awful lot of time…" It's a curious lapse in judgment, in an otherwise carefully nuanced book.

A couple of years ago, I wrote in this column about Michael Lewis's brilliant *Moneyball;* when I found during a recent trip to New York that Lewis had written a book about football, I was off to the till before you could say "Jackie Robinson." *The Blind Side* is very nearly as good, I think, which is saying something, seeing as *Moneyball* is one of the two or three best sports books I have ever read. It cleverly combines two stories, one personal, the other an account of the recent history of the game; Lewis explains how left tackle became the most remunerative position in the game, and then allows the weight of this history to settle on the shoulders of one young man, Michael Oher, currently at Ole Miss (I'm finding my effortless use of the American vernacular strangely thrilling). Oher is six feet six, weighs 330 pounds, and yet he can run hundreds of yards in fractions of seconds. He is, as he keeps being told, a freak of nature, and he is exactly what every football team in the U.S. is prepared to offer the earth for.

He has also had a life well beyond the realms of the ordinary, which makes his story—well, I'm afraid my knowledge of the terminology has already been exhausted, so I don't have the appropriate analogy—but in my sport we'd describe it as an open goal, and Lewis only has to tap the ball in from a couple of feet. I don't wish to diminish the author's achievement. Lewis scores with his customary brio, and the recognition of a good story is an enviable part of his talent. But who wouldn't want to read about a kid who was born to a crack-addict mother and part-raised in one of the poorest parts of one of America's poorest cities, Memphis, and ended up being adopted by a wealthy white Christian couple with their own private plane? This is material that provides the pleasures of both fiction and nonfiction. There's a compelling narrative arc, a glimpse into the lives of others, a wealth of information about and analysis of a central element of popular American culture. There's a touching central relationship, between Oher and his adoptive parents' young son, Sean Jr.; there is even a cheesy, never-say-die heroine, Oher's adoptive mother, Leigh Anne Tuohy, whose extraordinary determination to look after a boy not her own is Christian in the sense too rarely associated with the American South. This would make a great movie, although you'd need a lot of CGI to convince an audience of Michael Oher's speed and size.

The Blind Side is funny too. Michael's first game for his high school is

made distinctive by him lifting up his two-hundred-and-twenty-pound opponent and taking him through the opposition benches, across the cinder track
surrounding the pitch, and halfway across a neighboring field before he is
stopped by players and officials from both sides. (Oher had been irritated and
surprised by the opponent's trash-talking—he later told his coach he was going
to put the lippy kid back on his team bus.) And the formal interview between
Oher and an investigator from the NCAA, the organization whose job it is
to determine whether any illegal inducements have been offered to influence
a promising footballer's choice of college, is equally memorable. It's not just
Oher's attempts to list his brothers and sisters that baffle the investigator; it's the
opulence of his surroundings too. The Tuohys are Ole Miss alumni, desperate
for Michael to take the scholarship being offered by their alma mater, while
trying to avoid putting inappropriate pressure on him. But isn't Oher's whole
new life—the access to the jet, the new car, the pool, the exclusive private high
school—a form of inappropriate pressure? The baffled investigator eventually
decides not, but she is clearly perplexed by the atypicality of the arrangement.

Ian McEwan has hit that enviable moment that comes to a novelist only
very rarely: he has written himself into a position where everyone wants to read
his latest book *now, today,* before any other bastard comes along and ruins it.
He's genuinely serious and genuinely popular, in the U.K. at least, and in an age
where our tastes in culture are becoming ever more refined, and therefore ever
more fractured, he is almost single-handedly reviving the notion of a chattering
class by providing something that we can all chatter about. *On Chesil Beach* is,
for me, a return to top form after the unevenness of *Saturday.* It's unusual, on
occasions painfully real, and ultimately very moving.

Philip Larkin famously wrote that "Sexual intercourse began / In nineteen
sixty-three / (Which was rather late for me) / Between the end of the Chatterley
ban / And the Beatles' first LP." *On Chesil Beach* is set on a July night in 1962,
and sexual intercourse is about to begin for Edward and Florence, married that
afternoon, and painfully inexperienced. Edward wants it and Florence doesn't,
and that, pretty much, is where the drama and the pain of the novel lie.

On Chesil Beach is packed with all the period detail one might expect, and
occasionally it can feel as though McEwan's working off a checklist; there's the

bad food, the CND marches, the naïveté about the Soviet Union, the social-realist movies, the Beatles and the Stones... Hold on a minute. The Beatles and the Stones? "He played her 'clumsy but honourable' cover versions of Chuck Berry songs by the Beatles and the Rolling Stones." Well, not before July 1962 he didn't. (The sentence refers to the couple's courtship.) What's strange about this anachronism is that McEwan must, at some stage, have thought of the Larkin poem when he was writing this—it might even have inspired him in some way. So if the Beatles' first LP was released in the same year sexual intercourse was invented, what exactly was he playing her in the months leading up to July 1962? "Love Me Do" was released toward the end of that year, and there was nothing else recorded yet; the Stones, meanwhile, didn't produce anything until the following year. Does it matter? It didn't affect my enjoyment of the book, but I suspect that it does, a little. The Beatles really did belong to a different age, metaphorically and literally. I hereby offer my services as a full-time researcher.

On Chesil Beach is so short that it's actually hard to talk about without revealing more than you might want to know. You should read it, and be thankful that you grew up in a different age, where all matters sexual were a whole lot easier. Too easy, probably. Some of you younger ones are probably having sex now, absentmindedly, while reading this. You probably don't even know that you're having sex. You'll look down or up at the end of this paragraph and think, Eeek! Who's that? Well, that can't be right, can it? Surely things have gone too far the other way, if that's what's happening? I'm off to read some Jane Austen. ✶

AUGUST 2007

BOOKS BOUGHT:

* *The Ha-Ha*—Jennifer Dawson
* *Poppy Shakespeare*—Clare Allan
* *Yo Blair!*—Geoffrey Wheatcroft
* *Salmon Fishing in the Yemen*—Paul Torday
* *The Myth of the Blitz*—Angus Calder
* *This Book Will Save Your Life*—A. M. Homes

BOOKS READ:

* *Across the Great Divide: The Band and America*—Barney Hoskyns
* *Stasiland: Stories from Behind the Berlin Wall*—Anna Funder
* *Yo Blair!*—Geoffrey Wheatcroft
* *The Ha-Ha*—Jennifer Dawson
* *Coming Through Slaughter*—Michael Ondaatje
* *Poppy Shakespeare*—Clare Allan

On the face of it, the Stasi and the Band had very little in common. Closer examination, however, reveals the East German secret police force and the brilliant genre-fusing Canadian rock group to be surprisingly… Oh, forget it. I don't have to do that stuff in this column—or at least, if I do, nobody has ever told me. It goes without saying that the two wires that led me to the books by Barney Hoskyns and Anna Funder came from different sockets in the soul, and power completely different, you know, electrical/spiritual devices: *Stasiland* and *Across the Great Divide* are as different as a hair dryer and a Hoover. Yes. That's it. I'm the first to admit it when my metaphors don't work, but I'm pretty sure I pulled that one off. (I wish I'd hated them both. Then I could have said that one sucks, and the other blows. Regrettably, they were pretty good.)

The journey/length of cable that led me to the Hoskyns book began a couple of years ago, when I was just about to walk out of a music club. We'd gone to see the support act, but the headliners had this amazing young guitar player called James Walbourne, an unearthly cross between James Burton, Peter Green, and Richard Thompson; Walbourne's fluid, tasteful, beautiful solos drop the jaw, stop the heart, and smack the gob, all at the same time. We still walked out of the club, because we really wanted a pizza, and pizza always beats art, but I was determined to track him down and make sure that I hadn't been imagining it all. I've seen him a few times since—when he's not playing with the Pernice Brothers or Son Volt or Tift Merritt, he's been appearing with his own band in a pub not far from me—and he's recently taken to playing a cover of the Band's "Ain't No More Cane," a song off *The Basement Tapes*. So then I had a fit on the Band—I have pretty much listened to every single track on the box set that came out last year—and then I noticed that I had an unread 1993 biography on my shelves. Before long I was being taken from Stratford, Ontario, to the Mississippi Delta and on to Los Angeles.

In one crucial way, writing about the Band is difficult: Greil Marcus got there first, in his book *Mystery Train,* and Marcus's essay is still the best piece of rock criticism I have ever read. (There are thirty-seven separate index entries for Greil Marcus in *Across the Great Divide,* and yet Hoskyns still feels it necessary to get sniffy about a couple of factual errors that Marcus made in his writings. You'd have hoped that Hoskyns could have been more forgiving, seeing as how his own book would have been a lot shorter without Marcus's help.) And yet there's something irresistible about the story too, because it's the story of white rock and roll. Here's Robbie Robertson, aged sixteen, getting on a train and heading down to the American South from Canada, to play R&B covers with Ronnie Hawkins's Hawks; Robertson's pilgrimage from white Sleepytown to the birthplace of the blues was the one that millions of teenage guitarists made, in their heads at least, at the beginning of the sixties. (It may even still go on. I would imagine that James Walbourne has made exactly the same trip, and maybe not even symbolically. He lives in Muswell Hill, North London, which is sort of like Canada.) And here's Robbie Robertson, in his early thirties, bombed out of his head on cocaine, living with Martin Scorsese in a house on Mulholland Drive that had blackout covers on the windows so that the residents no longer knew or cared whether it was day or night. That, in a nutshell, is what happened to our music between the early sixties and the mid-seventies: the geographical shift, the decadence, and the obliviousness to the outside world. Thank heaven for punk. And Abba.

I may be the only person in the world who has just read *Across the Great Divide* after seeing James Walbourne play "Ain't No More Cane." I can't imagine I'm the only person in the world who has read *Stasiland* after seeing *The Lives of Others* in my local cinema. I left that film wanting to know more about the chilling weirdness of life in the old GDR, and Anna Funder's brilliant book is full of stories that not only leave you open-mouthed at the sheer lunatic ambition of the totalitarian experiment but break your heart as well, just as they should do.

Funder reviewed *The Lives of Others* in a recent issue of *Sight and Sound,* and argued persuasively that, while it was a great film on its own terms, it bore little resemblance to life as it was lived behind the Berlin Wall: the movie was too bloodless, and there never was and never could be such a thing as an heroic Stasi officer. Her book is personal and anecdotal: she tells the stories she has come across, some of which she discovers when she places an advertisement in a local newspaper in an attempt to contact former Stasi members. This approach is perfect, because you don't need anything other than personal anecdote to tell a kind of truth about the Stasi, because they knew everybody—that was the point of them. So who wouldn't have a story to tell?

I'd be doing you and the book a disservice if I recommended it to you simply as an outstanding work of contemporary history. I'm guessing that a fair few of you are writers, and one of the unexpected strengths of this book is the implausibility of the narratives Funder unearths—narratives that nevertheless, and contrary to all perceived wisdom, seem to resonate, and illuminate, and illustrate even greater truths. Frau Paul gives birth to a desperately sick baby just as the Wall is being built; one morning she wakes up to find that it has separated her from the only hospital that can help her son. Doctors smuggle him, without her permission, over the Wall. He lives in the hospital for the next five years.

Frau Paul is given only agonizingly sporadic permission to visit her child, and she and her husband decide, perhaps not unnaturally, that they will try to escape to West Berlin. Their plans are discovered; Frau Paul refuses to cut a deal that will endanger a young man in the West who has been helping her and others. She is sent to prison. Her son is nearly five years old when he is finally allowed home. (It's interesting, incidentally, that the central characters in *The Lives of Others* are all childless. I suspect children tend to limit the range of moral choices.)

There are, it seems, stories like this on every street corner of the old East Germany, insane stories, stories that defy belief and yet unfold with a terrible logic, and Anna Funder's weary credulity, and her unerring eye for the unimaginable varieties of irony to be found in a world like this, make her the perfect narrator. Believe it or not, there are some funny bits.

It was our prime minister's tenth anniversary recently, and by the time you get to read this he'll be gone anyway, so it seemed appropriate to give him a little bit of consideration. Not much—Geoffrey Wheatcroft's polemic is only 120-odd pages long—but the time it took me to read it was precisely the sort of time I wanted to give him. The title refers to your president's form of address during the disastrously revealing conversation Blair had with Bush during the G8 meeting in Russia last year, when an open mic revealed the true nature of their relationship to be something closer to the one between Jeeves and Bertie Wooster than that between two world leaders, although obviously Jeeves was less servile.

Wheatcroft overstates his case a little: however much you hate Blair, it's hard to hear that his soppy Third Way contains undertones of the Third Reich. But when you see the crimes and misdemeanors piled up like this, it's hard to see how we managed to avoid foreign invaders intent on regime change. It's not just Iraq and the special relationship with the U.S., although it's quite clear now that this is how Blair will be remembered. It's the sucking up to the rich and powerful (Berlusconi, Cliff Richard), the freeloading, the pathetic little lies, the broken promises, the apparent absence of any sort of conviction, beyond the conviction of his own rectitude. This book introduced me to a very handy word, *antinomian*. (Oh, come on. Give me a break. I can't know everything. Where would I put it? And think of all the other hundreds of words I've used in this column.) You are antinomian, apparently, when your own sense of self-righteousness allows you to do anything, however mean or vicious or morally bankrupt that thing might appear to be. It's been a while, one suspects, since this word could be legitimately applied to a world leader; even Nixon and Kissinger may have slept uneasily for a couple of nights after they bombed Cambodia.

Here is the best definition of a good novel I have come across yet—indeed, I suspect that it might be the only definition of a good novel worth a damn. A good novel is one that sends you scurrying to the computer to look at pictures of prostitutes on the internet. And as Michael Ondaatje's *Coming Through Slaughter* is the only novel I have ever read that has made me do this, I can confidently assert that *Coming Through Slaughter* is, ipso facto, the best novel I have ever read.

Regrettably, the pictures in question are by E. J. Bellocq, a central character in *Coming Through Slaughter,* which means that they have a great deal of redeeming cultural import (Susan Sontag wrote a brilliant introduction to a published collection of his work); when I read a novel that allows me to ransack the internet for prostitute pictures willy-nilly, this column will be awarding a prize worth more than any genius grant.

I had been having some trouble with the whole idea of fiction, trouble that seemed in some way connected with my recent landmark birthday; it seemed to me that a lot of novels were, to be blunt, *made up,* and could teach me little about the world. Life suddenly seemed so short that I needed facts, and I needed them fast. I picked up *Coming Through Slaughter* in the spirit of kill or cure, and I was cured—I have only read fiction since I finished it. It's sort of ironic, then, that Ondaatje's novel ended up introducing me to an important photographer anyway. (Oh, come on. Give me a break, I can't know everyone. Where would I put them? And think of all the other... No, you're right. You can only use this argument seven or eight hundred times before it begins to sound pathetic.)

Coming Through Slaughter, Ondaatje's first novel, is an extraordinary, and extraordinarily beautiful, piece of mythmaking, a short, rich imagining of the life of Buddy Bolden, a New Orleans cornettist widely regarded as one of the founders of jazz. It seems to me as though anybody who has doubts about the value of fiction should read this book: it leaves you with the sort of ache that nonfiction can never provide, and provides an intensity and glow that, it seems to me, are the unique product of a singular imagination laying its gauze over the brilliant light of the world. Ondaatje writes about the music wonderfully well: you couldn't ask for anyone better to describe the sound of the crack that must happen when one form is being bent too far out of shape in an attempt to form something else. And Bolden's madness—he is supposed to have collapsed during a carnival procession—provides endless interesting corridors for Ondaatje to wander around in. I am still thinking about this novel, remembering the heat it threw off, weeks after finishing it.

I am a literal-minded and simple soul, so since then I have read nothing but novels about mentally ill people. If it worked once, I reasoned, then there's no reason why it shouldn't work every time, and I was right. I have now taken a broad enough sample, and I can reveal that nobody has ever written a bad novel about insanity.

This is strange, if you think about it. You'd think the subject would give all sorts of people disastrous scope to write indulgent, carefully fucked-up prose asking us to think about whether the insane are actually more sane than the rest of us. Both Jennifer Dawson's *The Ha-Ha* and Clare Allan's *Poppy Shakespeare* miraculously avoid this horrible cliché; to crudify both of these terrific books, the line they take is that people suffering from a mental illness are more mentally ill than people who are not suffering from a mental illness. This, given the general use the subject is put to in popular culture, is something of a relief.

The Ha-Ha is a lost novel from 1961, recently championed by the English writer Susan Hill on her blog; *Poppy Shakespeare* was first published last year. Both are first novels, both are set in institutions, and both are narrated by young females attached to these institutions. *The Ha-Ha* is quieter, more conventional, partly because Jennifer Dawson's heroine is an Oxford graduate who speaks in a careful, if necessarily neurotic, Oxford prose. Clare Allan's N is a brilliant fictional creation whose subordinate clauses tumble over each other in an undisciplined, glorious rush of North London energy. I liked them both, but I loved *Poppy Shakespeare*. It's not often you finish a first novel by a writer and you are seized by the need to read her second immediately. Of course, by the time her second comes out, I'll have forgotten all about the first. But today, the will is there.

Anyway, hurrah for fiction! Down with facts! Facts are for the dull, and the straight, and the old! You'll never find out anything about the world through facts! I might, however, have a look at this Brian Clough biography I've just been sent. Football doesn't count, does it? ✱

SEPTEMBER 2007

BOOKS BOUGHT:

* ★ *Skellig*—David Almond
* ★ *Clay*—David Almond
* ★ *Tom's Midnight Garden*—Philippa Pearce
* ★ *Queuing for Beginners: The Story of Daily Life from Breakfast to Bedtime*
  —Joe Moran
* ★ *The Road*—Cormac McCarthy
* ★ *Better: A Surgeon's Notes on Performance*—Atul Gawande
* ★ *The Rights of the Reader*—Daniel Pennac

BOOKS READ:

* ★ *Skellig*—David Almond
* ★ *Clay*—David Almond
* ★ *Sharp Teeth*—Toby Barlow
* ★ *The Road*—Cormac McCarthy
* ★ *The Brambles*—Eliza Minot
* ★ *Queuing for Beginners*—Joe Moran
* ★ *American Born Chinese*—Gene Luen Yang

I had all sorts of clever introductions to this month's column written in my head, opening paragraphs that would have provoked and inspired and maybe even amused one or two of you, if you were in a really good mood. When I read the Eliza Minot novel, I started working up this riff about the joys of uncannily accurate impersonation; when I read the David Almond novels, I was going to tell you all to abandon adult fiction and turn to books written for kids and teenagers. And then I read the Cormac McCarthy novel, and they all seemed inappropriate, like trying to tell New Yorkers about my news first on September 11, 2001.

As you probably know by now—and more than eight million of you voted for it in the Believer Book Award—*The Road* may well be the most miserable book ever written, and God knows there's some competition out there. As you probably know by now, it's about the end of the world. Two survivors of the apocalypse, a man and his young son, wander through the scarred gray land-scape foraging for food, and trying to avoid the feral gangs who would rather kill them and eat them than share their sandwiches with them. The man spends much of the book wondering whether he should shoot his son with their last remaining bullet, just to spare him any further pain. Sometimes they find unex-pected caches of food and drink. Sometimes they find shriveled heads, or the remains of a baby on a barbecue. Sometimes you feel like begging the man to use his last bullet on you, rather than the boy. The boy is a fictional creation, after all, but you're not. You're really suffering. Reading *The Road* is rather like attending the beautiful funeral of someone you love who has died young. You're happy that the ceremony seems to be going so well, and you know you'll remember the experience for the rest of your life, but the truth is that you'd rather not be there at all.

What do we think about when we read a novel this distressing? *The Road* is a brilliant book, but it is not a complicated one, so it's not as if we can distract ourselves with contemplation; you respond mostly with your gut rather than your mind. My wife, who read it just before I did, has vowed to become more practical in order to prepare herself for the end of the world; her lack of culinary imagination when handed a few wizened animal gizzards and some old bits of engine has left her with the feeling that she'd be an inadequate mother if worse comes to worst. And I ended up thinking about those occasional articles about the death of the novel—almost by definition, seeing as our planet hasn't yet suffered this kind of fatal trauma, you cannot find a nonfiction book as compre-hensively harrowing or as provocative as this. Most of the time, however, you just experience an agonizing empathy, especially, perhaps, if you are a parent, and you end up wondering what you can possibly do with it, apart from carry it around with you for days afterward. "It is also a warning," one of the reviews quoted on the back of my paperback tells me. Well, after reading this, I defi-nitely won't be pushing the button that brings about the global holocaust.

It is important to remember that *The Road* is a product of one man's imagination: the literary world has a tendency to believe that the least consoling worldview is The Truth. (How many times have you read someone describe a novel as "unflinching," in approving terms? What's wrong with a little flinch every once in a while?) McCarthy is true to his own vision, which is what gives his novel its awesome power. But maybe when Judgment Day does come, we'll surprise each other by sharing our sandwiches and singing "Bridge over Troubled Water," rather than by scooping out our children's brains with spoons. Yes, it's the job of artists to force us to stare at the horror until we're on the verge of passing out. But it's also the job of artists to offer warmth and hope and maybe even an escape from lives that can occasionally seem unendurably drab. I wouldn't want to pick one job over the other—they both seem pretty important to me. And it's quite legitimate, I think, not to want to read *The Road*. There are some images now embedded in my memory that I don't especially want there. Don't let anyone tell you that you have a *duty* to read it.

So here's the introduction about mimicry. It goes something like this. Ahem. Believe it or not, I am not a good mimic. I can only do one impersonation, an actually pretty passable stab at Mick Jagger, *but only as he appears in the* Simpsons *episode in which Homer goes to rock and roll fantasy camp*. It's not much, I admit, but it's mine, and when I pull it off, my children laugh—simply, I guess, because it sounds so like the original, rather than because I am doing anything funny. (I never do anything funny.) Some of the considerable pleasure I drew from Eliza Minot's *The Brambles* was her enviable ability to capture family life with such precision that… Well, you don't want to laugh, exactly, because *The Brambles* is mostly about how three adult siblings cope with a dying father, but there is something about Minot's facility that engenders a kind of childlike delight: How did she *do* that? Do it again! One conversation in particular, in which a mother is attempting to explain the mysteries of death to her young children, is so loving in its depiction of the mess you can get into in these situations, and so uncannily authentic, that you end up resenting the amount of inauthentic claptrap you consume during your reading life. *The Brambles* isn't perfect—there's a plot twist that ends up overloading the narrative without giving the book anything much in return—but Eliza Minot is clearly on the verge of producing something special.

It's been a pretty significant reading month, now that I come to think about it. I read a modern classic that took away whatever will to live I have left, discovered a couple of younger writers, and then came across an unfamiliar genre that, I suspect, will prove of great significance for both my reading and my writing life. I recently completed my first novel for or possibly just about young adults, and my U.S. publishers asked me to go to Washington D.C., to read from and talk about the book to an audience of librarians. One of the writers on the panel with me was a guy called David Almond, whose work I didn't know; a couple of days before I met him, his novel *Skellig* was voted the third greatest children's book of the last seventy years. (Philip Pullman's *Northern Lights* was top, and Philippa Pearce's *Tom's Midnight Garden* came in second.)

I read *Skellig* on the plane, and though I have no idea whether it's the third greatest children's book of the last seventy years, I can tell you that it's one of the best novels published in the last decade, and I'd never heard of it. Have you? *Skellig* is the beautifully simple and bottomlessly complicated story of a boy who finds a sick angel in his garage, a stinking, croaking creature who loves Chinese takeaways and brown ale. Meanwhile, Michael's baby sister lies desperately sick in a hospital, fluttering gently between life and death.

The only problem with reading *Skellig* at an advanced age is that it's over before you know it; a twelve-year-old might be able to eke it out, spend a little longer in the exalted, downbeat world that Almond creates. *Skellig* is a children's book because it is accessible and because it has children at the center of its narrative, but, believe me, it's for you too, because it's for everybody, and the author knows it. At one point, Mina, Michael's friend, a next-door neighbor who is being homeschooled, picks up one of Michael's books and flicks through it.

> "Yeah, looks good," she said. "But what's the red sticker for?"
>
> "It's for confident readers," I said. "It's to do with reading age."
>
> "And what if other readers wanted to read it?… And where would William Blake fit in?… 'Tyger! Tyger! Burning bright / In the forests of the night.' Is that for the best readers or the worst readers? Does it need a good reading age?… And if it was for the worst readers would the best readers not bother with it because it was too stupid for them?"

Now that I come to think about it, Mina's observations might well summarize what this column has been attempting to say all along.

For the first time in the last three or four years, I read two books in a row by the same author, and though *Clay* isn't quite as elegant as *Skellig,* it's still extraordinary, a piece of pre-Christian mythmaking set in the northeast of England in the late '60s. And suddenly, I'm aware that there may well be scores of authors like David Almond, people producing masterpieces that I am ignorant of because I happen to be older than the intended readership. Is *The Road* better than *Skellig*? That wouldn't be a very interesting argument. But when I'd finished *Clay* I read an adult novel, a thriller, that was meretricious, dishonest, pretentious, disastrously constructed, and garlanded with gushing reviews; in other words, the best readers had spoken.

Meanwhile, the hits just kept on coming. Gene Luen Yang's *American Born Chinese* is a clever, crisply drawn graphic novel about the embarrassment of almost belonging; Toby Barlow's *Sharp Teeth* is a novel about werewolves in Los Angeles, and it's written in blank verse, and it's tremendous. I can't remember now if I've ever cried wolf, as it were, and recommended other blank-verse werewolf novels—probably I have. Well, forget them all, because this is the one.

I was sent a proof copy of *Sharp Teeth,* and when I saw it, I wished it well, but couldn't imagine actually reading it, what with it being a blank-verse novel about werewolves and all. But I looked at the first page, got to the bottom of it, turned it over, read the second page, and... You get the picture, anyway. You're all smart people, and you know the conventional way to get through a book. All I'm saying is that my desire to persist took me by surprise.

I had suspected that *Sharp Teeth* might not be serious—that it would turn out to be a satire about the film industry, for example (sharp teeth, L.A., agents, producers, blah blah). But the beauty of the book is that it's deadly serious; like David Almond, Toby Barlow takes his mythical creatures literally, and lets the narrative provide the metaphor. It's stomach-churningly violent in places (they don't mess around, werewolves, do they?), and tender, and satisfyingly complicated: there's an involved plot about rival gangs that lends the book a great deal of noir cool. The blank verse does precisely what Barlow must have hoped it would do, namely, add intensity without distracting, or affecting readability.

And it's as ambitious as any literary novel, because underneath all that fur, it's about identity, community, love, death, and all the things we want our books to be about. I'm not quite sure how Barlow can follow this, if he wants to. But there's every chance that *Sharp Teeth* will end up being clasped to the collective bosom of the young, dark, and fucked-up.

It seems years ago now that I dipped into Joe Moran's engaging *Queuing for Beginners: The Story of Daily Life from Breakfast to Bedtime.* Externally, I have only aged a month or so since I picked it up, but in the meantime I have endured an Altamont of the mind, and my soul feels five hundred years old. Post-McCarthy, it's hard to remember those carefree days when I could engross myself in anecdotes about the Belisha beacon, and short social histories of commuting and the cigarette break. (Eighty-nine percent of Englishmen smoked in 1949! And we were still a proper world power back then! My case rests.) And I suppose a sense of purpose and hope might return, slowly, if I read enough P. G. Wodehouse and sports biographies. I have nearly finished the Joe Moran, and I would very much like to read his final chapter about the duvet. But what's the point, really? There won't be duvets in the future, you know. And if there are, they will be needed to cover the putrefying bodies of our families. Is there anything funny on TV? ✶

OCTOBER 2007

The story so far: I have written a young-adult novel, and on a trip to Washington, D.C., to promote it, I met a load of librarians and other assorted enthusiasts who introduced me to a magical new world that I knew nothing about. I really do feel as though I've walked through the back of a wardrobe into some parallel universe, peopled by amazing writers whom you never seem to read about on books pages, or who never come up in conversations with literary friends. (The truth, I suspect, is that these writers are frequently written about on books pages, and I have never bothered to read the reviews; come to think of it, they probably come up frequently in conversations with literary friends, and I have never bothered to listen to anything these friends say.)

It was in D.C. that I met David Almond, whose brilliant book *Skellig* started me off on this YA jag; and it was in D.C. that Francesca Lia Block's *Weetzie*

Bat, first published in 1989, was frequently cited as something that started something, although to begin with, I wasn't sure what *Weetzie Bat* was, or even if the people talking about it were speaking in a language I understood, so I can't, unfortunately, tell you what *Weetzie Bat* is responsible for. When I got home, I bought it from Amazon (it doesn't seem to be available in the U.K.), and a few days later I received a very tiny paperback, 113 large-print pages long and about three inches high, and suspiciously, intimidatingly pink. Pink! And gold! The book is so short that you really don't need to be seen with it on public transport, but I wouldn't have cared anyway, because it's beautiful, and I would have defended its honor against any football hooligan who wanted to snigger at me.

Weetzie Bat is, I suppose, about single mothers and AIDS and homosexuality and loneliness, but that's like saying that "Desolation Row" is about Cinderella and Einstein and Bette Davis. And actually, when I was trying to recall the last time I was exposed to a mind this singular, it was Dylan's book *Chronicles* that I thought of—not because Block thinks or writes in a similar way, and she certainly doesn't write or think about similar things, but because this kind of originality in prose is very rare indeed. Most of the time we comprehend the imagination and intellect behind the novels we read, even when that intellect is more powerful than our own—you can admire and enjoy Philip Roth, for example, but I don't believe that anyone has ever finished *American Pastoral* and thought, Where the hell did that come from? *Weetzie Bat* is not *American Pastoral* (and it's not "Desolation Row"—or *Great Expectations,* while we're at it), but it's genuinely eccentric, and picking it up for the first time is like coming across a chocolate fountain in the middle of the desert. You might not feel like diving in, but you would certainly be curious about the decision-making process of the person who put it there.

Weetzie Bat is a young woman, and she lives in a Day-Glo, John Waters–camp version of Los Angeles. Eventually she meets the love of her life, whose name is My Secret Agent Lover Man, and they have a baby called Cherokee, and they adopt another one called Witch Baby, and… You know what? A synopsis isn't really going to do this book justice. If you've never heard of it (and of the six people questioned in the Spree offices, only one knew what I was talking about), and you want to spend about eighty-three minutes on an entirely different planet, then this is the book for you.

I read *Tom's Midnight Garden* because it finished one place above *Skellig* in a list of the greatest Carnegie Medalists of all time. (Phillipa Pearce's classic came runner-up to Philip Pullman. I'm sure the Pullman is great, but it will be a while before I am persuaded that sprites and hobbits and third universes are for me, although I'm all for the death of God.) Like everything else in this genre, apparently, it is a work of genius, although unlike *Weetzie Bat* or *Skellig*, it is unquestionably a story for children, and at the halfway mark, I was beginning to feel as though I might finish it without feeling that my life had been profoundly enriched. I mean, I could see that it was great and so on, but I was wondering whether my half century on the planet might be cushioning me from the full impact. But at the end of the book—and you've been able to see the twist coming from miles away, yet there's not a damned thing you can do to stop it from slaying you—I'm not ashamed to say that I cr... Actually, I am ashamed to say that. It's a book about a kid who finds a magic garden at the back of his aunt's house, and there's no way a grown man should be doing that.

They've been very disorienting, these last few weeks. I see now that dismissing YA books because you're not a young adult is a little bit like refusing to watch thrillers on the grounds that you're not a policeman or a dangerous criminal, and as a consequence, I've discovered a previously ignored room at the back of the bookstore that's filled with masterpieces I've never heard of, the YA equivalents of *The Maltese Falcon* and *Strangers on a Train*. Weirdly, then, reading YA stuff now is a little like being a young adult way back then: Is this Vonnegut guy any good? What about Albert Camus? Anyone ever heard of him? The world suddenly seems a larger place.

And there's more to this life-changing D.C. trip. While I was there, I learned about something called the Alex Awards, a list of ten adult books that the Young Adult Library Services Association believes will appeal to younger readers, and I became peculiarly—perhaps inappropriately—excited by the idea. Obviously this award is laudable and valuable and all that, but my first thought was this: You mean, every year someone publishes a list of ten adult books that are compelling enough for teenagers? In other words, a list of ten books *that aren't boring*?

Let me at it. I bought two of this year's nominees, Michael D'Orso's *Eagle Blue* and Ron Rash's *The World Made Straight,* having noticed that another of the ten was Michael Lewis's brilliant book about your football, *The Blind Side: Evolution of a Game,* and a fourth was David Mitchell's *Black Swan Green,* which I haven't read but which friends love. Whoever compiled this list knew what they were talking about. Who else might have won an Alex Award? Dickens, surely, for *Great Expectations* and *David Copperfield,* Donna Tartt, for *The Secret History,* Dodie Smith's *I Capture the Castle,* probably *Pride and Prejudice* and *Le Grand Meaulnes. This Boy's Life,* certainly, and *The Liar's Club,* Roddy Doyle for *Paddy Clarke Ha Ha Ha…* In other words, if a book couldn't have made that list, then it's probably not worth reading.

Like every other paperback, Rash's book comes elaborately decorated with admiring quotes from reviews. Unlike every other paperback, however, his Alex nomination gave me confidence in them. "A beautifully rendered palimpsest," said *BookPage,* and I'd have to say that this wouldn't entice me, normally. You can see how a book could be a beautifully rendered palimpsest and yet somehow remain on the dull side. But the Alex allowed me to insert the words *and not boring* at the end of the quote. "Graceful, conscientious prose," said the *Charlotte Observer—and yet not boring.* "Rash writes with beauty and simplicity, understanding his characters with a poet's eye and heart and telling their tales with a poet's tongue, *and not boring people rigid while he does it,"* said William Gay, almost. You see how it works? It's fantastic.

And *The World Made Straight* really is engrossing—indeed, the last devastating fifty-odd pages are almost too compelling. You want to look away, but you can't, and as a consequence you have to watch while some bad men get what was coming to them, and a flawed, likable man gets what you hoped he might avoid. It's a satisfyingly complicated story about second chances and history and education and the relationships between parents and their children; it's violent, real, very well written, and it moves like a train.

When I was reading it, I ended up trying to work out how some complicated novels seem small, claustrophobic, beside the point, sometimes even without a point, while others take off into the fresh air that all the great books seem to breathe. There would be plenty of ways of turning this book, with its drug deals and its Civil War backstory, into something too knotty to live—sometimes writers are so caught up in being true to the realities of their characters' lives that they seem to forget that they have to be true to ours too, however tangentially. Rash, however, manages to convince you right from the first page that his characters and his story are going to matter to you, even if you live in North London, rather than on a tobacco farm in North Carolina; it's an enviable skill, and it's demonstrated here so confidently, and with such a lack of show, that you almost forget Rash has it until it's too late, and your own sense of well-being is bound up in the fate of the characters. Bad mistake, almost. There is some redemption here, but it's real redemption, hard-won and fragile, rather than sappy redemption. *The World Made Straight* was a fantastic introduction to the Not Boring Awards. I was, I admit, a little concerned that these books might be a little too uplifting, and would wear their lessons and morals on their T-shirts, but this one at least is hard and powerful, and it refuses to judge people that some moral guardians might feel need judging.

Lawrence Weschler's *Everything That Rises: A Book of Convergences* is never going to be nominated for an Alex, I fear. Not because it's boring—it isn't—but it's dense, and allusive, by definition, and Weschler's thinking is angular, subtle, dizzying. I feel as though I only just recently became old enough to read it, so you lot will have to wait twenty or thirty years.

It's worth it, though. You know you're in for a treat right from the very first essay, in which Weschler interviews the Ground Zero photographer Joel Meyerowitz about the uncanny compositional similarities between his photos and a whole slew of other works of art. How come Meyerowitz's shot of the devastated Winter Garden in the World Trade Center looks exactly like one of Piranesi's imaginary prisons? Is it pure coincidence? Or conscious design? It turns out, of course, to be something in between, something much more interesting than either of these explanations, and in working toward the truth of it, Weschler produces more grounded observations about the production of art than you'd believe possible, given the apparently whimsical nature of the exercise.

And he does this time and time again, with his "convergences." No, you think in the first few lines of every one of these essays. Stop it. You are not going to be able to persuade me that Oliver Sacks's *Awakenings* can tell us anything about the recent history of Eastern Europe. Or: no, Newt Gingrich and Slobodan Milosevic have nothing in common, and I won't listen to you trying to argue otherwise. You got away with it last time, but this is too much. And then by the end of the piece, you feel stupid for not noticing it yourself, and you want Gingrich tried for war crimes. It's an incredibly rewarding read, part magic, part solid but inspired close practical criticism, and the best book about (mostly) art I've come across since Dave Hickey's mighty *Air Guitar*. When I'd finished *Everything That Rises* I felt cleverer—not just because I knew more, but because I felt it would help me to think more creatively about other things. In fact, I've just pitched an idea to Weschler's editor about the weird chimes between the departure of Thierry Henry from Arsenal and the last days of Nicolae Ceausescu, but so far, no word. I think I might have blown his mind. ✶

NOVEMBER / DECEMBER 2007

BOOKS BOUGHT:

- ★ *The Pigman*—Paul Zindel
- ★ *The Bethlehem Murders*—Matt Rees
- ★ *The Dud Avocado*—Elaine Dundy
- ★ *Singled Out*—Virginia Nicholson

BOOKS READ:

- ★ *Holes*—Louis Sachar
- ★ *The Fall-Out: How a Guilty Liberal Lost His Innocence*—Andrew Anthony
- ★ *A Disorder Peculiar to the Country*—Ken Kalfus
- ★ *Seeing Is Forgetting the Name of the Thing One Sees: A Life of Contemporary Artist Robert Irwin*—Lawrence Weschler (unfinished)
- ★ *Bridge of Sighs*—Richard Russo (unfinished)

Weirdly, I have had sackfuls of letters from *Believer* readers recently asking me—*begging* me—to imagine my reading month as a cake. I can only imagine that young people in America find things easier to picture if they are depicted in some kind of edible form, and, though one cannot help but find this troubling, in the end I value literacy more highly than health; if our two countries were full of fat readers, rather than millions of Victoria Beckhams, then we would all be better off.

As luck would have it, this was the perfect month to institute the cake analogies. The reading cake divided neatly in half, with Andrew Anthony's *The Fall-Out* and Ken Kalfus's *A Disorder Peculiar to the Country*, both inspired by 9/11, on one plate, and Richard Russo's *Bridge of Sighs* and Lawrence Weschler's biography of the artist Robert Irwin on the other. Louis Sachar's *Holes*, meanwhile, is a kind of nonattributable, indivisible cherry on the top. There. Happy now? I'm warning you: it might not work that satisfactorily every month.

Andrew Anthony is a former five-a-side football teammate of mine (he still plays, but my hamstrings have forced me into a tragically premature retirement), a leggy, tough-tackling midfielder whose previous book was a little meditation on penalty kicks. I'm not underestimating Andy's talent when I say that this book is a top-corner thirty-yard volley out of the blue; you're always surprised, I suspect, when someone you know chiefly through sport produces a timely, pertinent, and brilliantly argued book about the crisis in left-liberalism, unless you share a season ticket with Noam Chomsky, or Eric Hobsbawm is your goalkeeper.

Anthony (and if he wants a future in this business, he's got to get himself a surname) is a few years younger than I, but we have more or less the same political memories and touchstones: the miners' strike in the mid-'80s, the earnest discussions about feminism that took place around the same time, the unexamined assumption that the U.S.A. was just as much an enemy of freedom as the Soviet Union. *Liberalism* was a dirty word, just as it is in your country now, but in our case it was because liberals were softies who didn't want to smash the State. As Anthony points out, we would have been in a right state if anyone had smashed the State—most of us were dependent on the university grants or the dole money that the State gave us, but never mind. We wanted it gone. These views were commonplace among students and graduates in the 1980s; there were at least as many people who wanted to smash the State as there were people who wanted to listen to Haircut 100.

Anthony took it further than most. He read a lot of unreadable Marxist pamphlets, and went to Nicaragua to help out the Sandinistas. (I would have gone, but what with one thing and another, the decade just seemed to slip by. And also: I know this keeps coming up, but what are you supposed to do when there's a revolution on and you're a season-ticket holder at a football club? Just, like, not go to the games?) He also had it tougher than most: Anthony was a working-class boy whose early childhood was spent in a house without a bath or an indoor toilet—a common enough experience in the Britain of the 1930s and '40s, much rarer in the '60s and '70s. The things you learn about your friends when they write memoirs, eh? He had every right to sign up for a bit of class warfare. In the wearyingly inevitable name-calling that has accompanied the publication of his book, he has been called a "middle-class twat."

Anthony, however, has concluded that the class war is now being fought only by the deluded and those so entrenched in the old ideologies that they have lost the power of reason. Which economic and political system would we really prefer? Which economic system would the working class prefer? Which economic system gives women the best chance of fulfilling their potential? Nobody, least of all Anthony, is suggesting that the free market should go unchecked—that's why liberalism still matters. Post-9/11, however, all that old-left aggression, now whizzing round with nowhere to go, is being spent not on Iran, or North Korea, or any of the other countries that make their citizens' lives a misery, but on the U.S.—not your hapless president, but the place, the people, the idea. Anthony threads some of the most egregious quotes from liberal-left writers throughout the book, and when you see them gathered together like that, these writers remind you of nothing so much as a bunch of drunks at closing time, muttering gibberish and swinging their fists at anyone who comes remotely close. "It has become painfully clear that most Americans simply don't get it," wrote one on September 13, 2001 (which, as Anthony points out, means that he would have had to have finished his copy exactly twenty-four hours after the Twin Towers fell). "Shock, rage and grief there have been aplenty. But any glimmer of recognition of why... the United States is hated with such bitterness... seems almost entirely absent." Yes, well. Give them another day or so to get over the shock and grief, and they're bound to come round to your way of thinking. "When I look at the U.K., it reminds me of the Nazi era," said another, apparently in all seriousness. "While the killing of innocent people is to be condemned without question, there is something rather repugnant about those who rush to renounce acts of terrorism," said a third. (Are these rushers more or less repugnant than the acts of terrorism themselves? It's hard to tell.) By the time you get to the Index on Censorship editorial asking us to "applaud Theo van Gogh's death as the marvellous piece of theatre it was," you start to wonder whether some of these people might actually be clinically insane. Van Gogh, you may remember, was the Dutch filmmaker who was shot eight times and had his throat cut to the spine in broad daylight on a busy Amsterdam street. His last words were "Can't we talk about this?" How's that for censorship?

Sometimes, the doublethink necessary to produce observations and opinions like these can only produce disbelieving laughter. My favorite comic moment is provided by a leading Afro-Caribbean commentator, writing about the Asian immigrants expelled from Uganda by Idi Amin: "The Asians from Uganda came to what can only be described as the most inhospitable country on earth." The country he's talking about, of course, is Britain, the place the Asians fled to. This cannot literally be true, can it? However fierce our self-loathing, we must concede that, in this context at least, we came in a disappointing second place in the Most Inhospitable Country on Earth Cup. Uganda, the country that took everything the Ugandan Asians owned and forced them out under threat of death, won the gold medal fair and square.

This book has inevitably been misunderstood by many on the left as some kind of revisionist right-wing diatribe. It's true that Anthony owns up to believing in causes and systems that slowly revealed themselves to have been unworthy of anyone's belief, but this is an inevitable part of getting older. But *The Fall-Out* is really about the slippery relativist slope that leads tolerant, intelligent people to defend the right of unintelligent and intolerant people to be intolerant in ways that cannot help but damage a free society; I think we do a lot more of that in the U.K. than you do over there, possibly because the only people who have any real belief in an idea of England—invariably right-wing bigots—quite rightly play no real part in our political debate. Where is our Sarah Vowell?

Ken Kalfus's *A Disorder Peculiar to the Country* made a wonderful accompaniment to Anthony's book. You've probably read it already, so you know that it's about the frighteningly unpleasant, horribly believable end of a marriage, set during and after 9/11. The book opens with both parties having reason to hope that the other might have been killed, either in the Twin Towers or on a plane, and if you haven't read it already, then you will know from my synopsis of this narrative fragment whether you have the stomach for the rest of the novel. If the book has caught you at just the right point in your relationship, you'll wolf it down. And just in case my wife bothers to read this: I'm not talking about us, darling. At the time I wrote these words we were getting on well. I wolfed it down for entirely literary reasons. *A Disorder Peculiar to the Country* is a sophisticated piece of adult entertainment (and by the way, that last word is

never used pejoratively or patronizingly in these pages), full of mess and paranoia and an invigorating viciousness, and it takes narrative risks, too—a rare
quality in a novel that is essentially naturalistic and uninterested in formal
experiment. Not all of them come off, but when they do—and the vertiginous
ending is one that does, in spades—you feel as though this is a fictional voice
that you haven't heard before.

So the plate with the other half of the cake on it was, like, an art plate, and
I have to say that I haven't eaten it all yet. I'm two-thirds of the way through
Russo's *Bridge of Sighs* and about halfway through Weschler's Robert Irwin
book, and my suspicion is that I won't finish the latter. I'm so confused about
the house rules that I'm really not sure whether I'm allowed to say that or not,
even though it's a simple statement of fact; harboring a suspicion that you won't
finish a book is almost certainly a crime, and I'm almost certainly looking at
a one-month suspension, but I don't care. My reluctance to finish the book is
nothing to do with Lawrence Weschler—it's because I enjoyed *Everything That
Rises,* his brilliant collection of essays, that I went out (or stayed in, anyway)
and bought this one. It's more that the subject of his book is a minimalist artist,
and when it comes to minimalist art, I am, I realize, an agnostic, maybe even
an atheist.

I use these words because it seems to me that it's something you either
believe in or you don't—a choice you're not really given with a Hockney or a
Hopper or a Monet. Here's Irwin (clearly a likable, thoughtful man, incidentally) on his late line paintings, which consist of several straight lines on an
orange background:

When you look… at them perceptually, you find that your eye ends up
suspended in midair, midspace or even midstride: time and space seem to
blend in the continuum of your presence. You lose your bearings for a moment.
You end up in a totally meditative state.

Well, what if that doesn't happen to you? I mean, it doesn't happen to
everyone, right? What are you left with? And it occurred to me that Catholics
could make a similar claim about what happens when you receive communion.
There's a big difference between the body of Christ and a bit of wafer.

I shall write about Russo's absorbing, painstakingly detailed novel next month, when I've finished it. But I kept muddling up Irwin with Russo's artist character Noonan—not because the art they make is at all similar, but because the journey they take seems so unlikely. Noonan is a small-town no-hoper with a hateful father who grows up to be one of America's most celebrated painters; Irwin was a working-class kid from L.A. who loved cars and girls, went into the army, and then embarked on an extraordinary theoretical journey that ends with the blurring of the space-time continuum. When you read about the two lives simultaneously, one adds credibility to the other.

Louis Sachar's *Holes* is funny, gripping, and sad, a Boy's Own Adventure story rewritten by Kurt Vonnegut. Do you people ever do light reading, or is it all concrete poetry and state-of-the-nation novels? Because if you ever do take any time out, may I make a suggestion? These young-adult novels I've been Hoovering up are not light in the sense that they are disposable or unmemorable—on the contrary, they have all, without exception, been smart, complicated, deeply felt, deeply meant. They are light, however, in the sense that they are not built to resist your interest in them: they want to be read quickly and effortlessly. So instead of reading the ninth book in a detective series, why not knock off a modern classic instead?

P.S. Well, that didn't take long. I have been suspended for one issue. "Willful failure to finish a book," it says here, "thereby causing distress to a fellow author and failing in your duty to literature and/or criticism." Ho hum. This has happened so often that it's water off a duck's back. See you in a couple of months. ✲

JANUARY 2008

I have recently spent two weeks traveling around your country—if your country is the one with the crazy time zones and the constant television advertisements for erectile dysfunction cures—on a fact-finding mission for this magazine: the Polysyllabic Spree, the forty-seven literature-loving, unnervingly even-tempered yet unsmiling young men and women who remove all the good jokes from this column every month, came to the conclusion that I am no longer in touch with American reading habits, and sent me on an admittedly enlightening tour of airport bookshops. This is how I know that your favorite writer is not Cormac McCarthy, nor even David Foster Wallace, but someone called Joel Osteen, who may even be a member of the Spree, for all I know: he has the same perfect teeth, and the same belief in the perfectibility of man through the agency of Jesus Christ our savior. Osteen was on TV every time I turned it on—thank heaven for the adult pay-per-view channels!—and his book *Become a Better You* was everywhere. I suppose I'll have to read it now, if only to find out what you are all thinking.

True story: I saw one person, an attractive thirtysomething woman, actually buy the book, in the bookstore at the George Bush Intercontinental Airport in Houston, Texas, and, perhaps significantly, she was weeping as she did so. She ran in, tears streaming down her face and muttering to herself, and went straight to the nonfiction hardback bestsellers display. Your guess is as good as mine. I am almost certain that a feckless man was to blame (I suspect that she had been dumped somewhere between gates D15 and D17) and indeed that feckless American men are generally responsible for the popularity of Christianity in the United States. In England, interestingly, the men are not in the least bit feckless—and, as a result, we are an almost entirely godless nation, and Joel Osteen is never on our televisions.

I wrote this last paragraph shortly before going to the gym, where for twenty minutes or so I wondered how to link the story of the weeping woman to Tom Perrotta's *The Abstinence Teacher;* I just couldn't see a smooth way of doing it. As *The Abstinence Teacher* is, in part, about a feckless American male's rebirth as a Christian, I ended my session on the cross-trainer wondering instead whether my tour of U.S. airport bookshops has left me brain-damaged. I am almost sure it do has.

I should say that I read a U.K. proof copy of *The Abstinence Teacher,* and that on the cover it claims that Tom Perrotta is an American... Well, an American *me.* This is a high-risk, possibly even foolishly misguided, marketing strategy, and does no justice to Perrotta's talent. And it says a lot about my admiration for him, and my interest in what he has to say on what puzzles those over here most about the U.S., that I overcame my initial dismay and wolfed it down—albeit with the spine cracked, so that I could carry it around inside-out. Needless to say, I end up absurdly flattered by the comparison: *The Abstinence Teacher* is a clever, funny, thoughtful, and sympathetic novel.

Perrotta's initial focus is on Ruth Ramsey, a sex-education teacher who is having trouble with her school governors and the local evangelical church after telling her students, with a careless neutrality, that some people enjoy oral sex. When her daughter's soccer coach, a member of the church, leads the team in impromptu prayer after a victory, her outrage and grievance lure her into a confrontation that provides the bulk of the narrative, but what is particularly daring about *The Abstinence Teacher*, given Perrotta's constituency, is that he isn't afraid to switch point of view: it's all very well, and for Perrotta (I'm guessing) not particularly difficult, to give us access to the mind of a liberal sex-education teacher, but attempting to raise sympathy for a formerly deadbeat born-again is another matter. Perrotta's Tim is a triumphant creation, though, believable and human. It helps that he's a burned-out ex-musician who's turned to the Lord to help him through his various dependencies—there but for the grace of God go the readers and writers of this magazine, and certainly half the potential readership of a literary novel. And Tim's nagging doubt is attractive, too. Where Perrotta really scores, though, is in his detailed imagining of his character's journey. It seems entirely credible, for example, that Tim should have a particular problem with Christian sex: he knows that the drugs and the alcohol were harmful, and are therefore best avoided. But seeing as he has to have sex anyway, with his naïve and subservient Christian second wife, he cannot help but feel nostalgic for the old-school, hot and godless variety. I'm betting that this is exactly how it is for those who have followed Tim's path to redemption.

There was a similar collision between Christianity and liberalism in the canceled TV series *Studio 60 on the Sunset Strip*, but it didn't make much of a noise, mostly because the Christian character—or, rather, her determination to appear on a satirical liberal entertainment program weekly—constantly stretched our credulity, until our credulity tore right down the middle; Perrotta employs his considerable skill to ensure that Tim and Ruth are an accident waiting to happen.

Just recently, I read an interview with a contemporary literary novelist who worried—and I'm sure it was worry I heard in his voice, so the tone of lordly disdain was just mischievousness on the part of the interviewer—that books by me (and I apologize for repeatedly cropping up in this column as a writer, rather than as a reader) and other writers who use pop-culture references in their fiction would not be read in twenty-five years' time. And, yes, there's a possibility that in a quarter of a century, *The Abstinence Teacher* will mystify people who come across it: it's about America today, this minute, and it's chock-full of band names and movies and TV programs. (One or two passages may mystify people who live in soccer-playing nations now, but I enjoyed the book too much to take issue with Perrotta about his failure to grasp the insignificance of the throw-in.) Yet some fiction at least should deal with the state of the here and now, no matter what the cost to the work's durability, no? This novel takes on an important subject—namely, the clash between two currently prevailing cultures opposed to an almost ludicrous degree—that is in urgent need of consideration by a writer as smart and as humane as Tom Perrotta. My advice to you: don't read writers with an eye on posterity. They are deeply serious people, and by picking up their books now, you are trivializing them. Plus, they're not interested in the money. They're above all that.

I have been writing this column for so long that I am now forced to consider a novel by my brother-in-law *for the third time*. Irritatingly, it's just as good as the other two, although it's a lot less Roman than either *Pompeii* or *Imperium,* which may or may not show some encouraging signs of failure and/or weakness. In fact, *The Ghost* is Robert's first novel set in the present day, and, like *The Abstinence Teacher,* you don't want to wait twenty-five years to read it: it's about the relationship between Adam Lang, an ex–prime minister whose bafflingly close relationship with the U.S.A. has cost him a great deal, and his ghost writer, whose research uncovers things that Lang would prefer remain covered up. As the two of them work together in a wintry Martha's Vineyard, Lang's world starts to fall apart. *The Ghost* is one part thriller, one part political commentary, and one part the angry wish-fulfillment of an enraged liberal, and it has enough narrative energy to fuel a Combat Shadow. It also has a very neat GPS scene in it, the first I've come across in contemporary fiction. It has been said that Tony Blair is extremely vexed by *The Ghost,* so you don't even have to read it to feel its beneficent effects. If that's not a definition of great literature, then I don't know what is.

The last time I was here, I promised to return to Richard Russo's *Bridge of Sighs,* which I hadn't quite finished. Well, I finished it, and liked it (although not as much as I liked *Empire Falls,* which is an all-time favorite), and no longer feel competent to write about it. I started it on a sun-lounger in France, and it's now November, and Lou "Lucy" Lynch and his careful, gentle ruminations seem a lifetime ago. The same goes for Paul Zindel's *The Pigman,* this month's YA experience—I know I read it, but I'm not entirely sure I could tell you an awful lot about it. Maybe I should have done my book report the moment I finished it.

I recently discovered that when my friend Mary has finished a book, she won't start another for a couple of days—she wants to give her most recent reading experience a little more time to breathe, before it's suffocated by the next. This makes sense, and it's an entirely laudable policy, I think. Those of us who read neurotically, however—to ward off boredom, and the fear of our own ignorance, and our impending deaths—can't afford the time.

Speaking of which… Jeff Gordinier's forthcoming *X Saves the World* (subtitled *How Generation X Got the Shaft but Can Still Keep Everything from Sucking*) begins with an apposite quote from Douglas Coupland's novel *Generation X*: "My life had become a series of scary incidents that simply weren't stringing together to make for an interesting book, and God, you get old so quickly! Time was (and is) running out." *X Saves the World* starts with the assumption that the Boomers (born in the late '40s and '50s) have all sold out, and the Millennials are all nightmarish Britney clones who can't go to the toilet without filming the experience in anticipation of an MTV reality show. And that leaves Generation X, a.k.a. the slackers, a.k.a. the postmodern ironists, a.k.a. blah blah, to make something of the sorry mess we call, like, "the world." Gordinier, of course, is neither a Boomer nor a Millennial, which might in some eyes make his generalizations even more suspect than generalizations usually are, but I loved this book anyway: it's impassioned, very quick on its feet, dense with all the right allusions—Kurt Cobain, the Replacements, Susan Sontag, Henry James, and the rest of that whole crowd—funny, and, in the end, actually rather moving.

And it's convincing, too, although of course it's hard to talk about generational mores and attitudes without raising all the old questions about when generations begin and end, and how we as a collection of individuals, as opposed to a banner-waving mob, are supposed to fit into it all neatly. As far as I can tell, I'm supposed to be a Boomer, but I was twelve when Woodstock took place, nineteen when *Anarchy in the U.K.* was released, and always felt closer to Johnny Rotten (and hence to everything that came after) than to David Crosby, so where am I supposed to fit into all this? There were Boomers that never sold out, plenty of Xers that did, and lots of lovable Millennials who worry about global warming and literacy levels. There have always been relentless and empty-headed self-promoters, although in the good old days we used to ignore them, rather than give them their own reality show. Gordinier is right, though, I think, when he argues that Generation X (and I know that even naming you like this makes me sound cheesy and square, but I can't say "so-called" every time, nor can I raise my eyebrows and roll my eyes in print) has found another way of doing things, and that this way may well add up to something significant. This is a generation that not only understands technology but has internalized its capabilities, thus enabling it to think in a different way; this is a generation that knows that it can't change the world, a recognition that enables it to do what it can. Cinema, books, TV, and music have all produced something new as a result, so long as you know where to look.

I suspect that those who write about Gordinier's book will engage him in his argument, and that very few people will point out how much fun this book is to read, but it is; the last chapter, which uses Henry James's novella *The Beast in the Jungle* and the life and work of James Brown as the ingredients for a passionate rallying cry, is particularly fizzy.

In other news: nearly a third of the football season is over, and Arsenal, still undefeated, is sitting at the top of the Premier League, despite having sold Thierry Henry to Barcelona in the summer. These are golden days, my friends, for another couple of weeks at least. This is how to become a better you: choose Arsène Wenger, Arsenal's brilliant manager, as your life coach. I did, and look at me now. If I found myself weeping in an airport, that's the book I'd buy: *Think Offensively, the Arsène Wenger Way,* but he hasn't written it yet. (You'll be reading about it here first if he ever does.) Mind you, even Joel Osteen would be able to see that we need a new goalkeeper urgently. ✶

FEBRUARY 2008

BOOKS BOUGHT:

* *The Raymond Chandler Papers: Selected Letters and Nonfiction 1909-1959*—Tim Hinley, ed.

BOOKS READ:

* *What Sport Tells Us About Life*—Ed Smith
* *The Absolutely True Diary of a Part-Time Indian*—Sherman Alexie
* *The Darling*—Russell Banks
* *The Rights of the Reader*—Daniel Pennac

The best description I know of what it feels like to learn to read comes in Francis Spufford's brilliant memoir *The Child That Books Built*:

> When I caught the mumps, I couldn't read; when I went back to school again, I could. The first page of *The Hobbit* was a thicket of symbols, to be decoded one at a time and joined hesitantly together... By the time I reached *The Hobbit*'s last page, though, writing had softened, and lost the outlines of the printed alphabet, and become a transparent liquid, first viscous and sluggish, like a jelly of meaning, then ever thinner and more mobile, flowing faster and faster, until it reached me at the speed of thinking and I could not entirely distinguish the suggestions it was making from my own thoughts. I had undergone the acceleration into the written word that you also experience as a change in the medium. In fact, writing had ceased to be a thing—an object in the world—and *become* a medium, a substance you look through.

Firstly, we should note that the first book Spufford ever read was *The Hobbit*, a book that I still haven't picked up, partly because I am afraid I still won't understand it. Secondly, Spufford caught the mumps just as he turned six—he is one of the cleverest people I have ever come across, and yet some parents with young children would be freaking out if their kids weren't able to read by then. And lastly, I would just like to point out that you can't fake a memory like this. Learning to read happens once and once only for most of us, and for the vast majority of adults in first-world countries it happened a long time ago. You have to dig deep, deep down into the bog of the almost-lost, and then carry what you have found carefully to the surface, and then you have to find the words and images to describe what you see on your spade. Perhaps Spufford's amazing feat of recollection means nothing to you; but when I first read it, I knew absolutely that this was what happened to me: I too spooned up the jelly of meaning.

I turned back to Spufford's book because my five-year-old is on the verge of reading. (Yeah, you read that right, Spufford. Five! And only just! Francis Spufford was born in 1964 and this book was published in 2003, so by my reckoning my son will have produced something as good as *The Child That Books Built* by the year 2040, or something slightly better by 2041.) Writing hasn't softened for him: three-letter words are as insoluble as granite, and he can no more look through writing than he can look through his bedroom wall. The good news is that he's almost frenetically motivated; the bad news is that he is so eager to learn because he has got it into his head that he will be given a Nintendo DS machine when he can read and write, which he argues that he can do now to his own satisfaction—he can write his own name, and read the words *Mum, Dad, Spider, Man,* and at least eight others. As far as he is concerned, literacy is something that he can dispense with altogether in a couple of months, when the Nintendo turns up. It will have served its purpose.

Daniel Pennac's *The Rights of the Reader,* first published sixteen years ago in France, the author's native country, is a really rather lovely book about all the things parents and teachers do to discourage the art and habit of reading, and all the things we could do to persuade young people that literacy is worth keeping about one's person even after you've got it nailed. According to Pennac, we have spent most of our five-year-old son's life teaching him that reading is something to be endured: we threaten to withdraw stories at bedtime, and then never follow through with the threat ("an unbearable punishment, for them and for us," Pennac points out, and this is just one of the many moments of wisdom that will make you want him to be your adoptive dad); we dangle television and computers as rewards; we occasionally try to force him to read when he is demotivated, tired, bolshy. ("The lightness of our sentences stopped them getting bogged down: now having to mumble indecipherable letters stifles even their ability to dream," says Pennac sadly.) All of these mistakes, it seems to me, are unavoidable at some time in the average parenting week, although Pennac does us a favor by exposing the perverse logic buried in them.

What's great about *The Rights of the Reader* is Pennac's tone—by turns wry, sad, amused, hopeful—and his endless fund of good sense: he likes his canon, but doesn't want to torture you into reading it, and rights 2 and 3 (the Right to Skip and the Right Not to Finish a Book) are, we must remind ourselves, fundamental human rights. The French book about reading that's been getting a lot of attention recently is Pierre Bayard's *How To Talk About Books You Haven't Read,* which should surely be retitled *You Need Some New Friends, Because the Ones You've Got Are Jerks:* literary editors seem to think it's zeitgeisty, but out in the world, grown-ups no longer feel the need to bullshit about literature, thank god. Pennac's book is the one we should all be thinking about, because its author hasn't given up. *The Rights of the Reader* is full of great quotes, too. Here's one of my favorites, from Flannery O'Connor: "If teachers are in the habit of approaching a story as if it were a research problem for which any answer is believable so long as it is not obvious, then I think students will never learn to enjoy fiction." That one is dedicated to anyone who graduated from college and found themselves unable to read anything that came from the imagination.

Russell Banks's *The Darling* was recommended to me—*given* to me, even—by the owner of a wonderful independent bookstore, Rakestraw Books, in Danville, California; booksellers know better than anyone that talking about books you have read is much more persuasive than attempting to sound smart about books you haven't. It's the second great novel about Africa by an American writer that I've read in the last year (I'm forbidden from talking about the other one by internal bureaucracy), although the creative impulse behind Banks's book is much tougher to read. It's in some ways a peculiar novel, in that it tracks the journey of a 1960s radical, the daughter of a famous pediatrician, as she travels all the way from the Weather Underground to war-torn Liberia, where she marries a local politician and takes care of chimpanzees. A crude synopsis is only likely to provoke the question "What the *fuck*?" but then, synopses are rarely much use when it comes to novels. Whatever prompted Banks to write *The Darling*, the material here provides him with an enormous and dazzling armory of ironies and echoes, and his narrator, Hannah, by turns passionately engaged and icily detached, is inevitably reminiscent of a Graham Greene character. This is a novel that provides a potted history of Liberia, a dreamy, extended meditation on the connections between humans and apes, a convincing examination of the internal life of an American refusenik, and an acute portrait of a mixed-race, cross-cultural marriage, and if you're not interested in any of that, then we at the *Believer* politely suggest that you'd be happier with another magazine.

I nearly didn't read Sherman Alexie's *The Absolutely True Diary of a Part-Time Indian*, because I had decided that, as we had both had young-adult novels published at around the same time, we were somehow in competition, and that his book was the Yankees, or Manchester United, or Australia, or any other sporting nemesis you care to name. And of course hearing that Alexie's novel was great really didn't help overcome my reluctance—rather, it merely hardened it. I'd like to think that by reading the book I have demonstrated some kind of maturity, and come to recognize that books are not like sports teams and therefore can't play each other; mine can't advance to the next round by dint of all-round physical superiority, no matter how thoroughly I coach it, no matter what diet I put it on, no matter how many steroids I force down its little throat. (If I thought that giving my novel performance-enhancing drugs would help it in any way, I'd do it, though, and I'm not ashamed to admit it.)

Anyway, *The Absolutely True Diary of a Part-Time Indian* is, as I was told on my recent book tour by scores of unsupportive and thoughtless people, a terrific book, funny and moving and effortlessly engaging. The part-time Indian of the title is Junior, a hydrocephalic weakling whose decision to enroll at the white high school at the edge of his reservation costs him both his closest friendship and respect from his community; it's a coming-of-age story, but it's fresh: I for one knew nothing about the world that Alexie describes, and in any case Junior's voice—by turns defiant, worldly wise, sad, and scared—and Ellen Forney's cute and sympathetic drawings give the book the feeling of a modern YA classic. And, seeing as the best YA fiction (see previous columns) is as punchy and engaging as anything you might come across in a bookstore, it's for you, too. If you see Sherman Alexie's novel getting a beating somewhere—in the ring, at a racetrack, or anywhere else you're likely to see books competing—then demand a urine test, because somebody's cheating.

I have written about Ed Smith before: his last book, *On and Off the Field,* was a diary of his season, and as he's a cricketer, I presumed that my banging on about a sport you didn't know, understand, or care about would annoy you, in a satisfying way. It's great, then, that he has another book coming out, this time a collection of essays dealing with the areas where sport (quite often cricket) is able to shed light on other areas of life. In the first essay he explains why there will never be another Don Bradman, but as you lot don't even know that you've missed the first Bradman altogether, it's a waste of time and column inches going into any further detail, so that's what I'll do. Bradman's batting average, the *New York Times* concluded in its 2001 obituary after some fancy mathematics, meant that he was better than Michael Jordan, Babe Ruth, and Ty Cobb; nobody has got anywhere close to his record since, just as in baseball nobody has managed a .400 season since Ted Williams in 1941. (We weren't playing professional sports in 1941, you know. We were too busy fighting Nazis—an old grievance, maybe, but not one that anyone here is likely to forget for another few hundred years.) Smith argues that the increasing professionalism of sports means that it's much harder for sporting giants to tower quite as high over their peers: greater defensive competence and organization have resulted in a bunching somewhere nearer the middle. The bad players and teams are much better than they used to be, which means that the good ones find it harder to exert their superiority so crushingly. And when it comes to athletics, we can't get much faster, according to a Harvard evolutionary geneticist—"the laws of oxygen exchange will not permit it." Did you know that horses have stopped breaking racing records? They've now been bred to the point where they simply can't get any faster. I could eat this stuff up with a spoon.

You'll enjoy this: when the cricketer Fred Titmus made his professional debut, the tannoy announcer felt obliged to correct an error on the score card: "F. J. Titmus should, of course, read Titmus, F. J." An amateur player (a "gentleman," in the class-bound language of cricket) was allowed to put his initials before his surname; a player—in other words, a professional—had to put his initials after. Titmus was being put in his place—in *1949*. What a stupid country. This is why I have repeatedly turned down a knighthood. Knighthoods are no good to anyone, if they want to get on in Britain. I'm holding out for a lordship.

The chapter on what we can learn from amateurism (a word which, it's easy to forget, has its roots in the old-school, first-lesson *amo amas amat*) is of value to pretty much any of us who have managed to end up doing what we love for a living. Anyone in this privileged position who has never for a moment experienced self-consciousness, or endured a bout of second-guessing, or ended up wondering what it was they loved in the first place is either mad or isn't getting paid a living wage (and now I come to think about it, pretty much every writer I have ever met belongs in one of these two camps); Smith's entertaining exploration of creativity and inspiration would be every bit as useful to a poet or a songwriter (and he ropes Dylan in to help make his case) as it would be to an opening batsman. Ha! So you might actually have to read this book about cricket! Even better!

Next month, apparently, this column will be entitled "Stuff I've Been Watching" (for one issue only). I only watch *30 Rock* and *Match of the Day*. I'd skip it, if I were you, unless you want to know whether Lee Dixon is a better postmatch pundit than Alan Shearer. Actually, I'll tell you now, and save you the trouble: he is. Defenders are always better analysts than forwards. In this, as in so many other areas, sport is exactly like life. ✶

MARCH / APRIL 2008

FILMS WATCHED:
- ★ *The Simpsons Movie*
- ★ *Juno*
- ★ *This Is England*
- ★ *Unnamable*
- ★ *I'm Not There*
- ★ *And When Did You Last See Your Father?*

FILMS BORROWED FROM POSTAL DVD LIBRARY:
- ★ *Midnight Cowboy*
- ★ *Downfall*

At first I was afraid. In fact, I was, indeed, petrified. "Stuff I've Been Watching"? Are they sure? Even... this? And *that*? And if I own up, will they still let me write about stuff I've been reading? Or will the stuff I've watched count against me, on the grounds that anyone who watches either this or that is highly unlikely to know which way up you hold a book? I should admit straightaway that "this" and "that" contain no pornographic content whatsoever. "This" is likely to be, in any given month, a football match between two village teams battling for a chance to play in the first qualifying round of the FA Cup; "that," on the other hand, could very well be a repeat of a 1990s quiz show—*Family Fortunes,* say—broadcast on one of the U.K.'s many excellent quiz-show rerun channels. This isn't all I watch, of course. There are the endless games between proper football teams, and the first-run quiz shows, but I'm not embarrassed about watching them. Like many parents, I go to the cinema rarely, because going to the cinema means going without dinner, and no film is worth that, really, with the possible exception of *Citizen Kane,* and I saw that on TV.

As luck would have it, however, I have been asked to write about stuff I watched in December, and in December I watch screener copies of movies on DVD. I am a member of BAFTA, the British Academy of Film and Television Arts, which means that at the end of the year, every half-decent film that might have half a chance of winning an award is pushed through my letterbox. For free. The DVDs are piled high on a shelf in my living room, new films by Ang Lee and Paul Thomas Anderson, adaptations of books by Ian McEwan and Monica Ali, and they look... You know what? They look pretty daunting. Stacked up like that, they look not unlike books, in fact: already some of them are starting to give off the same slightly musty, worthy smell that you don't really want to associate with the cinema. Every year, some of them—many of them—will go unwatched. We're getting through a few of them, though. (And please welcome the first-person-plural pronoun to this column. Books are "I," but movies are "we," because that's how they get watched. Any views expressed herein, however, are mine, unless I manage to offend somebody in Hollywood with power and wealth, in which case that particular view was hers. She won't care. She's only an independent film producer.) So, from the top...

Just before Christmas, I was browsing the biography section of a chain bookstore, hopelessly looking for presents, when, suddenly and bewilderingly, the color drained out of the book jackets: they had all turned sepia or white. I was almost certain that I'd been stricken by a rare medical condition until I realized that I had reached the section reserved for the genre known in the U.K. as the "misery memoir." These books, all inspired by the enormous success of Dave Pelzer, seem to deal exclusively with childhood hardship and abuse, and have titles like *Please Daddy, Put It Away;* the jackets are white or sepia, apart from a washed-out photo, because Pelzer's books look like that. Anyway, in this chain bookstore, these memoirs had all been bunched together in a section called "Real Lives"—as if Churchill or Katharine Hepburn or Tobias Wolff or Mary Karr had lived unreal lives.

I was reminded of the "Real Lives" section when I was watching *This Is England,* a British independent film by the talented young English director Shane Meadows: there is a similarly hubristic claim to authenticity in the movie's title. Is the country depicted really England? Like, the whole of it? I've lived in England all my life, but I didn't recognize Meadows's version. He'd say that this is because I've spent my time in the soft south of the country, and he's made a film about the gritty north, and that's fair enough, although I'd be resistant to any argument that his England is more real than mine. What concerned me more is that some of the details on which any claim to authenticity must rest felt a little off to me. Why did the characters all have different regional accents, when the film is set in one depressed suburb of a northern English city? Were young no-hoper English skinheads really listening to Toots and the Maytals in 1983, or would they have stuck to their Madness and Bad Manners records? And did they really have instant access to the mythology of Woodstock when they were teasing their peers about clothes and haircuts? *This Is England* is a semi-autobiographical film about a twelve-year-old falling in with a dodgy crowd around the time of the Falklands War, when Margaret Thatcher's repulsive jingoism got roughly translated by some disenfranchised working-class kids into the violent and racist language of the far right. It's never less than gripping, not least because Meadows gets exemplary performances from all his actors, especially thirteen-year-old Thomas Turgoose as Shaun. Any film that ends with the one black character being kicked half to death by a psychotic skinhead is always going to be hard to adore, but I'm glad I watched it.

We watched... Actually, I'd better just check something. Hey, Spree! Do the same rules apply to movies as to books? We still have to be nice? Or say nothing at all? Yes? OK. So, we watched a film directed by a famous director and starring famous people, and—as film agents say—we didn't love it. (Top tip: if a film agent ever tells you that he or she didn't love your novel or script, then you might as well kill yourself, because you're dead anyway.) This particular film was about unpleasant people doing unkind things for increasingly contrived reasons, and though that's pretty much the dominant Hollywood genre, this one felt particularly phony. It was gloomy and portentous, too, which is presumably why it's being pushed through letterboxes during the awards season.

I did, however, love Todd Haynes's clever, thoughtful, frequently dazzling meditation on the subject of Bob Dylan, *I'm Not There,* which, as you must surely know by now, stars Cate Blanchett as one of six actors taking on Dylan's various incarnations and personas. If you'd decided not to see it because it sounded gimmicky or just plain daft, then you should think again: I can't guarantee that you'll like it, obviously, but I'm positive that you won't dislike it on the grounds that Cate Blanchett and a fourteen-year-old black kid called Marcus Carl Franklin are being asked to interpret the career of someone who doesn't resemble them physically. On the contrary, one of the film's many triumphs is that you never question it for a second—or rather, any questioning you do is on the filmmakers' own terms and at their behest, and as a consequence this helps you to engage with the endless complexity of both the material and Dylan himself.

None of these characters is called "Bob Dylan." Blanchett is Jude, the electric speed-freak *Don't Look Back*–era Bob (and her sections are occasionally reminiscent of Pennebaker's shaky handheld documentary, when they're not borrowing from Richard Lester or *Blowup*); the character's name is suitably androgynous, and of course contains an echo of that famous 1966 taunt, which comes in handy when the moment arrives. Franklin plays a folksinger called Woody, who rides trains with hobos and carries around a guitar case bearing the familiar legend THIS MACHINE KILLS FASCISTS. "It's 1959 and he's singing about boxcars?" a kindly woman who has taken Woody in and fed him asks witheringly, right at the start of the picture. "Live your own time, child. Sing your own time." This is a pretty good example of how Haynes has externalized and dramatized all the internal conversations Dylan must have had with himself over the last fifty-odd years, but it also provides the quest for all the characters: what and where is one's own time? Richard Gere's Billy the Kid is lost in a Pat Garrett/Lily, Rosemary Old West full of robber barons and the disenfranchised poor, and Jude, the most "modern" of any of the versions available, ends up running back into his/her own head. Meanwhile Heath Ledger's Robbie, living in the here and now, splits painfully, *Blood on the Tracks* style, from Charlotte Gainsbourg. So what use is the here and now, if all it can do is break your heart? Haynes has enormous fun with, and finds great profit in, the iconography of Dylan—there's so much of it that even a casual shot of a young couple huddled together against the cold, or a jokey montage scene showing Ledger bashing into a couple of dustbins while learning to ride a motorbike, teems with meaning. It's the best film about an artist that I've ever seen: it's meltingly beautiful and it has taken the trouble to engage its subject with love, care, and intelligence. What more do you want? Even if you hate every decision that Haynes has taken, you can enjoy it as the best feature-length pop video ever made. Who wouldn't want to watch Heath Ledger and Charlotte Gainsbourg making love while "I Want You" plays on the sound track?

There were two visits to cinemas this month, a family outing to see *The Simpsons Movie,* and a rare adults-only evening out for *Juno.* I can tell you little about *The Simpsons Movie* because—and I'm not big enough to resist naming names—Mila Douglas, five-year-old best friend of my middle son, was scared of it, and as her parents weren't with her, it was me that had to keep taking her out into the foyer, where she made a miraculous and immediate recovery every time. Scared! Of the Simpsons! I will cheerfully admit that I have failed as a father in pretty much every way bar one: my boys have been trained ruthlessly to watch whatever I make them watch. They won't flinch for a second, no matter who is being disemboweled on the screen in front of them. Mila (who is, perhaps not coincidentally, a girl) has, by contrast, clearly been "well brought up," by parents who "care," and who probably "think" about what is "age-appropriate." Yeah, well. What good did that do her on an afternoon excursion with the Hornby family? From what I saw, the movie was as good as, but no better than, three average *Simpsons* episodes bolted together—an average *Simpsons* episode being, of course, smarter than an average Flaubert novel. It could well be, though, that I was sitting in the foyer listening to Mila Douglas's views on birthday-party fashion etiquette during the best jokes.

By the time you read this, there's probably a *Juno* backlash going on, and smart people are describing it as too cute and kooky for its own good. Well, I'm stuck in 2007, and in 2007 we still think that *Juno* is charming and funny and that Michael Cera is a comic genius. *Juno* also features the first but almost certainly not the last cinematic reference to a quarterly magazine based not too far from Believer Towers. We at the *Believer* are used to being talked about in the movies—there was a surprisingly well-informed conversation about our decision to take advertising in *Live Free or Die Hard,* and an affectionate spoof of the Spree in *Alvin and the Chipmunks.* It's about time our poor relations caught up.

I'm in the middle of watching *And When Did You Last See Your Father?* as we speak—I stopped last night just when I got to the bit about fecal vomit, but

I'll watch Jim Broadbent die of bowel cancer this evening, if my morale is high enough. This movie was produced by a friend, directed by another friend, and stars a third. It was adapted by a neighbor from a memoir written by a guy I see from time to time and whose book I admired very much. What do I think of it so far? I think it's brilliantly produced, directed, acted, and written, and the source material is fantastic. Also, it's really good. ⋆

MAY 2008

Last month, I wrote about stuff I'd been watching, and while I was writing about stuff I'd been watching, I was thinking about the stuff I wasn't reading. I wasn't not reading because of the watching; I was simply not reading. Or rather, I was simply not reading complete books. I tried, several times; I began Martin Gayford's *The Yellow House*, about the nine weeks that Gauguin and van Gogh spent as roommates, and Matt Ridley's *Genome*, and Dickens's *Barnaby Rudge*, and Meg Wolitzer's *The Position*, and Irmgard Keun's *Child of All Nations*, and Roberto Saviano's *Gomorrah: Italy's Other Mafia*, and John Mullan's *Anonymity*, and I read a couple of entries in Clive James's *Cultural Amnesia*, and nothing took. None of this, of course, is the fault of these fine authors or their almost certainly brilliant work. I was just itchy and scratchy and probably crusty, too, and I began to wonder whether I had simply lost the habit—the skill, even—of reading. I was beginning to feel that this one long, pained explanation would have to serve as my last in this space, which I would then simply hand over to someone young enough to plow all the way through to the end, or at least the middle, of anything they start. (Although isn't that supposed to be one of the problems with young people? That their brains have been so rotted by internet pornography and Nintendo that they are physically incapable of reading anything longer than a cereal packet? Maybe I will prove impossible to replace, and as long as I read a few opening paragraphs every month, this gig is mine forever.) At least I have some facts at my disposal. Did you know that if you wrote out the human genome, one letter per millimeter, the text would be as long as the river Danube? Did you know that the most expensive living artist in 1876 was Meissonier, one of whose paintings went for nearly four hundred thousand francs? These are two of the many things I've learned by reading the beginnings of this month's books. I am beginning to think that this new regime will be ideal for my dotage. I can read the beginnings of a few books, sit at the bar at my local and regale people with fascinating nuggets of information. How can I fail to make friends if I know how long the human genome is?

Just as I was beginning to despair—and let's face it, a man who is tired of books is looking at an awful lot of *Rockford Files* reruns—a book lying on a trestle table in a local bookshop managed to communicate to me its desire to be read in its entirety, and I bought it, and I swallowed it whole. Quite why Graham McCann's *Spike & Co.*, about British comedy writing in the 1950s, should have succeeded in its siren call where scores of others failed remains mysterious. I had absolutely no previous desire to read it—I didn't even know it existed before the morning I bought it—and though I love a couple of the writers McCann discusses, I hadn't thought about them in a long while. Maybe the book nutritionists are right (and I'm sure that those of you who live in California probably have book nutritionists working for you full-time, maybe even living in your ubiquitous "guesthouses"): you need to listen to what your soul needs.

Spike & Co. is about a group of writers who formed a company called Associated London Scripts (they wanted to call themselves Associated British Scripts, but the local council turned them down on the grounds that they weren't big enough) who operated out of offices above a greengrocer's in Shepherd's Bush, and went on to change the course of British and American TV and radio writing. Out of these offices came *The Goons,* John Lennon's favorite radio show and a direct inspiration for Monty Python, *Steptoe and Son,* which became *Sanford and Son* in the U.S., *'Til Death Us Do Part* (known to you lot as *All in the Family*), and the sci-fi series *Doctor Who,* which is still running, in an admittedly snazzier form, today. I have known and loved these shows for much of my life, and yet I had no idea about the greengrocer aspect of it all, which seems to me extraordinary. Two of my favorite writers—and I'm not talking about writers of TV and radio comedy, but writers of all denominations—Ray Galton and Alan Simpson, met in a TB sanatorium, and I didn't know that, either. They were both desperately ill teenagers, neither expected to live much into his twenties; they met toward the end of their stay in the late 1940s, and by the mid-'60s had produced *Hancock's Half Hour* and *Steptoe and Son,* two series that have helped form the psyche of contemporary Britain. The chapter on Spike Milligan, meanwhile, provides an invaluable writing tip. "Once he had started work on a script he disliked ever having to stop; he wrote as he thought, and if he came to a place where the right line failed to emerge, he would just jab a finger at one of the keys, type 'FUCK IT' or 'BOLLOCKS,' and then carry on regardless. The first draft would feature plenty of such expletives, but then, with each successive version, the expletives grew fewer and fewer, until by about the tenth draft, he had a complete, expletive-free script..." I have found this more helpful than I am prepared to talk about in any great depth, possibly because I can build my own inadequacies right into the page, rather than let them hover around the edges.

I can't hope or imagine that you'll enjoy this book as much as I did. Much of it will be incomprehensible to you, and in any case, you're not me. John Carey points out in his book *What Good Are the Arts?* that there are millions of tiny decisions and influences, over the course of a lifetime, that help us form our relationships with books and music and the rest of it, and if you shared even half a dozen of them, I'd be surprised. Even if you'd bought the book at the same time at the same store, you couldn't have spent the previous hour on my analyst's couch—I would have noticed, because I'd have been lying on top of you. But as a direct result of *Spike & Co.,* two things happened: (1) I bought a signed commemorative Galton and Simpson print off the internet, and (2) I emailed a friend and asked him if he wanted to have a go at writing something with me, even though neither of us has TB or indeed any life-threatening infectious disease—*Spike & Co.* is a hymn to the joys of collaboration, and I suddenly became dissatisfied with the solitary nature of my day job. Such is the way of these things that nothing will come of it, of course, but we're having fun, and it's not often that you can say that about a day spent at a computer.

I read *The Shadow Catcher* and Junot Diaz's *The Brief Wondrous Life of Oscar Wao* because I had to: I agreed to judge the *Morning News's* Rooster competition, in which the best books of last year are drawn against each other in a knockout competition. At the time of writing, there is no overall winner, but I can tell you that Diaz unsportingly thumped Marianne Wiggins in my round. He's twenty years younger and, as far as one can tell from the jacket photos, a lot tougher than Wiggins, but he didn't let any of that stop him. I hope he's ashamed of himself. His book, incidentally, is brilliant.

The reading hiatus came during and after all the film watching, but luckily for you, I read a couple of books before it, so you can't leave just yet. Alec Wilkinson's *The Happiest Man in the World* is a study of Poppa Neutrino, and the book's title worked on me just as it was supposed to: I wanted to know his secret. I was once sent a self-help book called *Should You Leave?*, which was kicking around the house, in the way that books sometimes do, for months. Visitors would look at it, smile, pick it up, put it down, and then eventually start flicking through it. Nobody actually asked which page contained the answer, but you could see that they were hoping to stumble upon it without looking as though they were trying. It strikes me that anyone caught reading *The Happiest Man in the World* is owning up to a similar sort of dissatisfaction. I'm not sure, though, that Poppa Neutrino, a kind of Zen hobo who has spent his life rafting across the Atlantic, inventing new football plays, etc., can provide the answers we might be looking for. "He has begun to bleed constantly from his backside, so there is always a dark stripe down his pants…" "The box was six feet long, four feet tall and four feet wide… He came and went from the box only when no one was around, because he didn't want anyone to know he was living in it." I was unable to put myself in Neutrino's position and imagine myself as anything other than thoroughly miserable, so I quickly gave up on the idea of discovering the route to my future happiness and looked instead for the source of his. This, too, remains elusive—indeed, Poppa Neutrino seems to spend so much time starving, having heart attacks, living in boxes, and bleeding from his backside that you can't help wondering whether there was a terrible mix-up, and whether the text belonging to this particular title is inside the cover of an altogether less-promising-looking book. And there is a sleight of hand played here, too. The reason that many of us cannot live a life free of grinding obligation is because we have mortgages, children, parents, friends, and so on. Presumably the mortgage payments on boxes are not onerous, but Neutrino certainly has children, few of whom are mentioned at any great length; this raises the suspicion that it's easier to avoid grinding obligation if one simply chooses to ignore it. Those who read the *New Yorker* will know that Alec Wilkinson is incapable of writing anything dull, or inelegant, and his obvious fascination with the subject gives the book a winning energy. That fascination, however, is not always entirely comprehensible.

The Happiest Man in the World made me think, though. Mostly I ended up thinking about the nature and value of experiences and memories, although I didn't get very far. Crossing the Atlantic on a raft or staying in to watch TV... It's all the same, in the end, isn't it? There comes a time when it's over, and all you can do is talk about it. And if that's the case, then... I'm sorry. If you bother with this column at all, it's probably because you're looking for book tips. You probably don't want to hear that all human endeavor is pointless.

Here's a tip: M. T. Anderson's *Feed*. This is yet another book that can be added to an increasingly long list entitled "YA Novels I'd Never Heard of But Which Turn Out to Be Modern Classics," and *Feed* may well be the best of the lot. It's a sci-fi novel about a world in which everybody is plugged directly into a never-ending stream of text messages, shopping recommendations, pop music, and movie trailers—this is metaphor rather than prediction—and as a consequence Anderson's characters are frighteningly malleable and disturbingly inarticulate. Even the president of the U.S. has trouble with words! *Feed* is funny, serious, sad (there's a heartbreaking doomed romance at the center), and superbly realized; the moment I finished it I bought Anderson's latest novel, which is completely different. (It's set in 1775, and it's about a boy who's raised by a group of rational philosophers, so it sounds like the author has allowed himself to be seduced by the promise of a quick buck.) I haven't even read the beginning of it yet, though. It's a novel, so I very much doubt whether there will be any interesting facts in the opening pages. I rather fear that I'm turning into my father. ✶

SEPTEMBER 2008

BOOKS BOUGHT:

* ★ *Pictures at a Revolution: Five Movies and the Birth of the New Hollywood* —Mark Harris
* ★ *The Pumpkin Eater*—Penelope Mortimer
* ★ *Daddy's Gone a-Hunting*—Penelope Mortimer
* ★ *The Last Campaign: Robert F. Kennedy and 82 Days that Inspired America* —Thurston Clarke
* ★ *Lush Life*—Richard Price
* ★ *The Greek Way*—Edith Hamilton
* ★ *Nixonland: The Rise of a President and the Fracturing of America* —Rick Perlstein
* ★ *Netherland*—Joseph O'Neill

BOOKS READ:

* ★ *Pictures at a Revolution: Five Movies and the Birth of the New Hollywood* —Mark Harris
* ★ *The Studio*—John Gregory Dunne
* ★ *The Pumpkin Eater*—Penelope Mortimer
* ★ *Lush Life*—Richard Price
* ★ *The Last Campaign*—Thurston Clarke
* ★ *Cary Grant: A Class Apart*—Graham McCann

If you were given a month to learn something about a subject about which you had hitherto known nothing, what would you choose? Quantum physics, maybe, or the works of Willa Cather, or the Hundred Years' War? Would you learn a language, or possibly teach yourself how to administer first aid in the event of a domestic accident? I ask only because in the last month I have read everything there is to read, and as a consequence now know everything there is to know, on the subject of the film version of *Doctor Dolittle*, and I am beginning to have my doubts about whether I chose my specialism wisely. (I'm talking here, of course, about the 1967 version starring Rex Harrison, not the later Eddie Murphy vehicle. I don't know anything about that one. I'm not daft.)

This peculiar interest happened by accident rather than by design. I read Mark Harris's book *Pictures at a Revolution,* which is about the five movies nominated for the 1967 Best Picture Oscar, and Harris's book led me to John Gregory Dunne's *The Studio,* first published in 1969. Inexplicably, *Doctor Dolittle* was, in the opinion of the Academy, one of the five best films—along with *The Graduate, Bonnie and Clyde, In the Heat of the Night,* and *Guess Who's Coming to Dinner*—of 1967. (I say "inexplicably" because I'm presuming the film was tosh—although this presumption is in itself inexplicable, because when I saw it, in 1967, I thought it was a work of rare genius.) In *The Studio,* a piece of behind-the-scenes reportage, Dunne was given complete access to the boardrooms and sets of Twentieth Century Fox, a studio that happened to be in the middle of making *Doctor Dolittle* at the time.

Fortunately, *Doctor Dolittle* is worth studying, to degree level and possibly beyond. Did you know, for example, that in today's money it cost $190 million to make? That Haile Selassie visited the set in L.A., and Rex Harrison asked him, "How do you like *our* jungle?" That the script required a chimpanzee to learn how to cook bacon and eggs in a frying pan, a skill that took Chee-Chee—and his three understudies—six months to acquire? (I'm pretty sure I picked it up in less than half that time, so all those stories about the intelligence of apes are way wide of the mark.) Some of these stories should be engraved on a plaque and placed outside Grauman's Chinese Theatre in Hollywood, as a monument to the stupidity, vanity, and pointlessness of commercial moviemaking.

Pictures at a Revolution is one of the best books about film I have ever read, and if you're remotely interested in the process of making movies—in the process of making anything at all—then you should read it. Of course film-making has an enormous advantage when it comes to insider accounts, because every movie could have taken a different path, had crucial elements not fallen into place at crucial times. Robert Redford wanted to star in *The Graduate;* the writers of *Bonnie and Clyde* were desperate for Truffaut to direct their script, and Warren Beatty, one of the producers, saw Bob Dylan and Shirley

MacLaine as the leads. (If only literature could be this interesting. You know, "John Updike was scheduled to write *Catch-22* until right at the last moment. He pulled out when he was unexpectedly offered the first of the Rabbit books, after Saul Bellow's agent couldn't get the deal he wanted for his client..." As usual, books get stiffed with all the dull stories: "He thought up the idea. Then he wrote it. Then it got published." Who wants to read about that?) But Harris certainly exploits this advantage for all it's worth, and he does it with enormous intelligence, sympathy, and verve. He builds his compelling plotlines through painstaking accumulation of minute detail, but never lets the detail cloud his sense of momentum, and the end result is a book that you might find yourself unable to put down.

Like the best of those nonfiction books that take a moment in time and shake it until it reveals its resonance, *Pictures at a Revolution* turns out to be about a lot of things. The subtitle indicates one of Harris's theses—that 1967 was a pivotal year in cinema history, the year that the old studio system started to collapse, to be replaced by an independent producer-led culture which still thrives today, although not all of these producers are making *The Graduate* or *Bonnie and Clyde.* Sidney Poitier's emergence as a star with real box-office clout allows Harris to weave the subject of race into his narrative. Poitier starred in two of these five movies, and only just avoided having to appear in *Doctor Dolittle,* too, and he ended up being attacked for letting his side down—the bland liberal pieties of *Guess Who's Coming to Dinner* were deemed particularly offensive—while living in fear of his life whenever he ventured below the Mason-Dixon line. Meanwhile, the influx of saucy European movies that had hip Americans flocking to the cinemas had put ruinous strain on the curious, church-controlled U.S. censorship system, and Harris has fun with all the illogicalities and incongruities that were being backlit by the freedom of the '60s: a bare breast was tolerable in *The Pawnbroker* because it was a movie about the Holocaust, but the naked girls in Antonioni's *Blowup* were unacceptable. Harris even finds room for the slow death of one form of movie criticism, as exemplified by the stuffy Bosley Crowther of the *New York Times,* and the sharper, fresher style that Pauline Kael introduced.

Pictures at a Revolution is smart, then, and it feels real, but these qualities are not what make it such an absorbing read—not for me, anyway. I should perhaps admit at this point that for the last four years or so I have been working on a film script, a labor of love that, like all such projects, occasionally looked as though it was unloved by anybody but me. To cut a long, boring, occasionally maddening and frequently depressing story short, it's now being made into a film, as we speak, and I'm sure that the sudden metamorphosis of script into movie made me relish this book even more than I might otherwise have done: on top of all its other virtues, *Pictures at a Revolution* captures perfectly the long, meandering, dirty, and bewildering path from inspiration to production. There's no guarantee, of course, that anyone will ever see this film I've been involved in, but the great thing about Harris's book is that it has twenty-twenty hindsight, and it makes you feel as if anything might be possible. Who knew that the unemployable twenty-nine-year-old actor that Mike Nichols perversely cast in *The Graduate* would turn into Dustin Hoffman? Who could have predicted that the difficult young actress nicknamed, cruelly, "Done Fadeaway" by Steve McQueen would turn out to be the Oscar-winning star of *Network*? In other words, this book creates the illusion of shape and destiny, always useful when you have no sense of either.

As an added bonus, Harris introduced me to a novel that turned out to be a neglected minor classic. Immediately before Anne Bancroft took the part of Mrs. Robinson in *The Graduate,* she appeared in a small and apparently highly regarded British film called *The Pumpkin Eater*, adapted by Harold Pinter from a 1963 novel by Penelope Mortimer. It's a strange, fresh, gripping book, the story of a woman with five children by three different husbands, now married to a fourth, a successful scriptwriter named Jake Armitage who is sleeping around. If the setup stretches credulity, it should be pointed out that the plot is scrupulously, dizzyingly autobiographical. Or at least, Penelope Mortimer had a lot of children by several different men—not all of whom she was married to—before marrying the successful English novelist, playwright, scriptwriter, and lawyer John Mortimer. One of the many achievements of *The Pumpkin Eater* is that it somehow manages to find the universal truths in what was hardly an archetypal situation: Mortimer peels several layers of skin off the subjects of motherhood, marriage, and monogamy, so that what we're asked to look at is frequently red-raw and painful without being remotely self-dramatizing. In fact, there's a dreaminess to some of the prose that is particularly impressive, considering the tumult that the book describes and, presumably, was written in. Penelope Mortimer's books are mostly out of print, although the wonderful people at Persephone, a publisher that specializes in forgotten twentieth-century novels by women (*Miss Pettigrew Lives for a Day* is one of its notable successes in the U.K.), are bringing back a couple of them this year.

I'm sorry this section is so gossipy, but *The Pumpkin Eater* sheds an extraordinary light on a story that fascinated both the broadsheets and the tabloids in the U.K. a while back. In 2004 Sir John Mortimer, as he is now, was apparently surprised but delighted to learn that he had fathered a child with the well-known and much-loved British actress Wendy Craig at the beginning of the 1960s, while married to Penelope; father and son met for the first time in 2004, and have since formed a bond. (Imagine, I don't know, Garrison Keillor owning up to a child conceived with Shirley Jones of the Partridge Family and you will get a sense of the media interest in the story.) And yet in *The Pumpkin Eater,* Jake Armitage impregnates a young actress, just as his wife is being sterilized—a detail that sounds implausibly and melodramatically novelistic, but which is also, according to *A Voyage Round John Mortimer,* Valerie Grove's recently published biography, drawn from life. It is difficult to understand how his illegitimate son could have been a complete surprise to him, given that his wife had written about it in a novel forty-two years before he is supposed to have found out. If Sir John's surprise is genuine, then he is guilty of a far greater crime than infidelity: he never read his wife's stuff. This is unforgivable, and, I would have thought, extremely good grounds for divorce. If I ever caught my wife not reading something I'd written, there'd be trouble.

I have read other things these last few weeks—Graham McCann's intelligent biography of Cary Grant; the great Richard Price's new novel, *Lush Life,* which is typically absorbing, real, and breathtakingly plotted; Thurston Clarke's inspiring book about RFK's drive for the Democratic nomination in '68, *The Last Campaign.* But I'm not going to write about them, because this is my last column in the *Believer,* at least for a while, and I wanted to leave some space to bang on about how much I've enjoyed the last five years. In 2003, when

I began "Stuff I've Been Reading," I hadn't read *David Copperfield* or Edmund Gosse's *Father and Son*. I'd never read a word by Marilynne Robinson, and *Gilead* hadn't been published. I hadn't read Dylan's *Chronicles*, *Citizen Vince*, *The Dirt*, *How to Breathe Underwater*, *Hangover Square*, *Feed*, *Skellig*... (And, on a more mournful note, two of my favorite contemporary writers, Lorrie Moore and Elizabeth McCracken, have managed to avoid being included in the Books Read list through the simple but devious method of not writing anything since the column began.) I have been reading great books since I was sixteen or so, which means that I should have described one seventh of my most memorable reading experiences in these pages, but it really feels like more than that: you, dear reader, have helped me to choose more wisely than I might otherwise have done, and to read a little bit more vigorously. And quitting (because, despite all the fistfights and legal problems I've had with the Polysyllabic Spree, they never did have the guts to fire me) worries me, because there must be a chance that I'll sink back into my old reading habits: until 2003, I lived exclusively on a diet of chick-lit novels, Arsenal programs from the 1970s, and my own books. At the moment, though, I am telling myself that I'm leaving because I want to read lots of Victorian novels that you wouldn't want to read about, a lie that lets me walk out with dignity, and hope for the future. Thank you for listening, those of you that did—I'll miss you all. ✱

MAY 2010

It's never easy, returning home after failing to make one's way out in the world. When I left these pages in 2008, it was very much in the spirit of "Goodbye, nerdy losers! I'm not wasting any more time ploughing through books on your behalf! I have things to do, places to go, people to see!" Ah, well. What can you do, if the people don't want to be seen? I have now become that pathetic modern phenomenon you might have read about, the boomerang child—the kid who struts off (typically and unwisely with middle finger raised), spends a couple of years screwing up some lowly job on a magazine or in a bank, and then comes back, tail between his legs, to reclaim his old bedroom and wonder how come his parents have more fun than he on a Saturday night.

"What's a parent to do?" bewails a terrifying (for me) article dealing with this very issue on the website *eHow.com*. "It's hard to turn your children away. The best thing a parent can do is help them understand that they are adults now and the rules have changed." The new rules for parents, the piece goes on to say, should include charging rent and refusing to buy toiletries and other incidentals. I'm pretty sure I'm going to end up getting my own way on the incidental toiletries, should it come to that. It's pretty hot here at Believer Towers, and I suspect that the Polysyllabic Spree, the 115 dead-eyed but fragrant people who edit this magazine, will cave in long before I do. Still. It wasn't what I expected when I left: that eighteen months later, I'd be working for free deodorant. What's particularly humiliating in my case is that, unlike most boomerang children, I'm considerably older than those who have taken me back in. They're not as young as they were, the Spree, but even so.

I have decided to vent my spleen by embarking on a series of books that, I hope, will be of no interest whatsoever to the readership of this magazine. David Kynaston's superlative *Austerity Britain* is more than six hundred pages long and deals with just six years, 1945–51, in the life of my country. The second volume in the series, *Family Britain, 1951–57,* has already been published, so I plan to move on to that next; Kynaston is going to take us through to Margaret Thatcher's election in 1979, and I'm warning you now that I plan to read every single word, and write about them in great detail in this column.

I am less than a third of the way through *Austerity Britain,* but I have read enough to know that this is a major work of social history: readable, brilliantly researched, informative, and gripping. Part of Kynaston's triumph is his immense skill in marshaling the resources at his disposal: it seems at times as though he must have read every novel written in the period, and every autobiography, whether that autobiography was written by a member of the postwar Labour government or by a member of England's postwar cricket team. (On page 199 of my paperback, he quotes from former Labour deputy leader Roy Hattersley, Stones bassist Bill Wyman, and cookery writer Elizabeth David, all on the subject of the miserable, bitter winter of 1947.) And it goes without saying that he's listened to every radio program, and trawled through every newspaper.

The effect Kynaston achieves is extraordinary: Britain changes month by month, like a child, and you end up feeling that every citizen of the world should have the opportunity to read a book this good about their own country. I'm glad that not everyone in the U.K. has read it (although it has sold a lot of copies), because you can steal anecdotes from it and pass them off as your own. One of my favorites so far is David Lean's account of showing *Brief Encounter* at a cinema in Rochester, Kent, to a tough audience full of sailors from the nearby Chatham dockyards. "At the first love scene one woman down in the front started to laugh. I'll never forget it. And the second love scene it got worse. And then the audience caught on and waited for her to laugh and they all joined in and it ended in absolute shambles. They were rolling in the aisles." *Brief Encounter* is a much-loved British film, often taken out of a back pocket and waved about when someone wants to make a point about how we have changed as a nation, and what we have lost: in the old days, we spoke better, emoted less, stayed married, didn't get naked at the drop of a hat, etc. We are cursed with an apparently unshakable conviction that we are all much more knowing than people used to be, back in the Pre-Ironic Age, so it is both instructive and humbling to learn that, half a century ago, Rochester sailors didn't need the *Onion* to tell them what was hilarious.

The best stuff of all Kynaston has taken from Britain's extraordinary Mass Observation project, which ran from the late 1930s to the mid-'60s. The creators of MO—the anthropologist Tom Harrisson, the poet Charles Madge, and the filmmaker Humphrey Jennings, among others (even the formidable, and formidably clever, literary critic William Empson was involved somewhere)—got five hundred volunteers to keep diaries or reply to questionnaires, and the results provide the best record of what the war and its aftermath meant to ordinary Britons. True, there were some peculiar types involved; Henry St. John, a civil servant living in Bristol, scrupulously described each opportunity for masturbation, as and when it arose. A visit to London's Windmill Theatre, famous for its nude tableaux vivants, elicits this observation: "I delayed masturbation until another para-nude appeared seen frontways, with drapery depending between the exposed breasts." The day after Hiroshima sees Henry returning to a public lavatory in the northeast "to see if I could masturbate over the mural inscriptions." Say what you like about the internet, but for a certain class of underemployed male, life has become warmer, and more hygienic.

It's not all about wanking, of course. *Austerity Britain* is about the morale of a battered, broke nation, and its attempts to restore itself; it's about food rationing and town planning, housing and culture, socialism and aspiration, and it never forgets for a second that its (mostly gray and brown) tiles make up a big, big mosaic of our tiny, beleaguered island. And if you read or write fiction, you may be gratified to see how Kynaston relies on the contemporary stuff to add color and authenticity to his portrait of the times. The received wisdom is that novels too much of the moment won't last; but what else do we have that delves so deeply into what we were thinking and feeling at any given period? In fifty or one hundred years' time, we are, I suspect, unlikely to want to know what someone writing in 2010 had to say about the American Civil War. I don't want to put you off, if you're just writing the last paragraph of a seven-hundred-page epic novel about Gettysburg—I'm sure you'll win loads of prizes and so on. But after that, you've had it.

It's been a month of enjoyment in unlikely places, if David Kynaston will forgive me for wondering whether an enormous nonfiction book with the word *austerity* in the title was going to be any fun. Francis Spufford's forthcoming novel, *Red Plenty,* is about Nikita Khrushchev's planned economy, and it contains the phrase (admittedly in the extensive footnotes at the back) "the multipliers on which Kantorovich's solution to optimisation problems depended," and it's terrific. Yes, reading it involves a certain amount of self-congratulation— "Look at me! I'm reading a book about shortages in the early '60s Soviet rubber industry, and I'm loving it!" But actually, such sentiments are entirely misplaced, and completely unfair to Spufford, who has succeeded in turning possibly the least-promising fictional material of all time into an incredibly smart, surprisingly involving, and deeply eccentric book, a hammer-and-sickle version of Altman's *Nashville,* with central committees replacing country music. (*Red Plenty* would probably make a marvelous film, but I'll let someone else pitch the idea to the Hollywood studio that would have to pay for it.) Spufford provides a terrific cast, a mixture of the real and the fictional, and hundreds of vignettes that illustrate how Khrushchev's honorable drive to bring enough of whatever was needed to his hungry and oppressed countrymen, impacted on the lives of economists, farmers, politicians, black-marketeers, and even hack writers. (There was, of course, no other type, seeing as you wrote what you were told to write.)

Francis Spufford's name has come up in this column before: his *The Child That Books Built* is a brilliant memoir about what we read when we're young and why. And though I am not alone in thinking that he has one of the most original minds in contemporary literature, there really aren't as many of us as there should be. His own fantastic perversity is to blame for this—apart from *Red Plenty* and the memoir, he's written books about ice and English boffins—but you always end up convinced that the fusty-looking subject he's picked is resonant in all sorts of ways that you couldn't possibly have foreseen. One of his themes here is the sheer brainpower required for the extraordinary experiment that was Soviet communism; we know now that it was an experiment that failed, but controlling all aspects of supply and demand is a lot more complicated than sitting back and letting the market sort everything out. It turns out that genius is required. Not quite as much was necessary for the conception, research, and writing of this extraordinary novel, but that's only because novels don't need as much as entire economic systems. Oh, come on. They really don't.

A year or so back, my coeditor and I selected a story by Philipp Meyer for a collection we were putting together. (It came out, this collection. It was one of the many moneymaking schemes of the last eighteen months that failed to make money. Short stories by mostly young, mostly unknown American writers! For publication in the U.K. only! What could have gone wrong? Nothing, that's what. Which is why I suspect that I've been diddled, and that my coeditor is currently snorting cocaine and buying racehorses in Florida.) It was pretty good, this story, so when I saw Meyer's first novel, *American Rust,* reviewed ecstatically in the *Economist,* of all places, I... well, I was going to say, self-aggrandizingly, that I hunted it down, like some kind of implacable bibliomaniac Mountie, but we all know that nowadays hunting books down takes about two seconds.

The cover of my copy of *American Rust* sports blurbs by both Patricia Cornwell and Colm Tóibín, which positions it very neatly: *American Rust* is one of those rare books that provides the reader with not only a big subject—the long, slow death of working-class America—but a gripping plot that tunnels us right into the middle of it. Isaac and Poe, early twenties, both have plans to escape their broken Pennsylvania town, full of rotting steel mills (the book is crying out for a quote from Springsteen to go alongside those from Tóibín and Cornwell). Isaac is smart, and wants to go to a California college; Poe has been offered a sports scholarship that he's too unfocused to accept. And then Isaac kills someone, and it all goes to hell.

There is nothing missing from this book that I noticed, nothing that Meyer can't do. His characters are beautifully drawn and memorable—not just Isaac and Poe, but the sisters and parents and police chiefs, even the minor characters, the Dickensian drifters and petty criminals that Isaac meets during his flight from Pennsylvania. The plot is constructed in such a way that it produces all kinds of delicate moral complications, and none of this is at the expense of the book's sorrowful, truly empathetic soul. And, unlike most first novelists, Meyer knows that we're all going to die, and that before we do so we are going to mess our lives up somehow. There. I hope that's sold it to you.

You have to admit that when three books this good get read back to back, I'm the one that has to be given most of the credit. Yes, I appreciate the craft that has gone into these books, the research, the love, the patience, the imagination, the immense skill—just as I appreciate the craft that goes into the making of a perfectly spherical and lovingly stitched football. But, with the greatest of respect to Kynaston, Spufford, and Meyer, it's the reader who sticks the ball in the back of the net, the person who really counts. He shoots, he scores. Three times. A hat trick, in his first column back! He's still got it. ★

JUNE 2010

S o this last month, I went to the Oscars. I went to the Oscars as a *nominee*, I should stress (apparently in underlined italics), not as some loser, even though that, ironically, was what I became during the ceremony, by virtue of the archaic and almost certainly corrupt academy voting process. And my task now is to find a way of making the inclusion of that piece of information look relevant to a column about my reading life, rather than gratuitous and self-congratulatory. And I think I can do it, too: it strikes me that just about every book I've read in the past few weeks could be categorized as anti-Oscar. *Austerity*

Britain? That one's pretty obvious. Both words in that title are antithetical to everything that happens in Hollywood during awards season. You're unlikely to catch a CAA agent in the lobby of the Chateau Marmont reading Andrew Brown's thoughtful, occasionally pained book about his complicated relationship with Sweden; Elif Batuman's funny, original *The Possessed: Adventures with Russian Books and the People Who Read Them* is populated by people who spend their entire lives thinking about, say, the short stories of Isaac Babel, rather than Jennifer Aniston's career. (I'm not saying that one mental occupation is superior to the other, but they're certainly different, possibly even oppositional.) And even Patti Smith's memoir, which could have been glamorous and starry, is as much about Genet and Blake as it is about rock and roll, and is suffused with a sense of purpose and an authenticity absent even from independent cinema. Oh, and no fiction at all, which has got to be significant in some way, no? If you want to ward off corruption, then surely the best way to do it is to sit by a swimming pool and read a chapter about Britain's postwar housing crisis. It worked for me, anyway. I can exclusively reveal that if you sit by a swimming pool in L.A., wearing swimming shorts and reading David Kynaston, then Hollywood starlets leave you alone.

Finishing *Austerity Britain* was indisputably my major achievement of the month, more satisfying, even, than sitting in a plush seat and applauding for three and a half hours while other people collected statuettes. A month ago I had read less than a third of the book, yet it was already becoming apparent that Kynaston's research, the eccentric depth and breadth of it, was going to provide more pleasure than one had any right to expect; there were occasions during the last few hundred pages when it made me laugh. At one point, Kynaston quotes a 1948 press release from the chairman of Hoover, and adds in a helpful parenthetical that it was "probably written for him by a young Muriel Spark." The joy that extra information brings is undeniable, but, once you get to know Kynaston, you will come to recognize the pain and frustration hidden in that word *probably*: how many hours of his life, you wonder, were spent trying to remove it?

While I was reading about the birth of our National Health Service, President Obama was winning his battle to extend health care in America; it's salutary, then, to listen to the recollections of the doctors who treated work-ing-class Britons in those early days. "I certainly found when the Health Service started on the 5th July '48 that for the first six months I had as many as twenty or thirty ladies come to me who had the most unbelievable gynaecological conditions—I mean, of that twenty or thirty there would be at least ten who had complete prolapse of their womb, and they had to hold it up with a towel as if they had a large nappy on." Some 8 million pairs of free spectacles were provided in the first year, as well as countless false teeth. It's not that people were dying without free health care; it's that their quality of life was extraordinarily, needlessly low. Before the NHS, we were fumbling around half-blind, unable to chew, and swaddled in giant homemade sanitary napkins; is it possible that in twenty-first-century America, the poor are doing the same? Two of the most distinctive looks in rock and roll were provided by the NHS, by the way. John Lennon's specs of choice were the 422 Panto Round Oval; meanwhile, Elvis Costello favored the 524 Contour. What, you think David Kynaston would have failed to provide the serial numbers? Panto Round Oval, by the way, would be a pretty cool name for a band. Be my guest, but thank me in the acknowledgments.

My parents were in their twenties during the period covered in *Austerity Britain,* and it's easy to see why they and their generation went crazy when we asked for the simplest things—new hi-fis, chopper bikes, Yes triple-albums—when we were in our teens. They weren't lying; they really didn't have stuff like that when they were young. Some 35 percent of urban households didn't have a fixed bath; nearly 20 percent didn't have exclusive access to a toilet. One of the many people whose diaries provide Kynaston with the backbone to this book describes her father traveling from Leicester to west London, a distance of over a hundred miles, to watch the 1949 FA Cup Final, the equivalent of the Super Bowl back then. He didn't go all that way because he had a ticket for the game; it was just that he'd been invited to watch a friend's nine-inch black and white television. We stayed in the Beverly Wilshire for the Oscars, thank you for asking. It was OK.

I haven't read *Puzzled People,* the Mass Observation book published in 1947 about contemporary attitudes to spirituality, all the way through. (As I explained last month—please keep up—Mass Observation was a sociological experiment in which several hundred people were asked to keep diaries, and, occasionally, to answer questionnaires; the results have provided historians, including David Kynaston, with a unique source of information.) And you don't need to read the whole thing, anyway. The oblique first-person responses to metaphysical matters are ideal, if you have a spare moment to dabble in some found poetry—and who doesn't, really?—much as the surreality of the Clinton/Lewinsky testimony led to the brilliant little book *Poetry Under Oath* a few years back. ("I don't know / That I said that / I don't / I don't remember / What I said / And I don't remember / To whom I said it.") Here are a couple I made at home:

THE PURPOSE OF LIFE
Now you've caught me.
I've no idea.

My life's all work
And having babies.

Well, I think we're all cogs
Of one big machine.

What I'm wondering is,
What is the machine for?

That's your query.
JESUS
I wouldn't mind
Being like Him

But he was too good.

Didn't he say
"Be ye perfect"

Or something like that?

Well,
That's just
Ridiculous

I bought *Fishing in Utopia* because I found myself in a small and clearly struggling independent village-bookshop, and I was desperate to give the proprietor some money, but it was a struggle to find anything that I could imagine myself reading, among all the cookbooks and local histories. And sometimes imagination is enough. Surely we all occasionally buy books because of a daydream we're having—a little fantasy about the people we might turn into one day, when our lives are different, quieter, more introspective, and when all the urgent reading, whatever that might be, has been done. We never arrive at that point, needless to say, but *Fishing in Utopia*—quirky, obviously smart, quiet, and contemplative—is exactly the sort of thing I was going to pick up when I became someone else. By reading it now, I have got ahead of myself; I suspect that the vulgarity of awards season propelled me into my own future.

And in any case, the Sweden that Andrew Brown knew in the late '70s and early '80s is not a million miles, or even forty years, away from Austerity Britain. Our postwar Labour government was in some ways as paternalistic, and as dogged and dour in its pursuit of a more egalitarian society, as Olof Palme's Social Democrats, and one can't help but feel a sense of loss: there was a time when we were encouraged to think and act collectively, in ways that were not always designed to further individual self-interest. In England after the war, no TV was shown between the hours of six and eight p.m., a hiatus that became known as the Toddler's Truce; the BBC decided that bedtime was stressful enough for parents as it was, and, as there was only one TV channel in the U.K. until 1955, childless viewers were left to twiddle their thumbs. In Olof Palme's Sweden, you bought booze in much the same way as you bought pornography: furtively, and from the back of a shady-looking shop. It would be nice to think that we have arrived at our current modus vivendi—children watching thirty-plus hours of TV a week, young people with a savage binge-drinking problem, in the U.K. at least—after prolonged national debates about individual liberty versus the greater good, but of course it just happened, mostly because the free market wanted it to. I may not have sold *Fishing in Utopia* to you unless you are at least a bit Swedish and/or you like casting flies. But Andrew Brown demonstrates that any subject under the sun, however unpromising, can be riveting, complex, and resonant, if approached with intelligence and an elegant prose style. He even throws in a dreamy, mystical passage about the meaning and consolations of death, and you don't come across many of those.

Despite my affection for my German publishers, and for Cologne, the city in which my German publishers live, I wasn't particularly looking forward to reading at LitCologne, the hugely successful literary festival that takes place there every March. I had been traveling a lot (I was actually nominated for an Academy Award this year, believe it or not, and that necessitated quite a lot of schlepping around), and the novel I was reading from feels as though it came out a lifetime ago, and I hadn't written anything for the best part of a year. And then, the morning after my reading, I was in Cologne Cathedral with Patti Smith and our German editor, admiring the beautiful new Gerhard Richter window, and I remembered what's so great about literary festivals: stuff like that usually happens. It's not always Patti Smith, of course, but it's frequently someone interesting, someone whose work has meant a lot to me over the years, and I end up wondering what I could possibly have written in these twenty-four hours that would have justified missing out on the experience. I started *Just Kids* on the plane home and finished it a couple of days later.

Like Dylan's *Chronicles*, it's a riveting analysis of how an artist ended up the way she did (and as I get older, books about the sources of creativity are becoming especially interesting to me, for reasons I don't wish to think about), and all the things she read and listened to and looked at that helped her along the way. And it was a long journey, too. Smith arrived in New York in the summer of '67, and her first album was released in 1975. In between there was drawing, and then poetry, and then poetry readings with a guitar, and then readings with a guitar and a piano... And yet this story, the story of how a New Jersey teenager turned into Patti Smith, is only a subplot, because *Just Kids* is about her relationship with Robert Mapplethorpe, the young man she met on her very first day in New York City, fell in love with, lived with, and remained devoted to for the rest of his short life. One of the most impressive things about *Just Kids* is its discipline: that's Smith's subject, and she sticks to it, and everything else we learn about her comes to us through the prism of that narrative.

There is a lot in this book about being young in New York in the 1970s—the Chelsea Hotel, Warhol and Edie Sedgwick, Wayne County and Max's Kansas City, Tom Verlaine and Richard Lloyd, Gregory Corso and Sam Shepard. And of course one feels a pang, the sort of ache that comes from being the wrong age in the wrong place at the wrong time. The truth is, though, that many of us—most of us—could have been right outside the front door of Max's Kansas City and never taken the trouble (or plucked up the courage) to open it. You had to be Patti Smith, or somebody just as committed to a certain idea of life and how to live it, to do that. I felt a different kind of longing while reading *Just Kids*. I wanted to go back to a time when cities were cheap and full of junk, and on every side street there was a shop with dusty windows that sold radiograms and soul albums with the corners cut off, or secondhand books that nobody had taken the trouble to value. (Smith always seems to be finding copies of *Love and Mr Lewisham* signed by H. G. Wells, or complete sets of Henry James, the sale of which pays the rent for a couple of weeks.) Now it's just lattes and bottles of banana foot lotion, and it's difficult to see how banana foot lotion will end up producing the Patti Smiths of the twenty-first century; she needed the possibilities of the city, its apparently inexhaustible pleasures and surprises. Anyway, I loved *Just Kids,* and I will treasure my signed hardback until I die—when, like all my other precious signed first editions, it will be sold by my sons, for much less than it will be worth, probably to fund their gambling habits. And then, perhaps, it will be bought secondhand by a rocking boho in some postcapitalist thrift store on Fifth Avenue or Oxford Street, and the whole thing will start up all over again. ✳

JULY / AUGUST 2010

BOOKS BOUGHT:

* ★ *The Lodger Shakespeare: His Life on Silver Street*—Charles Nicholl
* ★ *The Birds on the Trees*—Nina Bawden
* ★ *The Driver's Seat*—Muriel Spark
* ★ *Peter Pan*—J. M. Barrie
* ★ *Fire from Heaven*—Mary Renault
* ★ *Live from New York: An Uncensored History of Saturday Night Live*
  —Tom Shales and James Andrew Miller
* ★ Too many other Muriel Spark novels to mention without embarrassment

BOOKS READ:

* ★ *Who Is It That Can Tell Me Who I Am?: The Journal of a Psychotherapist*
  —Jane Haynes
* ★ *The Birds on the Trees*—Nina Bawden
* ★ *The Driver's Seat*—Muriel Spark
* ★ *The Prime of Miss Jean Brodie*—Muriel Spark
* ★ *A Far Cry from Kensington*—Muriel Spark

I f you are reading this in the U.S., the presumption over here in the U.K. is that you have either just come out of a session with your shrink or you're just about to go into one, and for reasons best known to ourselves, we disapprove— in the same way that we disapprove of the way you sign up for twelve-step programs at the drop of a hat, just because you're getting through a bottle of vodka every evening after work and throwing up in the street on the way home. "That's just life," we say. "Deal with it." (To which you'd probably reply, "We are dealing with it! That's why we've signed up for a twelve-step program!" So we'd go, "Well, deal with it in a less self-absorbed way." By which we mean, "Don't deal with it at all! Grin and bear it!" But then, what do we know? We're smashed out of our skulls most of the time.)

Recently I read an interview with a British comic actress, an interesting, clever one, and she articulated, quite neatly, the bizarre assumptions and prejudices of my entire nation when it comes to the subject of the talking cure. "I have serious problems with it… The way I see it is that you're paying someone, so they don't really care about you—they're not listening in the way that someone who loves you does."

There's a good deal in that little lot to unpack. The assumption that if you give someone money, then, ipso facto, they don't care about you, is a curious one; the chief complaint I have about my dentist is that he cares too much, and as a consequence is always telling me not to eat this or smoke that. According to the actress, he should just be laughing all the way to the bank. And how does she feel about child care? Maybe she can't bring herself to use it, but in our house we're effectively paying someone to love our kids. (Lord knows, it wouldn't happen any other way.) But the real zinger is in that second argument, the one about "not listening in the way that someone who loves you does." Aaaargh! Der! D'oh! That's the whole point, and to complain that therapists aren't friends is rather like complaining that osteopaths aren't pets.

One of the relationships described in *Who Is It That Can Tell Me Who I Am?*, psychotherapist Jane Haynes's gripping, moving, and candid memoir, is clearly a defining relationship in her life, a love affair in all but the conventional sense. The affair is between Haynes and her own therapist, and the first half of the book is addressed to him; he died before their sessions had reached a conclusion, and Haynes's grief is agonizing and raw. So much for the theory that a bought relationship can't be real. In the second half of the book, Haynes describes the problems and the breakthroughs of a handful of her patients, people paralyzed by the legacies of their personal histories, and only the most unimaginative and Gradgrindian of readers could doubt the value of the therapeutic process. Pills won't work for the patient whose long, sad personal narrative has produced an addiction to internet pornography; pills didn't work for the woman who was saved from suicide, tragicomically, only because of a supermarket bag she placed over her head after she'd taken an overdose. (The maid cleaning her hotel room would have presumed she was sleeping had it not been for the fact that her face was obscured by an advertisement for Tesco.) As Hilary Mantel says in her quite-brilliant introduction, we don't enter the consulting room alone, "but with our parents and grandparents, and behind them, jostling their ghost limbs for space, our ancestral host, our tribe. All these people need a place in the room, all need to be heard. And against them, our own voice has to assert itself, small and clear, so that we possess the narrative of our own lives." In a bravura passage, Mantel goes on to describe what those narratives might read like: "For some of us, they are a jerky cinema flickering against a rumpled bedsheet, the reels out of order and the projectionist drunk. For some of us they are slick and fake as an old dance routine, all high kicks and false smiles and a desperate sweat inside an ill-fitting costume... For others, the narrative is the patter of a used-car salesman, a promise of progress and conveyance, insistently delivered with an oily smirk... There is a story we need to tell, we think: but this is not how; this is not it." If you think you can find a friend who is prepared to listen hour after hour, year after year, to your painful, groping attempt to construct your own narrative, then good luck to you. Me, I have friends who are prepared to listen for ten minutes to my list of which players Arsenal Football Club needs to mount a serious challenge next year—but then, I'm an English bloke. My therapist, however, has tolerated more agonized, baffled nonsense than any human being should endure. And yes, I pay him, but not enough.

Perhaps unsurprisingly, given the tenor of Mantel's introduction and the nature of psychotherapy itself, with its painfully slow storyboarding of life's plot twists, there is a good deal in this book about the value of literature. Haynes repeatedly claims that she'd find her job impossible without it, in fact—that Shakespeare and Tolstoy, J. M. Barrie (there's an extraordinary passage from *Peter Pan* quoted here, hence its appearance in Books Bought), and Chekhov have all created grooves that our narratives frequently wobble into, helpfully, illuminatingly. So even if you have no time for Jung and Freud, there's something for the curious and literate *Believer* reader, and as I can't imagine there's any other kind, then this book is for you. It's occasionally a little self-dramatizing, but it's serious and seriously smart, and Haynes allows her patients a voice, too: Callum, the young man addicted to pornography, makes an incidental but extremely important observation about the "pandemic" that the internet has helped spread among men of his generation. (Haynes quotes the psychoanalyst Joan Raphael-Leff, who says that sex "is not merely a meeting of bodily parts or their insertion into the other but *of flesh doing the bidding of fantasy*." So what does it say about those who use pornography, I wonder, that they are prepared to spend so much time watching the insertion of body parts?) I'm going to stop banging on about this book now, but I got a lot out of it. As you can probably tell.

In 1971, the Booker Prize suddenly changed its qualification period. Up until then, the prize had been awarded to a work of fiction published in the previous twelve months; in '71 they switched it, and the award went to a book released contemporaneously. In other words, novels published in 1970 weren't eligible for the prize. So somebody has had the bright idea of creating a Lost Booker Prize for this one year, and as a consequence our bookstores are displaying a short list of novels that, if not exactly forgotten (they had to be in print to qualify), certainly weren't terribly near the top of British book-club reading lists—and I'm betting not many of you have read Nina Bawden's *The Birds on the Trees*, J. G. Farrell's *Troubles*, *The Bay of Noon* by Shirley Hazzard, *Fire from Heaven* by Mary Renault, *The Driver's Seat* by Muriel Spark, or Patrick White's *The Vivisector*. I bought three of them, partly because it was such a pleasure to see books published forty years ago on a table at the front of a chain store: British bookshops are desperately, crushingly dull at the moment. Our independents are almost all gone, leaving bookselling at the mercy of the chains and the supermarkets, and they tend to favor memoirs written, or at least approved, by reality-TV stars with surgically enhanced breasts, and recipe books by TV chefs. To be honest, even memoirs written in person by reality-TV stars with entirely natural breasts wouldn't lift the cultural spirits much. If asked to represent this magazine's views, I'd say we favor natural breasts over augmented, but that breasts generally are discounted when we come to consider literary merit. And if I have that wrong, then I can only apologize.

Nina Bawden's *The Birds on the Trees* is what became known, a few years later, as a Hampstead Novel—Hampstead being a wealthy borough of London that, in the imagination of some of our grumpier provincial critics, is full of people who work in the media and commit adultery. My wife grew up there, and she works in the media, but... Actually, I should do some fact-checking before I finish that sentence. I'll get back to you. Nobody would dare write a Hampstead novel anymore, I suspect, and though its disappearance is not necessarily a cause for noisy lamentation—there is only so much to say about novelists having affairs, after all—it's interesting to read an early example of the genre. *The Birds on the Trees* is about a middle-class media family (the wife is a novelist, the husband a journalist) in the process of falling apart, mostly because of the stress brought on by a son with mental-health problems. People drink a lot of spirits. Marshall McLuhan is mentioned, and he doesn't come up so much in fiction anymore. There are lots of characters in this short book, all with tangled, knotty connections to each other—it feels like a novel-shaped Manhattan at times—and, refreshingly, Bawden doesn't feel the need to be definitive. There's none of that sense of "If you read one book this year, make it this one"; you get the sense that it was written in an age where people consumed new fiction as a matter of course, so there was no need to say everything you had to say in one enormous, authoritative volume.

None of the Lost Booker books are very long; I chose to read Muriel Spark's *The Driver's Seat* (a) because I'd never read anything by Muriel Spark before, and she has the kind of reputation that convinced me I was missing out, and (b) her novel was so slim that it is almost invisible to the naked eye. And, if you look at the Books Bought and Books Read columns this month, you will see, dear youthful writer, that short books make sound economic and artistic sense. If Spark had written a doorstopper of a novel, I probably wouldn't have bought it; if I'd bought it, I wouldn't have gotten around to picking it up; if I'd picked it up, I wouldn't have finished it; if I'd finished it, I'd have chalked her off my to-do list, and my relationship with Muriel Spark would be over. As it is, she's all I read at the moment, and the income of her estate (she died four years ago) is swelling by the day. What's the flaw in this business plan? There isn't one.

My only caveat is that your short novels have to be really, really good—that's the motor for the whole thing. (If you're going to write bad short books, then forget it—you'd be better off writing one bad long one.) *The Driver's Seat*, which is pitched straight into the long grass somewhere between Patricia Highsmith and early Pinter, is a creepy and unsettling novella about a woman who travels from Britain to an unnamed European city, apparently because she is hell-bent on getting herself murdered. I couldn't really tell you why Spark felt compelled to write it, but understanding the creative instinct isn't a prerequisite for admiring a work of art, and its icy strangeness is part of its charm. *A Far Cry from Kensington* came later but is set earlier, in a West London boarding-house whose inhabitants are drawn toward each other in strange ways when one of them, an editor at a publishing house, is rude to a talentless hack. (She calls him a "*pisseur de copie,*" an insult that is repeated gleefully and satisfyingly throughout the book. Spark is fond of strange, funny mantras.) *The Prime of Miss Jean Brodie* is her most famous novel, at least here, where the movie, star-ring Maggie Smith as an overbearing and eccentric teacher in a refined Scottish girls' school, is one of our national cinematic treasures. I probably enjoyed this last one the least of the three—partly because I'd seen the film, partly because Miss Brodie is such a brilliantly realized archetype that I felt I'd already come across several less-successful versions of her. (Influential books are often a disappointment, if they're properly influential, because influence cannot guar-antee the quality of the imitators, and your appetite for the original has been partially sated by its poor copies.) But what a writer Spark is—dry, odd, funny, aphoristic, wise, technically brilliant. I can't remember the last time I read a book by a well-established writer previously unknown to me that resulted in me devouring an entire oeuvre—but that only brings me back to the subject of short books, their beauty and charm and efficacy. *A Far Cry from Kensington* weighs in at a whopping 208 pages, but the rest are all around the 150 mark. You want your oeuvre devoured? Look and learn.

At the end of *The Prime of Miss Jean Brodie,* one of Miss Brodie's girls, now all grown up, visits another, and attempts to tell her about her troubled marriage. "'I'm not much good at that sort of problem,' said Sandy. But Monica had not thought she would be able to help much, for she knew Sandy of old, and persons known of old can never be much help." Which sort of brings us full circle.

In next month's exciting episode, I will describe an attempt, not yet begun, to read *Our Mutual Friend* on a very modern ebook machine thing. It's the future. Monday, in fact, probably, once more Spark oeuvre has been devoured. ✳

SEPTEMBER 2010

BOOKS BOUGHT:

* *Our Mutual Friend*—Charles Dickens
* *Brooklyn: Historically Speaking*—John B. Manbeck

BOOKS DOWNLOADED FOR NOTHING:

* *Our Mutual Friend*—Charles Dickens
* *The Adventures of Huckleberry Finn*—Mark Twain
* *Babbitt*—Sinclair Lewis

BOOKS READ:

* *Live From New York: An Uncensored History of Saturday Night Live*
  —Tom Shales and James Andrew Miller
* *Brooklyn*—Colm Tóibín
* *The Girls of Slender Means*—Muriel Spark
* *The Given Day*—Dennis Lehane (half)
* *Loitering With Intent*—Muriel Spark (half)
* *The Finishing School*—Muriel Spark (half)
* *Tinkers*—Paul Harding (one-third)

Four years ago to the very month, as I'm sure you will remember, this column daringly introduced a Scientist of the Month award. The first winner was Matthias Wittlinger, of the University of Ulm, in Germany, who had done remarkable things with, and to, ants. In an attempt to discover how it was that they were able to find their way home, Wittlinger had shortened the legs of one group and put another group on stilts, in order to alter their stride patterns. Shortening the legs of ants struck us, back in 2006, as an entirely admirable way to spend one's time—but we were younger then, and it was a more innocent age. Despite the huge buzz surrounding the inaugural award, Wittlinger received nothing at all, and is unlikely even to know about his triumph, unless he subscribes to this magazine. And to add insult to injury, there was no subsequent winner, because the following month we forgot about the whole thing.

Anyway: it's back! I am absurdly pleased to announce that this month's recipient, Rolando Rodríguez-Muñoz, is employed at a university right here in England, the University of Exeter. Together with his colleague Tom Tregenza, Rodríguez-Muñoz has been studying the mating strategies of crickets; they discovered, according to the *Economist,* that "small males... could overcome the handicap of their stature and win mates through prodigious chirping." In other words, being the lead singer works for the nerdy and the disadvantaged in other species, too.

Rodríguez-Muñoz has shaded it over Tregenza because, after he and his colleagues had "captured, marked, released and tracked hundreds of crickets," they filmed sixty-four different cricket burrows; Rodríguez-Muñoz watched and analyzed the results, two hundred and fifty thousand hours of footage. A quarter of a million hours! Just under three years of cricket porn! Presumably crickets, like the rest of us, spend much more time trying to get sex than actually having it, but even so, he must have seen some pretty racy stuff. Some of the sterner members of the judging panel tried to argue that because Rolando had watched the film on fast-forward, and on sixteen monitors at once, he had cut corners, but I'm not having that; as far as I'm concerned, watching crickets mate quickly is even harder than watching them mate in normal time. No, Rolando Rodríguez-Muñoz is a hero, and fully deserving of all the good things about to come his way.

There was a hurtful suggestion, four years ago, that the Scientist of the Month was somehow tangentially connected to the World Cup. He hasn't read enough to fill up a whole column, because he's spent the entire month watching TV, the argument went; so just because he stumbled upon an interesting article in a magazine between games, he's invented this bullshit to get him out of a hole. I resent this deeply, not least because it devalues the brilliant work of these amazing scientists. And though it is true that, at the time of writing, we are approaching the end of another World Cup, and reading time has indeed been in shorter supply, I can assure you that the sudden reappearance of this prestigious honor is pure, though admittedly baffling, coincidence.

The effect of the World Cup on the books I intended to read has been even more damaging in 2010 than it was in 2006. In '06, I simply didn't pick any up, and though I was troubled by the ease with which a game between Turkey and Croatia could suppress my hunger for literature, at least literature itself emerged from the tournament unscathed. This time around, as you can see from the list above, my appetite was partially satisfied by grazing on the first few pages of several books, and as a consequence, there are half-chewed novels lying all over the place. At least, I'm presuming they're lying all over the place; I seem to have temporarily lost most of them. When the World Cup is over, and we clear away the piles of betting slips and wall charts, some of them will, presumably, reappear. I wrote in this column recently about Muriel Spark's novels, their genius and their attractive brevity, but there is an obvious disadvantage to her concision: her books tend to get buried under things. I can put my hands on Dennis Lehane's historical novel *The Given Day* whenever I want, simply because it is seven hundred pages long. True, this hasn't helped it to get itself read, but at least it's visible. I didn't lose *The Girls of Slender Means,* and it was as eccentric and funny and sad as the bunch of Spark novels I read last month.

At the end of the last column, I vowed to have read *Our Mutual Friend* on an e-reader, and that didn't happen either. This was partly because of the football, and partly because the experience of reading Dickens in this way was unsatisfactory. It wasn't just that a Victorian novelist clearly doesn't belong on a sleek twenty-first-century machine; I also took the cheapskate route and downloaded the novel from a website that allows you to download out-of-copyright novels for no charge. I helped myself to *Babbitt* and *The Adventures of Huckleberry Finn* at the same time. The edition squirted down to me came without footnotes, however, and I rather like footnotes. More to the point, I *need* footnotes occasionally. (You may well work out for yourself eventually that the "dust" so vital to the plot is household rubbish, rather than fine grains of dirt, but it saves a lot of confusion and doubt to have this explained clearly and plainly right at the beginning of the novel.) The advantage handed the e-reading business by copyright laws hadn't really occurred to me before I helped myself, but it spells trouble for publishers, of course; Penguin and Co. make a lot of money selling books by people who are long dead, and if we all take the free-downloading route, then there will be less money for the living writers. In a spirit of self-chastisement, I bought a copy of *Our Mutual Friend* immediately, even though I have one somewhere already. It won't do any good, in the long run, because clearly books, publishers, readers, and writers are all doomed. But maybe we should all do what we can to stave off impending disaster just that little bit longer.

I was attempting to read *Our Mutual Friend* for professional reasons: I'm supposed to be writing an introduction for a forthcoming edition. I read Colm Tóibín's *Brooklyn* for work, too: I was asked to consider taking on the job of adapting it for the cinema, and as about a million critics and several real people had told me how good it was, I took the offer seriously. It's not the best circumstance in which to read a novel. Instead of admiring the writing, thinking about the characters, turning the page to discover what happens next, you're thinking, Oh, I dunno, and, Yay, I could chop that, and, Miley Cyrus would be *great* for this, and, Do I really want to spend the next few years of my life wrecking this guy's prose? It is a tribute to Tóibín's novel—its quiet, careful prose, its almost agonizing empathy for its characters, its conviction in its own reality—that pretty soon I forgot why I was reading it, and just read it. And then, after I'd finished it, I decided that I wanted to adapt it—not just because I loved it, but because I could see it. Not the movie, necessarily, but the world of the novel: the third-class cabin in which his protagonist travels from Liverpool to New York in the early 1950s, the department store she works in, the dances she attends. They are portrayed with a director of photography's relish for depth and light and detail.

The laziest, most irritating book-club criticism of a novel is that the reader "just didn't care" about the characters or their predicament, a complaint usually made in a tone suggesting that this banality is the product of deep and original thought. (It never seems to occur to these critics that the deficiency may well lie within themselves, rather than in the pages of the books. Perhaps they feel similarly about their friends, parents, children. "The trouble with my kid is that she doesn't make me *care* enough about her." Are we all supposed to nod sagely at that?)

It is not intended to be a backhanded compliment when I say that Tóibín doesn't care whether you care about Eilis, his heroine; it's not that the book is chilly or neutral, or that Tóibín is a disengaged writer. He's not. But he's patient, and nerveless, and unsentimental, and he trusts the story rather than the prose to deliver the emotional payoff. And it does deliver. *Brooklyn* chooses the narrative form of a much cheaper kind of book—"one woman, two countries, two men"—but that isn't what it's about; you're not quite sure what it's about until the last few pages, and then you can see how carefully the trap has been laid for you. I loved it. Will I wreck it? It's perfectly possible, of course. It's a very delicate piece, and Eilis is a watchful, still center. I won't have to hack away at its complicated architecture, though, because it doesn't have one, so maybe I have half a chance. By the time you read this, I should have started in on it; if you have a ten-year-old daughter with ambitions to be an actor, then she might as well start trying to acquire an Irish accent. In my experience of the film business, we'll be shooting sometime in 2020, if it hasn't all collapsed by then.

In a way, I read *Live From New York,* an oral history of *Saturday Night Live,* because of work, too. Earlier in the year I got an American agent, a lovely, smart woman whose every idea, suggestion, and request I've ignored, more or less since the moment we agreed she'd represent me. Anyway, she recommended Tom Shales and James Andrew Miller's book, and my feeling was that if I'm not going to make her a penny, I could at least follow up on her book tips. And I'm pretty sure that if it had to be one or the other, money or successful recommendations, she'd go for the recommendations. That's what makes her special.

I read the book despite never having seen a single minute of *Saturday Night Live,* at least prior to Tina Fey's turn as Sarah Palin in 2008. The show was never shown in the U.K., so I hadn't a clue who any of these people were. Will Ferrell? Bill Murray? Adam Sandler? Eddie Murphy? John Belushi? Chris Rock? Dan Aykroyd? It's sweet that you have your own TV stars over there. You've probably never heard of Pat Phoenix, either.

When it's done well, as it is here, then the oral history is pretty unbeatable as a nonfiction form—engrossing, light on its feet, the constant switching of voices a guarantee against dullness. Legs McNeil's *Please Kill Me: The Uncensored Oral History of Punk,* George Plimpton's Edie Sedgwick book, Studs Terkel's

Working... These are books that I hope to return to one day, when I've read everything else. *Live From New York* is probably just a little too long for someone unfamiliar with the show, but if you want to learn something about the crafts of writing and performing, then you'll pick something up every few pages. I am still thinking about these words from Lorne Michaels:

> The amount of things that have to come together for something to be good is just staggering. And the fact that there's anything good at all is just amazing. When you're young, you assume that just knowing the difference between good and bad is enough: "I'll just do good work, because I prefer it to bad work."

Michaels's observation contains a terrible truth: you think, at a certain point in your life, that your impeccable taste will save you. As life goes on, you realize it's a bit more complicated than that.

While I was reading *Live From New York,* I realized that G. E. Smith, the show's musical director, was the same G.E. Smith who sat next to me on a plane from New York to London, sometime in 1976 or 1977. I was just returning to college after visiting my dad; Smith was on tour with Daryl Hall and John Oates, who were up in first class. He was the first musician I'd ever met, and he was charming, and generous with his time. And he sold me on *Abandoned Luncheonette,* Hall and Oates's heartstoppingly lovely folk-soul album, recorded well before the disco years (which were pretty good, too, actually). He wouldn't remember a single second of them, but the conversations we had on that flight helped feed the idea, just sprouting then, that I didn't want a proper job. It was a pretty seminal flight, now that I come to think about it. I still love *Abandoned Luncheonette.* ✶

OCTOBER 2010

O n the day I arrived at last year's Sundance Film Festival, amid the snow and the painfully cold sponsored parties, I met a screenwriter who wanted to talk, not about movies or agents or distribution deals, but about this column, and this column only. Given the happy relationship between books and film, and the mutual understanding between authors and those who work in the movie industry, I presumed that this would be the first of many such conversations about the *Believer;* indeed, I was afraid that, after a couple of days, I would begin to tire of the subject. I didn't want to be asked, over and over again, what the members of the Polysyllabic Spree were really like, in real life; I wanted the chance to offer my opinion on Miramax's troubles, or the potential weaknesses in the new setup at WME. I made it my policy from that moment on to engage only with people who didn't look like *Believer* readers. It was a policy that proved to be amazingly successful.

So Michael was the one who slipped under the wire, and I'm glad he did. He wanted one shot at a book recommendation—presumably on the basis of the fact that my own had ruined his reading life over the last few years—and hit me with John Williams's novel *Stoner*. (To my relief, the title turned out to refer to a surname rather than an occupation.) *Stoner* is a brilliant, beautiful, inexorably sad, wise, and elegant novel, one of the best I read during my grotesquely unfair suspension from these pages. So when Michael, emboldened by his triumph, came back with a second tip, I listened, and I bought.

Don Carpenter's *Hard Rain Falling* is, like *Stoner,* part of the NYRB Classics series, but it didn't begin its life, back in 1966, wearing that sort of smart hat. Search the title in Google Images and you'll find a couple of the original covers, neither of which give the impression that Carpenter could read, let alone write. One shows a very bad drawing of a hunky bad boy leaning against the door of his jail cell; the other is a little murky on my screen, but I'm pretty sure I can see supine nudity. And of course these illustrations misrepresent Carpenter's talents and intentions, but they don't entirely misrepresent his novel: if you'd paid good money for it back in '66, in the hope that (in the immortal words of Mervyn Griffith-Jones, the hapless chief prosecutor at the Lady Chatterley trial in 1960) you might be picking up something that you wouldn't want your wife and servants to read, then you wouldn't have asked for your money back.

A lot of books containing descriptions of sex have been written since the 1960s, and I pride myself on having read at least part of every single one of them, but there was something about Carpenter's novel that dated the dirty bits, and sent me right back to my 1960s childhood. Every now and again, I would, if I delved deep enough in the right drawers, come across books that my father had hidden carefully away—John Cleland's *Fanny Hill,* for example, first published in 1749, but still being read surreptitiously, in the U.K. at least, over two hundred years later. (Wikipedia tells me that *Fanny Hill* was banned in the U.K. until 1970, but I found the family edition long before that, so I don't know where my father got his copy. He has gone up even further in my estimation.) We are long past the time when literature was capable of doubling as pornography, and I doubt whether twenty-first-century teenage boys with access to a computer bother riffling through *The Godfather* and Harold Robbins paperbacks as assiduously as I did in the early '70s. These days, regrettably, sex in novels must contain a justifying subtext; what dates the coupling in Carpenter's novel is that, some of the time at least, the couples concerned are simply enjoying themselves. I can't remember the last time I read a description in a literary novel of a couple doing it just for fun. (And if you have written exactly such a novel yourself, I am happy for you, and congratulations, but please don't send it to me. It's too late now.)

Hard Rain Falling is a hard-boiled juvenile-delinquent novel, and then a prison novel, and then a dark Yatesian novel of existential marital despair, and just about every metamorphosis is compelling, rich, dark but not airless. Carpenter is, at his best, a dramatist: whenever there is conflict, minor characters, dialogue, people in a pool-hall or a cell or a bed, his novel comes thrillingly alive. The energy levels, both mine and the book's, dipped a little when Carpenter's protagonist Jack Levitt finds himself in solitary confinement, where he is prone to long bouts of sometimes-crazed introspection. Form and content are matched perfectly in these passages, but that doesn't make them any more fun to read. Most of the time, though, *Hard Rain Falling* is terrific—and if you're reading this, Michael, then I'd like you to know you have earned a third recommendation.

I finished *Hard Rain Falling* in Dorset, in a wonderful disused hotel which pitches its atmosphere halfway between *Fawlty Towers* and *The Shining's* Overlook. I was there with family and friends, and, though I never forgot that I am a reader—I read, which helped to remind me—I completely forgot that I am a writer. This meant that the flavor of *The Conversations,* a collection of Michael Ondaatje's erudite, stimulating, surprising interviews with the film editor Walter Murch, was different from what it would have been had I devoured it during the rest of the year. In these pages a couple of months ago, I said that books about creativity and its sources are becoming increasingly important to me as I get older, but this has to be something connected with work—when I read these books (Patti Smith's memoir was the most recent, I think) I try to twist them into a shape that makes some kind of sense to me professionally. There is so much that is of value to writers in *The Conversations;* any book about film editing that manages to find room for the first and last drafts of Elizabeth Bishop's "One Art," in their entirety, has an ambition and a scope that elude most books about poetry. If I'd been in a different mode—in the middle of a novel, say—I'd have been much more alert to the book's value as a professional aid; and just occasionally, something that one of these two clever men said would jerk me out of my vacation and back to my computer all those miles away. Murch's reference to "Negative Twenty Questions," for example, a game invented by the quantum physicist John Wheeler to explain how the world looks at a quantum level and much too complicated to tell you about here… something about the way Murch used the game to illustrate the process of film editing dimly reminded me of how writing a book feels, if you end up plotting on the hoof.

But mostly I read the book simply as someone who has seen a lot of films, and as Murch edited *Apocalypse Now* and *The Godfather* and *The Conversation* and *The English Patient* (and reedited Welles's *Touch of Evil* using the fifty-eight-page memo that Welles wrote to the studio after he'd seen the studio's cut of the film), then I was in experienced hands: this book is a dream, not just for cineasts, but for anyone interested in the tiny but crucial creative decisions that go into the making of anything at all. At one point, Murch talks about recording the sound of a door closing in *The Godfather*—a film, you suddenly remember, whose entire meaning rests on the sound of a door closing, when Michael excludes Diane Keaton from the world he promised he'd never join. If Murch had gotten that wrong, and the door had closed with a weedy, phony click, then it's entirely possible that we wouldn't still be reading about his career today. And there's tons of stuff like that, discussions that seem like the nerdy fetishization of trivia, until the import of that trivia becomes clear. Harry Caul in *The Conversation* was going to be called Harry Caller (after *Steppenwolf*'s Harry Haller), until he decided that "Caller" was an insufficiently oblique name for a professional bugger. So "Caller" became "Call," which became "Caul" after a secretary's misprint, which in turn gave Coppola the idea of dressing Gene Hackman in his distinctive semitransparent raincoat. And Murch is reminded of this by a story of Ondaatje's about W. H. Auden, who saw that a misprint in a proof produced a line better than his original: "The poets know the name of the seas" became "The ports know the name of the seas"… Oh, boy. If you're who I think you are, you would love *The Conversations*. Strangely, though, every friend I've pressed it upon so far has already read it, which suggests (a) that it's clearly one of those books whose reputation has grown and grown since it was first published, in 2002, and (b) my friends think I'm some kind of dimbo who only reads football reports and the lyrics of Black Sabbath songs.

And, in any case, it turns out that editing is kind of a metaphor for living. Our marriages, our careers, our domestic arrangements... so much of how we live consists of making meaning out of a bewildering jumble of images, of attempting to move as seamlessly as we can from one stage of life to the next.

There comes a time in the life of every young writer of fiction when he or she thinks, I'm not going to bother with plot and character and meaningless little slivers of human existence—I've done all that. I'm going to write about *life itself*. And the results are always indigestible, sluggish, and pretentious. If you're lucky, you get this stage over with before you're published—you have given yourself permission to rant on without the checks of narrative; if you're unlucky, it's your publisher who has given you enough rope with which to hang yourself, usually because your previous book was a brilliant success, and it can be the end of you.

Tinkers is Paul Harding's first novel, and it's pretty much about life itself, and it won him the Pulitzer Prize; he got away with it because he has a poet's eye and ear, and, because he's a ruthless self-editor, and because he hasn't forgotten about his characters' toenails and kidneys even as he's writing about their immortal souls. (That's just an overexcited figure of speech, by the way, that bit about toenails and kidneys. There are no toenails in *Tinkers,* that I remember. I don't want to put anyone off.) Harding was at the Iowa Writers' Workshop, and I don't know whether he was taught by Marilynne Robinson, but if he was, then I would have loved to sit in on their tutorials; *Tinkers,* in its depth, wisdom, sadness, and lightly worn mysticism, is reminiscent of Robinson's *Housekeeping.* (And I'm not suggesting for a moment he ripped her off, because you can't rip Marilynne Robinson off, unless you too are wise and deep and possessed of a singular and inimitable consciousness.)

Tinkers is about a dying man called George Crosby; he's an old man, coming to the end of his natural life, and he's hallucinating and remembering, failing to prevent the past from leaking into the present. And George's dying is linked to his father, Howard's, life, and eventual death. Howard sold household goods off the back of a wagon toward the beginning of the last century—he was a tinker. George repaired clocks. It's breathtakingly ambitious in its simplicity, but Harding is somehow able, in this novel that runs less than two hundred pages, to include the moments on which a life turns, properly imagined moments, moments grounded in the convincing reality of the characters. I was going to say that it's perhaps not the best book to take on holiday, because who wants to be reminded of his own mortality while he watches his children frolicking in the icy British surf? But then again, who wants to be reminded of his own mortality after he's wasted a day messing around on the internet instead of writing a very small section of a superfluous novel, or a screenplay that probably won't get turned into a film? On reflection, the holiday option is probably the better one: when my time comes, I hope that my children frolic before my eyes. I certainly don't want to see an unedited paragraph of a superfluous novel. ✷

NOVEMBER / DECEMBER 2010

Something has been happening to me recently—something which, I suspect, is likely to affect a significant and important part of the rest of my life. The grandiose way of describing this shift is to say that I have been slowly making my peace with antiquity; or, to express it in words that more accurately describe what's going on, I have discovered that some old shit isn't so bad.

Hitherto, my cultural blind spots have included the Romantic poets, every single bar of classical music ever written, and just about anything produced before the nineteenth century, with the exception of Shakespeare and a couple of the bloodier, and hence more Tarantinoesque, revenge tragedies. When I was young, I didn't want to listen to or read anything that reminded me of the brown and deeply depressing furniture in my grandmother's house. She didn't have many books, but those she did own were indeed brown: cheap and old editions of a couple of Sir Walter Scott's novels, for example, and maybe a couple of hand-me-down books by somebody like Frances Hodgson Burnett. When I ran out of stuff to read during the holidays, I was pointed in the direction of her one bookcase, but I wanted bright Puffin paperbacks, not mildewed old hardbacks, which came to represent just about everything I wasn't interested in.

This unhelpful association, it seems to me, should have withered with time; instead, it has been allowed to flourish, unchecked. Don't you make yogurt by putting a spoonful of yogurt into something-or-other? Well, I created a half century of belligerent prejudice with one spoonful of formative ennui. I soon found that I didn't want to read or listen to anything that anybody in any position of educational authority told me to. Chaucer was full of woodworm; Wordsworth was yellow and curling at the edges, whatever edition I was given. I read Graham Greene and John Fowles, Vonnegut and Tom Wolfe, Chandler and Nathanael West, Greil Marcus and Peter Guralnick, and I listened exclusively to popular music. Dickens crept in, eventually, because he was funny, unlike Sir Walter Scott and Shelley, who weren't. And, because everything was seen through the prism of rock and roll, every now and again I would end up finding something I learned about through the pages of *New Musical Express*. When Mick Jagger happened to mention that "Sympathy for the Devil" was inspired by Bulgakov's *The Master and Margarita,* off I trotted to the library. It didn't help that I was never allowed to study anything remotely contemporary until the last year of university: there was never any sense of *that* leading to *this.* If anything, my education gave me the opposite impression, of an end to cultural history round about the time that Forster wrote *A Passage to India.* The quickest way to kill all love for the classics, I can see now, is to tell young people that nothing else matters, because then all they can do is look at them in a museum of literature, through glass cases. Don't touch! And don't think for a moment that they want to live in the same world as you! And so a lot of adult life—if your hunger and curiosity haven't been squelched by your education— is learning to join up the dots that you didn't even know were there.

In some ways, my commitment to modernity stood me in good stead: those who cling to the cultural touchstones of an orthodox education are frequently smug, lazy, and intellectually timid—after all, someone else has made all their cultural decisions for them. And in any case, if you decide to consume only art made in the twentieth century and the first part of the twenty-first, you're going to end up familiar with a lot of good stuff, enough to last you a lifetime. If your commitment to the canon means you've never had the time for Marilynne Robinson or Preston Sturges or Marvin Gaye, then I would argue that you're not as cultured as you think. (Well, not you. You know who Marvin Gaye is. But they're out there. They're out here, in Britain, especially.)

Over the last couple of years, though, I've been dipping into Keats's letters, listening obsessively to Saint-Saëns, seeking out paintings by van Eyck, doing all sorts of things that I'd never have dreamed of doing even in my forties; what is even more remarkable, to me, at least, is that none of these things feel alien. There wasn't one single Damascene moment. Rather, there was a little cluster of smaller discoveries and awakenings, including:

1) Laura Cumming's magnificent book *A Face to the World: On Self-Portraits*, one of the cleverest, wisest books of criticism I've ever read. I wouldn't have picked it up in a million years if I hadn't known the author, and I ended up chasing after the self-portraits she writes about, which involved visiting galleries and old masters I'd carefully avoided until she taught me not to. (I read this book during my laughably unjust and almost certainly illegal suspension from these pages last year, so I was unable to recommend it to you then, but you should read it.)

2) The Professor Green/Lily Allen song "Just Be Good to Green." I am old enough to remember not only the Beats International version, "Dub Be Good to Me," but the SOS Band's original, "Just Be Good to Me." And I'm not saying that the Professor sent me off screaming toward Beethoven's late quartets (very good, by the way); I did, however, find myself wondering whether, when a song keeps coming round again and again and again, like a kid on a merry-go-round, there comes a point when you have to stop smiling and waving. Saint-Saëns is a new artist, as far as I'm concerned, with a big future ahead of him.

3) A new pair of headphones, expensive ones, which seemed to me to be demanding real food, orchestras and symphonies, rather than a wispy diet of singer-songwriter.

4) Jane Campion's beautiful film *Bright Star,* which turned Keats into a writer I recognized and understood.

5) During promotional work for *Lonely Avenue,* the project I've been working on with Ben Folds, the two of us were asked to trade tracks for some iTunes thing. Ben recommended an early Elton John album and the first movement of Rachmaninoff's Third Piano Concerto. I bought the Rachmaninoff, because the enthusiasm was so unaffected and unintimidating.

6) And now, Sarah Bakewell's biography of Montaigne, *How to Live.*

I had never read Montaigne before picking up Bakewell's book. I knew only that he was a sixteenth-century essayist, and that he had therefore willfully chosen not to interest me. So I am at a loss to explain quite why I felt the need first to buy and then to devour *How to Live.* And it was a need, too. I have talked before in these pages about how sometimes your mind knows what it needs, just as your body knows when it's time for some iron, or some protein, or a drink that doesn't contain caffeine or absinthe. I suspect in this case the title helped immeasurably. This book is going to tell me how to live, while at the same time filling in all kinds of gaps in my knowledge? Sold.

Well, *How to Live* is a superb book, original, engaging, thorough, ambitious, and wise. It's not just that it provides a handy guide to Hellenic philosophy, and an extremely readable account of the sixteenth-century French civil wars; you would, perhaps, expect some of that, given Montaigne's influences and his political involvement. (He became mayor of Bordeaux, a city that had been punished for its insurrectionist tendencies.) Nor is it that it contains immediate and sympathetic portraits of several of Montaigne's relationships—with his wife, his editor, and his closest friend, La Boétie, who died in one of the frequent outbreaks of the plague, and of whom Montaigne said, famously, "If you press me to tell why I loved him, I feel that this cannot be expressed, except by answering: Because it was he, because it was I." The conventional virtues of a biography are all there, and in place, but where Bakewell really transcends the genre is in her organization of the material, and her refusal to keep Montaigne penned in his own time. In just over three hundred pages, she provides a proper biography, one that takes into account the hundreds of years he has lived since his death; that, after all, is when a lot of the important stuff happens. And the postmortem life of Montaigne has been a rich one: he troubled Descartes and Pascal, got himself banned in France (until 1854), captivated and then disappointed the Romantics, inspired Nietzsche and Stefan Zweig, made this column possible.

He did this by inventing the medium of the personal essay, more or less single-handedly. How many other people can you think of who created an entire literary form? Indeed, how many people can you think of who created any cultural idiom? James Brown, maybe; before "Papa's Got a Brand New Bag" there was no funk; and then, suddenly, there it was. Well, Montaigne was the James Brown of the 1580s. In his brilliant book *A Year in the Life of William Shakespeare: 1599,* James Shapiro says that Montaigne took "the unprecedented step of making himself his subject," thus enabling Shakespeare to produce a dramatic equivalent, the soliloquy. Of course, you can overstate the case for Montaigne's innovative genius. It's hard to imagine that, in the five-hundred-odd years since the essays were first published, some other narcissist wouldn't have had the idea of sticking himself into the middle of his prose. Montaigne invented the personal essay like someone invented the wheel. Why he's still read now is not because he was the first, but because he remains fresh, and his agonized agnosticism, his endearing fumbles in the dark (he frequently ends a thought or an opinion with a disarming, charming "But I don't know"), become more relevant as we realize, with increasing certainty, that we don't have a clue about anything. I'd be surprised and delighted if I read a richer book in the next twelve months.

And then, as if Montaigne's hand were on my shoulder, I discovered Emily Fox Gordon's *Book of Days,* a collection of personal essays. I had read a nice review of them in the *Economist,* but had presumed that they'd be nicely written, light, amusing, and disposable, but that's not it at all: these are not blogs wrapped up in a nice blue cover. (And is it OK, given the *Believer*'s no-snark rule, to say that some blogs are better than others? And that one or even two have no literary merit whatsoever?) There are jokes in *Book of Days,* but the writing is precise, the thinking is complicated and original, and just about every subject she chooses—faculty wives, her relationship with Kafka, her niece's wedding—somehow enables her to pitch for something rich and important. If you are interested in writing and marriage—and if you're not, then I don't know what you're doing round here, because I got nothing else, apart from kids and football—then she has things to say that I have never read elsewhere, and that I will be thinking about and possibly even re-reading for some time to come. In Sarah Bakewell's introduction to *How to Live,* she quotes the English journalist Bernard Levin: "I defy any reader of Montaigne not to put the book down at some point and say with incredulity, 'How did he know all that about me?'" Well, I haven't yet had that experience with Montaigne, probably because in my admittedly limited excursions so far, I've been looking for the smutty bits, but I felt it several times while I was reading *Book of Days.* "The Prodigal Returns," the essay about Gordon's niece's wedding, turns into a brilliant meditation on the ethics and betrayals of memoir-writing, and contains the following:

> What *do* I enjoy? Not staying in hotels, apparently. Not gluttony, not parties, not flattery, not multiple glasses of white wine. What I seem to want to do—"enjoy" is the wrong word here—is not to have experiences but to think and tell about them. I'm always looking for excuses to avoid sitting down at my desk to write, but I "enjoy" my life only to the extent that even as I'm living it, I'm also writing it in my mind.

Well. Obviously that's not me, in any way whatsoever. I'm an adventurer, a gourmand, a womanizer, a *bon viveur,* a surfer, a bungee jumper, a gambler, an occasional pugilist, a Scrabble player, a man who wrings every last drop from life's dripping sponge. But, you know. I thought it might chime with one or two of you lot. Nerds. And it certainly would have chimed with Montaigne.

I'm afraid I am going to recommend yet another epic poem about the Mau Mau uprising—this time Adam Foulds's extraordinary and pitch-perfect *The Broken Word.* It will occupy maybe an hour of your life, and you won't regret a single second of it. Foulds has written an apparently brilliant novel, *The Quickening Maze,* about the poet John Clare, in whom I have obviously had no previous interest, but this has the narrative drive of a novel anyway. Set in the 1950s (*der*, say the people who know all about the Mau Mau, which I'm presuming isn't every single one of you), it tells the story of Tom, a young Englishman who, in the summer between school and university, goes to visit his parents in Kenya, and is drawn into a horrific, nightmarish suppression of a violent rebellion. If there were money to be made from cinematic adaptations of bloody, politically aware but deeply humanistic long-form poetry, then the film rights to *The Broken Word* would make Foulds rich.

Such is his talent that Foulds can elevate just about any banal domestic conversation. In the last section of the poem, Tom is attempting to seduce a young woman at university, and the dialogue is full of *nos* and *that's not nices*, the flat, commonplace rejections of a 1950s courtship. But what gives the passage its chilling power is everything that has gone before: how much of the violence Tom has seen is contained in him now? The control here is such that the language doesn't have to be anything other than humdrum to be powerful, layered, dense, and that's some trick to pull off. Why the Mau Mau uprising? At the end of the poem, Tom and the girl he has been forcing himself upon are looking in a jeweler's window; the children they would have had together, born at the end of the 1950s and early '60s, sent to English public schools, are as we speak running our banks and our armies, our country, even.

These are three of the best books I've read in years, and I read them in the last four weeks, and they are all contemporary—*How to Live* and *Book of Days* were published in 2010, *The Broken Word* was published in 2008. So despite all my showing off and name-dropping, a narrative poem published two years ago and set in the 1950s is the closest I've come to the ancient world. But then, that's the whole point, isn't it? Great writing is going on all around us, always has done, always will. ✻

JANUARY 2011

The advantages and benefits of writing a monthly column about reading for the *Believer* are innumerable, if predictable: fame, women (it's amazing what people will do to get early information about the Books Bought list), international influence, and so on. But perhaps the biggest perk of all, one that has only emerged slowly, over the years, is this: you can't read long books. Well, I can't, anyway. I probably read between two and three hundred pages, I'm guessing, during the average working week, and I have the impression—please correct me if I'm wrong—that if you saw only one book in the Books Read list at the top there, it would be very hard to persuade you to plough through what would, in effect, be a two-thousand-word book review. And as a consequence, there are all sorts of intimidating-looking eight-hundred-pagers that I feel completely justified in overlooking. I am ignoring them for your benefit, effectively, although it would be disingenuous to claim that I spend my month resenting you. On the contrary, there have been times when, watching friends or fellow passengers struggling through some au courant literary monster, I have wanted to kiss you. I once gave a whole column over to *David Copperfield*, I remember, and more recently I raced through David Kynaston's brilliant but

Rubenesque *Austerity Britain*. For the most part, though, there's a "Stuff I've Been Reading"–induced five-hundred-page cutoff.

In the interests of full disclosure, I should add that I am a literary fattist anyway; I have had a resistance to the more amply proportioned book all my adult life, which is why the thesis I'm most likely to write is entitled "The Shortest Book by Authors Who Usually Go Long." *The Crying of Lot 49, Silas Marner, A Portrait of the Artist as a Young Man*... I've read 'em all. You can infer from that lot what I haven't read. And in any case, long, slow books can have a disastrous, demoralizing effect on your cultural life if you have young children and your reading time is short. You make only tiny inroads into the chunky white wastes every night before falling asleep, and before long you become convinced that it's not really worth reading again until your children are in reform school. My advice, as someone who has been an exhausted parent for seventeen years now, is to stick to the svelte novel—it's not as if this will lower the quality of your consumption, because you've still got a good couple of hundred top, top writers to choose from. Have you read everything by Graham Greene? Or Kurt Vonnegut? Anne Tyler, George Orwell, E. M. Forster, Carol Shields, Jane Austen, Muriel Spark, H. G. Wells, Ian McEwan? I can't think of a book much over four hundred pages by any of them. I wouldn't say that you have to make an exception for Dickens, because we at the *Believer* don't think that you have to read anybody—we just think you have to read. It's just that short Dickens is atypical Dickens—*Hard Times,* for example, is long on angry satire, short on jokes—and Dickens, as John Carey said in his brilliant little critical study *The Violent Effigy: A Study of Dickens' Imagination,* is "essentially a comic writer." If you're going to read him at all, then choose a funny one. *Great Expectations* is under six hundred pages, and one of the greatest novels ever written, so that's not a bad place to start.

Some months ago, I agreed to write an introduction to *Our Mutual Friend*—eight or nine hundred pages in paperback form, a terrifying two-and-a-half thousand pages on the iPad—and I have been waiting for a gap in the *Believer's* monthly schedule before attempting to embark on the long, long road. The recent double issue gave me an eight-week window of opportunity to read Dickens's last completed novel (only the unfinished *The Mystery of Edwin*

Drood came after it) on top of something else, so I knew I couldn't put it off any longer.

I first read *Our Mutual Friend* years and years ago, and didn't enjoy the experience much, but I was almost certain that the fault was mine rather than the author's. Something was going on at the time—divorce, illness, a newborn, or one of the other humdrum hazards that turn reading into a chore—and *Our Mutual Friend* never really started to move in the way that the other big Dickens novels had previously done. (There's this moment you get a hundred or so pages in, if you're lucky and sympathetic to Dickens's narrative style and worldview, when you feel the whole thing judder into life and pick up speed, like a train, or a liner, or some other vehicle whose size and weight make motion seem unlikely.) So I didn't worry about taking on the commission. I am in reasonable health, my next divorce is at least a year or so away, and I have given up having children, so I was sure that, this time around, I'd see that *Our Mutual Friend* is right up there with the other good ones—in other words, I was about to read one of the richest, most inventive, funniest, saddest, most energetic novels in literature.

Two-thirds of the way through, I was having such a hard time that I looked up a couple of contemporary reviews. Henry James thought it "the poorest of Mr Dickens's works… poor with the poverty not of momentary embarrassment, but of permanent exhaustion." Dickens's loyal friend John Forster admits that it "will never rank with his higher efforts." In other words, everyone knew it was a clunker except me—and even I knew, deep down, given that my first reading had been so arduous. And now, presumably, I have to write an introduction explaining why it's so great. What's great is the fifth chapter, an extended piece of comic writing that's as good as anything I've ever read by him. (If you have a copy lying about, start it and end it there, as if it were a Wodehouse short story.) What's not so great about it is not so easy to convey, because so much of it relates—yes—to length, to the plot's knotty overcomplications, stretched over hundreds and hundreds of pages. "Although I have not been wanting in industry, I have been wanting in invention," Dickens wrote to Forster sadly, after the first couple of parts had already been published in magazine form, and, as a summation of what's wrong with the book as a whole, that confession is hard to beat. It's interesting, I think, that nothing in *Our Mutual Friend* has wandered out of the pages of the novel and into our lives. There's no Artful Dodger, Uriah Heep, or Micawber, no Scrooge, no Gradgrind, no "It was the best of times, it was the worst of times," no Miss Havisham, no *Jarndyce v. Jarndyce.* The closest we get is a minor character saying, apropos of another character's gift for story-telling, that "he do the Police in different voices"—but Dickens needed a little help from Eliot for that particular stab at immortality. As far as I can tell, the novel has recovered from its poor reception, to the extent that it has become one of Dickens's most studied books, but that, I'm afraid, is no testament to its worth: it has endless themes and images and things to say about greed and poverty and money—in other words, endless material for essays—but none of that makes it any easier to get through. He'll be back in my life soon enough, but next time I might go for early Dickens, rather than late.

It now seems a very long time ago that I read Meg Wolitzer's forthcoming novel, *The Uncoupling,* and Colum McCann's National Book Award winner, *Let the Great World Spin,* and trying to think about them now is like trying to look over a very high wall into somebody's back garden. I know I enjoyed them, and they both seemed to slip by in a flash, but Dickens stomped his oversize boots all over them. I'm hoping that eventually they will spring back up in my mind, undamaged, like grass. McCann's novel, as many of you probably know, is set in New York City in August 1974, the summer that Philippe Petit walked between the Twin Towers on a tightrope. Underneath him, and all touched in some way by Petit's act of inspired insanity, lives McCann's cast of priests and lawyers, prostitutes and grieving mothers. It's a rich, warm, deeply felt and imagined book, destined, I think, to be loved for a long time. Regrettably, however, McCann makes a very small mistake relating to popular music toward the beginning, and, as has happened so many times before, I spent way too long muttering at both the novel and the author. I must stress, once again—because this has come up before—that my inability to forgive negligible errors of this kind is a disfiguring disease, and I am determined to find a cure for it; I mention it here merely to explain why a book I liked a lot has not become a book that I have bought over and over again, to press on anybody who happens to be passing by. And it would be unforgivably small-minded to go into it...

Ach. Donovan wasn't an Irish folk singer, OK? He was a Scottish hippie, and I hate myself.

Meg Wolitzer, like Tom Perrotta, is an author who makes you wonder why more people don't write perceptive, entertaining, unassuming novels about how and why ordinary people choose to make decisions about their lives. Take away the historical fiction, and the genre fiction, and the postmodern fiction, and the self-important attention-seeking fiction, and there really isn't an awful lot left; the recent success, on both sides of the Atlantic, of David Nicholls's lovely *One Day* demonstrates what an appetite there is for that rare combination of intelligence and recognizability. *The Uncoupling* is about what happens when all the couples in a New Jersey town stop having sex. (A magical wind, which springs up, not coincidentally, during rehearsals for a high-school production of Aristophanes's sex-strike comedy, *Lysistrata,* freezes the loins of all the post-pubescent women.) It's a novel that can't help but make you think about your own relationship—about what it consists of, what would be left if sex were taken away, how far you'd be prepared to go in order to keep it in your life somewhere, and so on. I have written all the answers to these questions down on a piece of paper, but I have locked the paper away in a drawer, and I'm not showing it to you lot. You know how much I get paid for this column? Not enough, that's how much.

The only thing I have read since Mr. and Mrs. John Harmon moved into Boffin the Golden Dustman's splendid house—that's an *Our Mutual Friend* spoiler, by the way, but I'm hoping I've spoiled it for you already—is Darin Strauss's *Half a Life,* a book that, as far as I'm concerned, could easily be republished under the title *The Opposite of Our Mutual Friend.* It's a short, simple piece of contemporary nonfiction, which in itself would be enough to make it look pretty good to me; it also happens to be precise, elegantly written, fresh, wise, and very sad. Strauss was still in high school when he killed a girl in an accident: Celine Zilke, then aged sixteen, and a student at the same high school, inexplicably veered across two lanes before riding her bike right across his Oldsmobile. She died later, in the hospital. Strauss was completely exonerated by everybody concerned, but, for obvious human reasons, the accident came to define him, and *Half a Life* is a riveting attempt to articulate the definition.

Any moral or ethical objection you might have to *Half a Life*—what right has he got to produce a book out of this when that poor girl was the victim?—is dealt with very quickly, because, in part, *Half a Life* deals with the question of what right Strauss had to do anything at all. Was it OK to go back to school, laugh, go to the movies, look at anyone, feel sorry for himself, go to Celine's funeral, avoid her friends, talk to her parents, leave his bedroom? The author, a teenage boy, didn't have the answers to any of these questions, and they continued to elude him until well into adulthood. You could describe *Half a Life* as an elevated study of self-consciousness, in all senses of the compound noun—a book about a man watching his younger self watching his own every move, thought, feeling, checking and rechecking them before allowing them to escape into a place where they can be watched by other people—at which point the checking and rechecking start all over again. It's easy enough for us to say that what happened to Darin Strauss was a tragedy—not, of course, as big a tragedy as the one that befell Celine Zilke and her family, but a tragedy nonetheless. Easy enough for us to say, impossible for him to say—and therein lies Strauss's rich and meaningful material, material he works into a memorable essay. "Whatever you do in your life, you have to do it twice as well now," Celine Zilke's mother told him at the funeral. "Because you are living it for two people." Most of us can't live our lives well enough for one, but the care and thought that have gone into every line of *Half a Life* are indicative not only of a very talented writer, but of a proper human being.

And now Strauss has got me at it. I was going to end with a very good, if overcomplicated, joke about Dickens and a pair of broken Bose headphones, but I'm no longer sure it's appropriate. So I'll stop here. ✷

FEBRUARY 2011

BOOKS BOUGHT:

* *Let's Talk About Love: A Journey to the End of Taste*—Carl Wilson
* *Will Grayson, Will Grayson*—John Green and David Levithan

BOOKS READ:

* *The Anthologist*—Nicholson Baker
* *Brooklyn*—Colm Tóibín
* *Madcap: The Life of Preston Sturges*—Donald Spoto
* *Let's Talk About Love: A Journey to the End of Taste*—Carl Wilson

It's a wet Sunday morning, and I'm sitting on a sofa reading a book. On one side of me is my eldest son, Danny, who is seventeen and autistic. His feet are in my lap, and he's watching a children's TV program on his iPad. Or rather, he's watching a part of a children's TV program, over and over again: a song from *Postman Pat* entitled "Handyman Song." Danny is wearing headphones, but I've just noticed that they're not connected properly, so I can hear every word of the song anyway. On my other side is another son, my eight-year-old, Lowell. He's watching the Sunday-morning football-highlights program *Goals on Sunday*. I'm caught between them, trying to finish Nicholson Baker's *The Anthologist*.

"Look at this, Dad," Lowell says.

He wants me to watch Johan Elmander's goal for Bolton at Wolves, the second in a 3–2 win. It's one of the best goals of the season so far, and at the time of writing has a real chance of winning the BBC's Goal of the Month award, but I only have thirteen pages of the novel to go, so I only glance up for a moment.

"Close the book," Lowell says.

"I saw the goal. I'm not going to close the book."

"Close the book. You didn't see the replay."

He tries to grab the book out of my hand, so we wrestle for a moment while I turn the corner of the page down. I watch the replay. He's satisfied. I return to *The Anthologist,* football commentary in one ear and the *Postman Pat* song in the other.

Would Nicholson Baker mind? I'm pretty sure he wouldn't choose for me to be reading his work under these circumstances, and I'm with him all the way. I'd rather be somewhere else, too. I'd rather be on a sun-lounger in southern California, in the middle of a necessarily childless reading tour, just for the thirty minutes it's going to take me to get to the end of the novel. I would savor every single minute of the rest of a wet English November Sunday with three sons, just so long as I was given half an hour—not even that!—of sunshine and solitude. I hope Baker would be pleased by my determination and absorption, though. I wasn't throwing his book away by submitting it to the twin assaults of *Postman Pat* and *Goals on Sunday.* I was hanging on to it for dear life.

It's a wonderful novel, I think, unusual, generous, educational, funny. The eponymous narrator, Paul Chowder, is a broke poet whose girlfriend has just left him; he's trying to write an introduction to an anthology of verse while simultaneously worrying about the rent and the history of rhyme. Chowder loves rhyme: he thinks that the blank verse of modernism was all a fascist plot, and that Swinburne was the greatest rhymer "in the history of human literature." Indeed, *The Anthologist* is full of artless, instructive digressions about all sorts of people (Swinburne, Vachel Lindsay, Louise Bogan) and all sorts of things (iambic pentameter) that I knew almost nothing about. Chowder might be an awful mess, but you trust him on all matters relating to poetry.

I developed something of a crush on Elizabeth Bishop after reading *The Anthologist.* I downloaded an MP3 of her reading "The Fish," and on an overnight work trip to Barcelona I took with me a copy of Bishop's collected poems but no clean socks, which is exactly the sort of thing that Paul Chowder might have done. I would say that in my half century on this planet so far, I have valued clean socks above poetry, so *The Anthologist* may literally have changed my life, and not in a good way. Luckily, it turns out that you can buy socks in Barcelona. Nice ones, too.

Pretty much everything I have read in the last month is related to the production of art and/or entertainment. Unlike all the others, Colm Tóibín's *Brooklyn* is not *about* art (and don't get sniffy about Céline Dion until I tell you what Carl Wilson has to say about her); it's about a young girl emigrating to the U.S. from a small town in Ireland in the 1950s. But as I am currently attempting to adapt *Brooklyn* for the cinema, it would be disingenuous to claim that the production of art and/or entertainment didn't cross my mind while I was re-reading it.

I haven't read a novel twice in six months for decades, and the experience was illuminating. It wasn't that I had misremembered anything, particularly, nor (I like to think) had I misunderstood much, first time around, but I had certainly forgotten the proximity of narrative events in relation to each other. Some things happened sooner than I was prepared for, and others much later—certainly much later than I can hope to get away with in a screenplay. You can do anything in a novel, provided the writing is good enough: you can introduce rounded, complex characters ten pages from the end, you can gloss over years in a paragraph. Film is a clumsier and more literal medium.

One thing that particularly struck me this time around is that though Tóibín's prose is precise and calm and controlled, *Brooklyn* is not an internal book. This is good news for a screenwriter, in most ways, but it did occur to me that if you strip away, as I have to do, all the control, then the story becomes alarmingly visceral. When Eilis travels third class on a ship to New York and ends up getting violently seasick and expelling her dinner through every available orifice… Well, if we show that on-screen, it will lose Tóibín's Jamesian poise. What you'll see, in fact, is a poor girl shitting copiously into a bucket. And Colm's devoted fans, aesthetes all, will say, Jesus, what has this hooligan done to our beautiful literary novel? There might be art riots, in fact, similar to those that greeted *The Rite of Spring* when it was first performed, in 1913. People will throw stuff at me, and I'll be running out of the premiere shouting, "*There was diarrhea in the book!*," but nobody will believe me. I'm going to blame the director. Who made the *Porky's* movies? We should hire him.

The invention of the iPad means, as I'm sure you have discovered by now, that you can watch Preston Sturges movies pretty well anywhere you want. I have seen *Sullivan's Travels, The Lady Eve,* and *The Palm Beach Story,* and though *Sullivan's Travels* remains my favorite, the minor characters in *The Palm Beach Story* are Dickensian in their weirdness and detail. It occurred to me that

I know a lot more about, say, Montaigne and Richard Yates, having read very good books about them, than I do about Preston Sturges—a regrettable state of affairs, seeing as Sturges means more to me than either.

After reading Sarah Bakewell's brilliant *How to Live: A Life of Montaigne in One Question and Twenty Attempts at an Answer*, I came to understand how Montaigne invented soul-searching; after reading Blake Bailey's *A Tragic Honesty: The Life and Work of Richard Yates*, I saw why Yates's books are so incredibly miserable. Well, Donald Spoto's *Madcap: The Life of Preston Sturges* tells you everything you need to know about the pace of Sturges's movies: he lived that fast himself. He hung out with Isadora Duncan and Marcel Duchamp, took a job as assistant stage manager on Duncan's production of *Oedipus Rex*, traveled throughout Europe, ran branches of his mother's cosmetics company in New York and London, turned down a job as a one-hundred-dollar-a-week gigolo, and was honorably discharged from the U.S. military. And then he turned twenty-one, and things got really interesting.

Sturges didn't really start writing until he was thirty; he began work on his first successful play, *Strictly Dishonorable*, on June 14, 1929, and finished it on June 23. (According to his diary, he did no work on the fifteenth, sixteenth, or twenty-second.) He received a telegram from a producer on July 2 suggesting an August production, and *Strictly Dishonorable* was one of the biggest Broadway hits of the 1930s. It made him a fortune. Even so, we here at the *Believer* recommend a ten- or fifteen-year gestation period for a first novel, play, or screenplay, five years of writing, and then another five years of rewriting and editing. ("June 23: *Strictly Dishonorable* finished 5.40 this afternoon. Will polish tonight. Later: did so and drew set plans.") Yes, Sturges went on to write and direct *Sullivan's Travels*, and in 1947 was paid more than either William Randolph Hearst or Henry Ford II. But the slow, careful approach is unarguably more authentic and artistic, and will almost certainly result in a literary prize, or at least a nomination. (In defense of your creative-writing professors, Sturges did write a lot of stinkers for the stage. Robert Benchley, in the *New Yorker*, observed that "the more young Mr. Preston Sturges continues to write follow-ups to *Strictly Dishonorable*, the more we wonder who wrote *Strictly Dishonorable*." You're not allowed to write cruel lines like that in this magazine, which is the only reason why I don't.)

I had no idea that Sturges's life had been so dizzyingly eventful; no idea, either, that he had changed the history of cinema by becoming the first Hollywood writer/director. He crashed and burned pretty spectacularly, too. He sank every dollar he had and a few hundred thousand more into a money-pit of a club; and after a hot streak of seven good-to-great films between 1940 and 1944, it was effectively all over for him by 1949. He made only one more, apparently very bad, movie before he died, in 1959. Spoto's book can't help but zip along, although I did find myself skipping over the synopses of some of Sturges's Broadway farces. Farce, it seems to me, is curiously resistant to synopsis: "He then makes his move to seduce Isabelle, but the judge enters, claiming it's his birthday and everyone must have champagne... The opera singer then reenters with pajamas for Isabelle... Gus puts pajama top over her head, and as it slips down her teddy falls to the floor..." I am sure that, in 1930, *Strictly Dishonorable* was the hottest ticket in town, and that had I been alive to see it, I'd have promptly died laughing. But nothing, I fear, can bring the magic back to life now.

It is not stretching a point to say that the rapidly shifting sands of critical and popular approbation are the subject of Carl Wilson's brilliant extended essay about Céline Dion, *Let's Talk About Love: A Journey to the End of Taste,* another in the excellent 33⅓ series. Most of the others I've read (with the exception of Joe Pernice's novella inspired by the Smiths' *Meat Is Murder*) are well-written but conventional songs of praise to an important album in rock's history—*Harvest, Dusty in Memphis, Paul's Boutique,* and so on. This one is different. Wilson asks the question: why does everyone hate Céline Dion? Except, of course, it's not everyone, is it? She's sold more albums than just about anyone alive. Everyone loves Céline Dion, if you think about it. So actually, he asks the question: why do I and my friends and all rock critics and everyone likely to be reading this book and magazines like the *Believer* hate Céline Dion? And the answers he finds are profound, provocative, and leave you wondering who the hell you actually are—especially if, like many of us around these parts, you set great store by cultural consumption as an indicator of both character and, let's face it, intelligence. We are cool people! We read Jonathan Franzen and we listen to Pavement, but we also love Mozart and *Seinfeld*! Hurrah for us! In a few short, devastating chapters, Wilson chops himself and all of us off at the knees. "It's always other people following crowds, whereas my own taste reflects my specialness," Wilson observes.

Let's Talk About Love belongs on your bookshelf next to John Carey's *What Good Are the Arts?*; they both cover similar ideas about the construct of taste, although Wilson finds more room for Elliott Smith and the Ramones than Professor Carey could. And in a way, taking on Dion is a purer and more revealing exercise than taking on some of the shibboleths of literary culture, as Carey did. After all, there is a rough-and-ready agreement on literary competence, on who can string a sentence together and who can't, that complicates any wholesale rejection of critical values in literature. In popular music, though, a whole different set of judgments is at play. We forgive people who can't sing or construct a song or play their instruments, as long as they are cool, or subversive, or deviant; we do not dismiss Dion because she's incompetent. Indeed, her competence may well be a problem, because it means she excludes nobody, apart from us, and those who invest heavily in cultural capital don't like art that can't exclude: it's confusing, and it doesn't help us to meet attractive people of the opposite sex who think the same way we do.

Wilson's book isn't just important; it has good facts in it, too. Did you know that in Jamaica, Céline is loved most of all by the badasses? "So much that it became a cue to me to walk, run or drive faster if I was ever in a neighborhood I didn't know and heard Céline Dion," a Jamaican music critic tells Wilson. And did you know that the whole highbrow/middlebrow thing came from nineteenth-century phrenology, and has racist connotations? Why aren't I surprised?

I may well have to insist that you read this book before we continue our monthly conversation, because we really need to be on the same page. My own sense of self has been shaken, and from this moment on, there may be only chaotic enthusiasm (or sociological neutrality) where there was once sensible and occasionally inspired recommendation. I may go and have a look at that Elmander goal again. It might help to ground me. You can still have good goals and bad goals, right? Right? ✱

MARCH / APRIL 2011

BOOKS BOUGHT:
- ✶ *The Immortal Life of Henrietta Lacks*—Rebecca Skloot
- ✶ *The Last Englishman: The Double Life of Arthur Ransome*
  —Roland Chambers

BOOKS READ:
- ✶ *Game Change: Obama and the Clintons, McCain and Palin, and the Race of a Lifetime*—John Heileman and Mark Halperin
- ✶ *The Immortal Life of Henrietta Lacks*—Rebecca Skloot

In April 2010, I was a tragic victim of the volcanic ash cloud that grounded all flights into, out of, and across Europe for a few days. I am sure that other people have hard-luck stories, too: weddings, births, and funerals were missed, job opportunities went begging, feckless husbands given one last chance got home to find their underwear strewn across the street, and so on. Mine, however, was perhaps more poignant than any of them: my family, stranded in Tenerife, was unable to celebrate my fifty-third birthday with me. Can you imagine? Of all the birthdays to miss, it had to be the one I was looking forward to the most. All my life I had wondered what it would be like to turn fifty-three, to open presents suitable for a fifty-three-year-old—something from the excellent Bald Guyz* range of beauty products, for example, or a Bruce Springsteen box set—while an adoring family looked on. Well, my adoring family was stranded on an island in the Mediterranean, in a hotel that apparently laid on a chocolate fountain for breakfast. When they eventually made it home, my birthday was clearly an event to be celebrated when it came around again in 2011, rather

---

* Bald Guyz makes head wipes, moisturizing gel, and all kinds of great stuff for men who have chosen to live a hair-free life. The company has not paid for this endorsement, but I am very much hoping it will, or that it will send me a crate of free stuff.

than retrospectively. I have therefore decided, perhaps understandably, that this April I will be turning fifty-three again. It's not a vanity thing; it's simply that I'm owed a birthday.

Back in 2010, I had to make do with the cards I'd been dealt, and the cards were these: a small group of friends bought me champagne, which we drank in my garden on a beautiful spring evening, at a time when I would usually be embarking on some terrible, strength-sapping, pointless fight about, say, shampoo and/or bedtime; the same friends then took me to a favorite local restaurant and gave me presents. You can see why I might feel bitter even to this day.

Three of the presents my friends had bought me were book-shaped, and, miraculously, given the lack of deferred gratification in my book-buying life, I wanted to read them all, and didn't own any of them. I got a lovely first edition of Mordecai Richler's *The Apprenticeship of Duddy Kravitz,* a copy of *Game Change: Obama and the Clintons, McCain and Palin, and the Race of a Lifetime* by John Heilemann and Mark Halperin, and Marc Norman's history of screenwriting, *What Happens Next.* Is it too late and too hurtful to say that my fifty-third birthday was perhaps the best ever?

Several months later, and I have finally read one of the three, even though I wanted to read all three of them immediately. (What happened in between? Other books, is what happened. Other books, other moods, other obligations, other appetites, other reading journeys.) *Game Change,* as you may or may not know, is about the 2008 election in the U.S., and appeared in a couple of the best-of-year lists here in the U.K., so I was reminded that I owned it; when I read it, I was reminded that politicians are unlike anyone I have ever met in my life.

Maybe some of you know politicians. Maybe you hang out with them, went to school with them, exchange Christmas cards with them. I'm guessing not, though. Politicians tend not to hang out with people like you, almost by definition. Typically, someone interested enough in the arts to be reading the *Believer* has spent a lot of time doing things that disqualify you not only from a career in politics, but from even knowing people who have a career in politics. While you were smoking weed, sleeping around, listening to Pavement, reading novels, watching old movies, and generally pissing away every educational opportunity ever given to you, they were knocking on doors, joining societies, reading the *Economist,* and being very, very careful about avoiding people and situations that might embarrass them later. They are the people who were knocking on your door five minutes after you arrived at college, asking for your vote in the forthcoming student-representative election; you thought they were creeps, and laughed at them behind their backs. Meanwhile, they thought you were unserious and unfocused, and patronized you irritatingly if you ever had cause to be in the same room. I hope that, however old you are, you have already done enough to kill any serious political ambition. If you haven't wasted huge chunks of your life on art, booze, and soft drugs, then you've wasted huge chunks of your life, and we don't want you around here. Go away.

Many of the characters in *Game Change* are quite clearly creeps. They are not portrayed as creeps, for the most part. John Heilemann and Mark Halperin obviously like the people who want to govern us, and their book, which is an unavoidable, enthralling mix of the gossipy and the profoundly significant, reflects this affection. And yet I defy anyone from around these parts to read this book without thinking, over and over again, Who are these people? There's John Edwards, of course, whose affair with the extraordinary Rielle Hunter was conducted more or less entirely in full view of an increasingly incredulous staff; when Edwards eventually realized the damage he had done to himself and his campaign, he lambasted a young staffer because he didn't come to his boss "like a fucking man and tell me to stop fucking her." But there are plenty of other strange people, too—people who don't really seem to believe anything, but who are desperately anxious to know what the country wants to hear them saying.

Obama is different, of course, but it's still very difficult to fathom why anyone would want to become a world leader. It's really not a nice job. For four hundred thousand dollars a year—plus a nineteen-thousand-dollar entertainment budget, although I would imagine very little of that can go on CDs, books, and cinema tickets—you give up safety, family life, social life, sleep, a significant proportion of your sanity, and the esteem of approximately two in every three of your fellow citizens. I am not being flippant: this is an intolerable prospect, for anyone with any sense of an inner life. This means that the people who want to represent us are actually the least representative people in the world.

Here in Europe, we still love Obama. But right at the beginning of *Game Change,* when Halperin and Heilemann are describing his relationship with Hillary Clinton, there is a line intended to convey how close the two were, once upon a time, but that serves only to make you wonder about politicians as a species. "At one point, Obama gave her a gift: a photograph of him, Michelle, and their two young daughters, Sasha and Malia." So, hold on… Hillary was Barack's mother? Because if she wasn't, why on earth would he give her a picture of himself and his kids? Would you do that with someone you knew professionally? "Here's a framed picture of me. Put it up anywhere in your house. It doesn't have to be on your mantelpiece. Or put it up in your office, on the half a shelf you have available for photos of your loved ones." Try it, and see how often you're invited to after-work drinks.

Game Change isn't the book I thought it would be, perhaps because the nomination race and the presidential campaign were not what they looked like from across the Atlantic. I was expecting a thrilling and inspirational story, full of goodies and baddies, dizzying highs and dispiriting lows; instead, Heilemann and Halperin describe a long, strength-sapping, and bitter trudge to victory. Much of the book is taken up with the inevitability of Clinton's defeat, and her refusal to acknowledge it, while Obama waits with weary impatience. And the fight between Obama and McCain is a nonevent once Sarah Palin joins in and makes the sides uneven. This is not to say that *Game Change* is dull. It isn't, because every page feels like the truth. It's just that the truth isn't as uplifting as you want to believe.

It was the holiday season here in the U.K., which explains the brevity of the Books Read list: my intellectual life is utterly dependent on my children attending school. The holiday season doesn't explain why I didn't pick up any fiction, nor does it explain why I should choose to spend all my available reading time on the unpromising subjects of American politics and cancer cells. I will only regret it if *Game Change* and *The Immortal Life of Henrietta Lacks* turn out to be the last two books I ever read, because I don't think they illustrate the breathtaking range of my literary tastes. They make me look like the kind of nonfiction guy I meet on planes during book tours. "Should I have heard of you? See, I don't read many novels. I like to learn something I didn't know already." At the time of writing I am halfway through a short and very beautiful YA novel, the completion of which should recomplicate me; meanwhile, you'll have to forgive these pages of the *Believer* temporarily resembling the books section of *Business Traveller* magazine.

Maybe the business travelers know what they're talking about, though, because *The Immortal Life of Henrietta Lacks* is riveting, beautifully written, and, yes, educational. I learned stuff. I learned so much stuff that I kept blurting it out to anyone who'd listen. Do you know who Henrietta Lacks was? Have you ever heard of the HeLa cells? Did you know that they can be found in just about any research lab in the world? And so on. I'll tell you, you don't want to be living with me at the moment. I'm even more boring than usual.

Rebecca Skloot's extraordinary book is the story of a dirt-poor black woman who died an agonizing death from cervical cancer in 1951. Just before Henrietta died, however, a surgeon sliced off a piece of her tumor and gave it to a research scientist called George Gey, who had been trying to grow human cells for years. Henrietta's cells, however, grew like kudzu, for reasons that are still not entirely clear to scientists; they grew so fast, so uncontrollably, that when you look up HeLa on Wikipedia, the entry uses the word *contamination* in the first four lines. HeLa is so powerful and fierce and durable, so eager to reproduce itself, that it gets into everything.

After I had read the first three or four chapters, I was a little worried on Skloot's behalf: I thought she was telling the story too quickly. Henrietta's cells were duplicating, her place in medical history was assured… maybe the last couple of hundred pages would turn out to be the first one hundred rehashed and analyzed, and the book would lose its breathtaking opening momentum. But the author knows what she has, and what she has is a gold mine of material dealing with class, race, family, science, and the law in America. In fact, *The Immortal Life of Henrietta Lacks,* like Adrian Nicole LeBlanc's incredible *Random Family,* is about pretty much everything. (*Random Family* and Skloot's book both took a decade to research and write, perhaps not coincidentally. I suspect that in both cases, the subject matter grew richer and richer with each year of contemplation.) Skloot tells brief, vivid, and astonishing stories of medical-ethics cases; she follows the cells as they get blasted into space and help find a vaccine for polio; she weaves in the lives of Henrietta's children as they struggle through the decades following their mother's death. They had no idea that she had achieved immortality until the 1970s, because nobody had ever taken the trouble to tell them, or to ask their permission—a courtesy denied Henrietta herself, of course. And while you can go online this very second and buy HeLa cells, the Lacks family has struggled, mostly in vain, for employment, access to health care, and recognition for Henrietta's contribution to science. If I come across a book as good, as gripping, as well constructed, and as surprising as this in the rest of 2011, I will be a happy and grateful man.

Contemporary fiction is OK, but you don't really learn anything from it, do you? It's mostly written by a bunch of arty losers who couldn't be bothered to go out and get a proper job, and who don't know anything about the world anyway. Nonfiction, that's the thing. Or historical fiction, because you know when you're reading it that people have done a whole load of research into nineteenth-century brick-making. Or thrillers, because you can learn a lot of things about high-grade weaponry. My New Year's resolution is to get a job as a, you know, a business guy, and join a business-guy book club. Plus, I'm going to befriend an important politician, a minister or a secretary of state. If any of you ministers or secretaries of state out there subscribe to this magazine and read this column, then facebook me, OK? I am literally holding my breath, so hurry. ✶

MAY 2011

I first and last read John Updike when I was in my twenties: I devoured all the *Rabbit* books that had been published at that point, and looked forward to a time in my life when I would be old enough to understand them. All that adultery and misery and ambition and guilt looked completely thrilling back then, but mystifying, too. Where did it all come from? And why, aged twenty-five, was I not grown up enough to be experiencing any of it? What was wrong with me? I suspect I didn't read any more of Updike's novels after that point simply because they made me feel inadequate, in ways that I hadn't previously considered. New forms of inadequacy I could live without, seeing as I didn't know what to do with the ones I was already aware of.

I'm not quite sure why an unread copy of *Marry Me* winked at me from my bookshelves just before I flew to the U.S. for a work trip recently. On the cover of the book, Paul Theroux promises us that "Updike has never written better of the woe that is marriage," but I can assure you (and my wife) that it wasn't the cheery blurb that lured me in. Perhaps I wanted to test myself again, a quarter of a century after the last time: had I got any closer to adulthood? Would I now, finally, be able to see a reflection of my own domestic circumstances?

"'You dumb cunt,' he said, and bounced her into the mattress again and again, 'you get a fucking grip on yourself. You got what you wanted, didn't you? This is it. Married bliss.'

"She spat in his face, *ptuh,* like a cat, a jump ahead of thought; saliva sprayed back down upon her own face and as it were awakened her..."

I am embarrassed to say that life is only very rarely like this *chez nous.* There's the holiday season, obviously, and the occasional Saturday night, especially during January and May, when, typically, my football team Arsenal crash out of the major competitions. But, hand on heart, I could not claim that we scale these particular giddy heights of seriousness with the kind of frequency that would allow me to gasp with recognition. I was even more cowed by the way this scene concludes, half a page and fourteen lines of dialogue later:

"'You're a nice man.' She hugged him, having suppressed a declaration of love.

"Wary, he wanted to sleep. 'Good night, sweetie.'"

I don't like to point the finger, and in any case my wife is generally a pacific and forgiving person. But the truth is that whenever I do call her the *c*-word and bounce her into the mattress again and again, she has never once told me that I'm "a nice man"—she tends to remain cross with me for hours. This means, in turn, that I have never been able to find it in myself to say "Good night, sweetie," and put the whole unfortunate episode behind us. In other words, it's her fault that we are not yet Updikean. She's a forty-five-year-old child.

It wasn't just the rows I found hard to comprehend; some of the sex was beyond me, too. "Though Sally had been married ten years, and furthermore had had lovers before Jerry, her lovemaking was wonderfully virginal, simple, and quick." Ah, yes. That's what we gentlemen want: women who are both sexually experienced and alive to the touch, while at the same time not too, you know, trampy. "Wonderfully virginal"? My therapist would have more fun in fifty minutes than he'd ever had in his whole professional life were I to use that particular combination of adverb and adjective in a session.

Marry Me was, as you can probably imagine, totally compelling, if extraordinarily dispiriting in its conviction that trying to extract the misery out of monogamy is like trying to extract grapes from wine. We worry a lot about how technology will date fiction; it had previously occurred to me that books written in the last quarter of the twentieth century would lead me to wonder whether something fundamental has changed in the relationships between men and women. I'm not sure we do feel that husbands and wives are doomed to suspicion, enmity, and contempt any longer, do we? Or am I making a twit of myself again? I suppose it's the latter. It usually is.

Worryingly—and this must remain completely between us—I recognized myself more frequently in the checklist Jon Ronson refers to in the title of his book than I did in *Marry Me*. (I'm not going to repeat the title. You'll have to go to the trouble of glancing up at the top of the previous page, and maybe you won't bother, and then you'll think better of me.) "Glibness/superficial charm"? Well, I have my moments, even if I do say so myself. And have you lost some weight? "Lack of realistic long-term goals"? I wouldn't call literary immortality unrealistic, exactly. It's more or less happened to Chaucer and Shakespeare, and I'm miles better than either of those. "Grandiose sense of self-worth"? Ah, now there at least I can plead not guilty. "Need for stimulation/proneness to boredom"? I literally stopped in the middle of typing out that last sentence in order to play *Plants vs. Zombies,* although I did get bored of that after a couple of hours, so perhaps there is hope for me. "Poor behavioral controls"? Again, there is a glimmer of light, because I have just put out my last cigarette, and eaten my last biscuit.

Jon Ronson, as those of you who have read *Them* or *The Men Who Stare at Goats* will know, is a fearless nonfiction writer, so familiar with, and curious about, the deranged and the fanatical that he probably asks for his hair to be cut with a lunatic fringe. *Them* dealt with extremists of all hues, and *The Men Who Stare at Goats* was about that section of the American military who believe that one day wars might be won using mind-control and gloop. *The Psychopath Test,* as the title suggests, cuts straight to the chase.

It begins with a mystery: why were a group of academics, mostly neurologists, all sent a book by "Joe K" that consisted entirely of cryptic messages and holes? The perplexed neurologists believed that Ronson was the man to solve the puzzle, and their instincts were sound, because he does so. On the way, he meets a man who pretended to be mad in order to escape a prison sentence, and now cannot convince anybody that he is sane; several Scientologists engaged in a war on psychiatry, as Scientologists tend to be; Bob Hare, the man who devised the eponymous test; and a top CEO whose legendary ruthlessness leads Ronson to suspect that he might tick a few too many boxes. (It is Bob Hare's contention that psychopaths are all around us, in positions that allow them to exert and abuse their authority.) Like all Ronson's work, *The Psychopath Test* is funny, frightening, and provocative: it had never occurred to me, for example, that Scientologists had any kind of an argument for their apparently absurd war on science, but Ronson's account of the equally absurd experiments and treatments for which respected psychiatrists are responsible gives one pause for thought.

If you are a subscriber to this magazine, and a regular reader of this column, and you have very little going on in your life, and you're kind of anal, you may be thinking to yourself, Hey! It's eight weeks since he last wrote a column, and he's read exactly four books! There are various explanations and excuses I could give you, but the two most pertinent are as follows:

1) I have been cruelly tricked into cofounding a writing center for kids, with a weird shop at the front of it, here in London (and don't even think about copying this idea in the U.S. unless you want to hear from our lawyers— although why you would want to spend a thousand hours and a million pounds a week doing so I can't imagine).

2) I have spent way too much time watching the Dillon Panthers, the fictional football team at the heart of the brilliant drama series *Friday Night Lights.* (And yes, I know, I know—I have seen the fourth season. I am being respectful to those who are catching up.)

Reading time, in other words, has been in short supply, even during the day, and half the reading that has got done is directly related to the above. H. G. Bissinger's terrific nonfiction book, the source for a movie and then the TV series, is about the Permian Panthers, who represent a high school in Odessa, Texas, and regularly play in front of crowds of twenty thousand—or did, when the book was published in the early '90s. There is no equivalent of high-school or college football in Europe, for several reasons: there are no comparable sports scholarships, for a start, and, in a country the size of England, it's quite hard to live more than fifty miles from a pro team. And in any case, because your major sports have turned out to be so uninteresting to the rest of the world, young talent in the U.S. is governable; the young soccer players of London and Manchester no longer compete with each other for a place in a top professional team, but with kids from Africa and Asia and Spain. Over the last several years, Arsenal has routinely played without a single English player in their starting eleven. Our best player is Spanish; one of our brightest hopes for the future is Japanese and currently on loan to a club in Holland. So the idea of an entire community's aspirations being embodied in local teenage athletes is weird, but not unappealing.

The reality, as Bissinger presents it—and he went to live in Odessa for a year, hung out with players and coaching staff and fans, so he knows what he's talking about—is a lot darker, however. It turns out that there are not as many liberals in small-town Texas as the TV series would have me believe: in Dillon, people are always speaking out against racism, or talking about art, or thinking about great literature. (The adorably nerdy Landry Clarke can quite clearly be seen reading *High Fidelity,* my first novel, in an episode of the third season. This is almost certainly the greatest achievement of my writing career. And I'm sorry to bring it up, but I had to tell somebody.) In Odessa, Dillon's real-life counterpart... not so much racism gets confronted, or towering masterpieces of fiction consumed. Bissinger loves his football, and falls in love with the team, but is powerfully good on what the town's obsession with football costs its kids. It's not just the ones who don't make it, or become damaged along the way, all of whom get chucked away like ribs stripped of their meat (and catastrophically uneducated before they've been rejected); the kids who can't play football are almost worthless. The girls spend half their time cheerleading and cake-baking for the players, and the students with more cerebral interests are ignored. In the season that Bissinger followed the team, the cost of rush-delivered postgame videotapes that enabled the coaches to analyze what had gone right and wrong was $6,400. The budget for the entire English department was $5,040. And the team used private jets for away games on more than one occasion. Isn't it great how little you need to spend to inculcate a passion for the arts? Perhaps I have drawn the wrong conclusion.

David Almond's *My Name Is Mina* is an extraordinary children's book by the author of *Skellig,* one of the best novels written for anyone published in the last fifteen years. And this new book is a companion piece to *Skellig,* a kind of prequel about the girl who lives next door. It's also, as it turns out, a handbook for anyone who is interested in literacy and education as they have been, or are being, applied to them or their children or anybody else's children:

> Why should I write something so that somebody could say I was well below average, below average, average, above average, or well above average? What's average? And what about the ones that find out they're well below average? What's the point of that and how's that going to make them feel for the rest of their lives? And did William Blake do writing tasks just because somebody else told him to? And what Level would he have got anyway?

> "Little Lamb, Who mad'st thee?
> Dost thou know who mad'st thee?"

> What level is that?

Almond's wry disdain for the way we sift our children as if they were potatoes killed me, because I was once found to be below average, across the board, at a crucial early stage in my educational career, and I have just about recovered enough confidence to declare that this judgment was, if not wrong, then at least not worth making. I think that, like everybody, I'm above average at some things and well below at others.

My Name Is Mina is a literary novel for kids, a Blakean mystic's view of the world, a fun-filled activity book for a rainy day ("EXTRAORDINARY ACTIVITY—Write a poem that repeats a word and repeats a word and repeats a word and repeats a word until it almost loses its meaning"), a study of loneliness and grief, and it made more sense to me than half the fiction I usually read. This can't be right, and I won't allow it to be right. For literary purposes only, I am off to call my wife obscenities and bounce her up and down on a mattress. As I write, she's upstairs, helping my youngest son with his homework, so she's in for a shock. ✷

JUNE 2011

My friendship with the writer Sarah Vowell—history buff, TV and radio personality, occasional animated character—is now fifteen years old. For the first decade or so, it was pretty straightforward: whenever I was in New York, we would sit in a park staring at a statue of an obscure but allegedly important American figure, and she would talk about it while I nodded and smoked. Over the last few years, however, it has become complicated to the extent that it has started to resemble one of those Greek myths where the hero (in this case, me) is asked to perform tasks by some enigmatic and implacable goddess (her) or monster (also her). Vowell isn't as well known in the U.K. as she should be—we have different chat shows, for a start, and because of the awesomely uncompromising insularity of her writing, her books aren't published here. So, as one of her few English fans, I have been taking the literary challenges that she throws across the Atlantic personally. In my mind, at least, it goes like this. I tell her that I am an enormous admirer of her work, and she says, "In that case, I am going to write a book about the museums of the assassinated American presidents, excluding the most recent, and therefore the only one you are interested in. Will you read it?" I read it, loved it, told her so.

"I see that you are a worthy English opponent, so I will have to try harder. I will now make you read a book about New England Puritans— not the Plymouth Pilgrims, but the more obscure (and more self-denying) Massachusetts Bay crowd." I read it, loved it, asked her to hit me with something a little less accessible.

And now she has come roaring back with *Unfamiliar Fishes,* a history of Hawaii, although obviously it's not a complete history of Hawaii, because a complete history of Hawaii would not have intimidated the English reader to quite the required extent, and might have contained some fun facts about Bette Midler. Vowell wisely chose to concentrate on the nineteenth century, post-1820, when her old friends from New England sailed around the entire American continent in order to tell the natives that everything they had hitherto believed was wrong. (One of the many things I had never thought about before reading *Unfamiliar Fishes* was the sheer uselessness of New England as a home base for missionaries. It took them a good six months to get to anywhere uncivilized enough to need them.)

Unfamiliar Fishes tells the story of the battle for hearts and minds between the Massachusetts killjoys and the locals. In these wars, the liberal conscience always has us rooting for the locals, even though we invariably already know that we are doomed to disappointment, and that the locals, whoever and wherever they might be, are even as we speak tucking into Happy Meals, listening to Adele, and working for Halliburton. In Hawaii, though, there was a lot invested in the idea that a child born from the union between brother and sister was superior to a child conceived any other way, and this particular belief kind of muddied the water a little for me. I know, I know. Different times, different cultures. But I have a sister, and you too may well have a sibling who operates an entirely different genital system. And if you do, then you might find yourself unable to boo the meddling Christians with the volume you can usually achieve in situations like this.

And yet as Vowell points out, the whole foundation of royalty is based on the notion that one bloodline is superior to another, and therefore shouldn't be messed with. "The way said contamination is prevented is through inbreeding, which, of course, is often the genetic cause of a royal dynasty's demise through sterility, miscarriages, stillbirths, and sickliness. That would be true of the heirs of Keopuolani just as it was true of the House of Hapsburg."

In other words, one of the reasons that my own country is in such a mess is that there simply hasn't been enough in-breeding: if there had, we might be shot of our Royal Family by now. Incest is more complicated than it looks (and please feel free to go and get that printed on a T-shirt, if it's a slogan that grabs you). Like anything else, it's got its good points and its bad.

The one team we can all get behind in *Unfamiliar Fishes* is the crew of the English whaler *John Palmer*. They were so annoyed by the missionaries messing with their inalienable right to onboard visits from prostitutes that they started shelling the port. I am, however, grudgingly respectful of the Americans who, convinced of the Hawaiians' need for a Bible, first helped to invent a written Hawaiian language, and then translated the whole thing from the original Greek and Hebrew. It took them seventeen years. Finally I have a notion of what I might do when I retire. Anyway, I have sailed through yet another task set by the dark nerd-maiden from across the water; I don't think she is capable of writing anything that I wouldn't read, although I hope she doesn't take that as a provocation. And her history of whaling on the island was so enthralling that it got me through the entire first chapter of *Moby-Dick*.

The idea of this column, for those of you who have arrived eight years late, is that I write about what I have read in the previous month; for some reason, the books I read with my children have never been included. This last couple of months, however, we have been reading Andy Stanton's *Mr. Gum* series at bedtime, and as Stanton's books are providing as much joy to me as they do to the boys, their omission from these pages would be indefensible.

Mr. Gum is an evil, joyless, smelly old man who tries to poison dogs, and whose favorite TV program is *Bag of Sticks,* which is as exciting as it sounds.

His best friend is the evil butcher Billy William the Third, and his enemies are the entirely admirable Polly, Friday O'Leary, and the billionaire gingerbread man with electric muscles, little Alan Taylor. The books are a happy product of a tolerably nonincestuous relationship between Roald Dahl and Monty Python, and they are properly funny: Stanton has an eccentric imagination, and an anarchic verbal wit that occasionally redirects his narrative in directions that possibly even the author didn't expect.

My sons' enormous enjoyment of the books has been intensified through a series of superb readings by their father, readings that, in his mind at least, are comparable only to the performances Dickens is reported to have given at public events. Billy William the Third is rendered as an evil version of the great English comic actor Kenneth Williams, Alan Taylor as the football commentator John Motson, and Mr. Gum as a kind of ancient Cockney gangster paterfamilias. It seems ridiculous that performances with this level of invention take place night after night in a child's bedroom, in front of an audience of two; I may well have to throw them open to the public.

If you, like me, have been cursed by boy-children, you too may have found that their relationship with books is a fractious one, no matter how many times they see a male role model lounging around the house with his nose glued to a partial history of Hawaii. Andy Stanton's series has been a real break-through, and a testament to the importance and the power of jokes; we are just about to start the seventh of the eight books, and I'm already fearful of the Gumless future.

I don't have the heart to tell my sons that the older one gets, the less funny literature becomes—and they would refuse to believe me if I tried to explain that some people don't think jokes even belong in proper books. I won't bother breaking the news that, if they remain readers, they will insist on depressing themselves for about a decade of their lives, in a concerted search for gravitas through literature. Charles Portis is a *Believer* favorite (one of our editors wrote an enormous and completely excellent piece about him in the very early days of this magazine's life) partly because he takes his humor seriously: the Coen brothers' recent adaptation of *True Grit* was admirable in many ways, but it didn't really convey the comic brilliance of the novel, nor was it able to, as so much of it was embedded in the voice of the priggish, god-fearing Mattie Ross. I suspect that we have the Coen brothers to thank for the reappearance of Portis's first novel, *Norwood,* in bookstores, so they have done their bit for comedy anyway.

"Norwood" is Norwood Pratt, a marine who obtains a hardship discharge so that he can return to Texas to look after his incapable sister Vernell. Vernell promptly marries an unlikable disabled veteran called Bill Bird, however, thus liberating Norwood to go to New York, partly in an attempt to reclaim seventy dollars that an army friend owes him. So *Norwood* is a road-trip book, and the simplicity of its structure allows for a dazzling range of eccentric minor characters, and plenty of room for any number of terrific, short, often crazily pointless passages of dialogue. Here's Norwood, on a bus, trying to engage with a two-year-old called Hershel Remley:

> "I believe the cat has got that boy's tongue," said Norwood.
>
> "Say no he ain't," said Mrs. Remley. "Say I can talk aplenty when I want to, Mr. Man."
>
> "Tell me what your name is," said Norwood. "What is your name?"
>
> "Say Hershel. Say Hershel Remley is my name."
>
> "How old are you, Hershel? Tell me how old you are."
>
> "Say I'm two years old."
>
> "Hold up this many fingers," said Norwood.
>
> "He don't know about that," said Mrs. Remley. "But he can blow out a match."

There's so much to love here: the portrayal of the clearly slow-witted toddler, Mrs. Remley's desperate and hopeful pride, the author's merciless ear for disastrous parental anthropomorphizing... This is the third novel I have read by Charles Portis, and I am now completely convinced that he's a neglected comic genius. And here's a cool fact: in Nora Ephron's new book of essays, *I Remember Nothing,* she talks about dating Portis in the '60s. The relationship clearly didn't last, but it feels as though their children are everywhere anyway.

Tom Rachman's *The Imperfectionists,* which I suspect you may have read already, is an ingeniously structured work of fiction that manages to tell the entire history of an English-language newspaper based in Rome through a series of linked short stories about its members of staff. This to me makes *The Imperfectionists* a collection rather than a novel, despite the bald assertion on the cover ("A Novel"), and I slightly resented being misled, for entirely indefensible reasons; in most ways I haven't aged at all over the last quarter of a century, remarkably, but I seemed to have developed some kind of old-geezerish resentment of story collections. Is that possible? Is resentment of short fiction a sign of aging, like liver spots? And if it is, then why? As the end of one's life draws closer, surely one should embrace short fiction, not spurn it. And yet I was extremely conscious of not wanting to make the emotional effort at the beginning of each chapter, to the extent that I could almost hear myself grumbling like my grandmother used to. "Who are these people, now? I don't know them. Where did the other ones go? They'd only just got here." It's a great tribute to Rachman, to his sense of pace and his choice of narrative moment, that within a couple of pages I had forgiven him. And the world of the expatriate is, it occurred to me halfway through the book, rich with fictional possibilities; almost by definition, the characters are lost, restless, discontented—just the way we like them.

I feel that I cannot leave before explaining some of the more baffling choices in the Books Bought column. Lawrence W. Levine's *Highbrow/Lowbrow* was, along with John Seabrook's *Nobrow,* a recommendation from a reader who felt it might help me with some of the difficult issues raised by Carl Wilson's essay on Céline Dion; the book about Ronald Reagan's time at General Electric I bought after watching a riveting Reagan documentary on the BBC. The chances of me reading either of them are, I suspect, slim; as is so often the case, however, I am, at relatively modest expense, intent on maintaining a risible self-delusion about my intellectual curiosity. I know way too much about James Brown already, so I'll probably choose that one next. ✲

JULY / AUGUST 2011

BOOKS BOUGHT:

- ☆ *Mrs. Caliban*—Rachel Ingalls
- ☆ *Whoops!: Why Everyone Owes Everyone and No One Can Pay*
  —John Lanchester
- ☆ *Adventures of Huckleberry Finn*—Mark Twain
- ☆ *The Writer's Journey: Mythic Structure for Writers*—Christopher Vogler

BOOKS READ:

- ☆ *Sum: Forty Tales from the Afterlives*—David Eagleman
- ☆ *Ball of Fire: The Tumultuous Life and Comic Art of Lucille Ball*
  —Stefan Kanfer
- ☆ *Nothing to Envy: Ordinary Lives in North Korea*—Barbara Demick
- ☆ *Whoops!: Why Everyone Owes Everyone and No One Can Pay*
  —John Lanchester
- ☆ *Adventures of Huckleberry Finn*—Mark Twain

No time spent with a book is ever entirely wasted, even if the experience is not a happy one: there's always something to be learned. It's just that, every now and again, you can hit a patch of reading that makes you feel as if you're pootling about. There's nothing like a couple of sleepy novels, followed by a moderately engaging biography of a minor cultural figure, to make you aware of your own mortality. But what can you do about it? We don't choose to waste our reading time; it just happens. The books let us down.

It wasn't just that I enjoyed all the books I read this month; they felt vital, too. If you must read a biography of a sitcom star, then make sure the sitcom is the most successful and influential in TV history. You have a yen to read about a grotesquely dysfunctional communist society? Well, don't mess about with Cuba—go straight for North Korea. John Lanchester's *Whoops!* is a relatively simple explanation of the biggest financial crisis in history; Mark

Twain's *Adventures of Huckleberry Finn* is, according to Hemingway, the book from which all American literature derives. A month of superlatives, in other words—the best, the worst, the biggest, and the most important.

And, as a digestif, David Eagleman's *Sum,* which invites us to contemplate forty varieties of afterlife. It's such a complete package that it seems crazy to carry on reading, so I may well stop altogether. I'm not giving this column up, though. It pays too well.

Stefan Kanfer's *Ball of Fire* contains an anecdote which seems to me to justify not only the time I spent reading it, but the entire genre, every biography ever written. Kanfer is describing the early days of Ball's relationship with Desi Arnaz, which was stormy right from the off:

> Almost every Sunday night ended with a furious argument about each other's intentions and infidelities… It happened that two of the town's greatest magpies witnessed many of the quarrels. F. Scott Fitzgerald and his inamorata, columnist Sheilah Graham, used to watch the spats from Fitzgerald's balcony.

F. Scott Fitzgerald used to watch Lucille Ball and Desi Arnaz fighting? Why didn't I know this before? If this story is true—and there's no reason to doubt it—then all is chaos. No biography can be left unread, just in case there is a gem like this lying there, undiscovered, within its pages. Maybe Thomas Pynchon repeatedly bangs on Sarah Michelle Gellar's wall because she plays her music too loud! Maybe Simon Cowell and Maya Angelou are in the same book group!

The reason Kanfer's book works so well, and why it throws up so many good stories, is that Ball, like the fictional Mose Sharp and Rocky Carter in Elizabeth McCracken's brilliant *Niagara Falls All Over Again,* took the long road through the American pop-culture century. She worked in theater, film, radio, and TV. She dated Henry Fonda, worked with the Marx Brothers, knew Damon Runyon. A washed-up Buster Keaton helped her with her physical comedy. She found out that she was pregnant by listening to Walter Winchell on the radio—he'd obtained the information from the lab technicians even before they passed the information on to Ball's doctor. She attracted the attention of HUAC, the House Un-American Activities Committee, because she'd registered with the

Communist party in 1936 primarily to humor her socialist grandfather. Hers was an extraordinary journey, and just in case you need a little more, there was a long, tempestuous marriage at the center of it. (Ball rendered the first divorce from Arnaz null and void by jumping into bed with her ex-husband on the way back from the courthouse.) We didn't have a Lucille Ball in the U.K.; you have way more female comediennes than us. This is not a coincidence.

There wasn't any logic behind my decision to go straight from *Ball of Fire* to the banking crisis, although John Lanchester's *Whoops!* (published in the U.S. as *I.O.U.*) certainly bolstered the sense of elegiac melancholy that lingers after you've said goodbye to Lucy and Desi and the Golden Age of Television. We now have more to worry about than the end of wholesome, nation-uniting family sitcoms; it turns out that the Golden Age of Everything is over. One of Lanchester's contentions is that "Western liberal democracies are the best societies that have ever existed… Citizens of those societies are, on aggregate, the most fortunate people who have ever lived." I'll be comparing and contrasting with North Korea a little later, but when you consider that one of the indicators of poverty in the U.S. and the U.K. is obesity, you can see his point. Nobody is obese in North Korea.

Now, however, the citizens of the U.S. and the U.K. have some bills to pay. One authoritative market commentator puts the cost of the bailout in the U.S. at just over $4.5 trillion—a number "bigger than the Marshall Plan, the Louisiana Purchase, the Apollo moon landings, the 1980s savings and loan crisis, the Korean War, the New Deal, the invasion of Iraq, the Vietnam War, and the total cost of NASA's space flights, all added together—repeat, added together (and yes, the old figures are adjusted upward for inflation)." If you were thinking of knocking on the door of a government body because you're looking for a little help with your video installation… well, I'd give it a few weeks. Here in the U.K., the government is looking to make an unprecedented and almost certainly unachievable 25 percent cut in public services; we need to find in the region of £40 billion a year simply to service our debts.

There are plenty of numbers in *Whoops!* Most of them are scary, but some are funny, if your taste in humor leans toward the apocalyptic. In a brilliant chapter about the catastrophic failure of the mathematical models of risk used by bankers and economists, a chapter entitled The Mistake, Lanchester introduces us—well, me, anyway—to the notion of the sigma, a measure of probability. "A '3-sigma event' is something supposed to happen only 0.3 percent of the time, i.e., about once every three thousand times something is measured." According to the mathematical models, the 1987 Black Monday crash was a 10-sigma event; this means that, were the life of the universe repeated 1 billion times, it still shouldn't have happened. And yet it did. During the recent crash, the CFO of Goldman Sachs claimed that he was seeing twenty-five sigma events "*several days in a row.*" (My italics, but I'm sure I'm italicizing for all of us.) Lanchester tries to give us some sense of the numbers involved here, but it's basically hopeless: "Twenty sigma is ten times the number of all the particles in the known universe; 25-sigma is the same but with the decimal point moved fifty-two places to the right." Even if we presume that there are three particles in the known universe—and I'm no physicist, but I'm guessing that three is probably on the low side—then the number is still impossible to grasp. And these people saw events on this scale of incomprehensible improbability happening every day for a week. They would presumably also have been staggered by Brazil winning the next World Cup, on the basis that they didn't win it yesterday or the day before or on any of the four and a half thousand days since their last victory, in 2002. (For those of you who don't follow soccer: Brazil are quite good. They always have a decent chance of winning the World Cup. But the World Cup takes place only every four years, so… Oh, forget it.) Meanwhile, the reality underpinning the numbers and the credit swaps and the securitization was a whole bunch of people who had been persuaded to take out mortgages that they couldn't afford, and had to pay more for them than people with a credit history and a job, because they were riskier. One thing that had never quite sunk in for me is that, for Wall Street and the City, subprime mortgages and junk bonds are Good Things—or used to be, anyway—so it wasn't as though the unscrupulous were hiding shoddy goods under the more-attractive stuff. The shoddy goods were attractive, and they wanted in. The higher the risk, the more money you make. Lovely. And the bankers thought they'd fixed it so that this risk had no downside, ever, for anyone. Securitization and its trimmings were, almost literally, alchemy, as far as the banks could tell.

One of the reasons *Whoops!* has done well in the U.K. is that John Lanchester is One of Us. He's not a financial journalist; he's a novelist, and a critic, and an outsider when it comes to this stuff. His dad was a bank manager, though, and he has the necessary interest, and the necessary anxiety. I watched *Inside Job* this month, too, and between them, Lanchester and Charles Ferguson have achieved the impossible, and made me feel… not knowledgeable, exactly, but at least I can see the dim light of comprehension breaking somewhere over the horizon. I don't know you personally, but I'm sort of presuming that you know more about the Decemberists and Jennifer Egan than you do about Gaussian copula formulas. Is that right? If so, then this is the book for you.

Nothing to Envy is a book about what happens when an economy fails completely, to the extent that there is nothing left—no work, no infrastructure, no food, no anything. I bought it after a forceful recommendation from a friend, and after it won a nonfiction prize in the U.K., and I wasn't sure I'd ever read it. But on the very first page there is a startling satellite picture of the Korean peninsula, taken at night, and I was hooked in. In this picture, the South looks like the U.S. or the U.K. or just about any twenty-first-century country, mottled with light from its cities, and great puddles of the stuff in the area around Seoul. In the North, it looks as though someone has a single candle burning in the capital, Pyongyang. Much of North Korea has no electricity. It's packed up. It went sometime in the early '90s, and it never came back. Sometimes—typically on the birthday of the Great Leader—it wheezes back into life for an hour or two, but the rest of the time North Korea is lost in a blackness of its own making.

Barbara Demick has pieced together a picture of daily life in this poor benighted country from the testimonies of people who got out. They weren't dissidents, because dissidence doesn't really exist in North Korea. How can it, when its citizens have never been presented with an alternative way of thinking, and when they have no access to books, magazines, newspapers, movies, TV, music, or ideas from any other part of the world? Even conversation is dangerous, when you have no way of knowing whether your friends, neighbors, even children are informants. You don't have a telephone, and you can't write to anyone when you have no pen or paper, and even if you do, the postman may well burn your letters simply because there's nothing else to burn. Meanwhile, everyone is starving to death. (Much of the book is about life in the 1990s, but, as Demick's epilogue and the most cursory Google search makes clear, nothing much has changed.) One of Demick's interviewees was a kindergarten teacher who saw her class go from fifty to fifteen kids. There is literally nothing to eat; they're peeling the bark off trees and boiling it up for soup. This is a country whose inhabitants have literally shrunk, while the rest of the world has got taller: the average North Korean seventeen-year-old boy is five inches smaller than his counterpart in the South.

A review quoted on my paperback edition tells us that this book is "required reading for anyone interested in the Korean peninsula"; I've just spent a few hundred words telling you how harrowing much of it is. We're not selling it to you, I can tell. And yet *Nothing to Envy* does have resonance, and it does transcend its subject matter, if that's what you want it to do. Both *Whoops!* and *Nothing to Envy* make it clear just how utterly dependent we all are on systems; without them, our much-cherished quirky individuality and our sense of moral self mean nothing. And I know this sounds weird and possibly callous, but Demick's book was every bit as absorbing as *Ball of Fire*: both contain a multitude of extraordinary stories, stories you want to remember. In other words, there is a kind of pleasure to be gained from the pain of others. That's the trouble with good writers. Only the bad ones make you want to do the human thing and look away.

I have almost no room to talk about *Sum* or *Huckleberry Finn*. Briefly: *Sum* I enjoyed, although I wish it had come with instructions. Was I supposed to read all the forty essays in one lump, which is what I did? Or was I supposed to pepper my month with them, treat myself to a tiny contemplation of what the afterlife is or does or should be at odd moments of the day and night? I suspect the latter. I blew it. As for *Huckleberry Finn*, the most important novel in American literature: Meh. That Tom Sawyer is a pill, isn't he? ✱

SEPTEMBER 2011

BOOKS BOUGHT:

* ★ *Ten Thousand Saints*—Eleanor Henderson
* ★ *Elia Kazan*—Richard Schickel
* ★ *Monogamy*—Adam Phillips
* ★ *Your Voice in My Head*—Emma Forrest
* ★ *Young Stalin*—Simon Sebag Montefiore
* ★ *The Sex Diaries: Why Women Go Off Sex and Other Bedroom Battles* —Bettina Arndt
* ★ *Epitaph of a Small Winner*—Machado de Assis
* ★ *Furious Love: Elizabeth Taylor, Richard Burton, and the Marriage of the Century*—Sam Kashner and Nancy Schoenberger

BOOKS READ:

* ★ *Out Stealing Horses*—Per Petterson
* ★ *Ten Thousand Saints*—Eleanor Henderson
* ★ *Elia Kazan*—Richard Schickel
* ★ *Mating in Captivity: Sex, Lies, and Domestic Bliss*—Esther Perel

I know that you are younger than me, because more or less everyone is, nowadays. I am presuming, too, that if you have turned to this page of the *Believer* then you have an interest in books, and that if you read any of the rest of the magazine, then you are likely to have a deep passion for other forms of art. It is not too much of a stretch, then, to deduce from this information that your sexual relationships are complicated, morally dubious, and almost certainly unsavory, and I say that with as much neutrality as I can muster. So before I write about *Mating in Captivity*, Esther Perel's book about monogamous sex, I suppose I should clarify a couple of points for you.

Firstly: monogamy is this thing where you sleep with only one person. And I'm not talking about only one person during the whole length of Bonnaroo, or an art-film screening, or a poetry "happening," or whatever. Sometimes the commitment might last weeks, months even. (Married readers: in next month's column, I may introduce some more information, although I suspect they're some years away from being able to handle the dismal truth.) Esther Perel has cleverly recognized that a tiny minority of monogamists can occasionally feel a twinge of inexplicable and indefinable dissatisfaction with their chosen path— nothing significant, and certainly nothing that leads them to rethink their decision (monogamous relationships almost never fail, unless either partner is still sexually active)—and she has written a book that might help them through this tricky time. It's a niche market, obviously, the sexual equivalent of a guide for people whose pets have an alcohol-abuse problem. It's great that someone has done it, but it's not for everyone.

Secondly, I should also explain that I read this book for professional reasons, and professional reasons alone: I'm trying to write something about monogamy, god help me. I know that sounds dubious, but maybe you will believe me if I confess that my own marital problems lie beyond the reach of any self-help book available in a bookstore, or even on Amazon. They also lie beyond the reach of pills and tears, but perhaps I have said too much.

Mating in Captivity is a very wise book—I was going to say "surprisingly wise," because I have hitherto maintained the lit-snob assumption that nonfiction books that purport to improve your unhappy marriage or your failing career or your sickly spiritual well-being will actually do no such thing. (As we know around these parts, only Great Literature can save your soul, which is why all English professors are morally unimpeachable human beings, completely free from vanity, envy, sloth, lust, and so on.) Perel is very good on how the space between couples in which eroticism thrives, a space we are desperate to fill in the early days of a relationship, can be shrunk by domesticity and knowledge; there is a pragmatic understanding in her writing that is entirely winning and sympathetic.

She also has interesting things to say about the contemporary insistence that all intimacy is verbal intimacy, a cultural diktat that confuses and intimidates the kind of male whose inability to talk is then misinterpreted as an inability to commit, or a macho fear of weakness. Perel tells the rather sweet story of Eddie and Noriko, who literally couldn't communicate because they didn't speak the same language; Eddie had been ditched by scores of women who were impatient with his apparent unwillingness to bare his soul. "I really think that not being able to talk made this whole thing possible," Eddie tells Perel, twelve years into his marriage. "For once, there was no pressure on me to share. And so Noriko and I had to show how much we liked each other in other ways. We cooked for each other a lot, gave each other baths… It's not like we didn't communicate; we just didn't talk." MORE BATHS, LESS TALKING… If you're a woman who is currently and unhappily single, you could do a lot worse than put that slogan on a banner and march up and down your street.

"Some of America's best features—the belief in democracy, equality, consensus-building, compromise, fairness, and mutual tolerance—can, when carried too punctiliously into the bedroom, result in very boring sex," Perel says in a chapter entitled Democracy Versus Hot Sex. At the time of writing, Michele Bachmann has just announced her candidacy for the presidency, and another assumption I have made about you is that very few of you vote Republican. I don't think Esther Perel is encouraging you to do so, although if the unthinkable happens and Bachmann wins, there may well be some consolations, from the sound of it. (None of this applies to the British, of course, who live in a class-ridden monarchy, and as a consequence have hot sex every single day of their lives.)

My only complaint about this engaging and thoughtful book is that its author uses the word *vanilla* pejoratively too often, as a synonym for *bland, dull, safe.* This usage, I think, must stem from vanilla ice cream, which, typically, tastes of nothing and is certainly the unthinkable option if you're in an ice-cream establishment that offers scores of varieties. The flavor of the vanilla pod itself, however, is sophisticated, seductive, subtle. Have you tried the Body Shop Vanilla Shower Gel? I don't want to write advertising copy for multinational companies—not for free, anyway—but Body Shop Vanilla, it seems to me, is much more suggestive of deviance and light bondage than it is of the missionary position. And, guys, if you use that, could you credit the *Believer*? And also chuck them a few quid? Thanks.

I bought a couple of the books on the lists above after coming across a top-five that Woody Allen put together for the *Guardian*. I had never heard of Machado de Assis, and I probably wouldn't have thought of reading a biography of Elia Kazan had it not been for Allen's recommendation, but Richard Schickel's book chimed with the mood created by *Ball of Fire*, Stefan Kanfer's terrifically entertaining book about Lucille Ball, which I read recently.

Kazan, as you may or may not know, was the brilliant director of *On the Waterfront* and *A Streetcar Named Desire*. But he is now remembered almost as clearly because he chose to testify against former colleagues in front of the House Un-American Activities Committee (HUAC)—in 1952. Schickel begins his book, electrifyingly and provocatively, by coming out swinging on Kazan's behalf. I had never come across anyone attempting to do this before, and as a consequence I had always presumed that those who named names could safely be written off; god knows there are few enough examples of moral choices that are straightforwardly good or bad, and I had always valued the decision of Kazan and others as one of those that one didn't have to think about: they were wrong, full stop, and we are thus free to condemn them as viciously and as cheerfully as we want.

Yes, well. It turns out that it wasn't quite like that. Schickel's arguments are complicated and detailed, and I don't have the space to do them justice here, but then, complication and detail are precisely what have been lacking ever since the 1950s. Schickel describes the campaign against Kazan as "a typical Stalinist tactic—seize the high, easy-to-understand moral ground, then try to crush nuanced opposition to that position through simplifying sloganeering." I suspect that I'm not the only one who liked the look of that easy-to-understand moral ground, and there is a part of me that is actually irritated to discover that it's not as comfortable as it appeared. Schickel's jabs at the kidney—if that is where our fuzzy sense of morality is stored—are telling and sharp: naming names would have been fine if the names named had belonged to the Ku Klux Klan or the Nazi Party; there were lots of other, more-democratic leftist organizations that liberals could have signed up for; there were public protests against the Gulags as early as 1931, and there was really no excuse for those who defended Stalin in the 1950s; much of the outrage directed against Kazan was entirely synthetic. Rod Steiger, who appeared in *On the Waterfront* and was loudly and angrily opposed to the idea of Kazan receiving an honorary Oscar in 1999, told a reporter from *Time* that Kazan "was our father and he fucked us"; Schickel points out that the fucking was done well over a year before *On the Waterfront* started shooting—in other words, Steiger's moral objections came to the surface painfully slowly, and well after one of the most celebrated performances of his film career was safely in the can.

It was Dalton Trumbo, one of the writers blacklisted as a result of HUAC, who ended up making the best case for Kazan. The kind of person who testified, he said, was "a man who has left the CP to avoid constant attempts to meddle with the ideological content of his writing… a person whose disagreement with the CP had turned to forthright hostility and who, when the crunch came, saw no reason to sacrifice his career in defence of the rights of people he now hated…" All I want is one simple article of faith that is even less complicated than it looks. Is that too much to ask?

There is a lot more to Kazan than all this, of course. He directed the first production of *Death of a Salesman,* as well as the stage version of *A Streetcar Named Desire,* worked with Arthur Miller on several other occasions, slept with Monroe and Vivien Leigh, made *East of Eden,* and wrote a novel that sold four million copies in the U.S.—Kazan had a pretty impressive twentieth century. I wish Schickel's book had been just that little bit more gossipy, not just because gossip is fun, but because Kazan's relentless womanizing, it seems to me, needed some kind of explanation or context. Schickel's refusal to discuss Kazan's domestic arrangements seems indulgent, rather than high-minded; Kazan is given a guys-will-be-guys (or, perhaps, great-artists-will-be-great-artists) free pass that I don't think anyone ever really earns. From the index: "Kazan, Molly Day Thacher (first wife) husband's affairs and, 94–95, 388–89, 404." They were married for thirty years.

Philip Roth was recently quoted as saying that he doesn't read fiction anymore. "I wised up," he told an interviewer in the *Financial Times.* We all have moments like this: I have vowed, at various points, never to read any more novels, and books about sport, and thrillers where kids get murdered, and music biographies; but none of these decisions ever holds for very long. Moods change, tastes reassert themselves, and a great book always shakes off its genre and its subject matter anyway, although I fear that the desire to read about the dismemberment of children and young women may have left me forever. I'm not sure wisdom has much to do with any of this, and I'd hate for Roth's words to be given extra weight just because of his age, his accomplishments, and the veneration he inspires. I don't know if it's ever very wise to give up on Dickens. In my experience, a sudden panic about my own ignorance is followed firstly by the desperate desire to read nonfiction, and then, usually very swiftly, by a realization that any nonfiction reading I do is going to be hopelessly inadequate and partial. If I knew I was going to die next week, then I'd definitely be keen to read up on facts about the afterlife; in the absence of any really authoritative books on this subject, however (no recommendations, please), then I think I'd rather read great fiction, something that shoots for and maybe even hits the moon, than a history of the House of Bourbon.

It is, perhaps, a little unfair to ask Eleanor Henderson to provide a philosophical justification for an entire art form, especially as *Ten Thousand Saints* is her first novel, but she does a pretty good job anyway. She moves in extraordinarily close to her young protagonists, participants in the New York straight-edge punk scene of the 1980s, and in doing so taught me a lot of things I didn't know. (Straight-edge was never much of a thing in England, where sobriety is seen as a moral failing by all ages and tribes.) The big draw here, though, is Henderson's writing, which is warm, engaged, and precise; I don't think I have ever come across a gritty urban novel that is as uninterested in finding a prose style to complement its subject. That's a good thing, by the way. *Ten Thousand Saints* is the offspring of Lester Bangs and Anne Tyler, and who wouldn't want to read that baby?

Per Petterson's beautiful, truthful *Out Stealing Horses* seems to me a pretty good example of the sort of thing that nonfiction can never accomplish. It's about aging and childhood, memory and family, and it has things to say on these subjects. That Petterson can accomplish this while providing an ornate, time-shifting narrative that includes—spoiler alert and hopeless volte-face, all at the same time—dead children seems to me the reason why we should never stop reading novels, however old and wise we are. ✶

OCTOBER 2011

It is August, and as I write, burned-out buildings in London and other British cities are being demolished after several nights of astonishing and disturbing lawlessness. Meanwhile I am in the Dorset village of Burton Bradstock, listening to the sound of the wind-whipped sea smashing onto the shore, and to the young daughter of a friend playing "Chopsticks" over and over and over again on the piano belonging to the cliff-top house we have rented. It's unlikely that the riots would have made it into these pages at all had it not been for *Hellhound on His Trail,* Hampton Sides's book about the murder of Martin Luther King Jr. and the hunt for his assassin, James Earl Ray. Just as Tottenham and Hackney, just a couple of miles from my home, were being set alight, I was reading about the same thing happening in Washington, D.C., on the night of April 5, 1968, twenty-four hours after Ray shot King while he was standing on the balcony of the Lorraine Motel in Memphis. There were five hundred fires set in D.C. that night; the pilot who flew Attorney General Ramsey Clark back to the capital from Memphis thought that what he saw beneath him looked like

Dresden. And here in Burton Bradstock it became impossible not to compare London in 2011 with D.C. in 1968. It wasn't an instructive or helpful comparison, of course, because it could only induce nostalgia for a time when arson seemed like the best and only way to articulate a righteous and impotent fury. And while it is true that a violent death sparked our troubles (a black man named Mark Duggan was shot and killed by police), it was not easy to see the outrage in the faces of the delirious white kids helping themselves to electronic goods and grotesquely expensive sneakers. Luckily for us, every single politician, columnist, leader-writer, talk-show host, and letters-page contributor in Britain knows why all this happened, so we should be OK.

Hellhound on His Trail is a gripping, authoritative, and depressing book about a time when, you could argue, it was much easier to talk with confidence about cause and effect. James Earl Ray, King's assassin, was a big supporter of segregationist George Wallace and his independent push for the White House; Ray also liked the look of Ian Smith's reviled apartheid regime in Rhodesia. He was eventually arrested at Heathrow as he attempted to make his way to somewhere in Africa that would let him shoot black people without all the fuss that he had caused in the U.S. Sides has little doubt that he acted alone, and indeed one of the lowering things about his book is the reminder, if one needed it, that it takes very little to kill a man; you certainly don't need the covert cooperation of the CIA or the FBI or the KKK. You just need enough money to buy a decent hunting rifle.

Of course, there are lots of people who have a vested interest in persuading us that the recent past is easier to read than the present. Paul Greengrass, the director of *Green Zone* and *United 93,* has for some time been wanting to make a film about the last days of MLK, but this year the project collapsed, apparently because the guardians of the King estate objected to depictions of King's extramarital affairs in the script. "I thought it was fiction," said Andrew Young, who was with King on the night he died. And yet King's womanizing was, according to Sides, both real and prodigious; he spent the night before he died in room 201 of the Lorraine Motel with one of his mistresses, the then senator of Kentucky, Georgia Davis. Davis has even written a book, *I Shared the Dream,* about her relationship with King. I haven't read Greengrass's script, but it looks as though Andrew Young is attempting, four decades after Memphis, to sanctify his friend in a way that can only impede understanding. Jesse Jackson, meanwhile, attempted to impede understanding there and then: he told TV interviewers that he was with King on the balcony (he wasn't), and, according to Sides, smeared his shirt with King's blood before appearing on TV chat shows. The trouble with history, it seems to me, is that there are too many people involved. The next time something historical happens, someone should thin out the cast list. Oh, and by the way, did you know that James Earl Ray was arrested in London, by detectives from Scotland Yard? Oh, yes. Your guys had done some handy groundwork, though, we'll give you that much.

It has, it must be said, been something of a gloomy reading month, not least because my brother-in-law has written another novel. *The Fear Index* is his fifth since I started writing this column, back in 2003. I have managed only three in the same period, and though I have also managed to squeeze out a screenplay for a movie, so has he. As I write, he is lying by a swimming pool in the South of France, whereas I am looking through a window at the gray North Sea. I am looking through a window (a) because if I ventured outside I would be blown into the gray North Sea by the gale that is currently blowing and (b) because I have a column to write, and therein, I think, we find the root cause of my brother-in-law's superior output and income. "Stuff I've Been Reading" is now well over one hundred thousand words long, and if I could somehow take those words back and rearrange them into a stylish, ingenious, compelling, and intelligent contemporary thriller, then I would. But there you are. My commitment to your literary health is such that I'm prepared to let my children shiver in their little wetsuits, although I don't suppose you're the remotest bit grateful. I wish I could tell you that *The Fear Index* is a resounding failure that will lie in unsold heaps all over Europe and the U.S., but I can't. Actually, why can't I? It's my column, and there are very few other advantages to writing it, as I have very recently realized. *The Fear Index* is a resounding failure that will lie in unsold heaps all over Europe and the U.S. I'm not going to tell you what it's about. You'll only want to buy it.

I suppose it wouldn't be giving too much away to tell you that *The Fear Index* is a financial-crisis thriller, the second book about the terrifying instability of our banking system that I've read in the last couple of months. The other was John Lanchester's brilliant *I.O.U.*, in which Lanchester says that "Western liberal democracies are the best societies that have ever existed... citizens of those societies are, on aggregate, the most fortunate people who have ever lived." There isn't much downside to being the luckiest people in history, but in James Hynes's brilliant novel *Next,* which I read because the editors of this magazine gave it a prize, Hynes's protagonist, Kevin Quinn, is fiftyish and struggling— struggling, at least, with all the things there are to struggle with in prosperous contemporary America. His career has been nudged, gently and undramatically, into a backwater; he has a relationship with a younger woman he doesn't love. He spends most of his time, or most of the eight or nine hours covered in the novel, anyway, daydreaming about a couple of the standout sexual experiences of his life.

Quinn is traveling from Ann Arbor to Austin for a job interview, on a day when there have been major terrorist attacks in Europe. He's uncomfortable flying, as we all are in those periods, but this doesn't stop him mooning over the young, sexy Asian girl sitting next to him on the flight, and when he bumps into her again in Austin, he ends up killing the time before his appointment by trailing idly after her, in an aimless and unthreatening kind of a way. He gets very hot, and extremely lost, both in Austin and in his own underwhelming and regret-filled past. It's all very real and very familiar, at least to this fifty-plus male.

Hynes writes with the sort of knowing, culturally precise, motor-mouthed internal chatter that brings to mind David Gates's two monumental novels, *Jernigan* and *Preston Falls,* and I can think of no greater recommendation: Hynes and Gates populate their books with men I recognize. They're not the intimidatingly brainy and, to me, alienating creatures you find in Great American Novels by Great American Novelists. There's less rage, more doubt, more regret—and, in the case of Kevin Quinn, more of a sense that he is entirely the author of his own misfortune. His failure can't be pinned on an event, or on a scheming, ball-busting woman. Rather, it's due to too much introspection, distraction, indiscipline. Quinn hasn't worked hard enough at anything.

And *Next* takes a dizzying, heartbreaking, apocalyptic, and oddly redemptive turn. As it turns out, the atrocities are not confined to small European countries far away. As Kevin is, finally, on his way to his interview, the cab driver is listening on the radio to news of attacks much closer to home, in Minnesota, where he has a brother. The cabbie is nervous, distracted, upset; he makes frantic phone calls. Kevin, though, is oblivious to all of this. He's re-creating, in pornographic detail, a night he spent a long time ago with a girl called Lynda. "You need to pay attention, man," the cabbie tells him, devastatingly, at the end of his ride, but it's too late for Kevin.

Violent deaths take place in all three of the books described above—in fact, I can't recall a more distressing reading month. And most of the fatalities are deeply upsetting, rather than fun, although in *The Fear Index* my brother-in-law does get to bump off a sleazebag we don't like very much. So I needed the respite of Priscilla Gilman's *The Anti-Romantic Child,* which, though serious, contains no bloodshed, and is all the better for it. A memoir about raising a child with special needs would not have been improved by scenes of indiscriminate slaughter. (This is the sort of quality advice you'll be getting when you enroll in my online writing school, coming soon.)

As regular readers of this column may have noticed, I don't read many first-person books on this subject, despite, or almost certainly as a direct result of, being the father of a disabled child myself. There are many reasons for this, and I have a feeling I've droned through some of them before, so I'll give it a rest this time around. However, I would like to observe that it's hard to find books in this genre with ideas in them, and that's where *The Anti-Romantic Child* scores. It's not just about dealing with the tricky hand that the author has been dealt; this is also a book about literature, specifically Wordsworth and the Romantics, and how Gilman's literary heroes (she used to teach them) have both helped and hindered her understanding of what her child is and what she wanted him to be. It's smart, soulful, and involving, and it rang plenty of bells for me; I also ended up reading more Wordsworth than I have ever done in my entire life. I understand the appeal a little more than I did, but I would still argue that there is more in those poems about the natural world than is strictly necessary.

I haven't read as much in Dorset as I wanted to. Perhaps that is what happens when you invite thirty-five kids to share your holiday home with you. (I wish that number were satirical in some way, but it's not.) I have, however, discovered a new product, the Waboba ball, which bounces off water and is completely tremendous. I'm not sure I can make a case for its literary qualities, which may mean that it has no place in this magazine. But those of us who contribute to the *Believer* have found that we have enormous influence over the manufacturers of leisure products, and that whenever we mention one we are bombarded with offers of free samples, exotic trips to Caribbean resorts, and so on. I suspect that, completely inadvertently, I have just opened myself up to all sorts of tempting but corrupting inducements. A few Waboba balls won't make up for the villa on the Côte d'Azur that this column has cost me, but the Waboba Surf, coming soon to a store near you, looks excellent. ⋆

NOVEMBER / DECEMBER 2011

BOOKS BOUGHT:
* None

BOOKS READ:
* *Charles Dickens: A Life*—Claire Tomalin

I f I were walking home down a dark alley, and I got jumped by a gang of literary hooligans who held me up against a wall and threatened me with a beating unless I told them who my favorite writer was... Well, I wouldn't tell them. I'd take the beating, rather than crudify my long and sophisticated relationship with great books in that way. The older I get, the less sense it makes, that kind of definitive answer, to this or any other question. But let's say the thugs then revealed that they knew where I lived, and made it clear that they were going to work over my children unless I gave them what they wanted. (This scenario probably sounds very unlikely to American readers, but you have to understand the violent passions that literature excites here in the U.K. After all, we more or less invented the stuff.) First, I would do a quick head count: my seven-year-old can look after himself in most situations, and I would certainly fancy his chances against people who express any kind of interest, even a violent one, in the arts. If, however, there were simply too many of them, I would eventually, and reluctantly, cough up the name of Charles Dickens.

And yet up until a couple of weeks ago, I had never read a Dickens biography. I have read a biography of Thomas Hardy, even though I haven't looked at him since I was in my teens, when I was better able to withstand the relentless misery; I have read biographies of Dodie Smith and Richard Yates, even though much of their work is unfamiliar to me; I've read biographies of Laurie Lee and B. S. Johnson, even though I've never even opened one of their books, as far as I know. Every time, I was drawn to the biographer, rather than the subject. (The great Jonathan Coe wrote the B. S. Johnson book, for example.) Last year

I devoured Sarah Bakewell's brilliant book about Montaigne, *How to Live,* even though I can hardly make it through a sentence of Montaigne's essays without falling into a deep sleep. Expecting a biography to be good simply because you have an interest in the life it describes is exactly like expecting a novel to be good simply because it's set in Italy, or during World War II, or some other place and time you have an interest in. The only Dickens biography I have ever wanted to read until now was Peter Ackroyd's, but it is over a thousand pages long and made me wonder whether I'd be better off digging in to *Barnaby Rudge,* or *The Pickwick Papers,* or one of the other two or three novels I haven't yet got around to. In the end, inevitably, I read neither Ackroyd nor *Rudge,* a compromise I have managed to maintain effortlessly to this day.

Claire Tomalin is my favorite literary biographer; in the U.K., she's everybody's favorite literary biographer. (Everybody has one, here in lit-crazy Britain.) She's a clever, thoughtful, sympathetic critic, a formidable researcher, and she has an unerring sense of the reader's appetite and attention span. A publisher once explained to me that the First Law of Biography is that they always increase in length, because the writer has to justify the need for a new one, and demonstrate that something previously undiscovered is being brought to the Churchill/Picasso/Woolf party; and you can't leave out the old stuff, the upbringing and the education and all that, because the old stuff is, you know, The Life. But Tomalin's *Charles Dickens: A Life* is 417 pages long, without notes and index—a pretty thrilling length, given the importance of the man, his enormous output, and his complicated personal life. Top biographer + favorite novelist + under 500 pages = dream package, or so I thought. I have never once made this complaint here, but I ended up wishing it had been longer.

I am not the best person to review it for you, however, because I have no idea how it compares to the Ackroyd, nor to the Fred Kaplan, nor to the recent Michael Slater, nor to Dickens's friend Forster's three volumes. Who flogs through more than one book about the same person, apart from Bob Dylan fans? The reviewers in the posher papers will all have read the others, but out here in the real world, I'm presuming that if you've read one Dickens biography, you won't be reading another, and it's highly unlikely that you'll ever get around to any of them.

You'd be missing out, though, if you don't read Tomalin's contribution. It is a fantastic book about a working writer, in the same way, oddly enough, that the first of Peter Guralnick's two monumental volumes about Elvis was a fantastic book about a working musician. Tomalin, like Guralnick, ignores the myth and gets up close to the daily life—the walks that Dickens needed to take in order to write, the strange Victorian intensity of his male friendships, the money worries, the pro bono work, and, above all, the almost demented production of prose.

One thing is clear: Dickens wasn't thinking about posterity. In fact, I'm betting he would have said that he'd comprehensively blown his chance of a literary afterlife: he wrote too much, too quickly, to feed his family and his ego, and to please his public. He wrote *The Pickwick Papers* and *Oliver Twist* at the same time, providing 7,500-word installments of each every month; later, he then did the same with *Oliver Twist* and *Nicholas Nickleby*. He was also editing and contributing to a magazine, and he was up to his neck in dependents. (He supported his father and mother, and eventually had ten children, most of them unwanted. And his sons turned out to be as burdensome and feckless as his father had been.) He was nowhere near thirty years old.

As Tomalin makes clear, there was an artistic cost. *Nicholas Nickleby* has "a rambling, unplanned plot" and an "almost unreadable" last quarter; the plotting in *Barnaby Rudge* is "absurd," in *Martin Chuzzlewit* it is "improbable and tedious." The second half of *Dombey and Son* wastes the promise of the first with its "feeble plotting and over-writing." *Our Mutual Friend* is "sometimes tedious," and "the weakness of the plotting is a serious fault." (I re-read *Our Mutual Friend* recently, and the weakness to which Tomalin refers would have made a scriptwriter on *The Young and the Restless* blanche.) Only *David Copperfield*, *Great Expectations,* and *Bleak House* receive more or less unreserved praise, although the prissy, saintly women are always a problem, and he published *Great Expectations* with a crowd-pleasing feel-good ending. If you are feeling bad because you haven't read any Dickens and don't know where to start, Tomalin reduces your reading load by a couple of million words. The books survive because there is something of great merit on almost every page—a joke, an unforgettable description, a brilliant set-piece, a character so original and

yet so perfectly descriptive of human foibles that he has entered the language—
and because of the ferocious energy of just about every line he wrote. Oh, and
because he was loved, and is still loved, and has always been loved. Meanwhile,
Bleak House wasn't even reviewed in the serious magazines—they didn't bother
with old tosh like that.

If Dickens were writing today, some journalist somewhere would be obliged
to point out that he was living the rock-star life; there's always a slightly disap-
proving wistfulness to this observation when it's made about Neil Gaiman or
David Sedaris or one of the other authors who routinely pack out theaters
on reading tours, as if it betokens something unspeakably vulgar about our
modern world. And yet Dickens got there first: it's his template, and maybe
the learned thing to say is that Bono is living the successful Victorian novelist's
life. Gigantic tours of the U.S., with huge and exhaustingly adoring crowds
everywhere? Check. Income affected by illegal downloading? Absolutely—
American publishers were not obliged to ask permission to publish the novels,
nor to pay royalties for them, and Dickens spent a lot of time and energy trying
to right this wrong, to general American indifference. Prurient press interest
in the star's private life, combined with very unwise attempts on the part of
the star to manage said interest? Both the *London Times* and the *New York
Tribune* published extraordinary letters from Dickens absolving himself for the
failure of his marriage. Over-hasty adaptations of the work, designed to cash in
on a book's success? Dickens saw stage versions of novels that he hadn't even
finished. Business relationships that fractured because of the petulant, arguably
greedy behavior of the artist? Dickens fell out with publishers over advances
and royalties and delivery dates with a frequency that would exhaust even the
grabbiest, grubbiest contemporary agent. The glitzy international friendships?
He met presidents and royalty, and he seemed to know every contemporary
writer you've ever heard of. One of the most striking stories here describes
Dostoyevsky calling in on Dickens at his offices in Wellington Street in Covent
Garden; the Russian's consequent account of their meeting in a letter to a friend
provides a profound glimpse of what we would now describe as Dickens's
creative process:

There were two people in him, he told me: one who feels as he ought to feel and
one who feels the opposite. From the one who feels the opposite I make my evil
characters, from the one who feels as a man ought to feel I try to live my life.
Only two people? I asked.[1]

But it was enough. Quilp and Steerforth, Uriah Heep and Madame Defarge,
Fagin and Bill Sikes and scores of others... If these all came from Dickens's
shadow side, then we must all be grateful that psychotherapy hadn't yet been
invented. If it had, some well-meaning shrink would have got him to talk these
extraordinary half-human creatures into nothingness.

I found myself thinking a lot about Dickens's formative years, and the failure
of his parents to care for him properly. With no educational provision, he was
free to wander the streets, mapping out London in his head, registering how
short was the walk between the splendors of Regent Street and the poverty of
Camden and Covent Garden. He went to see his father, whose chronic misman-
agement of the family finances meant that he ended up in the Marshalsea
debtors' prison, where Little Dorrit's family lived. And Charles's time at the
blacking factory opened up a whole new world to him, a world in which children worked, and suffered. Pretty much all you have to do as a dad is earn some
money, stay out of prison, and make sure your kid goes to school; John Dickens
struck out on all three requirements, and is therefore directly responsible for
some of the greatest fiction in the English language. I'm not saying that it's
a good idea to piss your money away and let your eleven-year-old wander
through the mean streets of your nearest big city. But if you do take your eye
off the ball, don't beat yourself up about it: the chances are that it will all turn
out OK.

One of the things that did me no good at all in the formative years of my
career was prescriptive advice from established writers, even though I craved

---

1. There are so many things in Claire Tomalin's wonderful biography I could have chosen to write
about and enthuse over. But after publication, Tomalin came to the conclusion that this letter was
probably a hoax, and there may not have been a meeting between the two great men. You should
still read this book anyway.

it at the time. You know the sort of thing: "Write a minimum of fifteen drafts." "A good book takes five years to produce." "Learn *Ulysses* off by heart." "Make sure you can identify trees." "Read your book out loud to your cat." I cannot tell an oak from another tree, the name of which I cannot even dredge up for illustrative purposes, and yet I got by, somehow. Walk into a bookshop and you will see work by writers who produce a book every three months, writers who don't own a TV, writers with five children, writers who produce a book every twenty-five years, writers who never write sober, writers who have at least one eye on the film rights, writers who never think about money, writers who, in your opinion, can't write at all. It doesn't matter: they got the work done, and there they are, up on the shelves. They might not stay there forever: readers, now and way off into the future, make that decision. Claire Tomalin's wonderful and definitive book is, above all, about a man who got the work done, millions of words of it, and to order, despite all the distractions and calamities. And everything else, the fame, and the money, and the giant shadow that he continues to cast over just about everyone who has written since, came from that. There's nothing else about writing worth knowing, really. ✳

JANUARY 2012

One of the pleasures of visiting my half brother, who lives in a lovely house in Sussex, not far from the south coast, is that he knows someone who entertains the children by firing whole lemons from a homemade bazooka. He doesn't fire the lemons at anything, but that's the point: a piece of waxy yellow fruit shooting up hundreds of feet through a blue sky is one of the best spectacles Mother Nature can offer. (And let's face it, even then she needed the help of a man-made explosive device.) In Kevin Wilson's first novel, *The Family Fang*, Buster Fang becomes badly injured when, during the course of a magazine assignment, he gets his facial features temporarily rearranged by a potato fired from a very similar device. I am pretty sure I would have loved *The Family Fang* anyway, but sometimes you need this kind of unexpected, almost suspiciously friendly connection to a novel. Buster is blasted by the potato on page 32 of my hardback copy, just at the point where, if you are the kind of person who gives up on books, you might be asking yourself whether you're going to stick with it. And then, suddenly, like a sign from God, you're thinking, Hey! That's Sam's lemon gun! Except they're using potatoes! Earlier in my writing career, I contributed reviews regularly to some of the more respectable broadsheet newspapers; now you can see why I gave up. I could never figure out a way of shoehorning the lemon-gun stories into my otherwise careful, sober appraisals, and yet sometimes you need them.

I came across *The Family Fang* as a result of good old-fashioned browsing, an activity that the internet, the decline of bookshops, and a ludicrously optimistic book-buying policy (see every previous column in these pages) has rendered almost obsolete. I picked it up because of the great Ann Patchett's generous and enthusiastic blurb—"The best single-word description would be genius"—and it stayed picked up because, on further investigation, it appeared to be a novel at least partly about art and why we make it, and I love books on that subject. I walked it over to the tills because I had recently come to the conclusion that I needed to read books by younger writers, not out of a sense of professional duty but because I was feeling the lack of youth in my fiction diet. Over the last couple of months I've read James Hynes's *Next* and Per Petterson's *Out Stealing Horses,* both novels about older men looking back on their lives, and the veteran biographer Claire Tomalin's magisterial life of Dickens, and suddenly I wanted to know what, if anything, the young were thinking. This month, everyone I read was between the ages of thirty and forty, which is about as young as I can go without wanting to hang myself.

The Family Fang is pretty much the kind of novel you might dream of finding during an aimless twenty minutes in a bookstore: it's ambitious, it's funny, it takes its characters seriously, and it has soul—here defined as that beautiful ache fiction can bring on when it wants the best for us all while simultaneously accepting that most of the time, even good enough isn't possible. Buster and Annie Fang are the adult children of Camille and Caleb Fang, performance artists whose art involved and frequently embarrassed their children while they were growing up. A series of calamities (potato bazooka for Buster, accidental nudity and unwise sex for Annie) results in the children returning home to Tennessee, where their parents are still working, still hoping to convince their kids that family performance-art is their one true calling.

You can see how this setup might have gone very wrong in lesser hands. It might have been so unbearably quirky that you got toothache, or too pleased with itself, or all high-concept and no low detail, but Kevin Wilson steps around every pothole with utter confidence. He has fun with the premise—the Fangs' stunts are inventive and plausible—but in the end this is a novel about parents and children, so everything serves a more sober purpose, although the sobriety never slows the book down. *The Family Fang* has been and will be compared to the work of Wes Anderson, but Anderson has never struck me as someone who gets engrossed in the psychology of his characters, and in any case, despite the beatnik milieu, Wilson tells his story pretty straight. I was reminded more of Anne Tyler's painstaking verisimilitude, and the love she lavishes on her people, and the way their apparently particular missteps and misunderstandings and regrets can serve, somehow, as shorthand for the many and various ways we all mess up.

"Art, if you loved it, was worth any amount of unhappiness and pain. If you had to hurt someone to achieve those ends, so be it. If the outcome was beautiful enough, strange enough, memorable enough, it did not matter. It was worth it." These are the views of Caleb Fang, soon after he has shot his mentor as part of a particularly daring performance piece. I suspect, however, that most of us who spend our days making shit up have bought into a similar philosophy at some point—or have wished that we were ruthless enough and committed enough to be able to, at least. *The Family Fang* is a novel that wonders aloud whether this particular creation myth is such a good idea, while at the same time proving that art with a moral sense doesn't have to be square.

Joe Dunthorne's second novel, *Wild Abandon*, is set on a commune in Wales, but it has a great deal in common with *The Family Fang*. Dunthorne shares with Wilson the conviction that jokes don't necessarily compromise the seriousness of a novel, and indeed may actually help smooth the path between the writer and the reader by making the book more enjoyable. And, perhaps weirdly, both writers are interested in how a parental addiction to the unconventional might complicate the lives of the children. In *Wild Abandon*, Kate, a teenage girl who has spent her entire life on the Welsh commune, finds herself increasingly drawn to the semidetached suburban attractions of her slightly dull boyfriend's family; meanwhile, her precocious but inevitably unworldly younger brother, Albert, is preparing for the impending apocalypse, an event confidently awaited by one of the many people in his life who stand, somewhat unsteadily, in loco parentis.

My sister-in-law and her family live in Wales, and (here comes the bazooka-lemon moment), like Dunthorne's characters, they have to deal with WWOOFers and polytunnels on a regular basis. WWOOFers! Polytunnels! I had never even seen those words written down before reading this novel, and I was certainly unaware that one of them began, improbably and unnecessarily, with a double W. (You grow otherwise recalcitrant and unhappy plants in a polytunnel, and WWOOFers, from the organization World Wide Opportunities on Organic Farms, are young men and women who have an inexplicable desire to work on the land for no money.) Like *The Family Fang*, *Wild Abandon* isn't interested in satire, even though the world it depicts offers plenty of opportunity; both novels recognize and relish the occasional disaster, but the object is to get in close and examine what's being done to the head and the heart. And in achieving this goal, Dunthorne, who's also a poet and a frequent organizer of spoken-word events and an all-round good thing, proves that he's going to be around for the long haul. He's an elegant, accessible, and interesting comic novelist whose work, I suspect, will provide a great deal of pleasure to a great number of people for many years.

Is it unwise to rely on contemporary fiction as a source of news? Because the surprising information I gleaned from *Wild Abandon* and from Megan Abbott's *The End of Everything* is that teenage girls want to sleep with middle-aged men. (Novels have never been wrong about anything before, as far as I know. But even so, if you, like me, are a middle-aged man, then I'd advise you to double-check this before acting upon it in any way.) In *Wild Abandon*, Kate is less interested in her boyfriend, Geraint, than she is in his father, whom she attempts to seduce. And in *The End of Everything*, there is transgressive and occasionally sinister sexual chaos, most of it involving girls who have only just hit, or have been hit by, puberty. Abbott is an extraordinary writer who I discovered through the unlikely medium of Facebook, although I'm not sure exactly how. I'm currently halfway through one of her four noir thrillers, *Bury*

Me Deep, now, and it's brilliant, melancholy and feverish, and comparable to the historical fiction of Sarah Waters in the way it both respects and reinvents its genre influences. *The End of Everything* doesn't belong in that sequence: it's somewhere between conventional thriller and literary fiction, and it's psychologically subtle, gripping, and brave.

The mystery at the heart of *The End of Everything* is the disappearance of a teenage girl called Evie, and though the mystery is solved, that's not really what the novel is about. While Evie is gone, the narrator, her best friend and next-door neighbor, Lizzie, tries to make sense of it all; she provides the police with vital information in an unhelpful and deceitful way, and she worms her way into Evie's family's life and grief. She makes moves on Evie's father, even though she is only half-aware of what she's doing, and she competes with Evie's sister for attention. It seems more and more probable that Evie herself has gone off with another neighborhood father, possibly voluntarily, and meanwhile Lizzie's divorced mother is having a clandestine but shockingly observable late-night affair. Sex hangs over the suburb like some sort of tropical mist: it blurs the outlines of everything, slows everybody up, muddles thinking and feeling and the instinct for what is right and wrong. Everybody, it seems, is simultaneously both a victim and the author of his or, more frequently, her own misfortune. Only a woman could have written it, that's for sure. No man would want to suggest that girls right on the very edge of womanhood could be so complicit, so responsible for this fug of repressed sexual yearning. Abbott picks her way through this dangerous terrain with real skill: she knows what she's doing, even if her characters don't.

I had barely recovered from *The End of Everything* when I picked up Emma Forrest's memoir, *Your Voice in My Head.* There is a lot of doomed, dark sexuality in this book, too, mixed in with self-harming and suicide attempts and eating disorders and a deep, intractable sadness, and by the time I'd finished it, I had vowed never to talk to anyone who is or who has ever been a girl or young woman, just in case anything I say is misconstrued and used in evidence against me. I'm almost positive that I am not responsible in any way for Forrest's troubles, but when a young and pretty girl finds herself in trouble this deep, it's hard, as a man, not to feel obscurely guilty.

There are two men at the heart of this spare, admirably airy and riveting book. One is Forrest's therapist, the wise and loving Dr. R; the other is a Hollywood film-star boyfriend, referred to only by the letters *GH,* which stands for *Gypsy Husband.* Both men disappear on her: Dr. R dies, at the age of fifty-three, from a cancer that he hid, with extraordinary selflessness, from his patients; GH changes his mind about their intense and passionate relationship apparently during the middle of a transatlantic flight. An intensely irritating review of *Your Voice in My Head* that appeared in my newspaper of choice accuses Forrest of "showing off" about GH, but his celebrity is, of course, relevant to the affair, and to the brusqueness of its death. If I was the subject of an internet hate-campaign simply because of the fame and desirability of my partner, I'd want to write about it too.

Forrest's desperate lows seems to belong in the past, hence the memoir, but occasionally one worries about the currency of the references that meant something in the maelstrom—a song by the band Beirut, Obama's inauguration, Russell Brand. The worst of the pain may be over, but it's not old. Emma Forrest is such a winning, smart writer that one hopes it gets smaller and smaller and smaller in her rearview mirror, and she goes on to write scores of novels and screenplays in which her scars are no longer visible.

Well, I like the young. Four terrific books, full of life and thought and ideas, and, interestingly, no sign of any narrative tricksiness at all. That, to me, is not necessarily a bad sign, and not just because I'm hopelessly intolerant of experimentation in my own age: these people haven't got the time to worry about any of that. They've got too much to say, too many characters to worry about, too many jokes to make. Only one of them, regrettably, contains a home-made device designed to fire fruit and vegetables at incredible speeds, but the thing about literature—about all art—is that you need to find your own lemon bazookas anyway. ✶

MARCH / APRIL 2012

BOOKS BOUGHT:

* ✶ *A Daughter's Love: Thomas More and His Dearest Meg*—John Guy
* ✶ *Pauline Kael: A Life in the Dark*—Brian Kellow
* ✶ *Ready Player One*—Ernest Cline
* ✶ *Skylark*—Dezsö Kosztolányi
* ✶ *Townie*—Andre Dubus III
* ✶ *Pulphead*—John Jeremiah Sullivan

BOOKS READ:

* ✶ *The Train in the Night: A Story of Music and Loss*—Nick Coleman
* ✶ *You Never Give Me Your Money: The Beatles After the Breakup*
  —Peter Doggett
* ✶ *Pauline Kael: A Life in the Dark*—Brian Kellow
* ✶ *A Daughter's Love: Thomas More and His Dearest Meg*—John Guy

I have known Nick Coleman for something like thirty years. He is one of the few people in my life that ticks every single one of my conversational boxes. (For the record, the conversational boxes are: books, family and relationships, football, music, writing, films, television, and the health of the psyche, although not necessarily in that order.) I value what he has to say on any subject he chooses to address, but when he turns his attention to music, I am likely to make mental and sometimes even actual notes, because, even now—and the qualification is not an insult, as I'll explain later—Nick has fantastic ears. He loves all the people a serious popular-music critic is supposed to love, Marvin and Miles Davis and the Stones and Tom Waits and so on; but he listens without prejudice, too—he is so unwilling to judge, in fact, that he can even take pleasure from English folk music, a form that can create almost irrepressible homicidal urges in less-forgiving souls—and as a result, he is able to find gold in the most unpromising terrain. It was Nick who told me about *Eleven Kinds of Loneliness*, a Tanita Tikaram album that I still love to this day, at a time when everyone, me included, had made up their minds about Tanita Tikaram, in my case without having heard her. (And it was only years later, after *Revolutionary Road* had been republished in the U.K., that I realized she'd taken the title from a Richard Yates collection. That should have told me something, but I needed to be as well read as she was in order to understand it.) It was Nick who insisted that I gave Sade's achingly beautiful and bottomlessly soulful *Lovers Rock* album a chance, at a time when everyone, me included, had decided that Sade was best heard in a Body Shop in an earlier decade. You may already have come to your own conclusions about these two records, and as a result feel that you have Nick's number; well, you're wrong on both counts—unless, that is, you agree with us. I like to think that I can occasionally reciprocate with books that I know he will love, books he might otherwise have missed, and I know that I am wholly responsible for the clasping of *Friday Night Lights* to the Coleman family bosom. But music recommendations last in a way that book and TV recommendations never can, sadly; tracks pop up in the car on playlists, decades after they came into my life, and as a consequence, I probably thank Nick more times in an average month than he thanks me.

And then, a few years ago, something catastrophic happened to Nick's ears: one morning, he found that the hearing in one of them was gone, suddenly, with no warning. He lost his balance, he started throwing up, and the thuds and bleeps and wails of tinnitus made him feel as though his head was going to explode. And music, when it was not causing him physical pain, no longer sounded like music. Since that first terrifying day, some things have got better, slowly—he walks without a stick now, and he has found ways to hear and to listen; but he remains half-deaf. The perfection of the cosmic joke becomes apparent pretty quickly: what better way to create a wonderful memoir (and yes, Nick is a friend, but this is a wonderful memoir nonetheless) than to screw around with the hearing of a music writer—someone whose ability to describe sound and rhythm and feel is valued by a much wider circle than its owner?

The Train in the Night is about the distress of his loss, but it's about an awful lot more than that, too; the catastrophe has given Nick the opportunity to explore, at length and with enormous intelligence, the subject of taste. (I can't call him "Coleman," by the way, even though that's what you're supposed to do when writing about books, as though every writer is a lowly grunt in some literary army, and critics are officers, barking orders.) A couple of years ago, I told you all to read Carl Wilson's brilliant little book about Celine Dion, *Let's Talk About Love: A Journey to the End of Taste*, in the 33⅓ series, although I don't suppose you bothered. Well, Carl Wilson and Nick Coleman would find a lot to talk about other than love, although they'd probably get on to that in the end. Wilson wrote about whether taste can ever be trusted, or whether it's always the product of sociology and psychology and geography. Nick's book is about that too, but his brief is wider, and there's an urgent personal involvement. Taste here is a complicated edifice that has been under construction since the early 1970s, and it's now in danger of collapsing—not just because Nick's relationship with his stuff has had to change, but because, in the new digital world, just about every form of engagement with art is up for reevaluation. What will it mean, when we all have access to every worthwhile piece of music ever made, and none of us own any of it, and none of us have had to save up for it, to choose between one album and another, to leave our homes to obtain it, even? Does that make us all the same? And what happens when your libraries disappear into one of Apple's clouds, young people? How will you decide who to have sex with then, eh?

Sorry. *The Train in the Night* doesn't contain the answers to these questions, and it doesn't ask all of them, but this is the sort of thing it makes you think of. All that plus a fantastic description of the instrumentation on "I Heard It Through the Grapevine," and glancing, delicate examinations of a family under stress, and meditations on aging and mortality and grief... And on the back cover, there is a photograph of a plastic carrier bag that I never thought I'd see again. It's not that I'd spent a great deal of time lamenting its absence from my life, you understand, but I did get a little pang when I turned the book over. (There is a French author whose name I am supposed to invoke here, but I don't suppose a plastic carrier bag can be a biscuit. Or maybe it can. Maybe the whole point of the biscuit is that it *can* be a carrier bag, if you want. I'm not about to read some enormous novel sequence in order to find out, though.) The plastic carrier bag belonged to a very good independent record-shop in the university city where Nick and I used to live, and I used to see and hold one several times a week. I have often wondered why we insist on taking photographs of places we go to once in our lives, and ignore the places we go to every day of the week; the everyday places are the ones you miss, when they go—and everything goes, in the end. Right. That's it. When I go to buy milk from the corner store this weekend, I'm taking a camera with me. I hope this book is published in your country, wherever you live. If not, you should move to England, although if you haven't read Carl Wilson's book when I told you to, you're hardly likely to emigrate under instruction. Could you at least check for it on Amazon? Is that too much to ask?

The other music book I read this month, Peter Doggett's *You Never Give Me Your Money,* is about the Beatles, the greatest band in the history of the world etc., rather than Sudden Neurosensory Hearing Loss, and therefore you'd be forgiven for thinking that it was infinitely more likely to inspire and delight. You'd be wrong, though. It's not Doggett's fault, but rather the fault of the band itself: *You Never Give Me Your Money* is about the Beatles after the split, a subject I thought I might be interested in, but which only left me disliking intensely four people for whom I had only ever previously felt admiration and fondness. John and then Yoko, Paul, George, and Ringo spent most of the '70s and '80s suing— suing each other, suing management companies, suing record companies, suing computer companies with the temerity to name themselves after a piece of fruit that the Beatles had, inexplicably, been allowed to claim for themselves. This book gives the impression that the surviving Beatles are extremely likely to sue me for saying that they spent a lot of time suing. It had to be done, I suppose, a lot of it, and who is to say that any of us would have acted any differently? It's not like all four constituent parts of the band were identical. That was one of the reasons the Beatles worked, because if you couldn't identify with John, you'd be able to identify with Paul. Which Beatle were you? Or, more pertinently, which Beatle would you have sued like? Bitter John? Chippy Paul? Smoldering George? Or drunk Ringo? (Hey, good luck, *Believer* fact-checkers!) When the Beatles initially settled with Apple, by the way, the latter promised that it would never have anything to do with the music business. I don't really follow the ins and outs of Silicon Valley, so I have no idea whether this is a promise that has held up.

Doggett's grasp of the legal complexities is entirely admirable, and rather intimidating; ditto historian John Guy's elegant presentation of the philosophical conviction that led to Sir Thomas More's execution by Henry VIII in *A Daughter's Love,* a book I read for professional purposes too nebulous to go into here. In fact, this month, one of the lessons I have learned from my reading is that I am unlikely to try my hand at biography. I loved every page of Brian Kellow's *Pauline Kael: A Life in the Dark,* but the very first chapter, in which Kellow describes Kael's early life in a tiny rural town in California, contains the following half sentence (I did read the rest of it, eventually, but I became distracted):

> To Kenneth Kann, author of *Comrades and Chicken Ranchers,* an oral history of farm life in Petaluma, the town was "a community of idealists, people who were not so…"

Hold on a moment, you find yourself thinking. In order to write a biography of the *New Yorker*'s film critic—a pretty nifty way, it turns out, of writing about postwar cinema—Brian Kellow has to read oral chicken-ranch histories? Of course he does, because he's a thorough and serious biographer. But… *damn.* There's another job I can't do when I grow up.

Pauline Kael was one of the people who made me want to write in the first place. I had never read the *New Yorker* before I came across a collection of her reviews on one of my very first visits to the U.S., when I was still in my teens. And I can't remember now what made me pick the book up, other than that it was on the remainder pile in Barnes and Noble on Fifth Avenue in New York. But I loved her energy, her enthusiasm, her informality and her colloquialisms, her distrust of phoniness, even before I realized that these were qualities I wanted to steal from her. The art-house audience, she wrote in 1964, "accepts lack of clarity as complexity, accepts clumsiness and confusion as 'ambiguity' and as style." (She'd be amazed, I think, to find that she could write the same sentence nearly fifty years later, on just about any page of any reviews section.) Stuff like that made me want to read her standing up.

What's much harder to stomach is her frequent line-crossing: Kael, it seems, wanted to pal up with the important filmmakers of the day, while reserving her absolute right to excoriate them in print. "If Woody Allen finds success very upsetting and wishes the public would go away," she wrote in a review of *Stardust Memories,* "this picture should help him stop worrying." "After that, her friendship with Allen froze solid," says Kellow. You don't say. Meanwhile, Kael was frequently mystified and hurt by attacks that fellow critics and, occasionally, directors made on her. One of the most substantial came from Peter Bogdanovich, who forensically demolished her essay on *Citizen Kane* (an essay that relied heavily on the research of another, uncredited writer). It was Woody Allen who advised Kael on how she should respond: "Don't answer." Maybe Kael would have seen no contradiction in any of this. She wanted to hang out with people who made good movies, and when they stopped making good movies, she wanted to be able to tell them so, in print, and at length. Perhaps this is what good critics do, but that doesn't mean you have to like them. ✶

MAY 2012

I am a creative professional. The temptation to qualify that sentence with an "I suppose" or a "for want of a better description" or an "on a good day" or a "whatever you might think" or just a simple "not" is almost overwhelming; it feels as though I just began a column with the sentence "I am very good at sex." Actually, it's even worse than that. I am likely to have sex with only a very small minority of you, for various reasons that we don't need to go into here, some of them surprising, so word is unlikely to spread. But you can all buy or borrow a book or a movie or even an album I've written, and make up your own minds about my creativity. One of the many admirable things about Jonah Lehrer's *Imagine* is that he does not argue that to be creative is the same thing as to be special, or clever, or gifted, and that's what sounds uncomfortable about that opening sentence: I seem to be saying something more than "I make stuff up, and someone shells out for it." I'm not, though. Honestly.

The first half of *Imagine* is about what happens in our brains when we make stuff up, and it's riveting, especially, perhaps, if that's what you're paid to do. The frequent appearance in this column of biographies, typically biographies of artists, can be explained by my enduring interest in this very subject. The main reason I pick up those books in the first place is because I want to know how Preston Sturges or Richard Yates or Lucille Ball or, most recently, Charles Dickens did what they did; I want to know what it felt like to be them. Well, Lehrer's subject is the mother ship. This is the literary biography that bypasses the details of advances and failed marriages, leaves out the names, even, and attempts to deal with the literal source of all creativity. There are many reasons why Dickens became Dickens, but none of them would have counted for anything had it not been for the alpha waves emanating from the right side of his brain, the part of us that enables insight and epiphany, working in conjunction with his prefrontal cortex, where his (admittedly prodigious) working memory was kept. Coffee and alcohol might have helped, and his legendarily long walks played a part, too. Dickens wouldn't have known about amphetamines, which were first created in Germany in 1887, seventeen years after his death—is there nothing this column doesn't know? But if he had, he'd have shoveled them in like M&M's, which, incidentally, weren't actually patented until 1941. (OK, I'll stop now. It's not even actual knowledge I'm dispensing. It's bits of Wikipedia.) It also helped, Lehrer explains, that he traveled and lived in a city, and that he had to battle with constraints of form, in his case imposed by the monthly serialization of most of his books.

Most of us sense, vaguely, that a walk will clear our heads, that drugs and coffee might help us to concentrate, that we find it easier to create if some kind of boundary is placed around our imagination. When a teacher asks for a story about anything at all, then the student will struggle; tell a kid that you want a story about a talking sponge who wants to take part in the Olympics and you'll get something pretty cool. What's enthralling about Lehrer's book is that he has neuroscientific explanations for why our habits and dependencies work. Speed, for example, increases the amount of dopamine in the synapses, and this helps us to pay attention: suddenly everything seems interesting. This means it's an editing drug rather than a creative drug, because we suddenly find we're getting pleasure from, say, messing about with the rhythm of a single sentence. In one of the most thrilling parts of this book, Lehrer compares the taut, spare, simple (and brilliant) poetry Auden wrote while using Benzedrine with the long "vomit"—Dylan's word—of "Like a Rolling Stone," an epiphanic right-hemisphere production if ever there was one.

The breadth of reference in *Imagine* is a joy in itself: Auden and Dylan, Milton Glaser, Yo-Yo Ma, John Lasseter, Clay Marzo, and Arthur Fry, who came up with the Post-it note. But the real stars of the book are the scientific researchers. It turns out that there is no area of creativity that someone hasn't devised a test for. Brian Uzzi, for example, wanted to test the optimum conditions for group creativity, so he chose the Broadway musical as his ideal model, and produced a study of every musical staged between 1877 and 1990. He used reviews and box office as his indicators of success, and came up with a measure, Q, to quantify the density of the connections between the major collaborators, the director, producer, composer, librettist, and so on. How often had the people behind a production worked with each other before? How often did they admit new people into their working circle? And what he found was that you needed a medium Q score for a successful show. A flop was more likely with either a high or a low Q—a high Q possibly indicating staleness and a refusal to find room for fresh ideas and voices, and a low Q suggesting inexperience and unfamiliarity with the creative processes of colleagues. The conclusions are interesting, of course, but the fun comes when you attempt to imagine Brian Uzzi's working life, which for the last part involved poring over 1930s theater programs. Charles Limb at Johns Hopkins found a way to scan the brains of jazz pianists while they were improvising. Earl Miller has taught monkeys to press buttons when a picture of randomly scattered dots on a screen looks a little bit like another picture of random dots. Jonathan Schooler evaluated daydreaming by making subjects read one of the less-gripping passages from *War and Peace* after a slug of vodka. (And there we have it: the true value of literature. The stupor it induces results in creative thinking.) Joe Forgas at the University of New South Wales hid plastic animals and toy soldiers near the checkout counter of a stationery store on rainy days and made the shop play sad music, in order to collect data on whether people noticed more when they were depressed. (They did—four times as much.) These people, the Uzzis and the Schoolers and the Limbs, are all ingenious, charming, and almost certainly insane.

I'm happy that I do the job I do, but my bad days irritate the hell out of me—the hours spent playing (currently) *Jelly Defense,* the despair, the occasional petulant act of self-sabotage. What is simultaneously comforting and alarming about *Imagine* is that it turns out I'm doing more or less everything right. These aren't avoidable professional hazards at all, but tools of the trade, at least as essential as a computer. Oh, and 80 percent of writers at the Iowa Writers' Workshop interviewed by a neuroscientist in the early 1980s were properly, formally depressed. Who'd have thought the figure would be as low as that? The depressometer I invented and affixed to the underside of my desk never dips below three digits. I can't imagine that there are many readers of this magazine who won't want to quote great chunks of *Imagine* to a significant other, if only to excuse and explain recent awful behavior.

It would have been interesting to think about David and Caroline Stafford's biography of Lionel Bart, *Fings Ain't Wot They Used T' Be,* in the illuminating light cast by Jonah Lehrer's book. Regular readers, however, will already know that if there is an uninteresting way to think about something, this column will find it, and so I read the two books the other way round. There is an awful lot in the Staffords' book that is relevant to the work of both Jonah Lehrer and Brian Uzzi, however: Bart popped out a couple of moderately successful musicals before writing, with apparently vomitical speed and necessity, the astonishingly successful *Oliver!* in 1960, when he was thirty years old. Uzzi would have fun Q-crunching; Bart worked with the same people, mostly associated with the Theatre Royal Stratford East run by the extraordinary Joan Littlewood. Lehrer, meanwhile, would understand the apparent effortlessness of the show's appearance from thin air, its relationship to Bart's tough East End Jewish upbringing, and his eventually ruinous drug use. It's all pretty much downhill after *Oliver!,* though. *Twang!!*—and there is almost certainly a piece of research being conducted on the inverse relationship between exclamation marks and commercial success even as we speak—remains one of the most famous theatrical disasters of the twentieth century. Its calamitous failure destroyed Bart, not least because he invested past, present, and future earnings from *Oliver!* in it, despite all wise advice to the contrary. Any biography of a minor cultural figure stands or falls on the quality of its supporting roles, and Bart "cast up," as film people say—filled his life with just about anyone who was alive and talented and interesting in the 1960s. He knew Judy Garland and Noël Coward, the Beatles and the Stones. Michael Caine, Lucien Freud, Cassius Clay. But it was Joan Littlewood, who directed his first hit, the eponymous *Fings...,* whom I wanted to know more about, hence the appearance of her autobiography in the Books Bought list above. A similar, now entirely incomprehensible fascination with Ronald Reagan once led me to buy a book about his years working for General Electric. That book is on the shelves above my bed, so I am reminded of the brevity and idiocy of my enthusiasms every night of the week. I'm sure Joan will go the same way, but look at this:

> Joan Littlewood ran away to Paris, arriving just in time to enjoy the street riots of 1934, which left 15 dead... London, when she returned, seemed lacklustre, so she decided to go to America. With £9 to her name, fares were a sticking-point, but a few shillings could be saved if she walked to Liverpool, so she did just that... In Manchester, the BBC came to her rescue with an invitation to give a talk about being a lady tramp. There she met a man called Jimmy Miller. They married. Jimmy later changed his name to Ewan MacColl, and wrote "Dirty Old Town" and "The First Time Ever I Saw Your Face."

And this is all before she began the career for which she became famous, her revolutionary theater work in a disused theater she rented, cleaned up, and fitted herself, where she directed and produced *Oh! What a Lovely War,* and plays by Brendan Behan and Shelagh Delaney. (Is this all a bit too British? Well, tough. She was a big deal here.)

I am now convinced that every nonfiction book contains one weird fact which you want to put in your pocket and pull out to show friends at every available opportunity. Last year I learned that F. Scott Fitzgerald used to stand on his balcony watching Lucille Ball and Desi Arnaz fight; now I learn that Bart's father may well have been in an internment camp on the Isle of Man with a cranky old geezer who made everyone do the fitness exercises he'd invented, a chap called Joseph Hubertus Pilates. I'd always presumed Pilates was an obscure offshoot of Greek science.

Jess Walter, one of my favorite contemporary American novelists, has written a novel in which you half expect Lionel Bart to turn up at any second. *Oliver!* was written in 1959, in a fishing village in Spain; chunks of *Beautiful Ruins* are set in a fishing village in Italy three years later, and its characters include Richard Burton and Elizabeth Taylor, who would almost certainly have met Bart, maybe even attended one of his scary-sounding showbiz parties. I don't think I'm going to tell you what Burton is doing in this book, apart from filming *Cleopatra;* all you need to know is that *Beautiful Ruins* is a novel unlike any other you're likely to read this year. It jumps between the Italian village and contemporary Hollywood, and there's a long, sad love story in it that reminded me a little bit of *Love in the Time of Cholera,* and it's full of stories, in lots of different forms—pitches for movies, extracts from plays, chunks of fictional memoirs. And just when you're beginning to doubt whether Walter can pull it all together, he hits you with a sucker punch, a long, delirious ending that ties up all the strands while managing to say something about the beauty and brevity of our time on this planet. And if there's nothing in there that you find interesting, then there won't be much else for you in the rest of this magazine. Ever. I re-read Walter's *Citizen Vince* this month, too, for Professional Purposes, and was reminded not only of what a great book it is, funny, clever, and beautifully plotted, but of what a surprising writer Walter is: his last four novels really bear no resemblance to each other, except in their freshness and originality.

Ready Player One is set in a depressing, brilliantly imagined dystopic future, and though neither Lionel Bart nor Richard Burton would crop up in it, it's absolutely stuffed full of pop-culture references, all of them taken from '80s movies and music. Whenever I have tried to read science fiction before, I have become quite suicidally depressed by my own incomprehension, but I am proud to say that I understood every single word of Ernest Cline's book, and if his publishers want to use that as a blurb, they're welcome. *Ready Player One* is set in 2044. The world's resources have more or less run out, and Wade Watts, the book's teenage narrator, lives in a trailer park in which trailer has been piled upon trailer to form a teetering tower-block. Watts spends his time, like an awful lot of other people, living virtually. He goes to virtual school, and when he has the virtual money to travel, visits other virtual planets. I am going to stop using the word *virtual* now, but don't forget it, because it's needed to make sense of all other sentences from now on.

The deceased founder of the world (not, like, the actual world), James Halliday, richer than Steve Jobs and Bill Gates combined, has left his entire fortune to anyone who can solve the impossibly labyrinthine puzzle he has set, a puzzle entirely reliant on an obsessive familiarity with John Hughes movies and Rush concept albums, the stuff that Halliday loved in his youth. Years pass, and most people have given up; then Watts gets a break that gives him a shot at winning the money. The clues and tasks, increasingly more inventive and more difficult, are strewn all over the universe. (Not, you know…) *Ready Player One* is like a computer game, fun and addictive; however, it has the disadvantage of not making you feel sick with self-loathing. Now I have finished it, I will go back to playing *Jelly Defense* on my iPad, which will do the trick. As Jonah Lehrer will tell you, I have no chance of creating a masterpiece to rival *Great Expectations* without it. All these books are wasting my time. ✶

JUNE 2012

I have been writing in these pages for nearly ten years, on and off, so I'm long past the point where I'm worried about repeating myself. I hope you're long past that point too, if you've been here since the beginning. I hope you treat this column as if it were your favorite chocolate bar: you've consumed something not just similar but *exactly the same* in the last few weeks, but you like it, and it's been a while since the last one, so it's OK. And if you follow those serving suggestions, you may actually be surprised every now and again, because it's not as if I say the same things about the same books every month. The ingredients are the same, sure, but at least the column has the virtue of being wildly inconsistent.

As you have probably guessed, I am about to repeat myself. I have said it before, every time Tyler has published a novel in the last decade, and I hope I have many opportunities to say it again: Anne Tyler changed my life. Before I started reading her books, back in the 1980s, I had no idea that novelists were allowed to do what she did, and still does, namely, write with simplicity, intelligence, humor, and heart about domestic life. Many years later, I realized that she had been given permission because she's a genius, but the blessing and the curse of her gift is that it seems effortless, and as a consequence she makes lots of idiots, this one included, think that they can do it too. It has also, I suspect, led lots of other idiots to underrate her as a writer. Yes, she's won a Pulitzer, and she frequently gets ecstatic reviews, yet her seriousness and her craft are so user-friendly that she still doesn't get the credit she deserves. She is a living American great, right up there with anyone you can think of, but her sympathy for her characters, and her determination to find redemption even for the most hopeless of them, sometimes leads to her being patronized by those critics who need writers to make a song and dance about their profundity and their worth.

Tyler has had a career that, I suspect, is unrepeatable. In 1964, when her first novel was published, she decided that she felt uncomfortable talking about herself, and didn't give another interview for the next forty-odd years. She simply stayed at home in Baltimore, writing novels about Baltimore, and slowly built a readership—a large, adoring readership, eventually—in a way that is no longer an option for anyone starting out on a literary career now: any first-time novelist who refuses to tour or tweet or make imaginary friends on social-networking sites is effectively announcing to publishers and bookstores that he or she would prefer to do something else for a living. As you may already have noticed, I haven't read her latest novel yet. But I bought it in Oxford, the day before I heard her talk about her work to nine hundred devotees at the Oxford Literary Festival. I have a personalized, signed copy of both *The Beginner's Goodbye* and *The Accidental Tourist*. I have met Anne Tyler, and that is something I never thought I would say.

Some people claim that they have no desire to meet their heroes for fear of disappointment, but this seems nuts to me, or at least suspiciously affected. So it's 1869, and you're at a party, and you notice Dickens leaning against the mantelpiece banging on about penal reform. It turns out to be his last year on Earth. You don't go over and listen, in the hope that someone will introduce you? Yes, there is the possibility that you'll think he's a pompous twit, in which case you've got a story that you'll tell people forever. There's a chance that he'll think you're a boring nonentity, but you can edit that bit from your narrative. But seriously, dude? You're too cool to bother to talk to Dickens? What about Hemingway, Fitzgerald, Marvin Gaye, Cézanne, Babe Ruth, Orson Welles? No?

Wow. Well, good for you, I suppose. You're a deeply serious person, although you're almost certainly no fun at parties, and you may well be unhappily single. Me, I'm going to take every chance I get to make a nuisance of myself when somebody I admire is in the vicinity, and if that means wearing a builder's hardhat that made me look like an unsuccessful animated children's character, then so be it. (Thierry Henry, Arsenal's record goal-scorer, while the new stadium was being constructed in 2005, in case you're wondering.)

It's true, though, that the real privilege lay not in meeting Henry but in owning a season ticket that allowed me to see just about every single goal he ever scored in the home games. And the real privilege here was in listening to Tyler talk about her work, in the company of several hundred other people. Some of you may have heard writers being asked about their process before; some of you may even be writers who have answered the same question. Well, you've never heard anything like the description she gave us. She was hesitant while giving it, and she laughed nervously at a couple of points in her narrative, as the extent of her commitment to her work became apparent (perhaps to her, as well as to us). I can't quite remember how it went. I know it involved a long-hand draft, followed by an insane number of corrections, and then a draft on the computer. And there was an old stenography machine in there somewhere, too. It was when she introduced the notion of *the second longhand draft* that the audience gasped, and those of us there who until that moment had thought of ourselves as professional writers shrank as far down into our seats as physics and biology would allow. Why is Anne Tyler so good? Oh, it's just one of those freakish gifts—some people are born lucky. I am about to read her new novel, and I will write about it in the next issue, and I will introduce it by drawing attention to the repetitiveness of this column.

Anyone who has now developed a taste for maddening circularity may want to move on to James Lord's little book *A Giacometti Portrait,* in which Lord reports, in diary form, on his experiences sitting for his friend in 1964. It wouldn't have been much of a book if everything had gone according to plan; Giacometti wanted "an hour or two, an afternoon at most." At the end of that first afternoon, though, the artist's dissatisfaction with his work was such that he asked Lord to come back the following day. The second day, though, is equally dispiriting. "It's going so badly that it's not even going badly enough for there to be some hope," says Alberto cheerfully. On the third day, Giacometti is sufficiently discouraged to claim that he's been wasting his time for thirty years; on the fourth, he threatens to give up painting for good. "It's going very badly, my friend," he says on the fifth. "But what does it matter? There's no hope of finishing it anyway." There's a flicker of hope on the seventh day—"I've reached the worst now"—but by the tenth, the painting is "unbearable, abominable. I think I'll die from it." Even Samuel Beckett would have ended up telling him that worse things happen at sea. There are eighteen such days altogether. You start to feel that Giacometti is on some carousel in hell, and your job is to wave at him cheerfully every time he goes past. Every single one of the eighteen is patterned in the same way, by abject despair and, at the end of the session, a determination to continue, despite the apparent impossibility of the project. "No one else could do it. Moreover, no one else is even trying to do it," he says gnomically at one point. Unless I've misunderstood not only the book but the accompanying illustrations, Giacometti was trying to paint a man's head, but we'll have to take his claim to singularity at face value.

When Lord takes a peep at the work in progress, he comes to the conclusion that the artist's misery is at its peak when the painting is at its best. This is no consolation, however, because the misery invariably leads Giacometti to paint over the detail of the day's work, and the next day he begins more or less from scratch, with a gray, smudged outline, although he frequently claims to be able to "see an opening." Jonah Lehrer, whose wonderful book *Imagine* explains, among other things, the neuroscientific necessity of hopelessness as a precursor to artistic breakthrough, could more or less have scripted Giacometti's side of the conversation, but Lord's book is still worth reading. It's funny, and smart, and though it hardly demystifies the creative process, there is great virtue in its opposite achievement: you thought painting a portrait was a simple matter of bashing down what you see in front of you? Boy, are you in for a shock. An artist friend recommended this book to me, just before he asked me to sit for him. He's doing some quick, off-the-cuff, forty-five-minute portraits of people he knows. I was with him for four or five hours, but it didn't work out in the way that he'd hoped, so I'm going back in a couple of weeks. Just for half a morning. Probably. Oh, god.

Mohammad Khan, the central character in Amy Waldman's brave, measured, and gripping novel *The Submission,* is an architect, but the design of
complex buildings seems like a breeze compared to the torture of portrait-
painting. The difficulties for Khan all arise not from his work but from his
name; he wins a competition to design a 9/11 memorial, a garden intended for
the spot where the Twin Towers stood, and his ethnicity and religion make a
lot of people very unhappy. The bereaved are unhappy, politicians are unhappy.
Politicized Muslims are unhappy when it becomes clear that the politicians
may not allow Khan to win; Khan's white, liberal supporters are unhappy when
he seems reluctant to distance himself from some of the cultural undertones
in his own design.

There are a lot of ways, it seems to me, in which this book could have gone
wrong; it would have been disastrous if Waldman had privileged one special-
interest group—grieving families, say—over another, or taken the furious
arguments for and against Khan's design more or less seriously. Tom Wolfe's
The Bonfire of the Vanities is mentioned by one of the characters on page six
of *The Submission,* but whereas Wolfe's book charged headlong into all sorts
of complicated social issues, the stakes are higher now, and Waldman knows
it. She's just as ambitious with her cast of characters, but her careful navigation
through the almost impossibly difficult environment of the last ten years is
exemplary. I rewrote that last sentence about four times before I was satisfied
that it wouldn't unintentionally piss anyone off; I can only imagine the task
that was facing Waldman. And I don't want to give the impression that *The
Submission* is damaged by its balance, because it's not: it rocks along, and its
characters live and breathe.

It's been a month of fictional bravery, although not on my part, obviously.
All I did was read the stuff. *Grace Williams Says It Loud* is narrated by a spastic.
I know the word is no longer acceptable, but Grace Williams was born in 1947,
and most of the book is set in an age when that word was used unflinchingly,
and when a desire for circumlocution would have been very low on Grace's list
of priorities. She is institutionalized, she's visited infrequently by her family,
she's sexually assaulted, and she's treated with brutal indifference by those
charged with her health and welfare. But before you thank me for reading it on

your behalf and move on, I should point out that this bleak synopsis doesn't convey the charm of the book, nor Grace's extraordinary tenacity and buoyancy, nor the moments when she is able to transcend her crippled body: there are a couple of scenes in which Grace and her friend Daniel, an epileptic with no arms, manage to have sex, for example, and it's no big deal—or, rather, it's no bigger deal than it would be for the rest of us. Emma Henderson finds a calm, engaging, and credible voice for Grace, full of wordplay and ellipses, and a narrative full of surprising and rich incident. There's a fire, a stolen night in a B&B, and a whole Victorian patchwork of injustice and feeling. Emma Henderson had a sister like Grace, but this book feels like a novel, not thinly disguised memoir. I suspect that it has taken a long time, and a lot of internal processing, to get to a point where Grace Williams is a rounded fictional character rather than a painful tribute to somebody else.

Every now and again I am appalled enough by my ignorance of un-English literature to attempt to do something about it. *Skylark* was on somebody's list of little-known classics, and it's published by NYRB Classics, almost a guarantee of quality, and it's short. What did I have to lose? A weird thing happened as I was finishing it, though. One of the kids was watching a program on TV made by the Sport Relief charity, and I happened to look up from my book and see film of a little boy and the heroic, heartbreaking journey he has to make every day to get clean water. And *Skylark,* which is about the unexpectedly exciting week that an old married couple spend in their small Hungarian town when their spinster daughter goes away, just started to hiss, like a punctured beach ball, and go flat. (I should point out that the exciting week was exciting only in context, by the way, and the context is a stifling life of duty and self-denial.) Is it fair to ask novels to compete with real life in this way? Probably not, but sometimes they have to anyway.

Next month, I will be writing about the new novel by Anne Tyler, who is one of the people… Oh. OK. Point taken. ✶

BOOKS BOUGHT:

* *A Natural Woman*—Carole King
* *Crooked Letter, Crooked Letter*—Tom Franklin
* *Fiction Ruined My Family*—Jeanne Darst
* *White Cargo*—Felicity Kendal
* *Don't Eat Cat*—Jess Walter
* *The Getaway Car*—Ann Patchett
* *After Friday Night Lights*—Buzz Bissinger

BOOKS READ:

* *Crooked Letter, Crooked Letter*—Tom Franklin
* *Dare Me*—Megan Abbott
* *Something Like the Gods: A Cultural History of the Athlete from Achilles to LeBron*—Stephen Amidon
* *Brother of the More Famous Jack*—Barbara Trapido
* *Don't Eat Cat*—Jess Walter

How are writers going to make a living in ten, twenty, fifty years' time? If you're a writer (or a publisher, or an agent, or a critic, or maybe even a reader), then this question may have occurred to you. Conversations I've been having with people recently, people whose job it is to try and make sense of what's happening out there, are alarming: bookstores are closing all over the place, and even the big chains are unlikely to survive in their current form for much longer; publishers are slashing advances; books by first-time authors that don't sell in hardback are being offered an extended life in e-book rather than in paperback. Nobody knows how long our current publishing culture will last, but some very clever observers foresee profound change over the next five years, leaving us with very little that any of us, however old we are, will be able to recognize. The work of art that I keep thinking about in relation to all this is the 1951 Ealing Studios comedy *The Man in the White Suit*, starring Alec Guinness. Guinness plays a man who invents a material that never wears out and never gets dirty, to the horror of both the textile manufacturers and the unions. I haven't seen the movie for a long time, but I seem to recall that we're supposed to side with Guinness's character, the little man who's invented something for the benefit of humankind, and who has to battle the dark forces of vested interest. It's hard to see it that way now, though, if you work in books or music or movies or TV. I now support the dark forces of vested interest. Yes, digitization has brought us convenience and portability and access, and saved us billions, because music and TV and films and, one day soon, books, are all free. But even so, I wish we'd at least talked about arresting the people who invented it, and maybe pulling out their tongues and cutting off their hands. I mean, I would have been against it, on balance. But I'd have listened carefully to the arguments from the other side.

When I try to talk about any of this stuff with those who love books, however, the dialogue becomes very frustrating very quickly.

> ME: It's pretty worrying, all this iPad and Kindle stuff.
>
> NICE BOOK LOVER: Why?
>
> ME: It's not just the physical book that's under threat. Have you been on a plane or a train recently? Nobody's reading at all, in any form. They're all watching screens.
>
> NBL: Oh, I love books.
>
> ME: Yeah, I know, but…
>
> NBL: There's nothing like the experience of being immersed in fiction.
>
> ME: I agree, but…
>
> NBL: And I could never switch to a Kindle. I love the smell of a new book. The feel of it. I like to know where I am in a book, and…
>
> ME: I know you do, but…
>
> NBL: Plus, I love my local independent bookstore. The people there are so knowledgeable, and they recommend things that they know I'll—
>
> ME: *Yes, but there are only seventy-three of you in the entire country! You're fifty years old! Your kids don't even know which way up they should hold a book!*

The only reason people ever used to read in the first place was because they
had nothing else to do, and now they have a million things to do, even in a
dentist's waiting room! Will you shut the fuck up about you?
NBL: I think you should go home now. You're upsetting the other dinner guests.

It's like trying to talk about global terrorism to someone who isn't worried because he knows for a fact that he would never strap a bomb to himself and blow himself up, and neither would any of his friends or family. You're glad to hear it, but your worries have not been entirely eradicated.

And yet, every now and again something happens that makes me wonder whether everything is going to be as awful and as depressing as I fear it will be. I have wondered this a couple of times before—once in the mid-'80s, and again in the early noughties—and I was disappointed (I'm talking about the entire future here, not just the future of publishing); but there is a possibility that if we are smart, if we engage properly with what's going on and don't close our eyes and hope for the best, then it might not all be over. Some of the things listed in my Books Bought column this month are not books at all: Ann Patchett's *The Getaway Car,* Jess Walter's *Don't Eat Cat,* and Buzz Bissinger's *After Friday Night Lights* are all from the interesting-looking online publisher Byliner, do not exist in physical form, and are in any case too short to justify conventional publication. *Don't Eat Cat* is a six-thousand-word zombie story with a twist, yours for ninety-nine cents, and, unless your dentist is running very late, it might even fill up the time in the waiting room. And suddenly I had a vision of the future as a happy digital re-creation of the 1930s, where writers were well paid for short stories that appeared in "the slicks," *Esquire* and the *Saturday Evening Post*—Fitzgerald got four thousand dollars a shot for his. The vision didn't last long, though. The shutters came down, like they did on those public binoculars you used to find at places with a view. *After Friday Night Lights* became a free Starbucks download, and Amazon hit back by reducing the price to zero, as in nought dollars and nought cents. Byliner, understandably, decided that it didn't want its authors' work given away, and withdrew the piece from Amazon. I won't dare to dream about anything good happening for another couple of decades.

"Maybe it's *always* the end of the world," says the narrator of *Don't Eat Cat*, in a brilliant riff on our need to catastrophize that repays your ninety-nine-cent investment at a stroke. "Maybe you're alive for a while and then you realize you're going to die, and that's such an insane thing to comprehend, you look around for answers and the only answer is that *the world must die with you.*" Yes. Well. In this case, it's the only possible explanation. The world must die with me.

I met Tom Franklin a few years back, in Oxford, Mississippi. At that time he'd published a much-admired collection of short stories and a terrific novel, *Hell at the Breech,* and he was teaching creative writing. To be honest, when I picked up *Crooked Letter, Crooked Letter* in a London bookstore, it didn't occur to me for a moment that the author was the same Tom Franklin; this new one was the recipient of a British TV crime-writing award, and one of the quotes on the back had been provided by A. N. Wilson, an English novelist who… Let's just say that he'd probably be happier in our Oxford, the one with the dreaming spires, even though the American Oxford is much nicer and more interesting. And *Crooked Letter, Crooked Letter* is a crime thriller—or at least, it's being very successfully marketed as such—that has been on the *New York Times* best-seller list. I was delighted to learn that there is only one Tom Franklin, and it's the one I met, rather than an English impostor.

What's interesting, I think, is that Franklin hasn't had to sell out, or to reinvent himself, or to compromise his art, in order to find a large readership. He wasn't an uncommercial writer when I met him, and he isn't a commercial writer now. *Hell at the Breech* was a magnificent, gripping book about a bloody postbellum feud; *Crooked Letter, Crooked Letter* is set in contemporary Mississippi, and its cast of characters (and body count) is smaller, but it is every bit as ambitious, as thoroughly imagined, and as gripping as his earlier work. Genre is in the eye of the beholder, or at least in the eye of the publisher, but we all need the help.

Meanwhile, the brilliant Megan Abbott, who started her career writing steamy noir fiction, has been wandering right to the edge of genre territory and can now shake hands with Franklin without having to stretch. Her last novel, *The End of Everything,* was a dreamy, haunting novel about teenage sexuality, centered around the disappearance of a pubescent girl; *Dare Me,* the new book... Well, there are more teenage girls. And there's more sex. It's not dreamy, though. It's set in a high school, and it's about cheerleading. It's dark and vicious, and Abbott ventriloquizes a kind of gum-snap young-adult voice quite brilliantly. She gets up so close to these girls that, every now and again, I feel the need to explain to anyone who might be in the vicinity that it's OK for me to be reading it, because the author is a woman, and she's serious-minded and gifted, and, you know, teen sexuality is a subject like any other, although obviously more interesting than most, or indeed any. This is the third Megan Abbott novel I have read this year, and I can see that, given the synopses I have provided, my enthusiasm might be open to misinterpretation. I can only repeat, with all the sincerity I can muster, that she's really good, and is doing something that nobody else I've read is attempting. (I am hoping—*praying*—that Abbott's work bears some resemblance to my description of it. If her novels are in fact conventional analyses of middle-class, middle-aged marital discord in Connecticut, or imaginative accounts of Henry VIII's court, then I will give up reading altogether.)

I suspect that you don't need to be a practicing psychotherapist to understand why I read Stephen Amidon's *Something Like the Gods,* a short, interesting, and extremely useful history of sports, immediately after *Dare Me.* It is difficult to achieve a *corpore sano* simply through the act of reading, but clearly I was looking for something that might provide some kind of literary cold shower. This, I should hasten to add, is by no means the entire appeal of Amidon's book. But the access Abbott had provided to the girls' locker room left some residual awkwardness, and the mere act of reading about the utter nakedness of the young men in the original Greek Olympic games washed it away.

Something Like the Gods is full of information that you want to pass on immediately—I had no idea, for example, that the Greek Olympics had lasted for a thousand years, nor that we have a record of every single winner of the *stadion,* a 210-yard race, and the first Olympic event ever contested. But Amidon's political consciousness, his gleeful skewering of sport's perennial propensity for doing the wrong things at the wrong time, gives him a real head of steam. Here in London, we are planting antiaircraft missiles on residential tower blocks in careful preparation for the Olympics (I'm not even joking), and it's good to be reminded of the hopeless idiocy of the modern tournament—its tacit endorsement of Nazism in 1936, its reactionary exclusion of women (there was no female fifteen-hundred-meter race until 1972, and no marathon until 1984), its suspension of Tommie Smith and John Carlos for their black-power salute. There are many villains in *Something Like the Gods,* but if anyone ever made an Olympics movie, John Malkovich would be licking his lips at the meaty roles provided by Pierre de Coubertin, the founder of the International Olympic Committee, or long-serving IOC president Avery Brundage.

After the brief respite provided by Stephen Amidon, I was ready to return to the eternally interesting subject of young women and their sexual relationships. I'd been meaning to read Barbara Trapido's much-loved *Brother of the More Famous Jack* for some time, and a new paperback edition, with an introduction by Rachel Cusk, finally pushed me over the edge. It was the introduction that did it, and I haven't even read it yet; this kind of public enthusiasm and endorsement, it seems to me, is a very good way of ensuring the survival of our best books, and of our best writers. And *Brother of the More Famous Jack* is a wonderful novel, as lovable as *I Capture the Castle,* with as much potential, I'd have thought, to mean a very great deal to the right kind of young woman, even though it was published thirty years ago. It's not a very high-concept book: Katherine, the heroine, is introduced to a large, bohemian, occasionally exasperating family when she is eighteen, and spends her entire young adulthood escaping from them, and being pulled back to them. But such are Trapido's warmth and energy and wit that I wanted to return to it every chance I got, as if it were a genre thriller. It's about a lot of women and places that I know very well, and if you buy it and don't like it, then I can only presume that you're not from round here. You can probably find it for ten cents on Amazon. You can probably even get it for free, somewhere. As I was saying: it's the end of the world, and everything's turning to shit—unless, I suppose, you like reading wonderful novels and not paying very much for them. If that's the case, then you might think that the world is really OK. ✷

SEPTEMBER 2012

BOOKS BOUGHT:

* ★ *Wild: From Lost to Found on the Pacific Crest Trail*—Cheryl Strayed
* ★ *The Pilgrim Hawk: A Love Story*—Glenway Wescott
* ★ *The Austerity Olympics: When the Games Came to London in 1948*
  —Janie Hampton
* ★ *Persuasion*—Jane Austen
* ★ *XX—YY*
* ★ *Rosamond Lehmann*—Selina Hastings
* ★ *Bonk: The Curious Coupling of Science and Sex*—Mary Roach

BOOKS READ:

* ★ *Wild: From Lost to Found on the Pacific Crest Trail*—Cheryl Strayed
* ★ *Billy Lynn's Long Halftime Walk*—Ben Fountain
* ★ *The Pilgrim Hawk: A Love Story*—Glenway Wescott
* ★ *The Austerity Olympics: When the Games Came to London in 1948*
  —Janie Hampton

Here's the thing: Cheryl Strayed's *Wild* is one of the best books I've read in the last five or ten years, up there with David Kynaston's *Austerity Britain,* and Mark Harris's *Scenes from a Revolution,* and Jess Walter's *The Financial Lives of the Poets,* and Kevin Wilson's *The Family Fang*—or rather *in* there, because whereas the former preposition indicates some kind of indefensibly objective ranking system, the latter more accurately reflects what happens to our favorite books, I think: we separate them from the other books we've read—the ones we liked but didn't love, or admired but didn't connect with, or hated and didn't finish—and we place them on a special and infinitely extendable shelf somewhere within our souls. So *Wild* is now in this personal library, which consists of probably three or four hundred books, a number I intend to add to as often as I can for the rest of my life; it's "mine," in a way that *Sullivan's Travels* is mine, and the first Ramones album is mine. In other words, it's not mine at all, but such is my affinity with it that I've somehow ended up embarking on long and expensive legal battles in an attempt to get myself a co-credit. (Preston Sturges, by the way, is not an easy man to deal with, if you're thinking about going down that road yourself with *The Lady Eve* or *The Palm Beach Story.*) Anyway, we're lucky if we find one of these a year; my admiration for *Wild* means that this was a very good reading month, whatever else happened.

I put down Strayed's book and picked up *Billy Lynn's Long Halftime Walk,* and suddenly a very good reading month turned into a very difficult one. The problem was this: *I loved Fountain's novel as much as I had loved* Wild. So suddenly, all was chaos. Is it possible to read two modern classics back-to-back, without anyone having mentioned that they're modern classics? Did this mean that my standards were slipping? Did it mean that times are so tough in publishing that *only* modern classics are being published? Had I gone mad? And, more pertinently, what was I going to read next?

This last question became particularly troubling, not only because I was unlikely to be lucky a third time, and would thus end up feeling itchy and dissatisfied by anything that attempted to occupy the time happily devoted to *Wild* and *Billy Lynn,* but because I had this column to write. Younger visitors to this page may not recall the *Believer's* legendary and entirely laudable no-snark rule: the Polysyllabic Spree, the seventy-eight stunningly attractive but dismayingly solemn editors of this magazine, are constantly on the lookout for slighting references to writers and/or works of literature, however carefully encrypted. (Seven of the Spree are employed *full-time* on this task.) And this was why I was so upset by the brilliance of Fountain's novel—how could I avoid incurring their wrath now? Any praise for the next books I read was likely to be faint by comparison, and to the collective mind of the Spree, showering a book with faint praise is like peeing on it. (And just in case this simile leaves any room for confusion in the minds of our more "artistic" subscribers: they're against peeing on books. I'm pretty sure they are, anyway. TBC.) My subsequent fear and indecision resulted in a lot of books being purchased and a lot of books being abandoned after a couple of pages. And we also have a first in one of the lists that introduce "Stuff I've Been Reading"—an anonymous Book Bought.

Here's how that works. I think carefully about the next novel I'm going to read. One in particular comes highly recommended, by two different friends whose taste I trust. I buy it, and resolve to read it next, and then I walk into a party and a third friend with impeccable taste asks me whether I've read *XX* by *YY*, the novel in question. I tell her I haven't, and am about to launch into an explanation of its sudden importance in my life, and *she makes a face*. It was a "Meh" face rather than a "Bleeeugh" face, but even so… There was no way I could persist with *XX* after that. I'd be reading it in the wrong spirit, and in any case I needed a cast-iron, superstrength guarantee of brilliance, and I hadn't got it. I still haven't read a word of *XX*. In desperation, I turned to *Persuasion,* but it didn't have the tremendous kinetic energy of the Fountain novel, and its careful moderation wasn't likely to give me the bare-knuckle punch of Strayed's memoir.

In the end, Glenway Wescott and Janie Hampton dug me out of a hole. Wescott's slim novella was published in 1940, and in any case has already had classic status conferred upon it, by both the *New York Review of Books* and Michael Cunningham, who in his introduction calls it "a work of brilliance." Plus, Wescott died in 1987, and the Spree don't seem to care much what I say about dead authors—I remember being underwhelmed by Voltaire without receiving so much as an admonitory email. Nobody around here cares what I think of *The Pilgrim Hawk,* which is why I bought it in the first place. It's really good, though, odd and shape-shifting and compelling, despite having to labor under that deathly plain title. The narrative is simple: the narrator, Alwyn Tower, is staying with a rich expatriate friend in a French village; one afternoon they are visited by an Irish couple, the Cullens, and Mrs. Cullen's hawk, Lucy, whose eating habits and occasional bates tend to dominate the social occasion. The relationships between the characters are subtle and labyrinthine, however, and Tower is an acute observer, not only of his companions but of himself: one of the joys of *The Pilgrim Hawk* is the way that the bird's moods and appetites provide an opportunity for a dense and surprisingly melancholy internality. *The Pilgrim Hawk* is subtitled *A Love Story,* but there's a lot more about love's impossibility than its joys.

By the time you read this, the 2012 Olympics will be over, and Londoners will have literally nothing to look forward to ever again. Janie Hampton's *The Austerity Olympics* is a straightforward, cheerful, frequently amazing account of the last time my city hosted the games, in 1948, when food was scarcer than it had been during the war, British athletes were obliged to take a day's unpaid holiday to compete in their events, and, with air travel not yet an option, the New Zealand team took five weeks to get here. (The ship's carpenter built for the one Kiwi swimmer a cabinet that was filled with seawater every day, so that she could train; the cabinet was a foot longer than she was.) The first gold medal of the games was awarded to Micheline Ostermeyer of France, a discus-thrower who had picked up a discus for the first time a few weeks before the event—but then again, her day job as a concert pianist had probably taken up a lot of her time and attention. It was the last time medals were awarded for artistic endeavor—Stravinsky had judged the music category in the 1924 games—although most of the competitors had to settle for honorable mentions, due to the dismal standard of their entries. The temperature in London on the day of the ten-thousand-meter final was 94 degrees, the hottest recorded since 1911, and seventeen of the thirty-one runners collapsed—hardly surprising when you learn that the prevailing nutritional wisdom of the time advised athletes not to drink in the twenty-four hours before a race. These events took place nine years before I was born, in a city I live in, and yet they seem to have happened in a parallel, and much less knowing, universe.

So both Hampton and Wescott did a magnificent job for me in very trying circumstances, but at this point I feel I should turn my attention, reluctantly, to the books that gave me all this trouble in the first place. Strayed started it, with *Wild*, and I really didn't think she was going to cause me any grief, despite the inspiring, life-changing review by Dwight Garner in the *New York Times* that made me order the book in the first place; when it arrived I noted darkly that (a) it was a book about hiking, and (b) that it seemed to be a "decide-to" book—as in, Cheryl Strayed decided to walk the eleven-hundred-mile Pacific Crest Trail from the Mojave Desert to Washington State, and then write a book about it. There are a lot of "decide-to" books: people decide to have sex three times a day for a decade, or decide to marry the first person they see in the morning, or decide to eat an entire car, and the reason that they decided to do these things can never be articulated in their narrative: it's because they could get an advance from a publisher. Good luck to them and all, but I've never really wanted to read about the car-eating that they're being paid to do.

If this was ever Strayed's intention, she was playing a very long game. She walked the PCT back in the mid-'90s, and, as this extraordinary and unforgettable book makes clear, it was because she had no real choice: she'd been destroyed by the premature death of her beloved mother, but also by a difficult childhood, and by being married too young to a man she loved but didn't know how to be with, and by her subsequent drug abuse and promiscuity. The opening section of *Wild* is harrowing, but it convinces you of its authenticity and its necessity. And in those early pages, you also come to understand that Strayed was no hiker—that she was as directionless and damaged and unfit as just about anyone who reads this magazine regularly. Her incompetence for the task at hand is one of the themes of this book, in fact, and it gave me a way in. I'm pretty sure I'll never walk my own height on the PCT, and I'm just as sure I wouldn't be able to. But then, that was pretty much Strayed's position before she set off. And as a consequence, a lot of this book is funny, in a way that you wouldn't necessarily expect if you had mis-shelved it in the po-faced "women's inspirational nonfiction" section of your mental bookstore. Strayed's inexperience results in such spectacular overpacking that she literally cannot lift her own backpack; after she has invented a complicated calisthenic system whereby she winches herself onto her feet, she persists with it anyway. Among her vital supplies is a hopeful pack of twelve condoms, which she throws away when a stern old hand at a rest-stop forces her to lighten her load. (While his back is turned, she slips one of the twelve into her back pocket.) I loved *Wild* for its humor, but I loved it for a lot of other reasons, too. I loved the way Strayed conveys the glorious feeling of a shower hitting your body when your body is filthy and sore, for example, and what a drink feels like when you've been wondering where the next one is coming from, and (condom spoiler alert, almost) what sex feels like when you've been lonely. *Wild* is angry, brave, sad, self-knowing, redemptive, raw, compelling, and brilliantly written, and I think it's destined to be loved by a lot of people, men and women, for a very long time.

Billy Lynn's Long Halftime Walk contains pretty much exactly the same tonal palette, and maybe one of the reasons it took me so long to find a book to replace it was that I had no need to read for a while, just as I'm not hungry straight after a big meal. Fountain's novel is about Iraq, really, but despite being populated mostly by men, it's not one of those guys' novels that strains to be definitive about the way we live now—this one's got soul, and overwhelming empathy.

In his book about hip-hop, *Where You're At,* Patrick Neate quotes an observation that black kids in the Bronx "have more cultural capital than anybody on earth, and less actual power than anybody on earth too," and though the observer maybe needs to get out of North America more, you can see what he means. In *Billy Lynn's Long Halftime Walk,* the same point could be made about Lynn and his colleagues in Bravo Company, who have been flown back to the U.S. for a triumphant series of meet-and-greets after their part in a firefight. Half of the entire country, it seems—the red half—has something invested in Bravo's heroism; meanwhile, teenage Billy has nothing, and is a matter of hours away from returning to the front line. There are many judicious decisions that Fountain has made, but one of the best is to write an Iraq novel set entirely in Texas: it's an act of creative genius that enables him to examine both the bewildering set of projections Billy's country shines on him, and his haplessness, his doubt and despair.

This will be sold to you as the *Catch-22* of the Iraq War, and certainly Fountain has the satirical chops not to be flattened by the comparison. His approximation of the language of Texan patriotism post-9/11—*wore on terRr, double y'im dees, dih-mock-cruh-see,* the words and phrases that Billy hears over and over again until they no longer make any sense to him—is funny and pitch-perfect. And there's a very good running gag about Hollywood interest in Bravo, with a scarily credible producer who's sharp, cynical, and defeated, rather than just loud and dumb. (That's the thing about Hollywood that literature rarely gets right. These guys aren't stupid. It's not as simple as that.) But the satire isn't the whole novel, not even half. Billy Lynn broke my heart, and I think about him still.

So. There you go. And as I have said before in these pages, I don't know you, and I can't really tell what books you'll connect with and what you won't, and if what you take from this column is that you really, really want to read a book about the 1948 Olympics, then I'd be delighted, and I'd feel that my time here hasn't been entirely wasted. But I'd probably also end up thinking that you were a little obtuse, too. ✴

MARCH / APRIL 2013

BOOKS BOUGHT:

* ★ *Rod: The Autobiography*—Rod Stewart
* ★ *Unapologetic: Why, Despite Everything, Christianity Can Still Make Surprising Emotional Sense*—Francis Spufford
* ★ *Tiny Beautiful Things: Advice on Love and Life from Dear Sugar*—Cheryl Strayed
* ★ *Love Goes to Buildings on Fire: Five Years in New York that Changed Music Forever*—Will Hermes
* ★ *Gone Girl*—Gillian Flynn
* ★ *Alys, Always*—Harriet Lane
* ★ *The Yellow Birds*—Kevin Powers
* ★ *How to Stay Sane*—Philippa Perry

BOOKS READ:

* ★ *Rod: The Autobiography*—Rod Stewart
* ★ *Unapologetic: Why, Despite Everything, Christianity Can Still Make Surprising Emotional Sense*—Francis Spufford
* ★ *Tiny Beautiful Things: Advice on Love and Life from Dear Sugar*—Cheryl Strayed

The first column I wrote for the *Believer* was published in the September 2003 edition, so technically I shouldn't be celebrating for another few months, but never mind: woo-hoo. Woo-hoo for a whole lot of reasons, actually. Woo-hoo because this is the first time I've ever held down a job for a decade; woo-hoo because it's kind of incredible that, in the digital age, a beautiful print magazine about books and the arts has survived; woo-hoo that the insultingly young editors of this magazine have a very short attention span—although in their case, it's too much flash fiction and too many haikus, rather than too much Xbox and MTV—and that they only ever look at the first few pages of the magazine.

The truth is that they don't even know I'm still here, which is just as well for me and my enormous, shiftless family. They hate older people, and if they ever did read right through to the back I'd be taken out, shot, and boiled down for glue, like a lame cart-horse. If you're twenty-three, and you've made a sculpture of R-Patz out of Play-Doh, pastrami, and your father's old Pavement albums, then it's all like, "Oh, hey, come on in! We'll put you on the cover and do a ten-page interview with you!" If, however, all you've done is read books, quietly and patiently, on trains and planes and toilets, and accumulated valuable experience and wisdom over the decades, they don't want to know. You're placed so near the end of the magazine that you're not even in the same time zone as all the cool kids at the front. Ach. The carnival atmosphere seems to have gone flat in the very first paragraph.

In that first column I read a lot of Salinger, a biography of Robert Lowell, and a novel by my brother-in-law. Is there any evidence of flaming youth in that lot? The Salinger jag clearly indicates a youthful disposition, although as I was forty-five years old at the time, you could equally argue that an obsessive interest in the Glass family is a morbid symptom of arrested development. Is there any evidence of decrepitude in the Books Read list above? I rather fear that if the Polysyllabic Spree, the sixty-six staggeringly beautiful young women who control both the contributions to the magazine and the minds of some of the weaker contributors, ever decided to slum it at the back of the magazine, they might be able to use my recent reading matter as an excuse to cut me loose and reduce the payroll. (I haven't read Hanna Rosin's recently published book *The End of Men,* but men have certainly been ended at the *Believer.* There was one working there, years ago, but he was packed off to Missouri—*pour encourager les autres,* presumably.)

Granted, sixty-eight-year-old Rod Stewart is possibly not as fashionable as he once was, although what do I know? You be the judge: he plays Vegas, produces album after album of show tunes, and at Christmas puts on a dinner jacket and performs seasonal songs on prime-time British TV. Is he "in" or "out"? I thought you'd say that. Well, when I was a teenager, he made three or four deathless folk-rock records that are still loved even by those who weren't around when they were first released; and at the time he was the only rock star who managed to combine an interest in Sam Cooke and Bob Dylan with an interest in football, a combination and an endorsement that meant an awful lot to me in 1972. I doubt whether I'd have read his memoir, however, if a friend of mine hadn't written it (or, as Rod puts it in the acknowledgments, been a "wonderful editor and confidant"). Giles Smith is one of this country's funniest columnists, and his customarily dry, self-deprecating tone is ideal for Rod's rambunctious, incorrigible, occasionally baffling life: there's an extraordinary amount to be self-deprecating about, much of it involving drink, cars, and extraordinarily unknowing behavior in the domestic wings of the Stewart mansions. You wouldn't want to be married to Rod, and you wouldn't necessarily want him and his mates to attend your next poetry reading; on further reflection, there are many, many circumstances and environments where those of a sensitive literary disposition might find the Stewart presence unhelpful. If, however, you don't worry about any of this, and accept that he is safely confined within the covers of his own autobiography, then the book is enormously enjoyable, and Rod is clearly such a generous-spirited and sweet-natured soul that I found myself forgiving him a great deal, especially as he wanders through the narrative with his hands raised in rueful apology.

His attempts to woo back an ex, the model Kelly Emberg, are indicative of the chaotic Stewart decision-making process: he cheated on her several times, she left him, and he embarked on a summer of hedonism before learning that Emberg was seeing someone else, at which point he decided that he couldn't live without her. On learning that she was sailing up the West Coast with her new lover, Stewart booked a plane to fly after her, trailing a banner sporting a proposal of marriage. Between the booking and the romantic proposal, however—a fatal gap that included a Saturday night—Rod met someone else; unable to contact the pilot, he was obliged to hunker down and simply pretend that the offer of marriage had never been made. This is not exemplary behavior, and it certainly doesn't suggest an evolved moral intelligence, but I'm afraid it made me laugh. You could take a more judgmental line than mine, I suppose, but I'm not entirely sure what the point would be, and I doubt very much whether you're the kind of person who would pick up the book in the first place.

I'm almost certain that there was nothing in the pages of Stewart's autobiography that led me directly to Francis Spufford's book *Unapologetic: Why, Despite Everything, Christianity Can Still Make Surprising Emotional Sense,* and I should reassure you that you can read either one without having to commit to both; certainly it would be hard to make the claim that the former shone any light on the latter. It could well be, though, that my desire to read the Spufford book is another indication that I'm not as young as I was: I am fast approaching the age where I need the answers to questions of metaphysical speculation.

There aren't that many people I'd listen to on the subject of God, despite the increasingly pressing need to find out whether He is real, but Francis Spufford is one of the cleverest and most thoughtful nonfiction writers in England, and when he talks, I listen, no matter what the subject. And his subjects have become increasingly perplexing as his career has progressed: before *Unapologetic,* he has written books about ice, childhood reading, boffins, and Soviet five-year plans, so you could hardly claim that he is an evangelical monomaniac. (You couldn't claim that he writes only for the fame and the money, either.)

Unapologetic is exactly what those who've followed Spufford's career might have suspected it would be: an incredibly smart, challenging, and beautiful book, humming with ideas and arguments. What I wasn't prepared for was its tough-mindedness, its tendency to bleakness: this isn't a woolly book offering the promise of an afterlife so long as you say your prayers and stop watching online porn. As Spufford points out, Christianity is a religion of orthodoxy, "right thinking or teaching," rather than orthopraxy, like Islam and Judaism, "right doing." In Spufford's version of Christianity, an afterlife isn't even the point, particularly. In one of scores of asides that wiped the patronizing smile off this particular nonbeliever's face, he refers to the Christians who are banking everything on eternal bliss as the "conjectural idiots of atheist fantasy." It's all about forgiveness in the here and now, given what he calls "the human propensity to fuck things up," or, as he refers to sin throughout, HPtFtU. ("I don't need to point out that I am not any kind of spokesman for the Church of England, do I?" he says in his notes at the end of the book.) And note the difference between *potential* and *propensity:* he's saying—and he's saying that Christianity is saying—that we all fuck up, all the time; we can't avoid it. HPtFtU "isn't a list of prohibited actions you can avoid. Fucking things up is too sensitive to our intentions to be defined that way. The very same action may be a secret kindness, an indifferent bit of trivia, or a royally destructive contribution to the ruination of something delicate and precious, all depending on what we mean by it. (There are remarks that end marriages, and very often what makes them so decisively poisonous is that they're chosen to seem perfectly innocent and ordinary when uttered in public, no big deal, deniable, yet touch deliberately on a pain which only intimacy could know.)"

If I know anything about you, dear reader, then I suspect that your interest will be piqued by that elegant, shrewd, novelistic parenthesis, and there are plenty of purely literary reasons to read *Unapologetic*. The chapter entitled Yeshua is a brilliant, fresh, conversational retelling of the Gospels, which draws attention not only to the power of the story of Christ but to its essential oddness, too, its complications and its refusal to work at the level of myth. But the best reason to read the book is that it enables thought, specifically thought about who we are and what we're doing here and how we intend to negotiate the difficulties and tragedies that are unavoidably a part of being human. And we're all for enabling thought, right? I have not become a Christian as a result of reading this book, but I have a much greater respect for those who are. And I intend to read it again, soon; there was a lot of thought enabled—too much, maybe, for a tired man at the end of a hard year.

Cheryl Strayed won't thank me for saying this, I suspect, but there is something Christlike about her alter ego, the advice columnist Sugar, whose columns written for the *Rumpus* have been collected into a book entitled *Tiny Beautiful Things*. I don't want to accuse her of being messianic, although I suppose I must be doing precisely that, etymologically speaking: I'm sure Francis Spufford would have something interesting to say about how atheists have managed to spin a whole sneery complex out of the story of Jesus. I mean only that the people who write to her, all of them—like all of us, riddled with the HPtFtU—are listened to with tolerance and compassion, and answered with extraordinary wisdom and clarity. Yes, Sugar can be an unlikely Christ, just as Spufford comes across as an unlikely Christian. "The first time Mr. Sugar spanked me we'd been lovers for a week," one column begins. "The fuck is your life," another ends, lovingly but firmly, as a response to the question(s) "Wtf? Wtf? Wtf?" But nevertheless, Sugar is someone whose ability to hear every note of someone's pain and confusion can strike one as almost supernatural on occasion. And, like *Unapologetic, Tiny Beautiful Things* is a book that aids introspection, makes thought about our lives cut a little deeper, stretch us a little further.

There is remarkably little literature that does this satisfactorily, when you think about it. Fiction is supposed to do it, but invented stories so rarely chime with our own, and in any case novelists have so many other jobs to do during the course of a novel that they have very little time or room to spare a thought for our woes. Pyschotherapeutic books have agendas, self-help books are usually cynically conceived and deal with single, usually intractable issues... What else is there? Strayed deals with marital dissatisfaction, grief, ambition, self-loathing, sexual disaster, parental cruelty, and just about everything else that can go wrong during the course of our allotted time on this planet, and she simply refuses to accept that any situation is literally hopeless; it's part of her brief to offer hope, even if that hope is a very faint light at the end of a very long tunnel.

Tiny Beautiful Things hasn't yet been published in the U.K., and in many ways it's a very un-English book. There may be people here who dismiss Sugar's belief in redemption and autonomy as American; we prefer to think that nothing can ever change, so it's best just to shut up and plod on. The second essay in this book, however—though I doubt very much whether the English were on Strayed's mind when she wrote it—is the best, and most careful, dismantling of our philosophy of despair that I have ever read. A woman writes, heartbreakingly, to Sugar about her late-term miscarriage, and her inability to move on from it. Sugar's reply contains a long story about her experience mentoring a group of badly damaged girls at a middle school. Every day these girls talk about their horrendous home lives, and Sugar listens, appalled. She tells them that many of the abuses they are enduring are illegal, intolerable, and she will get something done about them; to her amazement and despair, she finds that the relevant authorities are uninterested and powerless. So now what?

Strayed tells one of the most afflicted girls that "escaping the shit would be hard, but that if she wanted to not make her mother's life her destiny, she had to be the one to make it happen… She had to *reach*. She had to want it more than she'd ever wanted anything. She had to grab like a drowning girl for every good thing that came her way and she had to swim like fuck for every bad thing." Because, really, what else is there to say, if you have any ambition left for anything or anybody? Sometimes, when reading this book, I was reminded of some of the monologues that Springsteen used to deliver onstage in the late '70s, just before blowing an auditorium up with a "Prove It All Night" or a "Badlands": there's the same theatricality, the same soul, the same sense that there is a way out, despite all appearances to the contrary, but it will take courage and sometimes just rage to find it. "Write like a motherfucker," Strayed tells one young literary hopeful at one point, and you'll find yourself wishing that she was talking to you. But then you realize that she is. *Tiny Beautiful Things* will make you want to read like a motherfucker, too, long after you've finished it. And that, I hope, is what I've spent a decade telling you to do, in my own pinched and muted way. ✮

MAY 2013

INT. BEDROOM. NIGHT.

A man—handsome, mid-fifties, balding, or even bald, if Bruce Willis is the only actor available—lies in bed reading a biography of Artie Shaw. His probably young and probably pneumatic wife is lying next to him, bored and a little petulant, because he is so gripped by the book that he's paying her no attention. (This guy has no kids, by the way. That's how he gets so much reading done. And also he has this incredible bedroom, with buttons that make lights dim and music come on and cinema screens drop from the ceiling and all sorts.) This is really weird, like something out of a science-fiction film, because Artie Shaw was a bandleader and a clarinettist, and this guy, the Bruce Willis guy, doesn't really like jazz, as far as we know. So immediately the audience is gripped and all like, WTF?

CUT TO

FLASHBACK—EXT. HOTEL POOL. MARRAKECH. DAY.

The same guy (Willis? Depp? Pitt?) is lying by a swimming pool in the North African sun. He's reading Will Hermes's book about New York music in the mid-'70s, *Love Goes to Buildings on Fire*. The mystery deepens. How has the Hermes book led to the Shaw biography? In just a few short weeks? Hold on to your hats! It's going to be a bumpy ride!

Maybe I have overplayed the extraordinary cultural journey that I have made since the last time I wrote in these pages; maybe the story of me sitting by a pool and/or in bed, reading and/or listening to my iPod, would not, after all, make for an entertaining but intelligent multiplex cinematic experience. I'm just trying to convey excitement, so shoot me.

Love Goes to Buildings on Fire was my holiday reading over a short winter break. (In Marrakech! I wasn't even changing locale to make it more cinematic!) Hermes's book is a prime example of the sub-genre that has probably emerged as my favorite over the last few years: readable, rich, and intelligent nonfiction about the roots of creativity. The subtitle is *Five Years in New York That Changed Music Forever,* and the cover illustration is one of those crowded black-and-white cartoons featuring a bunch of caricatures. And as I could make out all the key players—Jerry Harrison, David Johansen of the New York Dolls, Patti Smith, Joey Ramone—straightaway, I pretty much knew what these years meant. I was nineteen in 1976, and I bought all the relevant records pretty much the day they came out. So I was pretty sure I knew what I was getting, and I was prepared to abandon *Love Goes to Buildings on Fire* quickly if the stories seemed too familiar, or if the book was poorly written or lazy.

I didn't know what I was getting into. Hermes set himself the task of writing about *all* the music that was being made in NYC between 1973 and 1977: the CBGB's crowd, yes, but also the salsa of Eddie Palmieri and the Fania

All-Stars, the loft jazz of David Murray and Don Cherry, Steve Reich's "Music for Eighteen Musicians," the birth of the twelve-inch single, and the very beginnings of hip-hop. Hermes's diligence and enthusiasm are reminiscent of the work Mark Harris did for his phenomenal book about the five movies nominated for Best Picture in 1967, *Pictures at a Revolution:* there's that same sense of almost intimidating scholarship which somehow never manages to overwhelm the narrative. Movies are made independently of each other, however; music, especially music being made in the same crowded (and crumbling) city at the same time, leaks everywhere. Patti Smith and Bruce Springsteen played together at the Bottom Line, and were working next door to each other in the Record Plant, hence "Because the Night." Philip Glass invited the Talking Heads to *Einstein on the Beach* after he'd seen them play at the Kitchen. The disco DJs started picking up on the new salsa records that were being made. Of course, you ache to be there, hearing it fresh, but unless you are a frankly dislikable show-off who knows everything about everything already, a lot of the music described so thrillingly in this book will be fresh to you anyway. I ended up buying a half dozen salsa compilations, some unfamiliar disco tracks, (yet another) Television live album, and then… well, things got a little out of hand. By the pool in Marrakech I wanted to listen to something that sounded messed-up, like New York City in the mid-'70s; I had some Television on my iPod, and Tom Verlaine's lyrical, jagged guitar playing scratched the itch for a little while, but everything else sounded too orderly. When I got home I bought one of David Murray's free-jazz albums, but for someone who'd pretty much only ever listened to music in 4/4 time it was a little too scary. I dug out the little jazz I had—Miles Davis and John Coltrane, because I am a walking cliché—and listened to that for a while; but Hermes had somehow, and without even intending to, persuaded me to listen to pretty much every jazz record made between 1950 and 1965. So I've heard Mingus and Lee Morgan, Art Blakey and Hank Mobley, Coltrane and Gerry Mulligan, Art Pepper and Harold Land, Jackie McLean and Sonny Rollins, Sun Ra and Wayne Shorter, Horace Silver and Clifford Brown. I haven't listened to anything else for six weeks. I don't love them all, but I'm giving everything a shot, in the same way that you might give every film at a festival a shot.

Can literature change your life? Yes, I know it can, because this is the second time it's happened to me. The first time came when I wrote my first book; this resulted in a job as an author, a profound change, considering I had been hitherto unemployable. And then, twenty years later, along came Will Hermes, who cost me (and arguably owes me) several hundred pounds on iTunes and ruptured my relationship with guitars. So, you know. Kudos to the power of books.

I'd love you to read *Love Goes to Buildings on Fire,* but it might not be for everyone, even though it transcends its subject: Hermes has, with enormous patience and Stakhanovite research, portrayed an enormous chunk of the cultural life of an entire city at a crucial time in its history. I can't, however, pretend that those entirely uninterested in Grand Wizard Theodore's revolutionary needle-drop cuing technique will get a lot out of it. Hermes's appetite for the details of how and why cool stuff gets done, though, is what makes this an exemplary and gripping work of social history. We at the *Believer* have long argued that there's a whole lot more to say about works of art than whether they're good or bad. Doing what Will Hermes has done takes real thought and real work, however, so you can see why most people don't bother.

My constant companion during the Jazz Age has been the magnificent *Penguin Guide to Jazz,* and it was while browsing through the early pages (it works chronologically) that I came across a reference to Artie Shaw's "extraordinary life." A few days later, a quick search for "best jazz biographies" on the internet threw up a recommendation for Tom Nolan's book, and the one-two punch resulted in a one-click. It was a serendipitous buy: *Artie Shaw: King of the Clarinet* describes the life of a man who seemed to let the twentieth-century entertainment industry flow through him. Born in 1910, he was a professional musician by 1925; he was old enough to see Bix Beiderbecke play, and he employed Billie Holiday. He married, among others, Lana Turner, Ava Gardner, and Kathleen Winsor, the woman who wrote *Forever Amber;* he married Turner in the middle of the night in Las Vegas, after a first date that also somehow managed to find room for Shaw's friend Phil Silvers. The date only took place because Shaw's lover, Betty Grable, was out of town and he was bored; conveniently, Turner was free because she'd just had a fight with her fiancé. (Oh, and by marrying her, Shaw also managed to break Judy Garland's heart.) He hung out with Jack Kerouac, and bailed Arnold Schoenberg out of a financial crisis. He appeared on a chat show with Richard Burton and Lee Harvey Oswald's mother. He bought the film rights to *The Man Who Fell to Earth* and, appalled that Americans weren't able to see it, turned distributor for the British thriller *Séance on a Wet Afternoon*—the lead actor, Kim Stanley, ended up with an Academy Award nomination. If the book sounds nuts, it's because Shaw's life was nuts.

He quit music, apparently bored and intellectually frustrated, when he was in his mid-forties, and he spent the rest of his long life trying to write and becoming embroiled in increasingly unlikely lawsuits: the unfortunate director of a 1985 Oscar-winning documentary about him found herself in litigation for many years, with Shaw claiming that the film was "collaborative" and demanding half a million dollars for the co-labor. But for a quarter of a century Shaw was a brilliant, and enormously popular, bandleader, earning tens of thousands of dollars a week in the 1930s, playing six shows a day to frenzied jitterbugging teenagers. Nolan's book is a riveting picture of a world that you can hardly believe ever existed, and I would never have found it if it hadn't been for Will Hermes's mighty shove.

I cannot give him any credit, I think, for the two works of fiction I've read recently. Harriet Lane's first novel, *Alys, Always,* was a recommendation from a friend, and it was a good one: Lane's book, reminiscent of Zoë Heller's equally gripping *Notes on a Scandal,* is a disquieting, brilliantly observed, and admirably patient psychological...Well, it's not a thriller in the conventional sense. There's an accidental death, in the first chapter, but there are no guns, and there are no crimes, and it's set in the world of literary London, so there are only so many thrills that even a writer as good as Lane can wring out. One of her real achievements, in fact, is to exert a grip without ever bending out of shape what can be, let's face it, a pretty sleepy world. (And before American readers start feeling smug, I've spent some time in literary New York and literary San Francisco, too, and there aren't nearly as many uzis and orgies as you'd assume in those milieus, either.) (Unless I haven't been invited to the right parties, which is, I grant you, always a possibility.) Lane's narrator is an apparently harmless assistant on the books pages of a national newspaper who is given the chance to worm her way into the family of a famous writer, a chance she takes with a quease-inducing sangfroid; *Alys, Always* is about ambition and class and the sort of amour propre that is very particular to a certain kind of famous author, and Lane really nails it all.

I didn't know how to read my other novel, Padgett Powell's extraordinary *The Interrogative Mood*. I finished it, and loved it, but I have absolutely no idea if I did it right. There are, it seems to me, two ways of getting through it. There's the conventional, read-a-few-pages-in-the-bath-and-at-bedtime way; it's not long, and you'd be done in a few days. And then there's the other way, the way that it probably deserves: you think about the questions, the ones that are asking to be thought about, anyway, in which case this may well be the last novel you ever read.

The Interrogative Mood consists of nothing but questions, literally—paragraph after paragraph after paragraph of them. It is a novel, though, and not some kind of self-help questionnaire, because a character emerges from the relentless probing, and even a narrative, of sorts. Sometimes the questioner, Powell's fictional creation, lets slip a personal detail, through his personal interests, and the idiosyncratic phrasing of his queries. Some of them are cranky: "Is good amateur theatre oxymoronic?" "Wasn't the world better when the word 'haberdasher' was current?" Some of them make you laugh: "Do you credit that a man seriously advanced 'Cogito, ergo sum' with a straight face?" "Would you rather play a board game with a child all day or go over Niagara Falls in a barrel?" Some of them make you feel dumb and incompetent: "Do you know how gyroscopes function aeronautically?" "Can you take apart a clothes dryer and get it going right?" And some of them send you off into a reverie from which, were it not for jobs and children and the need to watch TV, you might never come back: "What period of history most interests you?" "Do you know the names of your first three lovers?" "Whom do you regard as a bona fide intellectual, and have you known anyone personally that you regard as a bona fide intellectual?" "What is the loudest noise you have ever heard?" "Would any particular failing on your part today be more painful than all other failings?" "Are you aware of a more likable kind of person than yourself that you would like to be like?" It's distracting, isn't it? It's just as well most literature doesn't make you think like that, over and over again, three or four times a page, or we'd never get anything read. I'm similarly grateful that most literature doesn't change your life, otherwise you'd be spun round like a sock in a tumble-dryer every time you sat on a bus or a toilet or wherever you do your reading. Does anyone know whether Lee Morgan made another decent album after *The Sidewinder*? ✷

BOOKS BOUGHT:

* *Watergate*—Thomas Mallon
* *Assholes: A Theory*—Aaron James
* *The Summer of Naked Swim Parties*—Jessica Anya Blau
* *Drinking Closer to Home*—Jessica Anya Blau
* *Bedsit Disco Queen*—Tracey Thorn

BOOKS READ:

* *Assholes: A Theory*—Aaron James
* *How to Get Filthy Rich in Rising Asia*—Mohsin Hamid
* *The Wonder Bread Summer*—Jessica Anya Blau
* *Note to Self*—Alina Simone

I can tell you for a fact that when you pick up a book called *Assholes: A Theory*, and you notice that there is a chapter entitled Naming Names, your heart starts to beat a little faster—or it does if you fear you might have done something to bring yourself to the attention of the author of the book, philosopher Aaron James. You have never met Aaron James, you don't think. (Except what if you did, somewhere, and didn't afford him the respect he deserved and still deserves, and snubbed him, like an asshole? And, just to be clear, you the Snubber would be the asshole in this hypothetical situation, not James the Snubbed.) Nevertheless, could writing books and columns and scripts be enough for James to decide that you were worthy of inclusion? Not that the act of writing automatically makes you an asshole—although there is, of course, a compelling argument to be made that, actually, it kind of does—but writing things that Aaron James might have found objectionable in some way, or giving an unguarded and obnoxious interview when tired and/or drunk, could well earn an Asshole Academy Award nomination. And then you take a little peek, before buying the book, and you see the names of Noel Gallagher,

Rush Limbaugh, Richard Dawkins, Henry VIII, Julian Assange, and Dick Cheney, and you think, What kind of asshole thinks he's famous enough to be included in a list of famous assholes? You feel terrible. You notice a chapter entitled Newer Asshole Styles, and you check to see whether the mortifying solecism you have just committed is indeed an indicator of a newer asshole style. There is a section entitled Delusional Asshole. Is this you? Oh, god. Kanye West is in there. But maybe you should go in there with him, for daring to think that you're as famously delusional as Kanye West…

You will notice two things about Aaron James's little book. The first is that one cannot write about it without using the word *asshole* over and over again, just as James was unable to write the book itself without using the word over and over again. This relentlessness induces a mild hysteria: there are striking references to "cable news assholes," "artist assholes," "his own inner asshole," "asshole avoidance," and surprising phrases such as "a reliable system for dampening asshole profusion," "Italy already qualifies as an asshole capitalist system," "a spike in the asshole population," and so on. One review of the book that I read decided for reasons of propriety to replace the word *asshole* with the word *twit* throughout, but, of course, a twit is something entirely different— one of the reasons this book works is that we intuitively know the defining features of an asshole, and no other word will do.

And the second thing to notice is that one reads it fearfully, through one's fingers, or I did, anyway. Can any of this possibly describe me? Or my partner, my children, my group of friends? But both the fear and the hysteria eventually subside, James's keen intelligence overwhelms you, and you realize that *Assholes: A Theory* is helpful, stimulating, and very timely: the banking crisis, social media, Fox News, and the internet have all combined to turn the early twenty-first century into the Golden Age of the Asshole.

An asshole is usefully defined as a person who "systematically allows himself to enjoy special advantages in interpersonal relations out of an entrenched sense of entitlement that immunizes him against the complaints of other people." (James argues persuasively that assholes are invariably men, although surely one of the triumphs of feminism is that many more women now fit this description than would have been the case forty or fifty years ago, even if female assholes clearly account for only a small percentage of the asshole population.) The book is in part an attempt to explain why we find the asshole so upsetting, given that the advantages he gains through his behavior are usually minor—he jumps a queue, he shouts at a waiter, he cuts people off in traffic. James reckons this is because "one's very status as a moral person goes unrecognized," and our moral status is a big deal to us, an important part of our sense of self. There is a possibility, however, that the gains made by assholes are going to become much more consequential: the gripping, devastating chapter entitled Asshole Capitalism argues that the assholes are hastening the end of the world as we know it. Who will participate in the manifestly and increasingly unfair version of capitalism we are faced with now, wherein asshole bankers get richer at the expense of the societies that have to bail them out? Why should non-assholes pay taxes and stay in line if they can see only material disadvantage?

There is much to engage with in *Assholes: A Theory,* and much to enjoy; one of the pleasures for me was the introduction it provided to the rich and extraordinary literature of moral philosophy. I found myself, for example, unexpectedly eager to read Bernard Williams's *Philosophical Papers, 1973–1980* (Cambridge University Press, 1981). It contains an essay entitled "Moral Luck," which deals, as far as I can work out, with the problem of whether we can forgive Gauguin for abandoning his family in order to go to Tahiti and paint. The trip produced art that we still value to this day; if it hadn't, Gauguin would presumably have been just another feckless asshole. But maybe he's an asshole anyway, regardless of the work he produced? Your call, but maybe Bernard Williams can help you make it. Oh, and Jonathan Richman fans, take note: guess what Pablo Picasso gets called in this book? One of Richman's most celebrated songs is thus neatly and, in my opinion, sadly rendered factually inaccurate.

It is, as you can see, only a short step from *Assholes: A Theory* to Mohsin Hamid's *How to Get Filthy Rich in Rising Asia,* although I suspect that Aaron James would focus on the rampant asshole capitalism that Hamid describes with such alarming brilliance, rather than on any individual assholes. Hamid, like Lorrie Moore in *Self-Help,* tells his story in the second person, as befits a how-to manual, but the genius of the book is that the second person who emerges is both richly individual and utterly authentic-seeming. Actually, there's quite a lot of genius floating round in here: *How to Get Filthy Rich in Rising Asia* is also deeply moving, a marvel of economy, and tells you a lot of stuff you probably don't know about a country very different from your own. Hamid's hero is born into poverty in a country that isn't named, but shares a lot of similarities with Pakistan, where Hamid grew up. He endures a crude education, gets himself a job delivering bootleg DVDs, falls in love with the local beauty, a woman he will play hide-and-seek with for his entire life. He starts to make money by selling tins of expired goods, the sell-by dates artfully changed, to retailers, before moving into the booming bottled-water trade; this involves bottling the water himself, although at least he boils it first. This business grows and grows, especially after he has made the necessarily corrupt political and military connections. He's not an asshole, I promise; he's just doing what he has to do to avoid being sucked down into the pit of poverty and disease that festers underneath him. He loses first one parent and then the other. He marries a woman whom the local beauty prevents him from ever properly loving. He grows older and poorer, and eventually he… Actually, I won't tell you what happens at the end. That's the story of existence itself, and hitherto you may somehow have avoided the bad news coming your way. If you can boil an entire life down to its essence, without losing any of the detail, shape, pain, or joy of that life, then it seems to me that you've done pretty much everything a novel is capable of doing.

I have been reading proofs and typescripts of novels by women writers previously unfamiliar to me, possibly because it's spring here in the U.K., and the blizzards and the subzero temperatures have obliged me to look for sunshine, hope, and rebirth elsewhere. I didn't find much of it in Alina Simone's *Note to Self,* although it's a very good first novel; Anna, Simone's central character, is thirty-seven, lonely, overweight, unemployed, and addicted to the internet, and I should warn you in advance that Simone is not the kind of writer who is in a hurry to rescue her heroine from these predicaments. I don't know whether it's fair to think of Lena Dunham's Hannah, but, whether it's fair or not, it's kind of unavoidable. Lena! Hannah! Alina! Anna! What's a chap to do? Anyway, Anna could be Hannah in a decade's time, if we didn't know already that Hannah is eventually going to soar off into the stratosphere, surfing on the jetstream of her creator. Anna, who lives in Brooklyn, just surfs:

She ate straight from the plastic container while reading the *Daily Beast*'s "Cheat Sheet" on her laptop. When she finished eating, she clicked over to *Culture Vulture*, then *Fishbowl NY*, then back over to her e-mail, where there were no new messages in her in-box. She considered checking *Newser* (though she didn't much trust Michael Wolff) or *PopEater* (even though it always made her feel guilty afterward). Then Anna wondered whether the *Daily Beast*'s "Cheat Sheet" had refreshed in the past half-hour...

Those of you who are gainfully employed might not recognize anything in that, may not even know what the hell Simone is talking about (and if this novel's still being read in two hundred years' time, the footnotes will be spectacular, as dense and tiny as the ones you see at the end of *The Rape of the Lock*). Those without a job—and that category includes writers—will burst into tears of recognition, and then go and hang themselves.

Anna does end up finding something to do, at least for the duration of the narrative. She hooks up with an asshole—and I know whereof I speak—called Taj, and gets involved in a video-art project that turns out to be unspeakably cruel. (Like Kevin Wilson's wonderful *The Family Fang*, *Note to Self* is full of imaginative and well-imagined art projects.) The flavors of the book are sharp and sour, like a Chinese soup, and Alina Simone, a singer/songwriter, is clearly a novelist, too.

The book that made me happiest this month was Jessica Anya Blau's picaresque, properly funny, unpredictable, and altogether irrepressible *The Wonder Bread Summer*; it made me so happy that after I'd read it, in two days flat, I bought everything I could find by the same author. Why can't I ever find novels like this? The last time I can remember feeling quite as buoyed by a work of fiction, and as charmed by a writer, was when I discovered Charles Portis, who wrote *True Grit* and *Norwood,* and Blau reminds me of Portis in lots of ways. Her characters and her set pieces would seem too giddy in the hands of a less talented writer, and I certainly couldn't synopsize thoroughly without doing her a grave disservice. But she has a steady nerve, as well as a wicked imagination, and she takes her craft seriously—her situations and her characters are real, to her and therefore to us, and it takes you a little while to realize that what you're reading is top-notch comic writing, because you're getting all the stuff you normally get in literary fiction as well: rites of passage, the complications of fractured family, the works.

The eponymous summer is the summer of 1983; the eponymous Wonder Bread is actually only a plastic bag; the bread has been removed, and in its place is a whole pile of cocaine belonging to a drug-dealing boutique owner called Jonas, who, as the novel opens, is exposing himself to one of his employees, twenty-year-old Allie, who's working in the boutique during her summer break from college. Allie does not wish to see Jonas's penis, particularly, and in any case is owed money; she grabs the Wonder Bread bag and disappears. That's the setup. I'd been sent a proof, and only really intended to do the author the courtesy of reading the first couple of pages, but wherever Allie was going, I wanted to go with her. One of the remarkable things about Blau's novel is that while she recognizes the vulnerability of attractive young girls, she doesn't allow it to cripple them; they deal with the hand they've been played, and as a consequence, Blau writes about sex with a perspective that seems fresh to me.

There are many passages that I would like to read to you—Allie's first hapless attempt to sell some of the cocaine she's stolen, without scales, or bags, or any clue as to the street value of any drug, is a joy—but perhaps the most surprising moment is when Allie meets Billy Idol, offers him cocaine (he accepts the offer with enthusiasm), and then has sex with him. I can't recall another novel in which a real living person turns up with quite such... *aplomb*. Mr. Idol, according to Ms. Blau, has "a dick... the size of two Babe Ruth candy bars, side by side," a description that may be flattering enough to ward off any awkward lawyers' letters. (Actually, what the hell do I know? We don't have Babe Ruth bars here in the U.K.) This is Billy Idol's only appearance in the books I read this month. There are, I can tell you, worse books to appear in, as Noel Gallagher and Henry VIII might tell you. ✶

INDEX OF STUFF HE'S BEEN READING

NICK HORNBY
CONTINUES READING

JOIN HIM!

In addition to Nick Hornby's monthly column, every issue of the *Believer* features columns by Daniel Handler and Greil Marcus, a full-color comics section, and original essays and interviews that are frequently very long and almost always quite untimely. Three annual special issues come with ever-changing bonus items, such as DVDs, art objects, and original music compilations. Simply fill out the form below for your special Hornbyphile discount!

or subscribe for no discount at all at **believermag.com/subscribe**

· ·

Send me one year of the Believer *(nine issues) for just $40!*

NAME: _____

STREET ADDRESS: _____

CITY: _____   STATE: _____   ZIP: _____

EMAIL: _____   PHONE: _____

CREDIT CARD #: _____

EXPIRATION DATE: _____   (VISA/MC/DISCOVER/AMEX)   CVV: _____

Make check or money orders out to the *Believer*, and mail this form to:
The Believer, 849 Valencia Street, San Francisco, CA, 94110